CCNA Security Study Guide

Exam IINS 640-553

OBJECTIVE	CHAPTER
Describe the security threats facing modern network infrastructures	
Describe and list mitigation methods for common network attacks	2, 6
Describe and list mitigation methods for Worm, Virus, and Trojan Horse attacks	2, 6
Describe the Cisco Self Defending Network architecture	2
Secure Cisco routers	
Secure Cisco routers using the SDM Security Audit feature	5
Use the One-Step Lockdown feature in SDM to secure a Cisco router	5
Secure administrative access to Cisco routers by setting strong encrypted passwords, exec timeout, login failure rate and using IOS login enhancements	3
Secure administrative access to Cisco routers by configuring multiple privilege levels	3
Secure administrative access to Cisco routers by configuring role based CLI	3
Secure the Cisco IOS image and configuration file	3
Implement AAA on Cisco routers using local router database and external ACS	
Explain the functions and importance of AAA	4
Describe the features of TACACS+ and RADIUS AAA protocols	4
Configure AAA authentication	4
Configure AAA authorization	4
Configure AAA accounting	4
Mitigate threats to Cisco routers and networks using ACLs	
Explain the functionality of standard, extended, and named IP ACLs used by routers to filter packets	7
Configure and verify IP ACLs to mitigate given threats (filter IP traffic destined for Telnet, SNMP, and DDoS attacks) in a network using CLI	7
Configure IP ACLs to prevent IP address spoofing using CLI	7
Discuss the caveats to be considered when building ACLs	7

Sybex®
An Imprint of
WILEY

OBJECTIVE	CHAPTER
Implement secure network management and reporting	
Use CLI and SDM to configure SSH on Cisco routers to enable secured management access	5
Use CLI and SDM to configure Cisco routers to send Syslog messages to a Syslog server	5
Mitigate common Layer 2 attacks	
Describe how to prevent layer 2 attacks by configuring basic Catalyst switch security features	6
Implement the Cisco IOS firewall feature set using SDM	
Describe the operational strengths and weaknesses of the different firewall technologies	7
Explain stateful firewall operations and the function of the state table	7
Implement Zone Based Firewall using SDM	7
Implement the Cisco IOS IPS feature set using SDM	
Define network based vs. host based intrusion detection and prevention	8
Explain IPS technologies, attack responses, and monitoring options	8
Enable and verify Cisco IOS IPS operations using SDM	8
Implement site-to-site VPNs on Cisco Routers using SDM	
Explain the different methods used in cryptography	9, 10
Explain IKE protocol functionality and phases	10
Describe the building blocks of IPSec and the security functions it provides	12
Configure and verify an IPSec site-to-site VPN with pre-shared key authentication using SDM	12

Exam specifications and content are subject to change at any time without prior notice and at Cisco's sole discretion. Please visit Cisco's website (www.cisco.com) for the most current information on exam content.

CCNA® Security
Study Guide

Tim Boyles

Wiley Publishing, Inc.

Acquisitions Editor: Jeff Kellum
Development Editor: Stef Jones
Technical Editors: Chris Carson, Billy Haines
Production Editor: Angela Smith
Copy Editor: Judy Flynn
Editorial Manager: Pete Gaughan
Production Manager: Tim Tate
Vice President and Executive Group Publisher: Richard Swadley
Vice President and Publisher: Neil Edde
Media Project Manager 1: Laura Moss-Hollister
Media Associate Producer: Doug Kuhn
Media Quality Assurance: Josh Frank
Book Designers: Judy Fung and Bill Gibson
Proofreader: Rebecca Rider
Indexer: Jack Lewis
Project Coordinator, Cover: Lynsey Stanford
Cover Designer: Ryan Sneed

To God and my family. Without the support and love from both, I would not be able to do what I do. Thanks for the many blessings.

Acknowledgments

When you take on a project like this, there are always a number of people involved, and this one is no exception. I could not have done this book without the help and support of several folks. First, I'd like to thank my technical editor, Chris Carson, for keeping me honest and offering candid feedback. Chris also contributed to this book by writing Chapter 10 and Chapter 11. His help was invaluable. I would also like to thank Patrick Conlan, who provided access to most of the equipment used in the writing of this book.

A special thanks goes out to Stef Jones, this book's developmental editor. Stef was the one to keep me in line and was a tremendous help in shaping up some of the more difficult chapters.

And last but not least, thanks to the team at Sybex for supporting me in this endeavor: Pete Gaughan, editorial manager; Jeff Kellum, acquisitions editor; and Jenni Housh, Connor O'Brien, and Angela Smith, who are all on the editorial team. I'm sure I gave Jeff plenty of cause for concern over the course of the better part of a year, but we all survived—I think. Also, thanks to copyeditor Judy Flynn, proofreader Rebecca Rider, and indexer Jack Lewis.

About The Author

Tim Boyles is an IT manager at a large retailer based in the Dallas–Fort Worth Metroplex. He has been involved in networking and security for over 20 years. He is the holder of many certifications, including CISSP, CISA, CISM, GCIH, GAWN, and of course CCNA and CCNA-Security. Tim has worked on many networking and security books. He was previously the security practice leader for the South Central operation of BT Global Services and has been engaged with consulting for a number of years with numerous large corporate clients. He is also a mentor instructor for the SANS Institute, having conducted sessions on CISSP training, Incident Handling, Wireless Penetration Testing, and Web Application Security.

About the Contributor

Chris L. Carson, CCIE #19511, is a principal at Ethical Networks, a network and security consulting provider in the Dallas–Ft. Worth area. He has been in the network and security industry for more than 17 years and holds over 20 industry certifications, including CCIE, CCSP, CEH, and CCNA-Security. Most of his career has been spent working for large Cisco Gold partners throughout the United States. Chris's previous position as a security practice manager and principal for one of the largest Cisco partners in North Texas has provided him with expertise in designing, implementing, and troubleshooting solutions for many Fortune 500 customers.

Contents at a Glance

Contents

Introduction

Welcome to *CCNA Security Study Guide*, a comprehensive guide that covers everything you need for Cisco's exam IINS 640-553. For readers who are new to Cisco certifications, there is a well-defined structure to the different levels that network administrators can achieve. Cisco's current certification structure has the following five different levels of certification:

- Entry level
- Associate
- Professional
- Expert
- Architect

This book is written for the associate level of certification. Cisco considers this level to be the "apprentice or foundation level" for network administrators.

Cisco has recently broadened its associate-level certifications to include not only a certification for routing and switching (CCNA) and one for design (CCDA) but also more targeted associate-level certifications for security (CCNA Security), wireless (CCNA Wireless), and voice (CCNA Voice). These new certifications target specific areas of Cisco technology and are to be used as stepping-stones for the professional and expert levels of certification that Cisco offers.

This book is a culmination of a year's worth of work that focused on the things you need to know to pass the CCNA Security exam, but I also hope to engage your mind on the discussion of security. Obviously everything can't be covered in one book, so it is incumbent on you, the reader, to enhance your knowledge as you see fit with other training materials. With this book, you will gain hands-on experience by performing the exercises included in each chapter, and I have provided the output of commands that you would see if you were connected to the router. All you really need to practice the techniques shown in the book are a couple of Cisco routers that support SDM. For the most part, you can get by with one, but in some cases you may want to have a second one to help with the real-world aspect of things.

The biggest problem for me was determining what is important for the exam without going into any one topic too deeply. At the end of the day, this is a study guide. There is a certain amount of background material, but I'm confident you will find that it includes the right amount of information to pass the test.

Cisco's Security Certifications

Cisco offers three distinct levels of Security certifications. This diagram shows that the CCNA Security certification is a building block to the professional- and expert-level security certifications:

This book covers the CCNA Security certification exam, IINS (Implementing Cisco IOS Network Security) 640-553. As this book goes to press, the exam costs $250 USD. The exam tests your knowledge in areas specific to Cisco hardware and software, both theoretical and technical.

Once you achieve your CCNA Security certification, you can choose to continue on the path and achieve higher certifications, such as the Cisco Certified Security Professional (CCSP) or the ultimate, CCIE Security. But even if you stop after achieving your CCNA Security certification, you will have demonstrated to your current or prospective employers that you have a sound knowledge of the interworkings of security and Cisco security technologies. This can only increase your value as an employee, and it might even make it easier to land that dream job you've always wanted!

What Skills Do You Need to Become CCNA Security Certified?

To meet the CCNA Security certification skill level, you must possess the following skills:

- A thorough knowledge of core security technologies; how to install, troubleshoot, and monitor network devices to maintain integrity, confidentiality, and availability of data and devices; and familiarity of the technologies Cisco uses in its security structure

- The ability to develop a security infrastructure, recognize threats and vulnerabilities to networks, and mitigate security threats

How Do You Become CCNA Security Certified?

If you are new to Cisco certifications, to get your CCNA Security certification, you must first obtain your CCNA certification. You can become CCNA certified one of two ways:

- Pass the 640-802 CCNA exam.

- Pass both the ICND1 (640-822) and ICND2 (640-816) exams.

Once you have your CCNA, you can take the CCNA Security exam. This book covers 100 percent of the exam objectives for Exam #640-553, Implementing Cisco IOS Network Security (IINS). You will need to take and pass this exam to become CCNA Security certified. You can take the exam at any Pearson VUE testing center. The exam is 90 minutes long and includes from 55 to 65 questions.

The one thing I recommend is that you will need some hands-on experience. All you really need to practice the techniques shown in the book are a couple of Cisco routers that support Security Device Manager (SDM). For the most part, you can get by with one, but in some cases you may want to have a second one to help with the real-world aspect of things.

Hands-on experience is very important for this or any CCNA. I've provided numerous hands-on exercises throughout this book. That is a good place to start, but don't hesitate to experiment or look for other ways to gain experience.

Who Should Buy This Book

I am making certain assumptions about the reader:

- You either have a CCNA or are in the process of getting one.
- You are comfortable working with Cisco routers.
- You have at least an idea about security concepts.

This book contains everything you need to know to pass the CCNA Security exam, 640-553. It does not include exhaustive coverage of each and every topic. What it does do is cover what you need to know for the exam.

In the appendices, there is information on some related topics that are not yet part of the exam. It's anybody's guess when they might be, but chances are they will when the next release of the exam comes out, so why not get a head start with an introduction to the topics. In Appendix D, you'll find a more extensive hands-on exercise.

What's Inside

Here is a glance at what's in each chapter:

Chapter 1, "Introduction to Network Security," begins with a discussion to give you a basic understanding of network security, including such topics as threats to network security, the objectives of network security, data classification, security controls, incident response, and law and ethics.

Chapter 2, "Creating the Secure Network," provides a discussion of operations security, including the SDLC process. Also discussed are security policy, risk management, the Cisco Self-Defending Network, and security awareness.

Chapter 3, "Securing Administrative Access," shows you how to configure secure access to your router. It includes an introduction to Cisco Security Device Manager (SDM). And you'll find information on privilege levels, security features of Cisco ISR routers, and securing configuration files.

Chapter 4, "Configuring AAA Services," covers the functions and importance of AAA services, including TACACS+ and RADIUS. A more detailed discussion of authentication, authorization, and accounting follow.

Chapter 5, "Securing Your Router," introduces you to locking down the router by using One-Step Lockdown with Cisco SDM and then via the command line with AutoSecure. Also covered in this chapter is configuring SSH access and Syslog via the command line and SDM.

Chapter 6, "Layer 2 Security," shows you how to use IOS features on the Catalyst switch to secure your layer 2 communications.

Chapter 7, "Implementing Cisco IOS Firewall," covers the evolution of firewalls, using access-control lists, a discussion of stateful firewall features, and a Cisco Firewall feature set implemented with Cisco SDM.

Chapter 8, "Implementing Cisco IOS Intrusion Prevention," provides a discussion of network and host based intrusion detection and prevention. You will use Cisco SDM to implement IOS Intrusion Prevention.

Chapter 9, "Understanding Cryptographic Solutions," explains the history of cryptograph and goes over the different methods used. Also covered is a discussion of symmetric encryption.

Chapter 10, "Using Digital Signatures," gives us a discussion of hashing values and a covers an overview of digital signatures.

Chapter 11, "Using Asymmetric Encryption and PKI," covers public key cryptography and a discussion of asymmetric encryption.

Chapter 12, "Implementing Site-to-Site IPsec VPN Solutions," gives us a discussion of the components of IPsec plus runs through the configuration of a site-to-site VPN using Cisco SDM.

How to Use This Book

The *CCNA Security Study Guide* is designed to prepare the reader to pass the 640-553 exam to achieve the associate-level certification in Cisco security technologies. To get the most out of this book, I recommend you use the following study methods:

1. Take the assessment test provided to you prior to Chapter 1 of this book. Try to answer each question without looking at the provided answers and explanations found at the end of the test.

 NOTE   The assessment test is also included on the companion CD and can be taken electronically.

The assessment test should give you an indication of your skill level prior to reading the book. Once you have completed the assessment test and graded yourself, take time to carefully read over the explanations for any question you get wrong and note the chapters in which the material is covered. This information should help you identify sections of the book that you need to spend additional time on. Keep in mind, however, that the book was designed such that the chapters should be read in order. Much of the material found in the chapters build on knowledge learned from previous chapters.

2. Prior to reading each chapter, make sure you review the test objectives listed at the beginning. They list what the exam taker must ultimately know in order to pass the CCNA Security exam.

3. Complete each written lab at the end of each chapter. These labs are created to make sure the reader fully understands key topics that are contained within the chapter. Using a written format as opposed to a multiple-choice format forces the reader to know the answers off the top of their head instead of just eliminating options, as we often do with multiple-choice questions.

4. Work through and fully understand the commands found in the hands-on labs. Not all chapters have hands-on labs, but the book focuses on the important tasks necessary for aspiring CCNA Security network administrators.

5. Answer all of the review questions related to each chapter. Once you have finished answering the questions, review the answers and explanations to not only understand the correct answers but also to understand why the incorrect answers are actually incorrect! Keep in mind that these review questions will not be the exact questions you'll find on the exam, but they help you to understand the material from which Cisco creates the actual exam questions.

6. Take time to review the bonus exams that are included on the companion CD. Questions in these exams appear only on the CD.

7. Test yourself using all the flashcards on the included CD. They can be viewed on both PCs and mobile PC, so now you can take your study material with you wherever you go!

Home Lab Setup

Having access to a lab at home is always great, if you can swing it. As a suggestion, the minimum setup would be an ISR router that supports SDM and a Catalyst switch that you can use for practice exercises. For the router, you can use any of the following that support SDM:

- Cisco 800 Series
- Cisco 1800 Series
- Cisco 1900 Series
- Cisco 2800 Series
- Cisco 2900 Series

For the switch, you can choose almost any Catalyst model from the last few years. As noted in the text, some switches have slightly different syntax on some of the commands, but that's to be expected.

Of course, you can add servers and PCs as you wish to make it more realistic, but that's entirely your option. What I've listed is the minimum you would need.

What's on the CD?

The CD included with this book includes many supplemental tools that you can use to further your studies and achieve your goal of becoming a CCNA Security certified administrator. You can use the content described in the following sections to further your studying.

The Sybex Test Engine

The Sybex test engine software lets readers take all of the review and assessment questions found in the book as well as two additional bonus exams that are found only on the CD. Potential test takers can practice in an electronic test-taking environment that is similar to the environment of the actual Cisco exam.

Electronic Flashcards for PCs and Mobile PC Devices

In addition to the Sybex test engine software, Sybex has included over 100 electronic flashcards for you to test yourself with on PCs and compatible handheld devices. These flashcards are designed to get the reader to quickly recognize and recall important CCNA security information that will be useful for them when taking the 640-553 exam.

CCNA Security Study Guide in PDF

Finally, the CD contains the entire *CCNA Security Study Guide* in PDF format so you can read the book on your PC or laptop or any handheld devices that reads PDF files.

Tips for Taking Your CCNA Security Exam

The CCNA Security exam contains anywhere from 55 to 65 questions and must be completed in 90 minutes or less. The exam is in English, Japanese, Chinese, Russian, Portuguese, Korean, French, and Spanish. This information can change per exam. A passing score varies according to the types of questions found in the exam, but it is probably best to assume you need to get approximately 85 percent of the questions correct to pass the exam.

When taking the exam, thoroughly read each question to make sure you know what answer it is looking for. Cisco exam questions tend to have answers that look identical. You will find, however, that there are small differences in the answers that can determine which is correct.

Also, keep in mind that you should choose the answer that Cisco believes is correct as opposed to what you or other vendors believe. This is a Cisco exam, after all, so the right answer is the one that Cisco recommends!

The 640-553 exam questions might be in any of the following formats:

- Multiple-choice, single answer
- Multiple-choice, multiple answer (Cisco will always tell you to choose two or three depending on the proper number of multiple correct responses.)
- Drag and drop
- Fill in the blank
- Simulations

Test-Day Tips for Certification Success

Here are some things to keep in mind as you prepare for the exam:

- Arrive at the exam center at least 30 minutes early. That way you can check in and mentally prepare for the exam without having to rush.

- Take the Cisco exam tutorial. This tutorial is offered prior to the official start of each exam before the test timer starts. It is an interactive tutorial that shows you the format of the exam and how to navigate through the different question types, including multiple choice, drag-and-drop, fill-in-the-blank, and simulation questions. Even if you have taken many Cisco exams, I highly recommend going through the tutorial in case something new has been added to the exam format since the last time you took an exam.

- Read both the questions and answers very carefully. Cisco often will intentionally lead the hasty test taker who simply glosses over a question to quickly choose the incorrect answer. Patience and careful thinking pay off greatly when taking Cisco exams!

- Be aware that you cannot go back to change an answer once you have moved on to the next question. Make sure the answer you choose is the one you want to stick with.

How to Contact the Author

I welcome feedback from you about this book or any topic for a future book. You may reach me by writing to me at ccnasecurity1@gmail.com.

Sybex strives to keep you supplied with the latest tools and information you need for your work. Please check the website at www.sybex.com, where we'll post additional content and updates that supplement this book should the need arise. Enter **CCNA Security** in the Search box or type the book's ISBN—**9780470527672**—and click Go to get to the book's update page.

Assessment Test

1. Which of the following is a group of computers that have been compromised and are controlled by a third party?

   A. Hotnet

   B. Botnet

   C. LANnet

   D. DOSnet

2. A smurf attack is an attack on which tenet of the network security objectives?

   A. Confidentiality

   B. Reliability

   C. Availability

   D. Integrity

   E. Repeatability

3. A piece of marketing data for an upcoming but not yet released marketing campaign for the private sector is accidentally released. What would be the classification for this data?

   A. Top Secret

   B. Confidential

   C. Secret

   D. Private

   E. Sensitive

4. If you were going to design a network and adhere to operation security best practices, what in the following list would *not* be a factor?

   A. Keep it simple.

   B. Look for single points of failure.

   C. Look for attack vectors.

   D. Find the lowest cost.

   E. Plan for the future.

5. A degree in information assurance from a four-year university would be an example of what in a security awareness program?

   A. Training

   B. Awareness

   C. Certification

   D. Education

   E. Motivation

6. If you configured an enable secret password, what would precede the password in the saved configuration?

A. 1

B. 7

C. 4

D. 6

E. 5

7. What command would you use from the command line to verify that the proper SDM files exist so that you can run SDM to configure your router?

A. `show directory`

B. `show files`

C. `show flash`

D. `show sdm`

8. What command would you use to deter a brute-force attack on your router by setting a minimum time (beyond the default) to wait before login commands would be accepted again after an unsuccessful attempt?

A. `login block-for`

B. `login delay`

C. `login wait`

D. `login wait attempt`

9. What can be described as who logged in, what they did, and for how long?

A. Authentication

B. Authorization

C. Logging

D. Accounting

E. Debugging

10. A network access server (NAS—which also stands for network attached storage) is another name for what? (Choose all that apply.)

A. Switch

B. Router

C. VPN concentrator

D. Firewall

11. Cisco Secure ACS for Windows runs which AAA services? (Choose all that apply.)

A. RADIUS

B. CDP

C. TACACS+

D. SDEE

12. When you run `auto secure` from the command line, a number of global services are disabled. Which of these is *not* one of the global services that is disabled?

A. Finger

B. PAD

C. Small servers

D. Service password-encryption

E. NTP

13. A Syslog server can be configured in Cisco SDM by utilizing what interface element? (Choose all that apply.)

A. Router Properties

B. Additional Tasks

C. Security Tasks

D. Logging

14. Network Time Protocol (NTP) uses what protocol and port to communicate?

A. UDP 321

B. UDP 123

C. UDP 514

D. TCP 514

E. TCP 123

15. Which of the following is a method of basic layer 2 security?

A. CDP

B. DHCP snooping

C. 802.1Q

D. PPP

16. What is used to elect a root bridge within a layer 2 switched environment?

A. Hello packets

B. STP update packets

C. BPDU

D. CDP

E. STP cost

17. ARP spoofing attacks depend on the use of what type of messages?

A. CDP updates

B. NTP

C. GARP

D. MAC

E. DAI

18. When discussing access list placement, which of the following is correct? (Choose two.)

    A. A standard access list should be placed as close to the destination as possible.

    B. An extended access list should be placed as close to the source as possible.

    C. A standard access list should be placed as close to the source as possible.

    D. An extended access list should be placed as close to the destination as possible.

19. True or false? RFC 1918 IP addresses should be blocked by ACL at an Internet-facing router heading inbound to the local LAN.

    A. True

    B. False

20. At what level of the OSI model does a circuit-level firewall operate? (Choose all that apply.)

    A. 2

    B. 3

    C. 4

    D. 5

    E. 7

21. The IDS and IPS sensor uses four different approaches to scan for and identify malicious traffic. Which of the following is *not* one of the four approaches?

    A. Policy approach

    B. Signature approach

    C. Honeypot approach

    D. Brute-force capture approach

    E. Anomaly-based approach

22. When IDS/IPS technology is discussed, which of the following types can be described as "using a predefined definition of known good network behavior, usually provided by the vendor"?

    A. Statistical

    B. Nonstatistical

    C. Honeypot

    D. Active

23. Cisco Security Agent can be described as what kind of system?

    A. NIDS

    B. HIDS

    C. HIPS

    D. NIPS

24. DES has two operating modes, block cipher and stream cipher. Which two of the following selections are part of the block cipher mode? (Choose two.)

    A. CFB mode

    B. CBC mode

    C. ECB mode

    D. OFB mode

25. Which of the Rivest Ciphers (RCs) is commonly used within Secure Sockets Layer (SSL)?

    A. RC2

    B. RC3

    C. RC6

    D. RC4

26. Which of the following encryption algorithms is not supported in Cisco IOS for IPsec implementations?

    A. 3DES

    B. AES

    C. DES

    D. IDEA

27. What function is a code that further secures a hash?

    A. MAC

    B. MD5

    C. HMAC

    D. HMC

28. Which of the following is not a feature of digital signatures?

    A. Integrity

    B. Confidentiality

    C. Nonrepudiation

    D. Authentication

29. What is the biggest drawback to using asymmetric encryption algorithms?

    A. Less security

    B. Slow computing time

    C. Greater key length

    D. Difficulty in administration

30. What is the main standard for digital certificates?

    A. X.11

    B. 802.af

    C. X.509

    D. H.323

31. When you're configuring Cisco Easy VPN, what is the difference between Network Extension Mode and Network Extension Mode Plus?

    A. A loopback address is configured.

    B. An access list is required.

    C. NATs are in use.

    D. Routable addresses are used.

32. What commands might you use to troubleshoot a site-to-site VPN tunnel? (Choose two.)

    A. `debug crypto isakmp`

    B. `show crypto isakmp sa`

    C. `show ip route`

    D. `debug isakmp`

33. When you're using the Cisco SDM tool to configure a VPN tunnel, which one of the following items is *not* shown on the VPN Connection Information screen?

    A. Interface Selection

    B. Peer Identity

    C. Authentication

    D. Preshared Key

    E. Traffic to Encryption

Answers to Assessment Test

1. **B.** A botnet is a group of computers that have been compromised by various means and are controlled by a third party through a command and control server. For more information, see Chapter 1.

2. **C.** During a smurf attack, a large number of small packets are directed to a single host, causing a denial of service, which would be an attack on availability. For more information, see Chapter 1.

3. **E.** This is somewhat subjective, but since there were no specific security aspects, marketing data that is not really confidential or private but not public either would have to be classified as sensitive. Options A and B are from the military classification system. For more information, see Chapter 1.

4. **D.** All of the options except D (find the lowest cost) would be an aspect of operation security. See Chapter 2 for more information.

5. **D.** There are three components of a security awareness program: training, awareness, and education. A formal degree program would be an example of the education component. For more information, see Chapter 2.

6. **E.** The answer is 5 because the enable secret password is an MD5 hash of the entered password. For more information, see Chapter 3.

7. **C.** The answer is `show flash`, which displays the files on the flash memory. For more information, see Chapter 3.

8. **B.** When you use the `login block-for` command by itself, it sets a default of 1 second to wait after an unsuccessful attempt to login. If you want to configure a different interval, you must use the `login delay` command. For more information, see Chapter 3.

9. **D.** AAA services include authentication, authorization, and accounting. Accounting involves keeping a record of who logged in, what they did, and for how long. Authorization involves who can perform what tasks, and authentication is concerned with who is allowed to log in. For more information, see Chapter 4.

10. **A, B, C, D.** A network access server can be any device that can run TACACS+. A router is commonly used as an NAS, but if you have a Cisco network with many devices, chances are they are all using TACACS+ for AAA. For more information, see Chapter 4.

11. **A, C.** Cisco Secure ACS for Windows can be both a TACACS+ server and a RADIUS server and both at the same time. See Chapter 4 for more information.

12. **D.** Service password-encryption is enabled during the auto secure process. The rest of the global services listed are part of those that are disabled. For more information, see Chapter 5.

13. **A, B, D.** This is a bit of a trick question, but after you click the Configure button, Additional Tasks is the correct task on the taskbar. Router Properties is selected on the selection tree and then expands to display the Logging selection. More information can be found in Chapter 5.

14. B. NTP uses UDP 123 to communicate. UDP is a connectionless protocol, best suited for things like updates on time and log messages. More information can be found in Chapter 5.

15. B. DHCP snooping is a layer 2 security feature that creates ports where DHCP responses are allowed; this is called a trusted port. See Chapter 6 for more information.

16. C. Bridge Protocol Data Units (BPDUs) are used to elect a root bridge, based on bridge priority. For more information, see Chapter 6.

17. C. ARP spoofing attacks depend on the use of Gratuitous ARP (GARP) messages, which offer up bogus ARP packets to replace correct ones in an ARP table on a host or router. For more information, see Chapter 6.

18. A, B. A standard access list should be placed as close to the destination as possible and an extended access list should be placed as close to the source as possible. See Chapter 7 for more information.

19. A. You should block RFC 1918 addresses as well as multicast addresses, localhost addresses, and the local LAN range of addresses. For more information, see Chapter 7 and also RFC 2827, "Network Ingress Filtering."

20. C, D. A circuit-level firewall operates at the Transport and Session layers of the OSI model, monitoring TCP and UDP port communications. For more information, see Chapter 7.

21. D. The four approaches to IDS and IPS usage are policy, signature, honeypot, and anomaly based. Brute-force refers to an attack methodology to crack encryption. For more information see Chapter 8.

22. B. There are two types of anomaly-based IDS and IPS sensors, statistical and nonstatistical. Statistical sensors "learn" the good network behavior over time. Nonstatistical sensors are preprogrammed and may be correct, or they might need lots of tuning. For more information, see Chapter 8.

23. C. Cisco Security Agent (CSA) can best be described as a Host Intrusion Prevention System (HIPS). Certainly it can alert like an IDS, but the difference is that it can take action to block malicious actions. For more information, see Chapter 8.

24. B, C. The block cipher mode uses the Cipher Block Chaining (CBC) type and the Electronic Code Book (ECB) type. For more information, see Chapter 9.

25. D. RC4 is the most commonly used Rivest cipher and is a variable key length stream cipher. For more information, see Chapter 9.

26. D. IDEA is not supported for Cisco IPsec implementations. For more information, see Chapter 9.

27. C. The Hash Message Authentication Code (HMAC) is another layer of security on top of a hash such as MD5 or SHA-1. Cisco uses the HMAC within its security protocols. See Chapter 10 for more information.

28. B. Digital signatures feature integrity, authentication, and nonrepudiation but do not address confidentiality. See Chapter 10 for more information.

29. B. The biggest drawback to using asymmetric encryption is the speed factor. Using it is significantly slower than using symmetric encryption. For more information, see Chapter 11.

30. C. The main standard for digital certificates is the X.509 standard and is specified in RFC 5280.

31. A. The only difference in the Network Extension Mode and the Network Extension Mode Plus is that the Network Extension Mode Plus has an additional IP address configured in the form of a loopback address. For more information, see Chapter 12.

32. A, B. Two of the most commonly used commands to troubleshoot an IPsec VPN tunnel are related to the ISAKMP exchange. You want to debug the crypto ISAKMP messages with the `debug crypto isakmp` command and then show the state of the security association with the `show crypto isakmp sa` command. For more information, see Chapter 12.

33. D. The preshared key is not part of the information needed on the VPN Connection Information screen; however, whether to use a preshared key or digital certificate is one of the choices. For more information, see Chapter 12.

Chapter 1

Introduction to Network Security

This chapter lays the foundation for future chapters covering the CCNA Security Exam objectives. In this chapter, I'll discuss the following topics:

- Threats to network security
- Network security objectives
- Classification of data
- Security controls
- Incident response
- Law and ethics

In Chapter 1, I'm going to explore some fundamental tenets of network security. It's important to have a foundation for the topics we will continue to explore in depth later on. I'll start with the threats to network security. Then I'll cover the objectives of network security and you'll learn some of the ways data is classified. Next, we will look at the types of controls that can be applied to help achieve network security.

In the two final sections, I will discuss the steps of incident response. Then we will briefly cover the law as it applies to computers and networks and the part ethics plays in network security.

Threats to Network Security

In today's world, the threat to computer networks is great. Because of the nature of the global communications network, threats can come from an increasing number of places and are constantly taking on new forms. An old joke in security circles goes, "What's the most secure computer in the world?" "The one that isn't turned on." It's even more true today than it was when it was first told.

The computer that isn't turned on isn't of much value to us, so we have to strike some balance between the usability of the computer network and the security controls that we apply.

Threats to network security are generally categorized into two basic types, external and internal. Along the lines of the joke I made earlier, the best way to secure the network from external threats is to disconnect it from external networks. Unfortunately, that isn't an option in today's business climate. Virtually every business these days is connected to the Internet. Even some military computer networks are connected to the Internet. The days of maintaining complete physical separation of internal and external networks are over.

Today we protect our networks by using firewalls, intrusion prevention systems, access lists, layer 2 controls, Application layer firewalls, proxies, and other systems to provide what is called *defense-in-depth*. That is to say, we layer on many types of defenses so that if an intruder defeats one security measure, there are many more that will continue to protect the network and its sensitive data. With defense-in-depth, intruders must work a lot harder to achieve their objective of penetrating the network.

External Threats

External threats come from anyone outside of your network who is trying to get in. They can take many different forms and are attempted by people with varying motives and skill sets, and there are new ways being discovered and exploited every day. The following list describes some of the means that are used to attempt to breach the perimeter of someone's network:

Social engineering   While not necessarily a technology-based attack, social engineering can definitely be categorized as an attack against confidentiality. Typically, the attacker will pose as someone from the technical staff at a company either where the victim works or where they might have an account, such as a bank. The attacker will try to glean personal information from the victim in order to exploit something. For example, the attacker might try to gain access to an online bank account or find out the password to the victim's computer account at the office.

Denial of service attacks   This is an attack that can disable or cripple the use of a system. It could just be a huge load of packets directed to the target, it could exploit a vulnerability in the operating system or code, or it could involve the use of incorrectly formatted data. There are several specific types of denial of service attacks:

SYN flood   A SYN floods is the result of using the TCP three-way handshake to cause a denial of service. The attacker sends many crafted packets with spoofed source IP addresses to a host or device, such as a firewall or router. Because the source IP is spoofed, when the router or firewall responds with SYN ACK, it is never received. The router or firewall holds that SYN conversation open, waiting for the ACK response from the sending host, which never comes. Multiply this many times and it chews up a lot of resources, which is the intent of the attack. The attack exhausts all of the resources of the router or firewall in order to effect a denial of service.

Smurf attack   You may be having visions of little blue people, but that's not what I'm referring to. In a smurf attack, a single host, using a spoofed source IP, sends a ping flood to a broadcast address. This is a form of denial of service attack. What happens is that every IP that receives the ping request in that broadcast domain sends a response in an echo reply to the spoofed IP, which is a real IP and the target of the denial of service attack. This attack is well known and was a common type of attack in the '90s. It can still be used today, but it is less common because routers can be configured to not forward broadcast requests through the use of the `no ip directed-broadcast` command. Also, hosts are generally configured to not respond to broadcasts.

Distributed denial of service (DDOS) attacks   Botnets are the weapon of choice in today's world when you want to conduct a DDOS attack. Heck, you can even rent one if you want to. But really, any group of computers under an attacker's direct or indirect control can be used to launch an attack using any of the aforementioned methods.

> A botnet is a group of computers that have been compromised in such a way that they can be controlled by a third party, sometimes known as a *bot herder*. A compromised computer's owner seldom knows that it has been compromised, which is why the computers are sometimes referred to as *zombies*. Zombies are usually infected via specially crafted viruses, worms, or Trojan horses. They are usually controlled via Internet Relay Chat (IRC) by a command and control computer, usually a server under the attackers' control. Botnets can comprise tens of thousands of computers; a few have as many as a million. They can be used for spreading malware, denial of service attacks, and so on. The owners of such bots sometimes lease them to others.

Man-in-the-middle (MITM) attack   This is a classic attack in which the attackers insert themselves into the middle of a conversation where they can observe traffic that goes from one computer to another. They can simply observe or manipulate traffic as it flows from source to destination and back.

Session hijacking   This is similar to a man-in-the-middle attack, but the attacker is able to take over a session that the victim has launched. This is done by observing, by guessing, or by some other means of gaining access to the session ID that is in use while a victim is connected. In some cases, once the victim has been granted a session ID, the attacker assumes the role of the victim by causing a denial of service against the victim so the victim is out of the picture as far as the session goes. Then the attacker continues on with the session, posing as the victim.

Brute force attack   A brute force attack involves trying all possible combinations until the correct one is found. This applies to passwords, encryption keys, and the like. An example of this type of attack occurs in the wireless world. It is now known that the Wired Equivalency Protocol (WEP) is subject to an attack in which the attacker breaks the WEP key. Once this is done, all traffic that is encrypted is available to the attacker, who is posing as another host on the wireless network. In a nutshell, this is done by exploiting a vulnerability in the WEP and capturing enough packets to run the exploit. This is just one type of brute force attack; there are many others.

These are but a few of the increasing number of ways that a network, computer, or application can be exploited.

Internal Threats

Internal threats to a network — in which network intrusion or data theft is carried out by people inside your organization — are generally considered the most dangerous type of threat because people inside your organization have more access and more knowledge about the network and the devices on the network. An internal threat could be something as simple as someone installing a keylogger on a coworker's computer and stealing a password to a system they want access to.

Internal threats have long been considered serious, but statistics are starting to show that this may not be the case. The CSI Computer Crime and Security Survey keeps track of losses attributed to computer crime and security breaches. In Figure 1.1, a graph from this study shows the loss due to insiders based on a survey size of 420 respondents.

FIGURE 1.1   Percentage of losses due to insiders

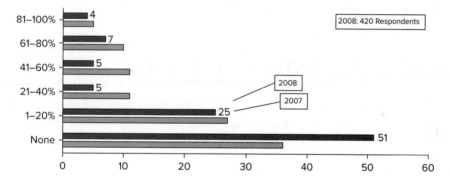

 You can sign up to receive a free copy of the CSI Computer Crime and Security Survey at the following Web page: http://www.gocsi.com/ forms/csi_survey.jhtml.

Internal threats are successful for a number of reasons:

- Improper patching
- Default configurations and default passwords
- Vendor best practices not followed

- Insecure programming practices
- Lax administration procedures

Application Security

Application attacks are attempts to gain control of a network or computer through a specific application, often a web browser or email application. Application attacks deserve special mention because they are said to account for 75 percent of all attacks carried out in today's networking environment. They are frequently successful due to a number of factors:

- Secure programming practices are not widespread. Programmers are usually under the gun to deliver code as quickly as possible, so security is often an afterthought. The best way to combat this is to use the Systems Development Life Cycle (SDLC) as a process to ensure that security is "built in" and not an afterthought.

- There's no firewall to crack through. With public facing web services, the application is already accessible.

- There are a growing number of security tools and applications that are built specifically for web attacks. And they are relatively easy to use.

Network Security Objectives

In a discussion about the tenets of network security, inevitably the CIA triad comes up (see Figure 1.2). CIA stands for confidentiality, integrity, and availability. These are collectively known as the objectives of network security.

FIGURE 1.2   The CIA triad

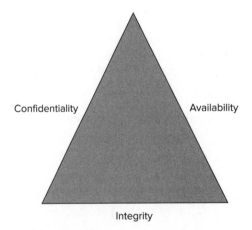

Confidentiality

Availability

Integrity

Let's discuss each of them briefly:

Confidentiality   Whether data is at rest or in motion, we are concerned about its confidentiality. Encryption is one way to protect data confidentiality. (Encryption will be covered in Chapter 9, "Understanding Cryptographic Solutions.") For example, when you make a purchase on the Web and you put in your credit card data, you should be concerned about the possibility of an unauthorized person seeing your personal details. That's why you should look for the use of HTTPS and/or the little lock symbol (depending on your browser) somewhere on your browser screen to indicate a secure session.

Integrity   Integrity refers to efforts made to ensure that data (whatever it may be) arrives at its destination unchanged. One method of checking integrity is to perform a check on the data using hash functions. A cryptographic hash function is defined as taking a string of variable length as input and producing a fixed-length hash. These checks help determine that the data that was originally sent is the same as the data that arrived.

Availability   Is data available? For example, if you are unable to access your Gmail account, which happed to me one morning recently, you have an availability problem. We have become a data-oriented society, and it's upsetting if our data isn't available.

So why do I mention the three objectives of information security? Think about the methodology a hacker uses to carry out an attack. When an attack takes place, it is against one of these three objectives. A denial of service attacks the availability of data. What about a simple defacement of a website? Wouldn't that be a simple attack against integrity? Let's take that example a bit further. Suppose someone adds false information to a Wikipedia entry and then someone else reads it and believes it to be true? Without getting into whether you should or should not believe everything you read on the Internet, such an action could be potentially damaging, and an attack against integrity. Finally, if someone breaks into a database and steals a load of credit card numbers, an attack against confidentiality has occurred.

Table 1.1 lists the network security objectives and some of the types of attack strategy used against each.

TABLE 1.1   Examples of Attack Types

Attack Category	Attack Strategy
Confidentiality	Man-in-the-middle, packet capture, port mapping
Integrity	Malicious code/data diddling, keylogger, proxy
Availability	DDOS, SYN flood, smurf attack

Classification of Data

Data classification is one of the first tasks an organization needs to embrace in order to adequately protect the data. If you don't know the value of the data that you are trying to protect, how can you know if you are assigning the appropriate controls? In many ways, it is enlightening to an organization to invest the time to determine what data they have, who owns the data, and how the data should be protected.

The following lists a number of important tenets surrounding data classification:

- All data is not equal.
- Some data might be embarrassing or damaging if made public.
- Some compliance measures require classification.
- You should focus your efforts on protecting the most critical data instead of trying to protect all data equally.

So what are the most important points to consider when classifying data?

First, if the organization goes to the trouble of classifying data, it sends a strong message about how dedicated it is to information security.

Second, the owners of the data get to determine what its sensitivity is. This helps system administrators and network security professionals determine the appropriate controls to safeguard the data.

Last, some types of data are subject to regulatory controls. Regulations may determine what controls should be used to safeguard the data.

Classification levels differ from organization to organization. Many firms try to follow a classification system similar to that of the many military organizations. Their classification system is shown in Table 1.2.

TABLE 1.2   Military Data Classifications

Classification	Description of Data
Unclassified	Data that has no confidentiality, integrity, or availability requirements. Not sensitive to the organization, so no need to secure.
Sensitive but unclassified (SBU)	Data that could provide some embarrassment to the organization if revealed, but no major security restrictions.
Confidential	Data that has the least-restrictive protection within the classified realm. This data must have confidentiality protection.

Classification	Description of Data
Secret	Data that must be secured at significant cost and effort. This data should be more restrictive that Confidential but less restrictive than Top Secret.
Top Secret	Data that must be secured with the most effort and cost, if necessary. Data at this level is usually available only to those who have been cleared at this level and who have a legitimate need to know.

Some organizations don't feel the need to have five levels of data classifications. Many organizations come up with their own scheme that fits their organizational needs. A common data classification scheme used in the private sector is shown in Table 1.3.

TABLE 1.3   Private Sector Data Classifications

Classification	Description of Data
Public	Data that is in the public domain, such as white papers, stock information, marketing information. No protection is required.
Sensitive	Very similar to the Sensitive But Unclassified (SBU) classification in the military model. An example might be a time-sensitive piece of data that could cause embarrassment if revealed early but would not cause a security breach.
Private	Data that is important to the organization and is protected accordingly. An employee directory might fall into this classification level. This information is not intended to be revealed to the outside world.
Confidential	The highest level within a private sector organization and afforded the highest level of security controls and expense. A trade secret, a formula, or non-public financial data are examples.

When an organization takes on the task of classification, it usually uses criteria like the following:

Value   This is the cornerstone of classifying data. What is the data worth to the organization? If you can't determine what it is worth, you have no basis on which to decide how much to spend to secure it.

Age   Ever notice that even the Pentagon declassifies certain data after a specific period of time? That's because it is no longer relevant from a security standpoint. An example might be a technology that was once secret but has now advanced well beyond its original form, so there is no reason to maintain the secrecy.

Usefulness   There's no reason to protect information no one cares about. For example, a three-year-old-financial report isn't really useful any more.

Personal data   This is protected by many different laws, so by definition, it has to be classified.

Once you decide on a scheme, you need to do some more tasks to finish the job of classifying data. Generally you need to identify who owns the data, how to classify it, and how best to secure it. Here's a checklist to help determine how to proceed:

1. Identify the custodian of the data.
2. Determine how the data is classified and labeled.
3. Identify the data owner and classify accordingly.
4. Identify any exceptions.
5. Identify specific controls to be used with each classification, if necessary.
6. Define the rules for declassifying data and disposal, if necessary.
7. Create a security awareness program that addresses information classification.

Are there times when data must be divulged, even though it is classified? As with everything else, there are certain gray areas or exceptions.

Court orders are one of the first things that come to mind in a discussion about divulging sensitive data. It is sometimes ordered that certain data be revealed to the court, including to court personnel. However, there is some expectation that the data would be divulged only to those with a need to know and that it would be protected while in the court's custody.

Here's another example. Suppose your company decided to outsource the HR department. The company would almost certainly need to turn over personnel records to the outsourcing company performing the HR function. This kind of data is generally protected legally through contractual obligations. This kind of situation calls for due diligence in that the outsourcing company must build in safeguards and determine effective controls. A good contract would specify the right to unannounced audits of security controls at any time.

Last, the roles that are played in an information security classification scheme are as follows.

Owner   The owner of the data is ultimately the person responsible for it, and it's usually a high-ranking member of management. The owner is generally different than the custodian.

Custodian The custodian is the person who takes care of the data, usually someone within the IT department. This is the person who maintains the server, the database, the backup tape, and so on.

User The user is someone who uses the data as part of their day-to-day duties. Users are generally governed by policies as to what they can or can't do with the data and how to handle it.

In the next section, we will look at the types of security controls that can be employed to protect the data after it's classified.

Security Controls

Security controls are measures applied to manage and reduce risk to your data. The strength of security controls and the type applied depend on the data being safeguarded. Security controls are generally lumped into three categories: administrative, technical, and physical.

Once data has been categorized and the owner has been identified, it is the custodian's responsibility to apply security controls to safeguard the data.

Security Controls by Type

Let's begin by examining the three basic types of security controls.

Administrative Administrative controls are typically associated with policies and procedures. Here are some examples of administrative controls:

- Security policies and procedures
- Awareness training
- Audits
- Change control procedures
- Background checks of employees
- Prudent hiring practices
- Job rotation
- Separation of duties

Administrative controls form the management layer of the control structure. If you don't have some policies and procedures, then the other two types of security controls are probably not going to work effectively.

Technical   Technical controls are usually hardware and software based, as are the following examples:

- Firewalls
- Intrusion prevention systems
- Router access Controls Lists
- Virtual private network (VPN) devices
- Identity management systems such as Terminal Access Controller Access-Control System Plus (TACACS+) and Remote Authentication Dial In User Service (RADIUS)
- Network admission control systems
- Tokens and smartcards

As with administrative controls, all of the technical controls in the world are worthless if they are the only line of defense. The combination of all three types helps to achieve data security.

Physical   Physical controls are typically mechanical in nature. The following are examples of physical controls:

- Locks
- Uninterruptible power supplies
- Diesel generators
- Security guards
- Motion sensors
- Alarm systems
- Safes
- Fire suppression systems

It must be said that even though there is a need for physical controls, human safety must come above all else. Doors and locks must have safeguards to allow exit in the event of an emergency.

Security Controls by Purpose

There is another way to categorize a security control — by its purpose. Each type of control mentioned earlier can also be categorized as follows:

- Preventative control
- Deterrent control
- Detective control

Sometimes a control can be in more than one of the preceding categories. For example, a security camera can be both a deterrent control (causing a would-be intruder to have second thoughts about breaking in) and a detective control (it can make a recording of what did happen so that security personnel have clues to an intruder's identity).

An example of a preventative control is proper hiring practices. When they are in place, human resource issues are prevented from arising because due diligence is put into the hiring process.

A security guard posted in the lobby of a bank is a great example of a deterrent control. Their main purpose is to make would-be robbers have second thoughts.

Finally, can you think of a detective control that is used in an IT environment? The first thing that pops into my mind is an Intrusion Detection System (IDS). This system alerts you after the fact that some anomalous condition occurred.

Incident Response

Responding to a security incident is an important part of security operations. How you respond is even more important. Maintaining one's composure and following a specific set of procedures is tantamount to success. There are typically six phases to incident response. You can remember these six phases by using the mnemonic word PICERL, as illustrated here:

- P - Preparation
- I - Identification
- C - Containment
- E - Eradication
- R - Restoration
- L - Lessons learned

We will explore each of these phases and then discuss some of the important facets of cybercrime.

Preparation

When we talk about the preparation phase from an incident handling perspective, we are talking about the steps required to get a team of people ready to handle incidents. It is through preparation that the elements come together. The following sections are not necessarily an exhaustive discussion but are meant to convey some of the key elements.

Policy

To prepare for future security incidents, there must be a firm policy in place and a list of procedures for what will happen when an incident occurs (as it inevitably will). Decisions must be made ahead of time about what will be done. It's of the utmost importance to have management buy in and sign off on both the policy and the procedures for handling an incident. Because an incident could potentially involve law enforcement, the legal team should be involved early on along with management to decide when, or even if, law enforcement should be called upon.

What happens when an incident takes place? Who gets notified and how? Is it a good idea to communicate over normal channels, or should there be an out-of-band method? These are some of the questions that need answers prior to jumping in. Usually there is a call tree of specific management personnel that need to be notified in the event of an incident. Because security incidents may compromise or break systems that are normally used to communicate, a secure, out-of-band method for communicating is strongly recommended.

Human Factors

When dealing with a potential security breach, it is easy to get worked up and make mistakes. The first order of business is to remain calm and think everything through. You should keep a notebook and take notes of everything that is observed and done. This will be valuable if an incident leads to criminal charges. It's important to keep a chronological record of what is happening so you don't have to recall it from memory while on the witness stand! If you take very good notes, the facts will be there in black and white for you to recall, complete with time and dates.

Also in the realm of human factors is the task of building a great team to react when an incident happens. It's best to pick a team from many disciplines so you have representation across the enterprise and the ability to look at any given issue with some level of expertise.

You should establish an organization that can support a response time service-level agreement of, say, 15 minutes to 30 minutes. It is largely up to management to determine their comfort level and how much money and manpower they want to allocate. If you have an incident at a remote location, either at another branch of your organization or at a company you work with, you need to decide if someone there can help you or if you need to send someone.

Additional Recommendations

A few other elements are key in the preparation phase. The following list lays out a number of recommendations:

- Establish a command post or war room from which to work.
- Establish a communications plan.
- Establish training and test runs.
- Coordinate with support desks and system administrators.
- Have emergency passwords and crypto keys available.
- Have a bag available with tools, drives, cables, USB keys, extra batteries, and so on.
- Have bootable media available with security tools and a laptop (or two).
- Have available cell phones and emergency call lists.

Identification

If something happens to your network, you need to decide how serious it is. In other words, you need to identify whether you have an *incident* (a serious breach) or an *event* (something happened, but it's not serious). This is analogous to someone running into the back of your car while you are stopped at a stoplight. You know something happened because you felt a jolt. But you don't know if it's a big deal until you get out and look at the bumper. You might find that there's no damage and you both go on your merry ways. On the other hand, you might know instantly that things are bad and you should call someone. It's the same for incident handling. For some things, it's intuitively obvious that there's a problem. For others, you might not know until you do some investigation.

In most cases, it's not wise to let just anyone declare that an incident has occurred. There should be established procedures about who can declare an incident. The responsible party should be someone who has been specifically trained and can quickly recognize if something is serious or not. That's not to say there is always someone who can recognize this. Keep in mind that it's better to declare an incident that turns out not to be one than it is not to declare one and have something serious happen and maybe cause damage.

How do you know if an incident has happened? Usually you have observed one or more suspicious events. For example, you observe a system log where a logon to the system has been attempted a hundred times in a row in a short period. That raises your eyebrows. First, no sane human being would try to log in to a system a hundred times. Second, it would be physically impossible for a human being to attempt the logon that many times in a short period of time. Something doesn't add up here. This would be a suspicious event, for sure. Other examples are unexplained new files or file modifications or missing logs.

So what happens after you declare an incident? You have gone through the preparation phase, so you know who to contact and who should do what; in other words, you follow the playbook.

Real World Scenario

A DNS Hack

While working at a transportation company several years ago, I ran into a situation one Friday afternoon. (Why do all these things happen on Friday?) The person who was responsible for administering the DNS servers called me and said that he couldn't log in as root anymore. Being the inquisitive type, I used my personal account to log in and started looking at the system. I noticed that the etc/password file had been modified 20 minutes earlier. I asked if there was any chance that he changed the password by accident, and the answer, of course, was no. Was there anyone else who had access? No, again. Well, it was time to call the boss and relay the bad news. It turned out the servers were scheduled to be updated with a patch over the weekend to close a security hole. Looked like the update was scheduled too late. The shelf life of vulnerabilities is getting shorter all the time.

Because there was no incident response team, the prudent decision at that time was to remove the servers from the network. The company was lucky that in the grand scheme of things, this action wasn't that critical. Imagine what might have happened if this had been a revenue-generation server, like an e-commerce server or credit card processing server. After much deliberation, the decision was made to rebuild the DNS servers over the weekend and be back in business on Monday morning.

The person who hacked in wasn't very smart. They could have created an account that wouldn't have been noticed, like an account with a variation of someone else's username. They could have lurked about for days or months without being noticed. They could have used their newfound access to do surveillance or launch attacks on other systems. The lessons learned here were to be cognizant of security patches and get them installed quickly. From an identification point of view, I was able to see that there was a serious problem almost immediately and quick action was taken.

In "A DNS Hack," identification was made by looking at a system. This is just one of the areas where identification is performed. It is also performed at the network perimeter and using firewall logs, IDS/IPS alerts, and router logs. There are also host file integrity products as well as antivirus products that can alert you to a problem.

Containment

Once you've identified the problem, it needs to be contained. You could do as I did and remove the system from the network. Safe move, but what if you wanted to observe the behavior? What if you need to do forensics? There are many factors to weigh when looking at an incident. Is it over or is it ongoing? How critical are the systems involved? Can you secure the area and still preserve evidence if you need to? Everyone handles these things differently, so be prepared. Can you filter the interloper at the perimeter with a router access control list (ACL)? Is the system stable enough to keep running? Lots of questions and the answers will depend on a lot of people's opinions, including management.

One thing that is almost always necessary is to do a backup as soon as possible. Usually a hard drive needs to be imaged multiple times. From a forensics standpoint, the original is kept for evidence. Backup copy 1 is then kept for possible production on a newly built system. Any other copies are made from backup copy 1 and could be used for forensics purposes.

Eradication

The next step is to decide how to get rid of the problem and get back to business. What's the first order of business when starting to get rid of the problem? If you guessed "find the last known clean backup," you hit the nail on the head. In today's environment, given the sophistication of many virus and worm writers, the chances that you are going to be rebuilding the system are pretty good. If that's the case, then you are definitely going to want the last good backup, because you're going to have to restore the data.

If you know how the attack happened, you will have to determine the best course of action to fix the system so the incident isn't repeated. If you don't know how it happened, maybe it's time to do a vulnerability assessment on the system to see if there are any big holes.

Recovery

Recovery is, simply put, getting the system back online and into production. The following steps are performed in the recovery phase:

- Restore the system.
- Validate the system.
- Put the system back into production.
- Monitor the system.

Lessons Learned

The final aspect of the incident response process is taking stock of the lessons learned. The goal here is to apply the knowledge learned during an incident to improve capabilities and hopefully the security.

This process should include a formal meeting at which a report should be presented explaining what happened, what was done, and how the situation can be improved to prevent a future occurrence.

Law and Ethics

In this section, we will explore the law as it relates to network security. We will cover the major types of law and how they might apply to a given situation. Intellectual property is a critical element in network security — I will briefly define the basic types. Ethics issues make big headlines in the news these days, and it plays an important role in how network security personnel work and how they are treated. In fact, it could be argued that the ethical standards of information security personnel need to be above and beyond those of other personnel. I'll wrap up this section with a discussion on major governance topics and how compliance with regulations fits into network security.

Legal Matters

The law is a driving factor behind policies at most organizations. To be more specific, compliance with certain laws and regulations is a motivating factor. Various regulatory agencies and the associated laws that they enforce make it necessary for anyone involved with information security to have at least a cursory knowledge of relevant aspects of the law. Depending on your job within information security, you might need to have more than just a cursory knowledge about the law. In particular, forensics specialists need to be conversant with rules of evidence, chain of custody, and other topics.

Let's begin by discussing the three basic types of law. Criminal law, civil law (also known as tort law), and administrative law are the three types typically found in most countries. That doesn't mean that they are all administered the same way or observed the same way in each country. This makes it more difficult to deal with a cybercriminal because more often than not, you are dealing with someone who might be operating in several countries.

Criminal Law

Criminal law involves transgressions of a jurisdiction's criminal code — laws against theft, murder, illegal drugs and other antisocial behavior. In the United States, these laws are enforced on local, state, and federal levels. Cop and lawyer shows on TV often portray the criminal law process, typically beginning when someone has committed a crime and then portraying the process as they travel through the justice system. Penalties can be probation, prison time, or fines and sometimes a combination of one or more.

As the computer/network industry continues to mature, more and more cases of criminal activity are starting to make headlines.

Generally speaking, prosecutors need to establish just three things to prove a criminal case in court:

Means   Were they capable of committing the crime?

Motivation   Was there a reason the culprit committed the crime?

Opportunity   Were they able to commit the crime?

You might ask why this is important. It ties directly into network security because evidence must be kept and a chain of custody of the evidence must be established. Evidence in a network security case could include, for example, physical hard drives, firewall logs, and intrusion detection messages.

Civil Law

Civil law deals with a perceived wrongdoing that is not necessarily criminal. It covers such matters as personal injuries, medical malpractice, slander, and business dealings. Civil law is usually about receiving money, although sometimes the court may require that an action be taken (or undone, in some cases). Prison is not an option in civil law.

Administrative Law

Administrative law usually involves the regulations and actions of government agencies. For instance, if a company was found to be negligent in paying its employees, a state or federal agency could force the company to correct the issue monetarily and could also levy an administrative fine as a punitive step.

Intellectual Property

Intellectual property is the largest asset of many companies. Therefore, it must be treated as confidential information and protected accordingly. Intellectual property may take one of the following forms:

Trademarks   A trademark is a word, a name, or a symbol that is used in trade and indicates where goods come from. It distinguishes one firm's products from another's.

Patents   A patent for an invention grants property rights to the inventor for a period of 20 years from the date the application was filed in the United States. U.S. patents are only valid inside the United States and its territories. A patent grants the right to prohibit others from making, using, or selling the invention.

Trade secrets   A trade secret is intellectual property that is not in the public domain. For example, the formula for Coca-Cola is a trade secret that is heavily protected. One of the tests to determine whether information is a trade secret is whether due care is taken to protect it.

Copyrights   A copyright protects original works, which include musical, literary, dramatic, and artistic works, whether they are published or unpublished. The Copyright Act of 1976 gives the owner of a copyright specific rights, including the right to control reproduction, distribution, and public performance or display.

For further information on intellectual property, visit the U.S. Patent and Trademark Office website at http://www.uspto.gov/web/offices/pac/doc/general/whatis.htm.

Ethics

Ethics refers to a set of standards and principles that are deemed to be higher than the law. Ethics involve morals and standards that are considered to be proper behavior in a given situation. Certain industry groups and professions usually have a code of ethics that they expect their members or constituents to abide by. Within the information security community, there are a number of ethics codes developed by industry organizations:

- International Information Systems Security Certification Consortium (ISC)^2 Code of Ethics
- Global Information Assurance Certification (GIAC) Code of Ethics
- Information Systems Security Association (ISSA) Code of Ethics
- Information Systems Audit and Control Association (ISACA) Code of Professional Ethics
- Internet Architecture Board (IAB)
- Generally Accepted System Security Principles (GAASP)
- Computer Ethics Institute

Review Questions

1. Which type of law is also called tort law?
   A. Administrative
   B. Criminal
   C. Judicial
   D. Governmental
   E. Civil

2. What is the guiding principle behind ethics instead of the law?
   A. Common sense
   B. The Golden Rule
   C. Morals
   D. Creed

3. What type of attack constitutes 75 percent of all attacks on today's networks?
   A. Internal
   B. External
   C. Application
   D. Password cracking
   E. Network

4. Which one of the following can be described as the "getting back to business" aspect of incident handling?
   A. Preparation
   B. Investigation
   C. Recovery
   D. Lessons Learned
   E. Containment

5. Which is *not* one of the things a prosecutor needs to prove in a cybercrime case?
   A. Means
   B. Money
   C. Opportunity
   D. Motivation

6. Which of the following is an external threat?

   A. An unpatched system

   B. Port scanning

   C. Default configurations

   D. Insecure programming practices

7. Which of the following would be part of the containment process?

   A. Investigating an incident

   B. Performing a backup

   C. Building a new server

   D. Formatting the hard drive

8. Which of the following is described as data that doesn't have any confidentiality, integrity, or availability requirements?

   A. Classified

   B. Secret

   C. Sensitive but unclassified

   D. Unclassified

   E. Confidential

9. Which of the following grants protections for 20 years in the United States?

   A. Trademark

   B. Patent

   C. Copyright

   D. Intellectual property

10. Which of the following is *not* one of the phases of incident response?

   A. Preparation

   B. Containment

   C. Identification

   D. Lessons learned

   E. Detection

P - **Preparation**

I - **Identification**

C - **Containment**

E - **Eradication**

R - **Recovery**

L - **Lessons learned**

Answers to Review Questions

1. E. Civil law is also known as tort law. This type of law involves the recovery of monetary damages.

2. C. Ethics can involve common sense, the Golden Rule, and creeds, but the best answer is morals, which are considered to be higher than the law.

3. C. Application attacks make up approximately 75 percent of all network attacks today.

4. C. Recovery describes the process of getting a server back into production and returning a business back to normal.

5. B. A prosecutor needs to prove means, motive, and opportunity.

6. B. Port scanning is usually done from outside, so that is your first clue that an attack is coming from outside the organization.

7. B. Performing a backup is part of the containment process because you may need to preserve evidence.

8. D. In the military data classification system, unclassified is the label for data that doesn't have any confidentiality, integrity, or availability requirements.

9. B. A U.S. patent is protected by law for a period of 20 years. Other types of intellectual property don't have the same protections.

10. E. Detection is not one of the phases of incident response. Remember the phases of incident response with the following mnemonic: PICERL.

Chapter

2

Creating the
Secure Network

**THE FOLLOWING CCNA SECURITY EXAM
OBJECTIVE IS COVERED IN THIS CHAPTER:**

✓ Describe the Cisco Self Defending Network architecture

The rest of the book discusses specific ways to secure a network from a Cisco perspective, but this chapter focuses on those things, from an operational perspective, that can be done to enhance network security. In this chapter I'll cover creating effective security policies and procedures, operations security, and the Cisco Self-Defending Network.

Creating a Security Policy

It is important that an organization takes the time to develop a comprehensive security policy. The policy must be enforced from the top levels of the company down and allow you to take the steps necessary to secure your company's information assets.

Goals of a Security Policy

The security policy sets out to define the following:

- The critical information assets of a company

- How they must be secured

- Appropriate use of the data and resources

The policy can be used to establish rules, set consequences for violations, suggest expected email etiquette and behavior, and so on.

A security policy establishes a baseline for what the security stance of the company will be. The baseline doesn't necessarily cover every single instance or every type of situation but lays out some basic rules. In most cases, the security policy is a living document because you will want to change or refine certain policies as your company's security posture matures as well as add new items as technology changes. For example, an antivirus policy that hasn't been touched for five years probably doesn't address the virus concerns of today.

What are the components of a good security policy? Well, for starters, it is not usually a single document, but a series of documents that target specific audiences. When I say the word *policy*, what I mean is the all-encompassing security direction or posture of the company as a whole.

A security policy should have at least three components: A governing policy, technical policies, and end-user policies. Let's look in more detail at the components.

Governing policy   The governing policy is a high-level document aimed primarily at managers and technical personnel. It covers the security items that are important to an entire organization. A typical governing policy covers the following topics:

- Identification of the issue
- The organization's position on the issue
- How the policy fits into the organization
- The roles and responsibilities of various members of the organization
- The level of compliance needed (i.e., what legal compliance measures apply to your organization)
- What actions are required and the consequences for noncompliance

Technical policies   Technical policies provide guidance for the IT staff, particularly security personnel. A backup policy is a good example of a technical policy. The person responsible for backups would use it to govern how backups are performed, stored, and so on.

End-user policies   As the name suggests, these are policies for the end user, and they cover company rules and guidelines such as, for example, the use of corporate email or the Internet. An email policy might contain such topics as whether it is acceptable to receive personal email at the office and not opening attachments from unknown persons.

One policy that is frequently discussed is the acceptable use policy (AUP), sometimes referred to as the appropriate use policy. If you've ever subscribed to an Internet or web service of any kind, you are probably familiar with the term. This policy lays out the dos and don'ts of using the service, whatever it might be. For example, a company might restrict employees from using stock ticker services during work hours. There might be restrictions on any nonbusiness use of the Internet during work hours, but there might be an exception for lunch time. If you sign up for an account with an Internet service provider, a prohibition on sending spam of any kind is usually part of the acceptable use policy. You get the idea: It's up to the company to decide how it wants the service to be used and what is and isn't acceptable. The AUP is a guiding document, but it can have security ramifications in that it might address issues about employees' use of the Internet and also how people from outside the company might use a company website.

Policies and Procedures

What is the difference between a policy and a procedure? A *policy* governs what should be done. For example, a policy might specify the need for a firewall to protect an organization from network attacks. A *procedure* is a step-by-step process describing how to actually perform a task — for instance, how to configure a specific firewall rule. Organizations typically have both. Procedures are sometimes identified by different names in different organizations, but the end result is the same. Policies by themselves are only high-level guidance; they do not tell you how to do something specifically.

Other Documents

There are other detailed documents that are used in an organization for security related tasks:

- **Standards:** Documents used to create consistency across the organization on how things are done. For example, there might be a router standard that specifies a hardening build. There also might be standards for server builds.

- **Guidelines:** Documents that suggest rather than require. For example, an end-user computing security guide might explain how to disable peer-to-peer file sharing.

Managing Risk

Some might say that managing risk is the embodiment of security, and I would have to agree. Although that is a simple statement to make, managing risk can be complex. How does one put a price on a piece of data? Sometime it's a simple enough task, and sometimes it's more difficult. The first priority when thinking about risk management should be to determine which data is worth protecting. The next step is to identify the systems on which the data is located.

Once you have identified those key pieces, you can begin to evaluate the threat against the systems and the data. This process is called *threat identification* or *threat modeling*. *Risk analysis* is then performed to determine the probability of a threat and what would happen if a threat were successful. Let's examine these a bit further.

Threat Identification

Let's look at an example of threat identification. Suppose you maintain the e-commerce site of a retail company that does $500 million worth of business a year, 50 percent of it over the Web. What kinds of threats do you face for this application? Building a list such as following is the first step in threat identification. It describes some of the threats an e-commerce application might face:

- Denial of service attack, which interrupts the revenue stream
- A system compromise that results in one or more of the following:

- Stolen credit card or banking data
- Loss of customer data
- Web defacement
- Deletion of transactional data
- Fraudulent transactions
- Public embarrassment and loss of trust

Risk Analysis

Once you have identified the threats, you need to do a risk analysis to determine the likelihood of the event occurring and what the ramifications could be. A risk analysis of the list of threats in the previous section might look like this:

Denial of service attack   The denial of service attack is easy to implement, and there is a high likelihood that it will happen. The tools are out there in great number and do not require a great deal of knowledge to use. The impact on an organization is potentially great because the ability to prevent and remedy denial of service attacks is limited in scope. Depending on the type of organization, the effects of a successful denial of service attack could range from mild annoyance to actual loss of revenue.

System compromise   A system compromise, in which someone gains access to the data on the system, is also highly likely, and the impact would be great.

Stolen credit card data could impact the company on a number of fronts, from Payment Card Industry (PCI) fines all the way to loss of public trust in the company. Loss of customer data would have some of the same effect on public trust and could cause a loss of business.

Web defacement is less of a concern in terms of the severity of consequences, but it is still embarrassing to the company.

Lost transactional data could hopefully be recovered through backups or an online duplicate copy, but it's still considered serious, largely because of the time it usually takes to restore data from backups.

Fraudulent transactions   Fraudulent transactions are all but a given in today's Internet environment and could have a great impact. They are accomplished through identify theft, system compromises, and insecure coding methods.

Public embarrassment and loss of trust   Public embarrassment is something very likely, given the sheer number of attacks. Impact could be very little to great, depending on what the issue is. For example, a very public loss of credit card data could be devastating to a credit card company but perhaps less so for a retailer. It depends largely on the type of loss, the consumer damage that was done, and the type of company. Loss of consumer trust in a company usually leads to loss of revenue, at least for a time.

What I have just outlined is an example *qualitative risk analysis*. This means that we looked at specific scenarios to determine where risk is and the likelihood of a risk event occurring. Consequences will likely be evaluated as well, and plans should be made to deal with an incident should it occur. But there is another type of risk analysis and that is *quantitative risk analysis*, which relies on mathematical formulas to determine assets, loss expectancy, and other values. This type of analysis is similar to what insurance companies do, from an actuarial basis. The values used in quantitative analysis are shown in Table 2.1.

TABLE 2.1   Quantitative Risk Analysis Values

Values	Description
Asset value (AV)	Value of an asset.
Exposure factor (EF)	The percentage of loss of an asset that would be realized if a risk event occurs.
Single loss expectancy (SLE)	The cost each time a risk event occurs. This is usually calculated for each threat.
Annualized rate of occurrence (ARO)	The estimated frequency of a risk event occurring — for example, how many times per year your website sustains a denial of service attack.
Annualized loss expectancy (ALE)	Expected amount of loss attributed to a single threat in a single year.

The relevant formulas when determining quantitative risk are as follows:

- Single loss expectancy (SLE) is the monetary cost each time a threat occurs for a given risk. SLE represents the asset value (AV) multiplied by the exposure factor (EF), or expressed mathematically, AV * EF = SLE.

- Annualized loss expectancy (ALE) is loss expectancy from a single threat in a given year in dollars. It's expressed mathematically as ALE = SLE * ARO. This figure can be used to justify the cost of security measures or controls applied to deter this threat.

Real World Scenario

Denial of Service Attack!

In the section "Threat Identification" earlier in this chapter, I gave you an example of a qualitative risk analysis for an e-commerce site for a retail company. This time we will look at it from the perspective of a quantitative analysis.

In this example, we will assume that the exposure factor (EF) is 70 percent; that is, if the web server resources or any part thereof were hit with a denial of service attack, only 30 percent of the site would be available. To get to an asset value, we need to look at what the annualized value of the revenue generated by the website would be. I stated earlier that it was 50 percent of the company's sales and that yearly the company's sales were around $500 million. That would make the asset value (AV) of the website $250 million. That means that the single loss expectancy (SLE) calculations are as follows:

$$AV\ (\$250,000,000) * EF\ (.70) = SLE\ (\$170,000,000)$$

So the SLE is $170 million for a denial of service attack. Some of the theory here doesn't match very closely with reality. What are the odds that only 30 percent of the website would be available for a whole year? The reality is that it's not likely at all. Could it happen for a few hours or days? Certainly. So you really need to multiply the calculated value by whatever time you think the website would be down in this case. Let's say that it's down an entire day. Assuming it's a 24/7 site, that's 1/365 of the value that we came up with earlier:

$$SLE = 1/365 * \$170,000,000 = \$465,763$$

Carrying this further, the annualized loss expectancy (ALE) is the product of the SLE multiplied by the annual rate of occurrence (ARO). The ARO is the number of times this action would be expected in a year. For the purpose of this example, let's use 3:

$$ALE = SLE\ (\$465,763) * ARO\ (3) = \$1,397,260$$

That means we would have no problems authorizing a fairly large sum of money to defend against a DoS attack. Because there is a lot of guesswork in these kinds of analyses, everything isn't always crystal clear.

Risk Management versus Risk Avoidance

In addition to threat identification and the two types of risk analysis are risk management and risk avoidance. *Risk management* is the process of determining risks and minimizing the negative consequences, and *risk avoidance* is the process of minimizing the exposure to a risk, which would be one form of managing it. Avoiding a risk by avoiding the risky activity altogether is usually not an option. To go back to the example of the retail company that does $500,000 worth of business a year, 50 percent of it over the Web, it's not likely that the business would want to avoid making $250 million a year. That means you manage the risk. Risk management involves the application of proper security controls to reduce the risk to acceptable levels.

There's a third category, and that's *risk transference*. If you don't want to manage the risk yourself, you can transfer the risk to someone else. For example, you could outsource your credit card processing for your website to a third party. If the hackers can't get to credit card numbers on your systems, then you have transferred that risk to someone else.

Secure Network Design

The concept of secure network design is important to security policies and risk management. The design can be affected by many things:

- Business requirements
- Security policy
- Risk analysis
- Security operations
- Operations security best practices

Let's explore these items a bit more:

Business requirements   Business requirements don't always include security concerns when they involve new systems. But you must find a way to keep a business running while still addressing security. This is probably the most important area of secure network design.

Security policy   As discussed earlier, a security policy addresses how systems need to be deployed.

Risk analysis   The risk from an insecure network needs to be analyzed to determine a cost should the risk be realized. You can then make an informed decision about how much you would be willing to spend to reduce that risk.

Security operations   This includes auditing, monitoring systems, and incident response.

Operations security best practices   Operations security best practices can help guide the design with solutions that have been deployed and proven elsewhere.

When designing a network, it is important to have a good set of assumptions going in. Sometimes it is necessary to "think like a hacker" and look at your network from that perspective. How would you attack this design if you were on the outside looking in? Here are some of the things you might want to focus on:

- Attack vectors. What are all of the ways that you can get into your network? You should include every possible path.

- Plan for the future. What security measures are going to be available in a year, three years, five years down the road and how will that impact your network design? It's hard to determine what these might be, but keeping up with thought leaders can help you.

- Plan for failure. Look for single points of failure and plan accordingly.

Keep your design simple. The more complex it is, the greater the possibility that you will misconfigure something. An entry point will be overlooked, a single point of failure will be missed, and something will be bypassed because the design was too complex.

Also, adhere to the principle of least privilege when doing secure network design. *Least privilege* means each person, software application, or item of hardware has the lowest privileges necessary to perform their required functions. This applies to many areas, including personnel, but let's focus on the network for the moment. Suppose you have an e-commerce web server that is physically in the demilitarized zone (DMZ) of your network. See Figure 2.1 for a diagram of this scenario.

FIGURE 2.1   Principle of least privilege

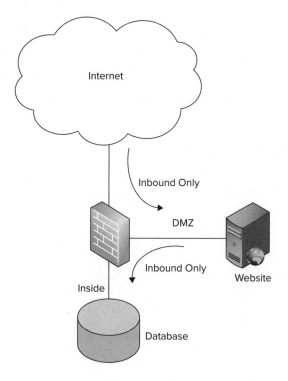

The web server needs to talk to a database sitting behind the DMZ on the inside of the network. How would you design this from a firewall perspective? Following the principle of least privilege, you would allow only traffic from the Internet into the web server. From the web server into the DMZ, you would allow only traffic to the database on the inside. There would be no traffic allowed out to the Internet originating from the web server, and there would be no traffic allowed from the database out to the DMZ. Therefore, only the traffic that is absolutely necessary to perform the function is allowed.

Creating Security Awareness

User awareness of security concerns at an organization is largely driven from the top down. The best organizations are what I call "security conscious" and the concept of security is ingrained in all that they do. How is that awareness distributed to the masses?

There are three components of any security awareness program:

- Awareness
- Training
- Education

Awareness

A security awareness program should be part of every employee's training, starting on the first day on the job. In addition, user security training should be periodically reinforced. Maintaining awareness is a combination of informing users about security policies and systems, keeping the user informed about current threats, and reinforcing good security habits. Tools for improving security awareness can include security posters, login banners, computer-based training, videos, and newsletters.

The key elements of an effective user awareness training program are as follows:

- Motivation of management and employees
- Administration of the program
- Maintenance of the program
- Evaluation of the program
- Identification of the scope and objectives
- Identification of the proper instructors
- Identification of the groups to receive the training

Training

Security training serves the purpose of providing current information and developing the skills of IT employees who are not necessarily directly involved in administering network security. Target audiences for this kind of training are members of management, audit staff, developers, system administrators, and the like. Training typically focuses on teaching skills, and the primary difference between training and awareness is that awareness focuses on drawing attention to a specific topic rather than pushing a specific skill.

Education

Education is the composite of a number of multidisciplinary skills that are taken as an overall program that lends itself toward the creation of a well-rounded security professional. Education is usually conducted at a college or university, with a degree conferred at the conclusion. While colleges and universities have more than just degree programs, taking a single or even multiple classes typically is more closely related to training than education. In other words, having a degree is one type of education, but in order to stay up-to-date and continue your education, ongoing training is required. You might also consider furthering your education — say, pursue an advanced degree — but the idea is to continuously learn.

Maintaining Operational Security

Operational security is defined as the security measures employed to protect systems (hardware), software, and the media that contains data. This commonly involves the actions of security personnel after systems and software have been installed. Now it is their job to monitor and secure those systems and applications, protecting from internal and external threats as well as operational threats in the environment. One of the ways that this can be done is by employing measures that control the way systems are deployed and software is written. One such measure is called the Systems Development Life Cycle (SDLC).

> The U.S. Department of Defense uses the term *operations security (OPSEC)*. This refers to measures taken to compartmentalize or secure information that would compromise operations if discovered by the enemy.

Defining the Systems Development Life Cycle

Depending on who you talk to, SDLC can be expanded to Systems Development Life Cycle or Software Development Life Cycle. For the purpose of this discussion, let's go with the Systems Development Life Cycle.

The SDLC is a methodology in which to build and deploy information systems. (It can also be used for writing software, hence the alternative definition, Software Development Life Cycle.) There are also a number of other methodologies that can be used, lest you think the SDLC is the only one. The SDLC process is illustrated in Figure 2.2.

FIGURE 2.2   The SDLC process

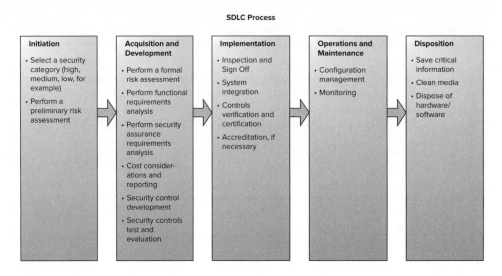

Initiation   Initiation is generally thought of as capturing two items: security categorization and risk assessment.

Security categorization occurs when the security of the system is assigned to one of several categories — generally high, medium, or low. The categories represent how severely a breach of security for the given system would affect the organization. Categorization helps determine the appropriate security controls to be used.

A preliminary risk assessment is what some might call a "ballpark" view of things. It is a very high-level assessment of the security requirements. A more detailed, formal risk assessment occurs later in the process.

Acquisition and Development   Acquisition and development covers a number of items, including the formal risk assessment process.

- The risk assessment process identifies protection requirements and refines the preliminary assessment that was done in the Initiation stage.

- Functional requirements analysis is another part of Acquisition and Development. This analysis looks at security policy, architecture, and functional security requirements.

- Continuing, security assurance is an analysis of the requirements that are required and assurance that security will work correctly. The analysis is based on legal and functional requirements and defines what assurance methods are required.

- A cost analysis is important to determine what security costs are associated with the development of the system.

- Security control development identifies planned or existing security controls, including policy, security training, incident response, and configuration management.

- Security controls test and evaluation tests security controls during development and after the system is developed.

Implementation   Implementation generally consists of four tasks. The inspection and sign-off process verifies that the deliverables meet the requirements. Any integration to be done with other systems is performed at this stage as well as enabling security controls settings to be used. Security certification controls are tested again to ensure that the operation functions as planned. Security certification involves testing for vulnerabilities in the system. Once that is complete, a system accreditation is performed. A senior member of the organization authorizes the implementation of the system and certifies that the risks have been identified and assurance made.

Operations and Maintenance   Operations and Maintenance consists of performing configuration management and control and then monitoring the system. Change management is part of this process to inform parties that use the system and any associated integrated system of impending changes. Monitoring is key in determining that a system is performing correctly and verifying security control effectiveness.

Disposition   Disposition is the final phase of the SDLC. Once the asset or system has reached the end of its life, a few things need to be taken care of. First, any information that was stored on the system needs to be evaluated for preservation purposes. Is there a legal or compliance need to keep the data on the system? Next, the media has to be destroyed or sanitized. What do you do with your used hard drives? There must be a procedure to sanitize or destroy the hardware. An example would be to degauss a hard drive before it is sold or reused. Last, proper procedures must be followed to dispose of any hardware or software that made up the system.

Review of Operations Security

The primary tenets of operations security involve the security and IT personnel assigned to safeguard IT assets. These principles are in place to ensure the following:

- Data remains intact and can be recovered in a disaster.

- No one person has too many privileges.

- Changes made to a system or systems do not impact an organization's security posture.

    Some of the best practices of operations security are shown in Table 2.2.

TABLE 2.2   Operations Security Best Practices

Practice	Description
Separation of duties	One person alone should not be allowed to compromise security. A *dual operator* or a *two-man control* system should be in place to avoid this issue. This may be difficult in smaller organizations.
Rotation of duties	A single employee cannot subvert security practices easily if employees' duties are rotated. Peer review can expose any issues. This also may be difficult in smaller organizations.
Trusted recovery	An organization must make backups, secure them, and test them regularly to be prepared for a disaster.
Configuration and change control	Change control is a necessity in any organization and is designed to prevent a change from impacting other functional areas inadvertently. Changes are usually reviewed by peers and backout plans are formulated.

Evolution of Threats

In the 1980s there were boot viruses, which took weeks and sometimes months to proliferate. They weren't terribly sophisticated, but they were effective. In 1988, the Morris worm was launched, proving that such a thing could be very effective and in a very short amount of time. This was just the beginning of what was to be.

 The Morris worm was launched in November 1988 and was the first occurrence of a malicious piece of code that installed itself one or more times and distributed itself via the Internet without user intervention. It spread rapidly and caused denial of service attacks on many Sun and Vax computers.

In the 1990s there were email viruses, denial of service attacks, and some limited hacking, but not to the extent we see today, by any means. In the early 1990s, viruses were mostly spread by sharing infected floppy disks. But then the Internet went commercial and email viruses became prevalent, as well as infected programs.

In the early 2000s we started to see self-replicating technology in viruses, worms, and malware. Malicious software took weeks and months to spread in the 1980s, days in the 1990s, and just minutes in today's world.

One of the earliest self-replicating worms in the early 2000s was the so-called Code Red worm, which debuted in mid 2001. It targeted a vulnerability in the indexing service of Microsoft's Internet Information Services (IIS) server. A patch had been issued for this vulnerability only a month earlier. This incident was the beginning of when people started to pay attention to patch management. The worm caused hundreds of thousands of machines to be infected in just a matter of days.

Another example of the speed in which worms spread is the SQL slammer incident, which happened in 2003. This was a piece of code that did very little other than send itself to random, self-generated IP addresses. It caused a denial of service condition that was exacerbated by the fact that if it found a specific vulnerability in Microsoft's SQL Server software, it would install itself on the server. This happened at a very fast rate; 90 percent of the vulnerable machines were infected within 10 minutes of launch.

Today's viruses, worms, and malware are particularly sophisticated, having the capability to shut down antivirus software, morph to avoid detection, and propagate in a number of ways. Because they use multiple ways of infecting and propagating, they are known as a *blended threat*. A blended threat may combine several different technologies to create a supervirus or worm. Attacks are starting to become more targeted, and the ability to send an attack from many hosts (botnets) to a single host can cause a massive denial of service.

So why is this such a threat today? There are a number of reasons, but one of the biggest is that the network perimeter is largely gone. It used to be that we could keep interlopers at bay by building a secure perimeter using several layers of defense. Now, there isn't only one area that connects into our network. We have multiple entry points, such as remote access virtual private networks (VPNs), business-to-business partner VPNs, portals, SSL VPNs, web mail front ends, wireless networks, smart phones, and so forth. You have to protect all of these.

Also, we allow more ports and services into our networks from the Internet than at any time before. To pick a basic example, port 80 is allowed into every website that is available from the Internet. This has given rise to Application layer attacks, which target web services and the systems behind web services, such as databases.

So we need a defense system that is adaptable to all of these kinds of threats without the worry that we are missing something when a new attack vector presents itself.

The Cisco Self-Defending Network

If you look at the history of the threat vector, you'll see that it used to move a lot slower than today's lightning quick worms and viruses. There was a time when you could react to a threat before it became a serious issue. That time is gone. So what do we do about it? Enter the Cisco Self-Defending Network.

The Self-Defending Network is an offering from Cisco that provides a defense-in-depth architecture by layering on several products that provide different security services. It is designed to be adaptable to threats and recognize attacks and thwart them.

Characteristics of the Cisco Self-Defending Network

There are three characteristics to the Cisco Self-Defending Network, as shown in Figure 2.3.

FIGURE 2.3   Core characteristics of the Cisco Self-Defending Network

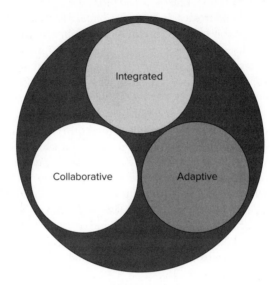

A self-defending network must be integrated, collaborative, and adaptive. What does that mean?

Integrated   First, all the parts must work together and should be designed that way from the start. It does no good if an intrusion detection system (IDS) sends alerts somewhere but none of the other systems are aware of it.

Collaborative   The systems need to cross more than one boundary within information technology groups.

Adaptive   The products must adapt to an ever changing security threat.

Other benefits to the Cisco Self-Defending network include the following:

- Comprehensive network defense that delivers threat intelligence and multivector threat identification
- Streamlined policy management
- Business protection

Let's have a look at the architecture of a self-defending network, which is shown in Figure 2.4.

FIGURE 2.4   Cisco Self-Defending Network architecture

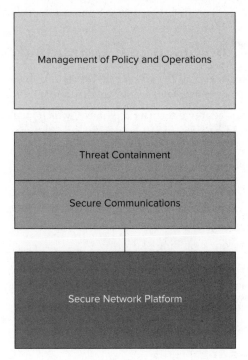

The foundation is the network, of course. There must be a secure network platform from which to build on. The next building block provides encryption, intrusion detection and prevention, and threat containment. And at the top is a management platform that provides control and oversight of all the pieces we just discussed.

Let's look at each of these in a bit more detail.

Secure network platform   This is the Cisco network consisting of the switches and routers that are in place and using the security features built into the IOS. An example would be utilizing Dynamic ARP Inspection (DAI) on layer 2 devices and access control lists on a router.

Secure communications   This can be achieved using Cisco's products which implement Secure Sockets Layer (SSL) and IPsec VPNs, for instance. These can be either site-to-site or remote-access solutions. For the purpose of this discussion, we are talking only about data in motion.

Threat containment   Using solutions such as Cisco Security Agent, which implements host security, is part of the way threats are contained. Viruses and spyware can be contained via email. Infrastructure threats can be contained via products such as firewalls, by protecting ports that shouldn't be exposed to third-party networks such as the Internet.

Management of policy and operations   The network management systems allow you to deploy policy in a more automated fashion, not to mention more accurately. They allow you to respond to threats in a quicker fashion and to gain a more global view of end-to-end security. Another benefit of operational control is improved workflow management.

Components of the Cisco Self-Defending Network

Here are some of the components of the Cisco Self-Defending Network. This is not an exhaustive list, but merely some of the components that you might commonly run into:

- Cisco ASA 5500 series adaptive security appliance, which includes the following models: 5505, 5510, 5520, 5540, 5550, and 5580
- Cisco 4200 series intrusion prevention appliance, also known as an intrusion detection system (IDS) or IDS sensor
- Cisco Integrated Service Routers (ISRs) and SDM software
- Monitoring, Analysis, and Response System (MARS) appliance, which receives alerts and does correlation across several different security platforms
- 6500 series switch, a core switching platform
- Cisco Security Manager (CSM), a management platform for security devices
- Cisco ACS Server, used for authentication, authorization, and accounting
- Cisco Security Agent (CSA) host intrusion prevention system
- Cisco NAC (network admission control) appliance

Summary

In this chapter, you learned about the three components of a security policy: a governing policy, technical policies, and end-user policies. You also learned about the differences between policy and procedures. We covered risk management and secure network design. Also discussed was the concept of operational security and the SDLC process as well as security operations best practices. Wrapping up the chapter was a discussion of the Cisco Self-Defending Network. The characteristics of the Cisco Self-Defending Network are that it is integrated, collaborative, and adaptive.

Exam Essentials

Understand the goals and components of a security policy.   The goals of a security policy are to identify the critical information assets of an organization, how they must be secured, and the appropriate use of data and resources. The components of a security policy are a governing policy, technical policies, and end-user policies.

Know the components of managing risks.   Threat identification and risk analysis are the underpinnings of managing risk. One element of risk analysis is quantitative analysis, which utilizes a formula that determines the annual loss expectancy (ALE) for a specific risk.

Know the best practices of operations security.   Separation of duties, rotation of duties, trusted backup, and configuration management and change control are the best practices of operation security. Adhering to these principles helps to ensure that data remains intact and can be recovered in a disaster. Also, they ensure that no one person has too many privileges. Finally, you need to make sure system changes do not impact other systems or compromise security for the organization.

Know the phases of the Systems Development Life Cycle process.   The SDLC process has five phases to it. It starts with Initiation, followed by acquisition and development, implementation, operations and maintenance, and finally, disposition. Using the SDLC process is part of operations security.

Understand the components of the Cisco Self-Defending Network.   The Cisco Self-Defending Network is a system of components that are adaptive, collaborative, and integrated. It has a base secure network layer followed by a threat containment engine and secure communications managed by an operational control and management policy layer. Hardware components of a Cisco Self-Defending Network include ISR routers, ASA series adaptive security appliances, Cisco MARS appliances, and IDS Sensors.

Written Lab

Write the answers to the following questions:

1. What are the five phases of the SDLC?
2. The acronym OPSEC was first used by whom?
3. Name the three components of a user awareness program.
4. Name two Cisco hardware components of the Cisco Self-Defending Network.
5. What is the formula for calculating the ALE?
6. What is the concept of least privilege?
7. The Cisco Self-Defending Network has three characteristics. What are they?
8. What is one component of managing risk?
9. Name the operations security best practices.
10. What are the three components of a security policy?

Review Questions

1. What product can be considered to be part of the threat containment architecture?

   A. MARS

   B. Catalyst switch

   C. ASA firewall

   D. Cisco Security Agent (CSA)

2. Which of the following is *not* a characteristic of the Cisco Self-Defending Network?

   A. Adaptive

   B. Collaborative

   C. Integrated

   D. Intelligent

3. Which of the following is the foundation component of the Cisco Self-Defending Network architecture?

   A. Effective management structure

   B. Dedicated firewalls

   C. Secure network

   D. Strong encryption

   E. Cisco Security Agent

4. Which would not be, by itself, a component of the Cisco Self-Defending Network?

   A. Cisco ASA 5510 adaptive security appliance

   B. Cisco 4200 IDS appliance

   C. Cisco 6500 switch

   D. Cisco MARS

   E. Cisco NetFlow

5. Which of the following is part of the management component of the Cisco Self-Defending Network?

   A. SAM

   B. ASA 5510

   C. IOS

   D. MARS

6. The SDLC process does not include which of the following components?

    A. Initiation

    B. Disposition

    C. Remediation

    D. Implementation

    E. Operations and maintenance

7. Which one of the following is *not* a component of operations security best practices?

    A. Least privilege

    B. Rotation of duties

    C. High availability

    D. Trusted recovery

    E. Configuration management and change management

8. Which one of the following is *not* a component of a good security policy?

    A. A governing policy

    B. User policies

    C. Technical policies

    D. User training

9. When performing a risk analysis, which of the following is the number of times an event might happen in a year?

    A. Guess

    B. ARO

    C. ALE

    D. SRO

10. Which one of the following is defined as a means to compartmentalize information such as not to compromise security?

    A. SDLC

    B. CIA

    C. OPSEC

    D. MARS

11. A document specifying that encryption must be used when transferring data over the Internet would be an example of what?

   A. Technical policy

   B. Technical guideline

   C. Governing policy

   D. End-user guideline

12. Which of the following is *not* a component of a security awareness program?

   A. Awareness

   B. Training

   C. Education

   D. Management

13. When discussing annual loss expectancy, which of the following would be described as the loss expectancy from a single threat in a given year in dollars?

   A. ALE

   B. SLE

   C. ARO

   D. LE

   E. SEL

14. Which is not a goal of an information security policy?

   A. Identify the critical information assets.

   B. Identify how the assets must be secured.

   C. Identify the appropriate use of data.

   D. Identify the risk to the data.

15. Which of the following products would be part of the secure communications component of the Cisco Self-Defending Network?

   A. MARS

   B. Cisco ACS server

   C. ISR router

   D. ASA security appliance

   E. Cisco NAC

16. The SDLC process includes a formal risk assessment. Which phase does it belong to?

    A. Initiation

    B. Disposition

    C. Acquisition and development

    D. Implementation

    E. Operations and maintenance

17. A computer virus that combines several different technologies is known as what?

    A. Polymorphic threat

    B. Blended threat

    C. Super threat

    D. Sophisticated virus

    E. Worm

18. Transferring credit card processing from your data center to a third-party processor is an example of what?

    A. Risk management

    B. Risk assessment

    C. Risk avoidance

    D. Risk transference

19. When performing a risk analysis, which of the following is the formula for determining the annual loss expectancy (ALE)?

    A. SLE * ARO

    B. ARO * AV

    C. ALE * EF

    D. EF * SRO

20. Which one of the following is *not* an OPSEC best practice?

    A. Trusted recovery

    B. Principle of least privilege

    C. Threat containment

    D. Rotation of duties

Answers to Review Questions

1. D. The best answer is Cisco Security Agent, largely because it is a host intrusion prevention system and is built so it can contain a threat, even if encountered.

2. D. The three core characteristics of the Cisco Self-Defending Network are integrated, collaborative, and adaptive.

3. C. A secure network platform is the foundation of the Cisco Self-Defending Network. Other components, such as encryption and intrusion prevention, are layered on top of the foundation component.

4. E. All of the components except for Cisco NetFlow could be considered components of the Cisco Self-Defending Network. The access point could be considered part of the secure network platform from which to build on.

5. D. The best answer is MARS, which stands for Monitoring, Analysis, and Response System. It describes an appliance that receives alerts from various security components and is able to compile, analyze, and respond, if necessary, to the security event at hand.

6. C . Remediation is not one of the fi ve phases of the Systems Development Life Cycle (SDLC). The missing one is acquisition and development.

7. C. High availability is not an operations security best practice; however, it is a good system design practice.

8. D. User training is not a component of a security policy, but user policies are.

9. B. The annual rate of occurrence (ARO) is the number of times a security risk event might take place in a year.

10. C. OPSEC stands for *operations security* and is borrowed from the U.S. Department of Defense. The term is adapted to mean that a user or administrator should have only the privileges they need to do their job and nothing else.

11. C. The best answer to this question is a governing policy. The reason it's a governing policy is that it tells you encryption must be used but doesn't tell you what strength or type of encryption to use. A technical policy might tell you what kind of encryption to use.

12. D. The three components of a security awareness program are awareness, training, and education.

13. B. The loss expectancy from a single threat in a given year in dollars is the single loss expectancy, or SLE.

14. D. The three goals of an information security policy are to identify the critical information assets of an organization, how they must be secured, and the appropriate use of data and resources.

15. C, D. The Cisco ISR router and Adaptive Security Appliance (ASA) product both support VPN capabilities, which would qualify as secure communications.

16. C. A formal risk assessment is performed during the acquisition and development phase.

17. B. A blended threat is a virus that combines several different technologies.

18. D. Risk transference is transferring risk to another party.

19. A. The annual loss expectancy is computed by multiplying the single loss expectancy (SLE) by the annual rate of occurrence (ARO).

20. C. Threat containment is not one of the OPSEC best practices. It is a principle of the Cisco Self-Defending Network.

Answers to Written Lab

1. Initiation, acquisition and development, implementation, operations and maintenance, and disposition

2. The U.S. Department of Defense

3. Awareness, training, and education

4. All of these are correct answers: adaptive security appliance (ASA); Integrated Service Router (ISR); IPS appliance; Monitoring, Analysis, and Response System (MARS) appliance

5. ALE = SLE * ARO

6. Having the least amount of privileges possible to do your job.

7. Integrated, collaborative, and adaptive

8. Threat identification or risk analysis

9. Separation of duties, rotation of duties, trusted backup, and configuration management and change control

10. A governing policy, technical policies, and end-user policies

Chapter

3

Securing Administrative Access

THE FOLLOWING CCNA SECURITY EXAM OBJECTIVES ARE COVERED IN THIS CHAPTER:

✓ Secure administrative access to Cisco routers by setting strong encrypted passwords, exec timeout, login failure rate and using IOS login enhancements

✓ Secure administrative access to Cisco routers by configuring multiple privilege levels

✓ Secure administrative access to Cisco routers by configuring role based CLI

✓ Secure the Cisco IOS image and configuration file

In this chapter, we'll explore the ways to secure administrative access to your router. We'll look at the Cisco Integrated Services Router (ISR) series of routers and the Cisco Secure Device Manager (SDM).

Securing Administrative Access

In this section, we explore the ways to secure administrative access to the router. This involves securing physical as well as virtual ports and setting passwords, levels of access, and levels of privilege.

Methods of Accessing the Router

There are many ways for a router administrator to communicate with a router:

- Console port on the router

- Virtual port over the network

- HTTP or HTTPS over the network

Generally, when you configure a router for the first time, you use the console port on the router because you are physically close to it.

Later, after the router is configured, you might gain access over the network using a virtual port—or, in Cisco parlance, a VTY port—with either Telnet or SSH. And then you might access the router over the auxiliary or AUX port when it is attached to a modem.

Let's talk a bit about the use of the VTY ports. You can use the Telnet program on your host computer to access the router via the VTY port; however, using Telnet is discouraged because you can see the username and password over the network in plain text. If you use a program such as Wireshark on your host computer, you can observe what I'm talking about. A better choice is SSH, which features an encrypted session, not observable over the network. In Chapter 5, "Securing Your Router," I discuss how to configure the VTY ports to allow only SSH.

The final alternative is to use HTTP or HTTPS on those routers that support a graphic environment such as SDM (which I will introduce later in this chapter). As you might expect, HTTPS is the better choice because it uses SSL encryption to protect your session.

Modes of Interaction with the Router

Now let's discuss the modes of interaction you can use on the router after you gain access. There are two modes: user mode and privileged mode.

Once you provide a username and password to gain access to the router, you are usually put into what is known as *user* mode. User mode generally doesn't allow you to make any changes to the configuration and is frequently used to perform show commands to query the router. User mode is indicated by the lack of a # prompt. You will see only the hostname when in user mode. This mode might be used by an operator at a network operations center to help isolate a problem during troubleshooting.

If you want to make changes to the configuration, you use the enable password to enter *privileged* mode. You must type **enable** (or the shortcut, **en**) to enter privileged mode. You will be prompted to enter the enable password and then you will enter privileged mode, which is indicated by a hash mark or # following the hostname at the prompt.

Password Guidelines

It is important to consider password strength when choosing passwords for your router, specifically the enable password, since it controls configuration aspects of the router.

Cisco recommends the following rules of thumb or guidelines when choosing passwords:

- Use a minimum of 10 characters.

- Use a mixture of upper- and lowercase text plus special characters and numbers.

- The password should not be a word that appears in a dictionary.

- Develop and implement a password policy that dictates the length of passwords and how often they must be changed.

One way to assure password length on the router is to configure the security-password min-length 10 command while in global configuration mode.

Also of note is that spaces are normally considered special characters and are recognized inside of passwords, but not on the leading edge of the text. Once the first character of text is added, spaces are legitimate characters and are recognized.

Password Types

Passwords are usually configured during the initial configuration of the router, either manually or by using the setup command. If you use the setup command, it will interactively prompt you to set the following passwords:

- VTY

- Enable

- Enable secret

Let's talk about the differences between the VTY, enable, and enable secret passwords.

VTY password You are prompted for the VTY password when you use SSH or Telnet to access the router. Depending on what is configured for the router, this action might send you to an AAA server (see Chapter 4, "Configuring AAA Services"). The VTY password might be configured manually on the router. The password is configured under the VTY lines section of the configuration. You will see the configuration in the next section, "Configuring Passwords."

Enable password   The enable password is the legacy backward-compatible password used for privileged mode, but it has security vulnerabilities because it is a Type 7 password. Type 7 passwords can be deciphered easily because they are just a Boolean exclusive OR or XOR function performed on the plain text. There are many programs that can automatically decipher a Type 7 password by just pasting in the ciphertext from the configuration. That means that anyone who is able to gain access to a copy of the configuration can gain access by deciphering the enable password.

Enable secret password   Because of the vulnerability in the enable password, Cisco came up with the enable secret password, which is an MD5 hash of the entered password. If you were to look at the configuration of an enable secret password, you would see a 5 in front of it, so these are commonly known as Type 5 passwords.

Another type of password is a Type 0, which indicates no encryption. Any password that is not encrypted in the configuration can be converted using the `service password-encryption` command.

Finally, you may want to assign a password to the AUX port on the router, which is usually configured with a modem for a router that is located remotely from the administrator.

Configuring Passwords

Let's look at the passwords from a configuration standpoint.

Starting with the console, you would need to enter line configuration mode to enter the password:

```
Router(config)# line con 0
Router(config-line)# password sup3rs3cr3t
Router(config-line)# end
```

That's the configuration for the console; now let's look at the AUX port, which is similar:

```
Router(config)# line aux 0
Router(config-line)# password mys3cr3t
Router(config-line)# end
```

There is another configuration that uses the line configuration mode, and that is the VTY or virtual TTY. By default on a Cisco router, there are five virtual TTY lines, numbered 0 through 4. So when configuring the VTY lines, you type **line vty 0 4** as your command:

```
Router(config)# line vty 0 4
Router(config-line)# password vtyp4ssw0rd
```

```
Router(config-line)# login
Router(config-line)# end
```

On the VYT configuration, you also need to add a `login` command to the configuration.

Moving on to the enable secret password, you will notice that when you type in the password, it is plain text, but when you show the running configuration, you will see the MD5 hashed ciphertext:

```
Router(config)# enable secret s3cr3tpass
Router(config)# end

Router# show running-config

hostname Router
!
enable secret 5 $1$Y21P$us4RNo7gQGPfoJdkJKNOf.
!
```

Now that you have seen what the encrypted text looks like, let's have a look at what I was discussing earlier, and that is the running configuration of the console, AUX, and VTY passwords. As you can see, they are shown in plain text:

```
Router# show running-config

hostname Router
!
line con 0
 password sup3rs3cr3t
 login
line aux 0
 password mys3cr3t
 login
line vty 0 4
 password vtyp3ssw0rd
 login
```

Now I am going to apply the `service password-encryption` command to add the level 7 encryption to the configuration. Let's look at the running configuration again:

```
Router# service password-encryption

Router# show running-config

hostname Router
```

```
!
line con 0
 password 7 06151A311F5C1A4A0605411F
 login
line aux 0
 password 7 03094218550C331F5A
 login
line vty 0 4
 password 7 08375857194D1604055B1E00
 login
```

As you can see, the passwords are now encrypted in the running configuration.

Configuring Privilege Levels

Sometimes larger organizations have the need for multiple levels of privilege on the router. For example, a large Network Operations Center (NOC) might have three levels of technicians. Levels 1 and 2 might be granted access to only certain commands, but the level 3 tech might have full access. Here's where privilege levels come in handy.

There can be 16 privilege levels on a Cisco router, but the default is to use only three: 0, 1, and 15. Levels 2 to 14 can be configured as custom privilege levels.

Here is a sample of a privilege level command:

```
Router(config)# privilege exec level 2 traceroute
Router(config)# enable secret level 2 p4ssw0rd
```

If the router is configured in this way, you would log in as level 2 using the following command:

```
Router enable 2
Password: p4ssw0rd
Router# show privilege
Current privilege level is 2
```

Once you've logged in, the router is configured to allow users who log in as level 2 to use the traceroute command.

CLI Views

In the Cisco IOS you have the ability to create command-line interface views. This is similar to configuring privilege levels, but it involves the use of AAA to define the views to apply to a particular user or role.

Views give someone who logs into a router a way to see what privileges they have.

The first thing you need to do to configure a view is to enable AAA, of course:

```
Router(config)# aaa new-model
```

> There is more to configuring the view than just enabling AAA services on the router. This section covers just the fact that AAA needs to be enabled before you can set up new views. The focus here is on the CLI view, not how to configure AAA for it. You'll find more information on AAA in Chapter 4.

The root view is the view that the administrator would have. A typical administrator would have level 15 command privileges, and indeed, that is a requirement to enable the root view. In the following example, the administrator is logged in and is in enable mode, referenced by the # symbol after the router name, and then enables the root view by typing enable view.

```
Router# enable view
```

```
Password:
Router#
```

Now that the view is enabled, you can configure additional views. In the following example, the command parser view is used to create a view called NOC, short for Network Operating Center, which is a practical example. You might want all of your NOC personnel to only be able to perform certain tasks on your routers.

```
Router# conf t
Router(config)# parser view NOC
Router(config-view)#
```

Next you need to set a password for the view. You can configure either a type 0 or a type 5 password. If you use type 0, it means no encryption in the configuration and you can see the password in plain text. If you use a 5 in your configuration, the password will be encrypted. In this example, you will use a type 0 password:

```
Router(config-view)# secret 0 n0cp4ssw0rd
```

Next you need to set the commands you want this particular view to be able to perform. In the following example, the ping and traceroute commands are extended to the view NOC:

```
Router(config-view)# commands exec include traceroute
Router(config-view)# commands exec include ping
```

Now that you are finished with the configuration, you can verify it by using the enable view command. Type a question mark to see what commands are available in this view:

```
Router# enable view NOC

Password:

Router# ?
Exec commands:
  <1-99>      Session number to resume
  enable      Turn on privileged commands
  exit        Exit from the EXEC
  ping        Send echo messages
  show        Show running system information
  traceroute  Trace route to destination
```

Securing Router Files

Cisco IOS allows an administrator to make a secure copy of the router configuration and the router image stored in a hidden location on the router. This feature is called Cisco IOS Resilient Configuration. The files themselves are called the *bootset*.

Follow these steps to create a secure copy of the router configuration and image:

1. Issue the **secure boot-image** command from global configuration mode. This creates a secure copy of the router image that is hidden from view of the normal directory listing.

2. Issue the **secure boot-config** command, also from global configuration mode. This archives the running configuration to persistent storage.

3. Verify the configuration using the **show secure bootset** command.

Login Features for Virtual Connections

The Cisco IOS Login Enhancements feature allows you to add some more security to your virtual login environment. You can configure your router to do the following:

- Add delays between successive login attempts.
- Shut down the login function if a DoS attempt is detected.
- Generate system logging messages for login attempts.

Delays between Successive Login Attempts

The default behavior of the Cisco IOS router is that any virtual connections will be processed as fast as the router can perform them. Therefore, if you want to protect the router from a brute-force attack, you can introduce a delay between any successive login attempts using the following commands:

- `login block-for`
- `login delay`

If you issue the `login block-for` command without any other commands, the default login delay is one second. To effect a further delay, you must use the `login delay` command to configure something other than 1 second.

Shut Down Logins When a DoS Attack Is Detected

If you configure a limit on the number of login failures within a specific time period and that limit is met, the router no longer responds to connection attempts for a given amount of time, called the *quiet period*. If, however, you have configured an access list to control host connections, anyone who matches that access list can log in during the quiet period.

To control host connections through the use of an access list, use the command **login quiet-mode access-class** from global configuration mode.

Generate System Logging Messages for Login Attempts

If you have configured login delays or login quiet-mode commands on the router, you can log messages about failed or successful attempts to connect as well as whether quiet mode has been entered or exited.

- Use the command `login on-success` in global configuration mode to log successful logins.
- Use the command `login on-failure` in global configuration mode to log unsuccessful logins.

If you used `auto secure` to secure your router, then messages for failed attempts will be logged. Successful attempts are only logged if you manually configure the router to do so.

Configuring a Banner Message

It's always a good idea to add a banner message when you're configuring a router. That means that anytime someone accesses the router, they see a message, usually something like "Access prohibited, violators will be prosecuted" or the like. It's wise to get the blessing of your legal counsel before you enter your particular banner message.

The command to use when you have the appropriate message ready is `banner motd` *delimiter message delimiter*.

The motd stands for *message of the day* and is derived from a command of the same name on Unix systems. The `delimiter` variable is a special character that would not be part of the message but instead signals the beginning or end of the message itself. In the following example, I will use a $ to delimit the text message.

```
Router(config)# config t

Enter configuration commands, one per line. End with CNTL/Z.
Router(config)# banner motd $

Enter TEXT message. End with the character '$'.
Warning! This router is private property and may only be accessed by
authorized users. All access is monitored and logged.
Violators will be prosecuted to the fullest extent of the law.

$
Router(config)# end
```

Now that the message of the day is configured, let's have a look at what the user would see when attempting to access the router. Assuming that the user accessed the router via an SSH session, this is what they would see:

```
Warning! This router is private property and may only be accessed by
authorized users. All access is monitored and logged.
Violators will be prosecuted to the fullest extent of the law.

User Access Verification

Password:
```

 Real World Scenario

Banners and Passwords

You have inherited a network to manage through an acquisition. Upon an audit of the configuration of the routers in the new network, you have found that they do not have banner messages upon login via SSH. Further, you have learned that even though all of the routers have a terminal server connected to the console port, none of the console ports have passwords configured. It's your job to configure the banner message and passwords necessary to secure the console port.

First, you will tackle the banner message. This time you will use an ampersand as the delimiter:

Router(config)# **banner motd &**

Enter TEXT message. End with the character '&'.
Warning! This router is private property and may only be accessed by
authorized users of this system. All access to this system is monitored and
logged.
Violators will be prosecuted to the fullest extent of the law.

&
Router(config)# **end**

Next you will configure a console password to secure the router through the console port:

Router(config)# **line con 0**
Router(config-line)# **password myroutersecret**
Router(config-line)# **login**

The next thing would be to make sure the password is encrypted, so you will use the service password-encryption command:

Router(config)# **service password-encryption**

Using this configuration as a template, you can roll this out to all the affected routers.

Cisco ISR Routers

Cisco Integrated Services Routers (ISRs) are offered in a wide variety of sizes, functionality, and features. The ISR routers integrate features such as voice, security, and quality of service. The models include the 800 series, 1800 series, 2800 series, and 3800 series. You might be noticing a pattern here: The third digit from the right in the names of all the ISRs is 8. Starting with the 800 series, meant for the small office, home office (SOHO) market, models can grow all the way up to the 3800 series, which is designed for medium to large offices.

Table 3.1 lists the high-level security features found in Cisco ISRs.

TABLE 3.1 Security features found in Cisco ISRs

Security Feature	Description
Stateful firewall	The Cisco IOS firewall feature set can be used for stateful inspection of packets.
Virtual private network (VPN)	Cisco routers support VPNs in Cisco IOS.
VPN Virtual Routing and Forwarding (VRF)–aware firewall	VRF-aware firewalls maintain separate routing tables for each VPN.
Intrusion prevention system (IPS)	Cisco IOS has an intrusion prevention system that can detect and prevent attacks before they are successful.

Cisco Security Device Manager (SDM)

In this section I will introduce the Cisco Security Device Manager (SDM), a graphical environment that facilitates configuring, using, and monitoring the IOS features on your Cisco ISR.

Because some tasks are more onerous than others when configuring routers, Cisco has provided the Cisco SDM to assist. One of the ways it helps is through the use of wizards to automate certain tasks. While the name implies that it performs only security tasks, the fact is that you can also use it for many of the everyday tasks of configuring and managing a router.

Prerequisites for Running SDM

Most routers today come already preloaded with Cisco SDM. But if your router is older or didn't come with it, you will need to load the software yourself. If you have a CD with the software, you can load it from there. The other alternative is to download it from Cisco CCO.

You may find that the process to load the software is a bit different than the way you may be used to doing it. SDM is installed via a wizard and can be installed on either the administrator's workstation or the router in flash memory, or you can do both.

SDM can be accessed via a web browser with either HTTP or HTTPS. There are a few commands associated with SDM configuration that you should acquaint yourself with. These are listed in Table 3.2.

TABLE 3.2   HTTP commands associated with SDM configuration

Command	Description
ip http server	Enables an HTTP server
ip http secure-server	Enable an HTTPS server
ip http authentication local	Enables local authentication for HTTP access
username *name* privilege 15 secret 0 *password*	Configures a username and password for local authentication

Let's look at a sample configuration of the commands in Table 3.2. For the purpose of this exercise, the username will be joe and the password will be cool:

```
Router(config)# ip http server
Router(config)# ip http secure-server
Router(config)# ip http authentication local
Router(config)# username joe privilege 15 secret 0 cool
```

The next step is to verify that the proper files are on the router. The command you need to use is the show flash command. This will display all the files on the flash. The following files are critical and required for SDM:

- home.tar
- home.shtml
- common.tar
- es.tar
- sdm.tar
- sdmconfig-*router_platform*.cfg

Assuming you have all of the correct files, it's now time to jump into SDM. One thing to keep in mind is that if you were to run SDM from the router's flash memory for the first time, you would be directed to the SDM express screen, where you can configure the initial settings.

The initial IP address of a new SDM router is 10.10.10.1. You would point your browser to http://10.10.10.1. Don't forget to use either a switch/hub or a crossover cable and configure your PC to be on the same subnet.

Once you perform your initial configuration, any subsequent connections to the router will be the full SDM, not the SDM Express. It's worth noting that some router platforms can run only SDM Express because of hardware limitations and flash memory size.

You can run SDM on your PC by choosing Start ➢ Programs ➢ Cisco Systems ➢ Cisco SDM.

Introduction to SDM

If you look at Figure 3.1, you will see the initial screen as you enter SDM. At the top of the screen you will see a toolbar, which has three basic views that you will primarily use, which are Home, Configure, and Monitor.

FIGURE 3.1   SDM Home screen

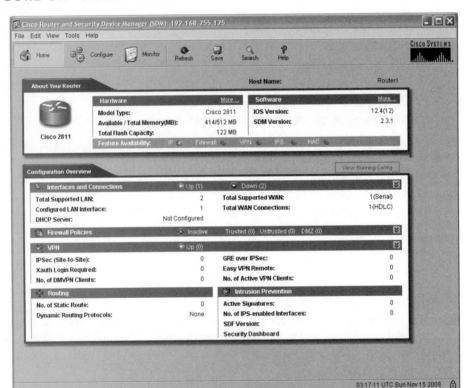

The Home view is a summary of information about the router. You get basic information such as router model, the amount of memory, the amount of flash, the IOS version, and the interfaces that the router has.

If you click the Configure button, you will see the screen in Figure 3.2.

FIGURE 3.2 The Configure screen with the Interfaces And Connections task displayed

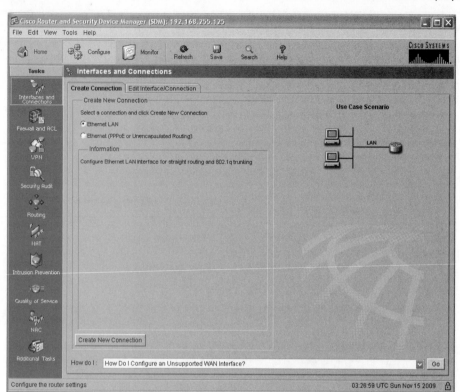

The Configure screen has a Taskbar that runs on the left side of the screen. As you can see, you start on the Interfaces And Connections task. Table 3.3 describes the available tasks in the Configure section of SDM.

TABLE 3.3 Tasks available in the Configure section of SDM

SDM Configuration Tasks	Description
Interfaces And Connections	Configure LAN and WAN interfaces.
Firewall And ACL	Configure IOS firewall settings.
VPN	Configure remote and site-to-site VPNs as well as Easy VPN and DMVPN.
Security Audit	Perform an audit of security features and functionalities. Can dynamically change the router to further secure it.

TABLE 3.3   Tasks available in the Configure section of SDM *(continued)*

SDM Configuration Tasks	Description
Routing	Configure RIP, EIGRP, and OSPF routing protocols.
NAT	Configure Network Address Translation.
Intrusion Prevention	Configure IOS IPS.
Quality Of Service	Configure quality of service.
NAC	Configure Network Admission Control.
Additional Tasks	Configure AAA, DNS, DHCP, and others.

The Additional Tasks item is shown in Figure 3.3.

FIGURE 3.3   Additional Tasks in the SDM Configure Section

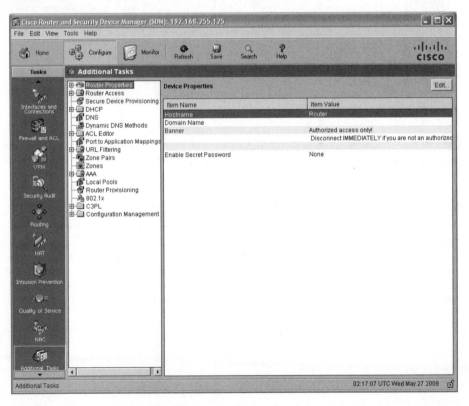

The last view that we will look at is the Monitor view. If you click the Monitor button, you will see the screen shown in Figure 3.4. From this screen you can keep track of various functions of the router, such as the firewall, IOS IPS, VPN, and logging, among others.

FIGURE 3.4 SDM Monitor Overview

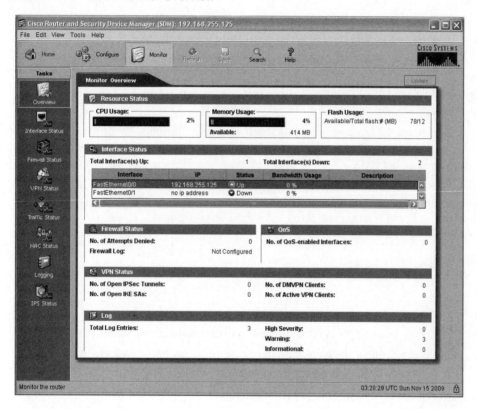

Since you will see the specifics of SDM in other chapters, I will end the introduction of SDM here and allow you to explore the tool at your leisure.

Summary

In this chapter you learned about securing administrative access to your Cisco router. The chapter also included an introduction to using the Cisco Security Device Manager, a graphical environment that is extremely useful in configuring your ISR router as well as monitoring usage. You also learned about the features that are available in an ISR router.

Finally, I showed you how to configure passwords for administrative access to the router, how to create banner messages, and how to protect router files.

Exam Essentials

Remember the features of the ISR that are available for use with Cisco SDM.   The security features of the Cisco ISR include stateful firewall, VPN, VRF-aware firewall, and IPS.

Know how to configure SSH as a transport method.   You need to specifically configure the VTY lines to use SSH instead of Telnet as the preferred transport method.

Understand how to configure secure administrative access.   The methods for secure administrative access are configuring privilege levels and configuring passwords for console, VTY, and HTTPS access. Other things to remember are CLI view, enable passwords, and login features for virtual connections.

Know how to use CLI to configure IOS Resilient Configuration.   Remember the commands to store the image and configuration files securely into a bootset and then the commands to show the secure bootset.

Remember the prerequisites for SDM and the wizards that are available within.   The prerequisites of running SDM include setting up an HTTP server and user login and password and ensuring that the correct files exist on the router.

Written Lab

Write the answers to the following questions:

1. Which type of encryption is used when configuring an enable secret password?

2. What is the name of the command to change the delay between login attempts?

3. Write the command to limit VTY connections to only SSH.

4. Write the command to change privilege levels.

5. Write the command to enable the use of SDM over HTTP.

6. Write the command to enable the root view.

7. Write the command to enable the CLI view named OPS.

8. Write the name for the secured image and configuration files used as part of Cisco IOS Resilient Configuration.

9. Write the command to set the inactivity time-out to never timeout.

10. Write the command to configure a minimum password length of 8.

(The answers to the written lab can be found following the answers to the review questions.)

Hands-on Lab

With this hands-on lab exercise, you can practice requirements for configuring passwords to protect your router.

Hands-on Lab 3.1: Configuring Passwords

In this lab you will manually configure the router for passwords for administrative access. You have been given the following information to use when configuring the passwords.

Console: guessthis?

VTY: dollar123

AUX: aboutf4ce

1. Log into your router and go into privileged mode by typing **en** or **enable**.

2. Enter global configuration mode by typing **config** t or **configure terminal**.

3. Type **line con 0** to enter line configuration mode.

```
Router# config t
Enter configuration commands, one per line.  End with
  CNTL/Z.
Router(config)# line con 0
```

Enter **password guessthis?** and then **end** to exit configuration mode.

```
Router(config-line)# password guessthis?
Router(config-line)# end
```

4. Enter line configuration mode again. Type the command **line vty 0 4** to enter the virtual TTY line mode. Then add **password dollar123** and then type **end** again.

```
Router(config)# line vty 0 4
Router(config-line)# password dollar123
Router(config-line)# end
```

5. Add a password to the AUX line. Once again, enter line configuration mode by typing **line aux 0**. Again, add the **password aboutf4ce** and then **end**.

```
Router(config)# line aux 0
Router(config-line)# password aboutf4ce
Router(config-line)# end
```

Review Questions

1. Which of the following is *not* a Cisco IOS security feature commonly found on Cisco ISRs?

   A. CDP

   B. IPS

   C. Stateful firewall

   D. VPN

   E. VRF-aware firewall

2. Which command can turn on logging of unsuccessful login attempts? (Choose two.)

   A. `auto secure`

   B. `logging failure`

   C. `login on failure log`

   D. `logging login failure`

   E. `auto log`

3. What is the name of the secure files used in conjunction with the Cisco IOS Resilient Configuration?

   A. configset

   B. bootset

   C. startup-config-secure

   D. running-config-secure

   E. config-set

4. Which of the following is the graphical user environment that is used to configure many router settings and provides several wizards to automate certain tasks?

   A. ACS

   B. ASDM

   C. STP

   D. SDM

   E. CDP

5. Which of the following is *not* one of the high-level tasks that you can perform from Cisco SDM?

   A. VPN

   B. Security Audit

   C. Configuration Management

   D. Interfaces and Connections

6. Cisco SDM can be installed where?

    A. On the administrator's PC

    B. On the router's flash memory

    C. On both the administrator's PC and router's flash memory

    D. In the running configuration

    E. In the startup configuration

7. You have been asked to configure SSH using the command-line interface. However, you have discovered that some keys were left over on the router. What command is used to clear the RSA keys so that you can regenerate them?

    A. Router1# `clear rsa keys`

    B. Router1# `(config)rsa clear keys`

    C. Router1# `(config)crypto key zeroize rsa`

    D. Router1# `crypto rsa key zeroize`

    E. Router1# `crypto key zeroize rsa`

8. Which command confers the traceroute command privileges to level 4?

    A. `privilege exec level 4 traceroute`

    B. `privilege level 4 traceroute`

    C. `privilege 4 traceroute`

    D. `authorization 4 traceroute`

9. Which of the following is the command to configure a minimum password length of 8 for any passwords configured on the router?

    A. `security password length 8`

    B. `security password min-length 8`

    C. `password length 8`

    D. `password security length 8`

10. Which of the following is the global configuration mode command to encrypt any plaintext passwords in a Cisco configuration?

    A. `service-password encryption`

    B. `service password-encryption`

    C. `service encryption-password`

    D. `service-encryption`

    E. `service level encryption`

11. Which of the following is *not* one of the files necessary to run Cisco SDM on your router?

    A. `es.tar`

    B. `sdm.tar`

    C. `common.tar`

    D. `sdm.bin`

12. What is the default delay between successive login attempts if the `login block-for` command is issued without further qualifications?

    A. 1 sec

    B. 10 sec

    C. 5 sec

    D. 15 sec

    E. 1 minute

13. What is the global configuration mode command that allows you to configure a banner message for use when attempting to access a router via Telnet or SSH?

    A. banner

    B. message banner

    C. motd

    D. banner config

    E. banner motd

14. What is the global configuration mode command that will allow you to specify the number of failed login attempts that trigger a quiet period?

    A. login block-for

    B. login exec timeout

    C. login block

    D. login timeout

    E. exec timeout

15. Which command would you enter to use Cisco SDM in a secure web session?

    A. ip http secure

    B. ip https

    C. ip https secure-server

    D. ip http secure-server

    E. ip secure-server

16. What is the command that will reset the RSA keys on a Cisco router?

    A. zero-out

    B. zeroout

    C. zeroize

    D. reset

    E. clear keys all

17. In generating RSA keys, what does Cisco recommend for the key modulus size?

    A. 512

    B. 2048

    C. 1024

    D. 4096

    E. 256

18. What feature must be enabled prior to configuring command-line interface (CLI) views?

    A. ACS

    B. CLI

    C. AAA

    D. NTP

19. Which of the following are *not* wizards that can be used with Cisco SDM? (Choose two.)

    A. VPN

    B. Security Audit

    C. BGP

    D. CDP

20. What type of encryption is used with a Type 5 encrypted password in a Cisco router configuration?

    A. SHA

    B. MD5

    C. SSL

    D. RC4

Answers to Review Questions

1. A. There are generally four categories of security features found in Cisco IOS. They are a stateful firewall, an IPS, VPN capabilities, and VRF-aware firewall.

2. A, C. You can use the `login on failure log` command if you are manually configuring it, but `auto secure` will also configure it (and a lot of other commands).

3. B. The secure files are collectively called the bootset.

4. D. The Cisco Security Device Manager (SDM) is the graphical user environment used to configure a Cisco router.

5. C. Configuration Management is not one of the choices from the main task list.

6. C. Cisco SDM can be installed on both the administrator's PC and the router's flash memory.

7. C. Clearing the keys is done from the global configuration menu. The correct command is `crypto key zeroize rsa`.

8. A. The `privilege exec` command allows commands to be assigned to privilege levels.

9. B. The command to configure a minimum password length of 8 is `security password min-length 8` in global configuration mode.

10. B. The correct answer is `service password-encryption`.

11. D. Except for HTML files, all the other files are in TAR format, therefore D is not one of the files necessary to run Cisco SDM on your router.

12. A. The default delay between successive login attempts if the `login block-for` command is issued in its default state is 1 second. You can configure a different delay if you use other options with the command.

13. E. The `banner motd` command is used to create a banner message. It also requires you to designate a delimiter to use for the purposes of identifying the message content.

14. A. The command `login block-for` can be used to specify the number of failed attempts to trigger a quiet period and how long that quiet period can be.

15. D. To use HTTPS with Cisco SDM, you must configure it from the command line with the command `ip http secure-server`.

16. C. The `zeroize` command will essentially remove any existing RSA keys on a Cisco router.

17. C. Cisco recommends a key modulus size of 1024.

18. C. AAA is required and must be enabled prior to configuring CLI views.

19. C, D. VPN and Security Audit are two of the choices that you have when choosing a wizard to use within Cisco SDM.

20. B. An enable secret password would have a Type 5 password, which is actually an MD5 hash.

Answers to Written Lab

1. MD5 hash

2. login block-for

3. transport input ssh

4. privilege exec

5. ip http server

6. enable view

7. enable view OPS from enable mode

8. bootset

9. exec timeout 0 0

10. security-password min-length 8

Chapter

4

Configuring AAA Services

THE FOLLOWING CCNA SECURITY EXAM OBJECTIVES ARE COVERED IN THIS CHAPTER:

- ✓ Explain the functions and importance of AAA

- ✓ Describe the features of TACACS+ and RADIUS AAA protocols

- ✓ Configure AAA authentication

- ✓ Configure AAA authorization

- ✓ Configure AAA accounting

In this chapter, I'm going to discuss how authentication, authorization, and accounting (AAA) services are used in a Cisco internetwork. We'll explore the functions of these services as they relate to network devices. Authentication, authorization, and accounting services allow you to dictate exactly who accesses your network and what privileges they have and to log how and when those services are used.

Cisco devices can use two kinds of AAA services, Remote Authentication Dial In User Service (RADIUS) and Terminal Access Controller Access-Control System Plus (TACACS+). Both of these will be discussed in detail and compared.

And finally, you will learn how to configure each of the AAA services in depth. We will start with configuration from a command-line interface perspective and then tackle the tasks using Cisco Security Device Manager (SDM.)

 For up-to-the-minute updates for this chapter, please see www.sybex .com/go/ccna-security.

Defining AAA Services

The components of AAA services are authentication, authorization, and accounting. Each has a different role. Depending on the protocol used, some can be used independently of each other.

Authentication Authentication is the most basic of the AAA services. It allows users to log in and prove that they are who they say they are. Although different methods can be used, the most basic is the use of a username and password. Hardware and software tokens and biometric devices can also be used.

Authorization Once authentication has taken place, authorization dictates what services are allowed and/or what resources a user can access. On a Cisco router, authorization allows the administrator to determine what commands can be used on a per-user basis.

Accounting After allowing access and authorizing what can be done, you need to log what happened. You might want to keep track of who logged in, how long they were logged in, and what they did while they were logged in. This record-keeping activity is called accounting.

In the next section, we will discuss the two AAA protocols that are supported on Cisco devices, RADIUS and TACACS+. While both are supported, they are each unique, which may influence when you use one over the other. I will discuss the differences and situations in which you might use each one.

Defining RADIUS and TACACS+

The two most frequently used AAA protocols are RADIUS and TACACS+. Either one can be used in a Cisco router environment:

- RADIUS is an open-source standard maintained by the Internet Engineering Task Force (IETF). The main RADIUS Requests for Comments (RFCs) are RFC 2865 and RFC 2866. There are many other associated RFCs, such as RFCs that address extensions to RADIUS and the use of SNMP.
- TACACS+ is a Cisco proprietary protocol that was implemented as an enhancement over RADIUS. In particular TACACS+ includes the ability to separate authorization from authentication and accounting.

Table 4.1 compares the two protocols.

TABLE 4.1 Comparison of RADIUS and TACACS+

RADIUS	TACACS+
Uses UDP as the transport.	Uses TCP as the transport.
Encrypts only the password.	Encrypts the entire body of the packet, excluding the header.
Combines authentication and authorization.	Separates the authentication from the authorization and accounting functions.
Limited support for certain protocols.	Full multiprotocol support.
Vendor implementations often differ (even though it is an open standard). Interoperability can be an issue.	Specific to Cisco equipment.
Traffic is minimal due to limited command support.	Traffic can be significantly higher than with RADIUS because TACACS+ supports more commands and capabilities.

RADIUS

Remote Authentication Dial In User Service (RADIUS) is an open-standard authentication scheme that was originally used in dial-up applications, hence the words *dial in* in the name. RADIUS implements all three of the AAA services, but it was originally used primarily for accounting, which allowed service providers to keep track of time used and bill accordingly.

If you remember back in the good old days (or were they the bad old days?), virtually everyone had to dial up to get to the Internet because this was the only means available. The point is that RADIUS was used throughout the industry as the way to authenticate and then bill for the time used.

RADIUS was originally developed at Livingston Enterprises, who had created a remote dial-in server as a product. It included a version of it with its Portmaster product, an early dial-in platform. RADIUS went through many iterations until it was finally issued as RFC 2058 in early 1997.

 A popular no-cost version of RADIUS is called FreeRADIUS and can be downloaded from `http://freeradius.org/download.html`.

RADIUS uses specific message types to establish communication between the device (in this case our router) and the RADIUS server itself.

 In RADIUS-speak, the device is called a NAS (network access server). I don't like using that terminology because it is easy to confuse with network attached storage, also abbreviated NAS. So I will just use the term *router*.

There are four message types:

ACCESS-REQUEST   This message commonly contains the username and password and can contain other attributes (see the description of attribute-value pairs after this list) and is the initial message sent from the router to the RADIUS server.

ACCESS-ACCEPT   This is the message provided by the RADIUS server that indicates that the username and password were correct.

ACCESS-REJECT   This is the message provided by the RADIUS server that indicates that the username and password were incorrect.

ACCESS-CHALLENGE   This message is provided when an additional form of authentication is employed, such as a token or a personal identification number (PIN). This message would be sent after the initial successful exchange. It can also be used in conjunction with setting up secure tunnels between the client and RADIUS server directly.

Attribute-values, often referred to as A-V pairs, include additional information sent within the message structure. The IETF defined approximately 50 attribute values in the initial RFC. In order to make the structure extensible, a vendor-specific attribute, attribute 26, was also included. This attribute allowed vendor customization. Cisco uses this attribute to enhance the RADIUS protocol for use with Cisco products.

Let's examine the operation of RADIUS in depth. Following is a step-by-step description of what happens in a typical RADIUS transaction, such as someone trying to log in to a router:

1. The client initiates the conversation by attempting to access the router.

2. That request prompts a username query from the router.

3. The client sends the username to the router.

4. The router requests the password.

5. The client then provides the password to the router.

6. The router takes the username and password information provided and sends it in an ACCESS-REQUEST message to the RADIUS server.

7. If the username and password are correct, the RADIUS server will provide an ACCESS-ACCEPT message back to the router and access is granted. If, on the other hand, the username and password combination are incorrect, the RADIUS server will pass back an ACCESS-REJECT message and the router will end the conversation.

 DIAMETER is the successor to RADIUS and was introduced in late 2003 as RFC 3588. At this writing, it has not been widely used.

TACACS+

Terminal Access Controller Access-Control System Plus (TACACS+) was created by Cisco to achieve a higher degree of control over the authentication process. In a sense, it's a better implementation of RADIUS specifically for Cisco environments. TACACS+ uses TCP port 49 to communicate and is supported by a large number of Cisco devices, such as routers, switches, firewalls, content engines, and wireless access points, to name a few. It works similarly to RADIUS but there are a few more steps, as shown here:

1. User makes a request to log in to a router.

2. The router requests the username from the TACACS+ server.

3. The TACACS+ server provides a username prompt to the router.

4. The router provides the username prompt to the user.

5. The user inputs the username at the prompt.

6. The router then forwards the username to the TACACS+ server.

7. The router requests a password prompt from the TACACS+ server.

8. The TACACS+ server provides a password prompt to the router.

9. The password prompt is then provided to the user from the router.

10. The user inputs a password at the prompt.

11. The router forwards the password to the TACACS+ server.

12. The TACACS+ server sends one of four response messages: ACCEPT, REJECT, ERROR, CONTINUE.

> The product incorporating TACACS+ is called Cisco Secure ACS version 4.0. This is a graphical user interface–based product that runs on the Windows platform. Cisco Secure ACS has support for routers, switches, Voice over IP (VoIP) platforms, firewalls, content engines, storage devices, and wireless access points (APs).

Each TACACS+ response code is described in the following list:

ACCEPT   The username and password were correctly authenticated.

REJECT   The username and/or password was incorrectly entered.

ERROR   An error has occurred somewhere along the way. This does not necessarily mean that the username or password is incorrect. Typically this is some kind of communication error. If an alternative method of authentication has been configured, the router will attempt the alternative method.

CONTINUE   This denotes that additional information needs to be provided by the user before authentication can take place.

> You can obtain a freeware version of TACACS+ by using your favorite search engine to search for "tac_plus freeware." Generally it is found in source code format to be compiled and run on a Linux host. It is not as full featured and doesn't have the nice GUI that you have in the Cisco products, but it will suffice for simple needs.

Configuring AAA Using Cisco Secure ACS

Cisco Secure Access Control Server (ACS) is a centralized identity management system that gives administrators of Cisco devices a way to be authenticated and to easily manage users of the devices.

In the following sections, I'll discuss what Cisco Secure ACS is, what it can be used for, the basic requirements for installation, and the installation procedure.

Although a local AAA database is easy to configure, it doesn't really scale well, and it confers a heavy administrative burden. You would have to administratively add each username and password. This is fine for a few usernames, but it doesn't work well for a lot. So, we need a way to allow hundreds or thousands of users access to resources. This system can take the form of three basic types:

- Cisco Secure ACS for Windows, a software-only product that installs on a Windows server

- Cisco Secure ACS Solution Engine, a high-performance appliance that runs a version of Cisco Secure ACS

- Cisco Secure Express, a smaller, single-purpose appliance that is meant for a fixed number of users

Introduction to Cisco Secure ACS for Windows

Cisco Secure ACS for Windows is a platform for managing administrative access to Cisco devices such as routers, firewalls, and switches, among many others. In addition, it supports Cisco's Network Access Control (NAC). Cisco NAC is part of an industry proposal by Cisco to enforce policy compliance on devices that wish to access network resources. NAC relies heavily on Cisco Secure ACS to enforce policy by performing authentication and authorization of the host attempting to access resources in the network infrastructure.

It is worth noting that there are two kinds of Cisco Network Access Control (NAC). The kind referred to in this section is the NAC Framework infrastructure and not the Cisco NAC appliance. The NAC appliance doesn't require the use of Cisco ACS.

By the time this goes to print, ACS 5.0 will be out. ACS 5.0 is supported as an appliance and can also be used as a virtual machine (VM) under VMware's ESX product line.

Cisco Secure ACS for Windows provides a high-performance, flexible, and scalable TACACS+ and RADIUS server. It also provides support for a highly intelligent NAC solution by managing users, administrators, and resources. Cisco Secure ACS provides authentication, authorization, and accounting services that, in concert with policy control, provide total network access security.

There are a number of advanced features in Cisco Secure ACS for Windows:

- 802.1x support, which includes all of the following Extensible Authentication Protocols (EAP): EAP-TLS, PEAP, LEAP, EAP-FAST, EAP-MD5

- Support for access control lists from routers, firewalls, and virtual private network (VPN) devices

- Lightweight Directory Access Protocol (LDAP) and Open Database Connectivity (ODBC) user authentication support

- Group profiles

- Ability to limit access by time of day and day of week

- Authorization support

- Database synchronization and automatic service monitoring

Cisco Secure ACS supports a broad range of Cisco's and other vendors' network devices:

- Routers

- Switches

- Access points

- Firewalls

- VPNs

- Storage devices

- VoIP

- Content engines

- Broadband access devices

- Intrusion Detection Systems (IDSs)

There are a number of additional features that you might want to deploy when using Cisco Secure ACS 4.2 for Windows:

Cisco NAC support Cisco NAC support is built into Cisco Secure ACS for Windows and acts as a policy enforcement tool. Cisco Secure ACS provides administrator-definable policies used to authenticate users and hosts.

Scalability Improvements The 4.x software version of Cisco Secure ACS for Windows supports, for the first time, an industry-standard relational database management system, which increases the number of devices that it can support by a factor of 10. Other improvements include performance increases measured in terms of transactions per second (TPS).

Network access profiles (NAPs) Network access profiles are a new feature of Cisco Secure ACS for Windows. They define access policies that can be tied to location, protocol types, device groups, or any other RADIUS attribute. One way in which this is important is that you can assign wireless users different rights than, for instance, LAN users.

Extended replication support   Another improvement in the 4.x software version of Cisco Secure ACS for Windows is that administrators can now replicate network access profiles and associated configuration items. The following elements can be replicated:

- AAA clients
- External database configurations
- Dictionaries
- Network device groups
- Shared-profile components
- Posture validation settings
- Additional logging settings

EAP-FAST enhanced support   Extensible Authentication Protocol-Flexible Authentication via Secure Tunnel (EAP-FAST) is a Cisco-developed 802.1x EAP type. Cisco developed this solution for customers who cannot enforce a strong password policy. The key components of this method are as follows:

- No requirement for digital certificates
- Support for a variety of usernames and passwords
- Support for password expiry and change
- Flexible and simple management

Machine Access Restriction (MAR)   Machine Access Restriction (MAR) is a way of additionally controlling authorization of Microsoft Windows authenticated EAP-Transport Layer Security (EAP-TLS), EAP-FAST, and Microsoft Protected Extensible Authentication Protocol (PEAP) users, based on machine authentication of the computer used to access the network.

Network access filters (NAFs)   Network access filters (NAFs) are groupings of AAA client configurations, network device groups, or IP addresses of specific AAA client devices. NAFs can be used to group together a disparate set of devices. In addition, you can differentiate user requests on the same type of device. For instance, you might want to filter users who have newer models of the same device that might have different capabilities.

Downloadable IP ACLs   IP access control lists (ACLs) can be downloaded on a per-user basis, for use with any device that supports ACLs, such as an Adaptive Security Appliance (ASA) firewall or router.

Certificate revocation list (CRL) support   Certificate revocation is supported through an X.509 CRL profile.

AD multiforest support   Active Directory (AD) multiforest support is available, starting in ACS 4.2.

Preparation and Installation of Cisco Secure ACS for Windows

Now I'll walk you through the installation of Cisco Secure ACS on a Microsoft Windows Server platform. Before you start your install, you need to be aware of a number of things.

The following list includes some of the information you will need to familiarize yourself with before you get started (detailed information will follow, where necessary):

- Hardware requirements
- Operating system requirements
- Browser requirements
- Network requirements
- TCP/UDP port requirements
- Answers to installation questions
- Administrator and database passwords

Installation Requirements

There are certain things you need to consider before installing Cisco Secure for Windows.

Hardware Requirements

A server that is going to be running Cisco Secure ACS for Windows 4.2 must meet the following requirements:

- A Pentium 4 processor at 1.8 GHz or greater
- A minimum of 1 GB of RAM
- A minimum of 1 GB of hard drive space — more if you are going to run the database on the same machine
- Minimum graphics resolution of 256 colors at 800×600 pixels
- CD-ROM
- 100 Mbps Ethernet controller

Operating System Requirements

Cisco Secure ACS 4.2 for Windows is supported by the following Microsoft operating systems:

- Microsoft Windows 2003 R2, Standard Edition
- Microsoft Windows 2003 R2, Service Pack 2 (SP2)
- Microsoft Windows 2003 Standard Edition, Service Pack 2 (SP2)

- Microsoft Windows 2003 Enterprise Edition, Service Pack 2 (SP2)
- Microsoft Windows 2003 Standard Edition, Service Pack 1 (SP1)
- Microsoft Windows 2003 Enterprise Edition, Service Pack 1 (SP1)
- Microsoft Windows 2000

 Cisco Secure ACS 4.2 does not support 64-bit operating systems.

Browser Requirements

The following browsers are supported for use with Cisco Secure ACS:

- Microsoft Internet Explorer version 6 with SP1
- Microsoft Internet Explorer version 5.5
- Microsoft Internet Explorer version 7 with SP2
- Netscape 7.0, 7.1, and 7.2

Other browsers are not supported, so if you decide to use one not listed here, you will be on your own.

There are also specific requirements for the Sun Java runtime environment. Check the release notes of your specific version to be up-to-date.

Network Requirements

The following network requirements should be met before you put your Cisco Secure ACS server into production:

- The Cisco Secure ACS server should be able to ping all AAA clients, which could be a router, switch, and so on.
- All non-LAN clients must be able to connect to all of the AAA clients.
- Firewalls and routers must be configured to allow the necessary ports through to facilitate any communication between AAA clients and the Cisco Secure ACS server.
- All network cards in the Cisco Secure ACS Server must be enabled.
- Non-Cisco clients must be configured with TACACS+, RADIUS, or both.
- If you want to grant Microsoft Windows users permission to dial in to the network (as a way of controlling VPN usage, among other things), you must configure the option in Active Directory Users and Computers.
- One of the supported browsers must be installed on the server where Cisco Secure ACS for Windows is installed.

Port Requirements

Table 4.2 lists the TCP and UDP ports used by Cisco Secure ACS for Windows for various types of communications, such as communications with AAA clients, other Cisco Secure ACS servers, and databases, to name a few.

TABLE 4.2   Ports used by Cisco Secure ACS

Feature	Protocol	Port(s)
TACACS+	TCP	49
RADIUS authentication and authorization	UDP	1645, 1812
RADIUS accounting	UDP	1646, 1813
Database replication	TCP	2000
Database synch	TCP	2000
Logging	TCP	2001
User password change web application	TCP	2000
Administrative HTTP port for new sessions	TCP	2002
Administrative HTTP port range	TCP	Configurable

Confirming Preparations Before Installing Cisco Secure ACS for Windows

During installation, a series of questions will be asked, asking you to confirm the following:

- The end-user clients can successfully connect to AAA clients.
- The Cisco Secure ACS server can ping AAA clients.
- One of the supported browsers is installed.
- The administrative password is available.
- The database password is available.

These questions will appear in a Before You Begin screen shortly after you start the setup program. See the next section.

Installing Cisco Secure ACS for Windows

To start the installation, follow the steps as outlined in this section. Some may be slightly different than described because of variations in versions of Cisco Secure ACS. When in doubt, see the release notes for the version that you have. Here are the steps:

1. Log on to the server using a local administrator account.

2. Click setup.exe in the root directory of the CD-ROM (if autorun is enabled, it will start automatically).

3. Depending on which version you are installing, you may have to click Install before you see the license agreement. Read the software license agreement and click Accept.

4. After the welcome screen, click Next.

5. Next pops up a Before You Begin dialog box, shown in Figure 4.1. Make sure you have checked all of the boxes and then click Next.

FIGURE 4.1   Before You Begin dialog box

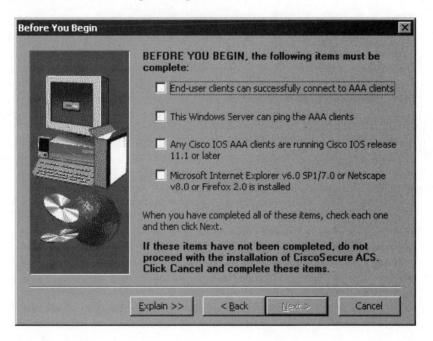

6. The Choose Destination Location dialog box appears next. If you want to change where the software is installed, here is where you change it. If you want to accept the default location, just click Next.

7. The next screen that appears is the Authentication Database Configuration dialog box. You have two different options here.

- You can use the internal database only, so if that's your choice, click Check The Cisco Secure ACS Database Only.

- If you want to use an Active Directory user database in addition to the Cisco Secure ACS internal database, you can perform the following steps:

  a. Click Also Check The Windows User Database. The Grant Dial-in Permission To User check box will become available.

  b. Click Yes if you want to allow access to users who have been given dial-in permission in the Windows users account. Then click Next.

8. The Advanced Options dialog box appears next. If you want any of the features, check the boxes. Click Next.

9. The Active Service Monitoring dialog box appears. Click Next.

10. The Database Encryption Password dialog box appears. Enter the password to be used and then click Next.

11. Then the Service Initiation Screen appears and you have the following options:

- Yes, I Want To Start The Cisco Secure ACS Service Now

- Yes, I Want Setup To Launch The Cisco Secure ACS Administrator From My Browser Following Installation

- Yes, I Want To View The Readme File

Select the options that you want and click Finish.

12. This ends the setup program. Now you can access the administration screen by using the Desktop icon, or alternatively, you can open a browser and enter **http://localhost:2002**.

Setting Up Remote Administration

Note that this is all done locally. If you would like to administer the Cisco Secure ACS server from the network, you will need to create an administrator account and enable it because it isn't done for you by default.

Here's how to create an administrative account:

1. Click the Administration Control box, which is always displayed on the left side of the screen with other options. (See Figure 4.2.)

FIGURE 4.2   Administration Control page

2.   Click Add Administrator.

3.   Add a username and password.

4.   Confirm the password.

5.   Select the Grant All option to choose all privileges, which an administrator should have.

 Note that you could choose to have multiple levels of administration with different privileges.

Configuring Authentication

Authentication is used to ensure that the users are who they say they are and helps secure the device that is being protected. This is the first step in protecting your network device. Here you will learn how to use a local database to authenticate users.

AAA Local User Authentication

We've talked a bit about TACACS+ and RADIUS, but what if you want to do local authentication on the router itself? You can configure local authentication with AAA directly on the router if you wish.

In this section, I'll show you how to configure AAA with local user authentication. You might wonder why you would do this. First and foremost, if you are using AAA servers, you want to have a way to get into the router if the configured AAA servers are down. It's a kind of back door, but it's still secure because you, the administrator, are the only one who knows the username and password. You might also want to do this if you will have only a few users and don't want the expense and administration of purchasing and configuring an AAA server. Or you might have a remote router that doesn't have access to the AAA servers used throughout the rest of the network (either by design or because the WAN is down).

To complete the bare minimum configuration, follow these steps:

1. Turn on AAA services using the `aaa new-model` command as shown here:

    Router1(config)# **aaa new-model**

2. Add a user name and password using the following syntax:

    Router1(config)# **username** *username* **password** *password*

    The username command syntax is covered in Chapter 3, "Securing Administrative Access."

3. Define the login default for AAA as a local database. Use the following syntax:

    Router1(config)# **aaa authentication login default local**

There are many other configuration options available to peruse in your spare time. You can use the built-in help within IOS to display the many options available, which are as follows:

```
Router1(config)#aaa authentication ?
  arap              Set authentication lists for arap.
  attempts          Set the maximum number of authentication attempts
  banner            Message to use when starting login/authentication.
  dot1x             Set authentication lists for IEEE 802.1x.
  enable            Set authentication list for enable.
  eou               Set authentication lists for EAPoUDP
  fail-message      Message to use for failed login/authentication.
  login             Set authentication lists for logins.
  password-prompt   Text to use when prompting for a password
  ppp               Set authentication lists for ppp.
  sgbp              Set authentication lists for sgbp.
  username-prompt   Text to use when prompting for a username
```

There are lots of options available here, but don't let it worry you. We are going to focus on just a few of them for now:

aaa authentication attempts   This is a valuable security feature to put limits on the number of logins that can be attempted before a user is locked out.

aaa authentication enable   This is usually combined with the `default` keyword to indicate that the enable password is used to authenticate.

aaa authentication ppp   This is usually used on a serial line to enable PPP authentication.

aaa authentication login   This option sets authentication to occur at login (as opposed to through PPP or another protocol).

Next I will cover the use of method lists to describe the type of authentication to be used.

Using Method Lists

It's important that we dive into the concept of method lists here. The *method* part of *method list* refers to the means of authentication. The options are numerous (local, enable, RADIUS, TACACS+, and line). The *list* part refers to the order in which these methods are attempted. This is an important concept to grasp. If you don't configure multiple methods of authentication, your odds of being locked out of the router or other device increase exponentially.

The following methods are available for authenticating the user:

- Local -The local username database is being used to authenticate the user.
- Enable - The enable password is being used to authenticate the user.
- RADIUS - A RADIUS server is being used to authenticate the user.
- TACACS+ - A TACACS+ server is being used authenticate the user.
- Line - A line password is being used to authenticate the user.

Let's imagine a scenario in which a method list with only one method has been specified; let's say RADIUS. What happens if the RADIUS server goes down? No authentication because there was only a single authentication method. You should always have a way to get into the router in an emergency. Usually that involves creating a local username and password on the router. Also you can use the `enable` password as a last resort.

You can configure a maximum of four methods within the context of a method list.

Let's examine an example of a method list.

```
aaa authentication login default group tacacs+ line enable
```

Can you guess how many methods are employed here? If you guessed three, you are correct. So, in order, I am going to try to use TACACS+ first; if that fails, I will use the `line` password; and finally, I will use the `enable` password.

Notice that the keyword `default` is used here. Replace that and you have the name of your list. The list named "default" applies to all interfaces unless specified elsewhere. You can override the default method list by defining a named list. So let's look at how this all works.

Suppose you want to configure AAA authentication for the console port. Here's an example of a method list for the console port:

```
aaa authentication login console_list local
```

In this case, I have designated a list called `console_list`. The word `local` means that this method list uses the local username database on the router to authenticate. Let's see how this list is applied to the console line:

```
Router1(config)# line console 0
Router1#(config-line) login authentication console_list
```

So what this means is that anyone attempting to use the console will have to authenticate to the router using a username and password that have been defined locally on the router.

Let's look at another example, this time using PPP:

```
aaa authentication ppp default local
```

In this example, I am using the local database to authenticate PPP connection requests. There are many other options to consider, but these are the primary ones to focus on.

Configuring Authorization

As stated earlier you can use authorization to define what commands can be used (in the case of TACACS+) or, for other methods, what types of access are defined. Let's take a look at the aaa authorization command to see what options there are. Again, we will look at the options available using the built-in help within the IOS. Here are the available options:

```
Router1(config)# aaa authorization ?
  auth-proxy       For Authentication Proxy Services
  cache            For AAA cache configuration
  commands         For exec (shell) commands.
  config-commands  For configuration mode commands.
```

```
configuration    For downloading configurations from AAA server
console          For enabling console authorization
exec             For starting an exec (shell).
ipmobile         For Mobile IP services.
network          For network services. (PPP, SLIP, ARAP)
reverse-access   For reverse access connections
template         Enable template authorization
```

As you can see, you have many options for configuring authentication. The best way of getting to know them is to explore a few sample configurations.

Here's a sample configuration of aaa authorization with the commands option.

```
aaa authorization commands 15 default local
```

So what did I just authorize? In this example, I am using the local database to grant commands available at privilege level 15 to the default method list. (Privilege levels are covered in Chapter 3.)

What if I used the network option? Here's a sample configuration of what that looks like:

```
aaa authorization network test1 local
```

This command allows the use of all network commands, such as PPP (Point-to-Point Protocol), SLIP (Serial Line Internet Protocol), and ARAP (AppleTalk Remote Access Protocol), for those who are authorized via the local database for the method list test1.

And last, there is an option to provide an EXEC shell to someone who has already authenticated.

```
aaa authorization exec test2 if-authenticated
```

So you can see that providing an EXEC shell to someone is a valuable option you can use to get very granular about what commands you need to allow for specific users. This is handy if you have a large number of administrators, some of whom may not be allowed to configure devices. See Chapter 3 for more information about specifying what commands an administrator can use.

Configuring Accounting

Now we get to the third *A* of *AAA*, which is accounting. Accounting allows you to provide audit trails of what is done on the network and also to bill for the usage of services. The syntax of aaa accounting is as follows:

```
aaa accounting {auth-proxy | system | network | exec | connection | commands
level} {default | list-name} {vrf vrf-name} {start-stop | stop-only | none}
{broadcast} group group-name
```

Here are the options the built-in help displays when you type a question mark after the aaa accounting command:

```
Router1(config)# aaa accounting ?
  auth-proxy        For authentication proxy events.
  commands          For exec (shell) commands.
  connection        For outbound connections. (telnet, rlogin)
  delay-start       Delay PPP Network start record until peer IP address is
                    known.
  exec              For starting an exec (shell).
  gigawords         64 bit interface counters to support Radius attributes
                    52 & 53.
  nested            When starting PPP from EXEC, generate NETWORK records
                    before EXEC-STOP record.
  network           For network services. (PPP, SLIP, ARAP)
  resource          For resource events.
  send              Send records to accounting server.
  session-duration  Set the preference for calculating session durations
  suppress          Do not generate accounting records for a specific type of
                    user.
  system            For system events.
  update            Enable accounting update records.
```

As I did with authorization, I will give a couple of examples for accounting. Here is a case in which I am using a TACACS+ server and tracking what is done by a user who executes level 15 commands:

```
aaa accounting commands 15 default stop-only group tacacs+
```

In the following example, I am using the auth-proxy option. With this option, you can have users authenticate for access either inbound or outbound. For example, a user trying to browse the Internet from their PC might be normally blocked by an access control list. But with auth-proxy, a temporary access list change is made allowing the outbound traffic:

```
aaa accounting auth-proxy default start-stop group tacacs+
```

Configuring TACACS+

We've tackled configuring a router for RADIUS, and now it's time to configure it for TACACS+. I will discuss the steps necessary to configure it both from a command-line interface and using Cisco Security Device Manager (SDM).

Configuring AAA Services from the Command Line

There are three basic steps to configuring a router to use a TACACS+ server:

1. Configure AAA services globally using the `aaa new-model` command.

2. Configure the server or servers you are going to use by specifying their IP addresses.

3. Configure an encryption key that prevents someone from putting a rogue TACACS+ server on the network.

   In this example of configuring a router, more than one TACACS+ server is configured and the same encryption key is used for both routers. The `single-connection` option specifies that the router and TACACS+ server maintain a single TCP connection rather than allowing the connection to be set up and torn down each time it is used. This is more efficient and allows more connections. Here are the commands:

```
Router1# aaa new-model
Router1# tacacs-server host 172.16.100.100 single-connection
Router1# tacacs-server host 172.16.100.101 single-connection
Router1# tacacs-server key mys3cret
```

   Let's say you want to be super-secure and have two separate TACACS+ servers and two separate encryption keys. In that case, you would include the key statement on the command line where you designate the TACACS+ server host. Here is a sample configuration:

```
Router1# aaa new-model
Router1# tacacs-server host 172.16.100.100 single-connection key mys3cret
Router1# tacacs-server host 172.16.100.101 single-connection key yours3cret
```

   If you use the built-in IOS help by listing a ? after the `tacacs-server` command, you see the full list of commands that are available:

```
Router1(config)# tacacs-server ?
  administration      Start tacacs+ daemon handling administrative messages
  directed-request    Allow user to specify tacacs server to use with `@server'
  dns-alias-lookup    Enable IP Domain Name System Alias lookup for TACACS
                      servers
  extended            Enable extended TACACS
  host                Specify a TACACS server
  key                 Set TACACS+ encryption key.
  last-resort         Define TACACS action if no server responds
  optional-passwords  The first TACACS request can be made without password
                      verification
  packet              Modify TACACS+ packet options
  retransmit          Search iterations of the TACACS server list
  timeout             Time to wait for a TACACS server to reply
```

Configuring AAA Services with Cisco SDM

If you're not a command-line aficionado, you might give the Cisco SDM tool a whirl. It's a really nice way to configure things and if you set up the SDM to display the commands that it is sending to the router, you might learn some command line configuration in the process! So let's jump right into it.

In this section, I'm assuming you've spent at least a little time with SDM, so I don't show you the introductory screens but instead jump right into the configuration screen.

To navigate to the Cisco SDM Additional Tasks screen, on the Configure tab, choose AAA from the Additional Tasks list, as shown in Figure 4.3.

FIGURE 4.3   The Cisco SDM Additional Tasks AAA screen

Something you'll notice right away is that AAA is disabled at the moment. So your first task is to enable AAA. If you were at the command line, you would be issuing the familiar aaa new-model command. But here you are going to click on the box at the upper-right corner labeled Enable AAA. When you do, the Enable AAA dialog box appears (Figure 4.4).

FIGURE 4.4   The Enable AAA dialog box

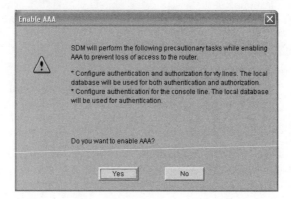

Notice that the screen advises that authentication and authorization will be configured for vty (Telnet) lines and authentication will be configured for the console line, both using the local database. So SDM makes your job a lot easier by reducing the amount of typing you have to perform.

A confirmation dialog box, shown in Figure 4.5, notifies you that AAA has been enabled.

FIGURE 4.5   Information dialog box showing that AAA has been enabled

Back at the main AAA screen, shown in Figure 4.6, it now shows that AAA has been enabled. Notice that no servers have yet been configured and the values for the other two entries have changed as proof of what the enable screen advised would be configured.

FIGURE 4.6   The Cisco SDM AAA(Enabled) screen

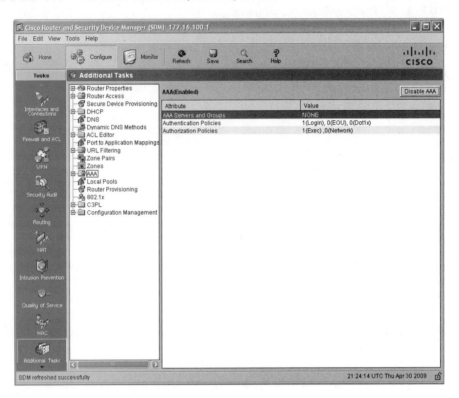

The next step is to add your AAA servers. If you click AAA in the list to the left and expand it, you will see AAA Servers And Groups. Expand that to see the AAA Servers option, shown in Figure 4.7. Click the AAA Servers options and that's where you will add your AAA servers.

FIGURE 4.7   The Cisco SDM AAA Servers screen

Click the Add button in the upper-right portion of the screen and the Add AAA Server dialog box appears (Figure 4.8).

FIGURE 4.8   The Add AAA Server dialog box

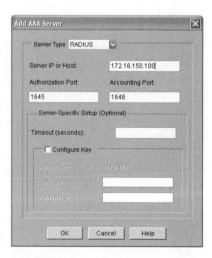

The Add AAA Server dialog box defaults to configuring a RADIUS server, as you can see. You can also choose to configure a TACACS+ server, and you will see this in a little bit. For now, we are going to configure a RADIUS server. Notice that the default ports are shown already. You can optionally configure a time-out value and encryption keys to use. I've added an IP address in the Server IP Or Host box, and other than that, accept the defaults and just click OK. You can see the result of adding the RADIUS server in Figure 4.9.

FIGURE 4.9   The Cisco SDM AAA Servers screen showing the RADIUS server

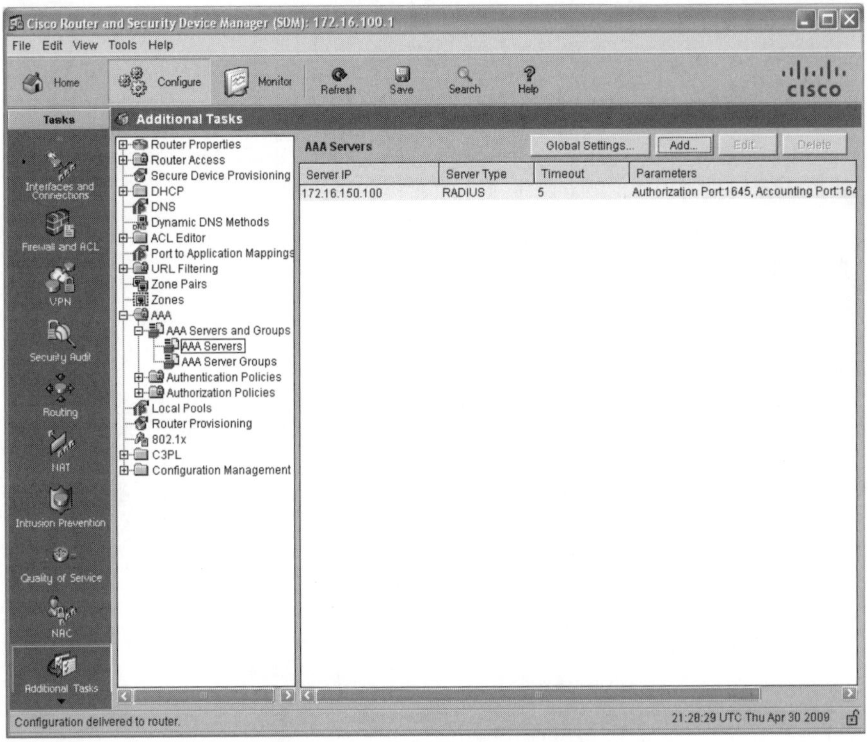

Let's go back and add a TACACS+ server. Once again, click the Add button. In the Add AAA Server dialog box, choose TACACS+ from the Server Type menu. Next, add a key by checking the Configure Key check box and then entering and confirming a key value. Note in Figure 4.10 that the key value is not displayed in the clear.

FIGURE 4.10 Adding a TACACS+ server

Click OK, and again, you are back to the AAA Servers screen (Figure 4.11), which shows the TACACS+ server that was just configured. (If you were wondering what happened to the RADIUS server we configured earlier, I removed it for clarity's sake.)

FIGURE 4.11 The Cisco SDM AAA Servers screen showing the TACACS+ server

Real World Scenario

AAA to the Rescue!

John is a network engineer at a medium-sized business in St. Louis, Missouri. He has just been asked by the CIO if there is a way to find out who is able to log in to the company's routers. The CIO was concerned about a preliminary finding in an auditor report for Sarbanes-Oxley compliance done by an outside firm. John wasn't immediately certain who had logged in because the company was somewhat decentralized and a number of people had access to the routers. He suddenly remembered from a training class he had attended that user authentication to the router could be controlled by AAA services. "Say," he thought to himself, "didn't someone install a Cisco TACACS+ server last year?" He didn't know what it was being used for, but he decided to look into it.

John found that the TACACS+ server had been purchased last year by an engineer who was no longer with the company. It had been installed but no one had been using it. John was able to get administrative privileges on the server and he added all known users of the company's routers. This would allow the company to have a record of who logged into the routers and keep anyone not authorized out.

Now there was just one thing left. John needed to configure all the routers in the network. He added the following configuration to each router to secure administrative access to them.

```
Router1(config)#aaa new-model
Router1(config)#aaa authentication login default group tacacs+ enable
```

For the purpose of this example, it is assumed that a TACACS+ or Cisco Secure ACS server has already been configured in the router.

Troubleshooting AAA on Cisco Routers

When troubleshooting AAA issues on a Cisco router, you should engage the debug command to assist you. Here's a list of all the possible debug options that are available to you:

```
Router# debug aaa ?
  accounting        Accounting
  administrative    Administrative
  api               AAA api events
  attr              AAA Attr Manager
```

authentication	Authentication
authorization	Authorization
cache	Cache activities
db	AAA DB Manager
dead-criteria	AAA Dead-Criteria Info
id	AAA Unique Id
ipc	AAA IPC
mlist-ref-count	Method list reference counts
per-user	Per-user attributes
pod	AAA POD processing
protocol	AAA protocol processing
server-ref-count	Server handle reference counts
sg-ref-count	Server group handle reference counts
sg-server-selection	Server Group Server Selection
subsys	AAA Subsystem

Let's use one of the options and do an actual debug to see what it looks like. In the following example, I am going to look at the authentication of a username and password from a local database on the router itself:

```
Router# debug aaa authentication
113147: May 13 10:02:48.145 CST: AAA/MEMORY: create_user (0x619C4940) user=''
Ruser'' port='tty1' rem_addr=async/81560' authen_type=ASCII service=LOGIN
priv=1
113148: May 13 10:02:48.145 CST: AAA/AUTHEN/START (2784097690): port='tty1'
list=''
action=LOGIN service=LOGIN
113149: May 13 10:02:48.145 CST: AAA/AUTHEN/START (2784097690): using
"default" list
113150: May 13 10:02:48.145 CST: AAA/AUTHEN/START (2784097690): Method=LOCAL
113151: May 13 10:02:48.145 CST: AAA/AUTHEN (2784097690): status = GETUSER
113152: May 13 10:02:48.145 CST: AAA/AUTHEN/CONT (2784097690): continue_login
(user='(undef)')
113153: May 13 10:02:48.145 CST: AAA/AUTHEN (2784097690): status = GETUSER
113154: May 13 10:02:48.145 CST: AAA/AUTHEN/CONT (2784097690): Method=LOCAL
113155: May 13 10:02:48.145 CST: AAA/AUTHEN (2784097690): status = GETPASS
113156: May 13 10:02:49.985 CST: AAA/AUTHEN/CONT (2784097690): continue_login
(user='test1')
113157: May 13 10:02:49.985 CST: AAA/AUTHEN (2784097690): status = GETPASS
113158: May 13 10:02:49.985 CST: AAA/AUTHEN/CONT (2784097690): Method=LOCAL
113157: May 13 10:02:49.985 CST: AAA/AUTHEN (2784097690): status = PASS
```

This is just one example of the level of detail you can see using the debug command. In this snippet, you can see that the method used is LOCAL, which means that the local database is used. Later in the snippet, you see that the user is 'test1'. Immediately after that the password is requested. You can see that the password that was provided was authenticated, indicated by the status = PASS message. You will not see the password shown. Always know that when you're having problems, debug can be your friend.

Summary

In this chapter, you learned about AAA services and the operation of RADIUS and TACACS+ servers. AAA services are key to device control, user access, and accounting functions.

When it comes to configuring authentication, authorization, and accounting functions, remember that authentication covers who can access the resource, authorization covers what the user can do, and accounting tells you what the user has done and when they did it. In particular, I covered TACACS+ configurations. It's important to be able to configure TACACS+ for basic functions. You should now be able to enable AAA on a router, define the TACACS+ servers, configure a method list, define and configure a local database, and be able to enable basic troubleshooting with debug.

Finally, you used the Cisco Security Device Manager (SDM) to configure AAA servers on a Cisco router. The Cisco SDM is an important tool for the CCNA Security exam. It's good to familiarize yourself with it, especially if you don't have lots of experience on the command line.

Exam Essentials

Remember the three components of AAA: authentication, authorization, and accounting. The components of AAA are important because they offer robust services that are used in many applications today. Know the two types of AAA servers covered in this chapter, which are RADIUS and TACACS+.

Know the differences between RADIUS and TACACS+. A primary difference is that RADIUS uses UDP and TACACS+ uses TCP. Also, TACACS+ can separate authentication, authorization, and accounting, whereas RADIUS combines authentication and authorization.

Understand how to enable AAA via command line on the router. By using the command aaa new-model, in global configuration mode, you can enable AAA on the router.

Remember how to configure local authentication via the command line on the router. Make sure you know how to add a username and password on the router and then define local authentication using the aaa `authentication` command.

Understand how to configure local authorization via command line on the router. Make sure you know how to add a username and password on the router and then define local authentication using the aaa `authorization` command.

Know how to configure AAA authentication on the router. Make sure you know how to configure AAA accounting on the router. Options such as commands and `auth-proxy` are key.

Understand how to configure a TACACS+ server using either the command line or SDM. The command line method is `tacacs-server` *ip address*. Using the SDM, you navigate to the AAA section of Additional Tasks on the Configure menu. Under that menu, click the Add box.

Remember how to enable AAA services using SDM. Recall that when you navigate to the AAA portion of the SDM, it tells you whether AAA is enabled or not in the upper-left portion of the screen. If it is not enabled, there is the option to do so in the upper-right section of the screen.

Know how to add an AAA server using SDM. You must expand the AAA section of the SDM Configure screen to get to the AAA Servers menu. From there you have the option to add a server. Click the Add box and you can add either a RADIUS or a TACACS+ server.

Written Lab

Write the answers to the following questions:

1. What is the command to enable AAA on a Cisco router?
2. What is the command to configure authentication using a local database for login to the router?
3. What is the command to add a TACACS+ server to a Cisco router?
4. What protocol is used at the transport layer of RADIUS?
5. How many methods can be used in a method list to do authentication?
6. What attribute number does the IETF assign for vendors to use to extend the protocol?
7. What command is used with AAA accounting to allow a user to authenticate to the router for access purposes, for instance, to the Internet?
8. What is the name of the option applied to the aaa `authorization` command to allow users to perform functions based on EXEC levels?

9. When using RADIUS to perform authentication, what would the proper response message be to a successful username and password entered?

10. What is the name of the successor to RADIUS?

    (The answers to the written lab can be found following the answers to the review questions.)

Hands-on Labs

Use these hands-on lab exercises to practice using basic AAA commands on a router. Because I state assumptions about certain aspects of the exercises, you will need only a single Cisco router that supports AAA, which is pretty much any of them.

If you want to use any of the SDM features discussed earlier in the chapter, you will need a Cisco ISR router, such as an 800 series or an 1800 series, but an ISR router is *not* required for these hands-on labs. There are other models as well, but these are a couple of the lower-end models that are more affordable if you happen to be footing the bill for them.

Hands-on Lab 4.1: Configuring AAA Authentication with a Local Database

In this lab, you will configure a local database and then enable AAA and use that local database for authentication.

1. Log in to your router and go into privileged mode by typing **en** or **enable**.

2. Enter global configuration mode by typing **config t** or **configure terminal**. Then enter the usernames **user1** and **user2** and their respective passwords as shown:

    ```
    Router#config t
    Enter configuration commands, one per line.  End with
      CNTL/Z.
    Router(config)#username user1 password test1
    Router(config)#username user2 password test2
    ```

    At this point, you have a local database to use. Next, you'll configure the AAA commands.

3. While still in global configuration mode, type **aaa new-model** to turn on AAA services.

4. Now that you have AAA services running, you are going to configure authentication using the local database you just created. Again, while still in global configuration mode, type the command **aaa authentication login default local**.

Now you have completed the configuration of AAA authentication using a local database.

Hands-on Lab 4.2: Configuring TACACS+ Authentication, Authorization, and Accounting

In this lab, you will configure a router for AAA using TACACS+, where you will configure basic authentication, authorization, and accounting.

1. Log into your router and go into privileged mode by typing **en** or **enable**.

2. Enter global configuration mode by typing **configure terminal** or **config t** and then enter the command **aaa new-model** to turn on AAA services.

   ```
   Router#config t
   Enter configuration commands, one per line.  End with
     CNTL/Z.
   Router(config)#aaa new-model
   ```

3. For the purpose of this exercise, you are going to assume that you have a TACACS+ server at IP address 172.16.54.100. You are going to enter in the TACACS+ server using the following command:

   ```
   Router(config)#tacacs-server host 172.16.54.100
   ```

4. While still in global configuration mode, type **aaa authentication login default group tacacs+**.

5. Now that authentication services are configured, you need to configure authorization and accounting. Add the following commands: **aaa authorization exec default group tacacs+ if-authenticated**.

6. And finally, add the following commands for accounting services: **aaa accounting exec default start-stop group tacacs+**.

Review Questions

1. What protocol is used with TACACS+ when it is used to authenticate users of a network device?

   A. ICMP

   B. UDP

   C. FTP

   D. TCP

   E. RTP

2. In RADIUS, which IETF vendor-specific attribute is used by Cisco to add functionality?

   A. 39

   B. 25

   C. 26

   D. 56

   E. 19

3. Which IOS command sequence is used to turn on AAA services on a router? What IOS user exec command should you issue?

   A. `Router1(config)#aaa`

   B. `Router1(config)#aaa enable`

   C. `Router1(config)#aaa new-model`

   D. `Router1(config-if)#aaa new-model`

   E. `Router1(config)#aaa service enable`

4. Which of the following is a valid response from the TACACS+ server to the correct user-name and password being entered by the user? (Choose all that apply.)

   A. REJECT

   B. ACCEPT

   C. ERROR

   D. CONTINUE

5. Your new boss tells you that you need to set up AAA services on a router in a remote office. You have only the SDM at your disposal to perform that task. Which menus would you use?

   A. On the Configure tab, choose AAA.

   B. On the Configure tab, choose AAA from the Services list.

   C. On the Configure tab, choose AAA from the Security list.

   D. On the Configure tab, choose AAA from the Additional list.

   E. On the Configure tab, choose AAA from the Additional Tasks list.

6. Which of the following are methods used in AAA method lists? (Choose all that apply.)

   A. login

   B. local

   C. SLIP

   D. PPP

   E. TACACS+

7. What is the maximum number of methods that can be designated in a method list?

   A. 2

   B. 3

   C. 4

   D. 5

8. When configuring a method list using PPP, which one of the following command sequences is correct?

   A. `aaa authentication ppp login`

   B. `aaa login ppp`

   C. `aaa authentication ppp default local`

   D. `aaa authentication local`

9. When you use SDM to enable AAA, what also happens? (Choose all that apply.)

   A. Vty authentication

   B. Login authentication

   C. Console authentication

   D. Console authorization

10. You have successfully configured a router with AAA services. Unfortunately, the TACACS+ server keeps crashing and you now need to add another method to authenticate. Which one of the following commands should you implement?

   A. `aaa authentication default`

   B. `aaa authentication login`

   C. `aaa authentication login default tacacs+ enable`

   D. `aaa authentication default tacacs+ enable`

   E. `aaa authentication login default group TACACS+ line enable`

11. If you want to configure AAA authentication, which mode should you be using?

   A. User

   B. Privileged EXEC

   C. Configuration

   D. Global configuration

12. What is the name of the function that allows you to specify the type of authentication to use and in what order?

    A. List

    B. Method list

    C. Authentication list

    D. AAA-list

13. You have successfully started up the Cisco SDM and have accessed a router. Now you have to configure a TACACS+ server. What must you do? Assume that you are using a brand-new router. (Choose all that apply.)

    A. Configure the router IP addresses.

    B. Click Configure ➢ Additional Tasks ➢ AAA and then click on the Enable AAA box.

    C. Configure IP accounting.

    D. While in the AAA Servers section, click the Add button and add a TACACS+ server.

    E. Add the correct SNMP community string.

14. Which of the following is not a service that would be allowed by a TACACS+ server if used for authorization?

    A. PPP

    B. SLIP

    C. EXEC

    D. SSH

    E. Telnet

15. Which of the following is not a feature of TACACS+?

    A. Support for TCP

    B. Separates each of the AAA processes

    C. Encryption of the password only

    D. Allows specific commands to be passed down to the user

16. You find a configuration that a previous engineer had put onto a router in a remote building. A portion of the configuration is shown here:

```
tacacs-server host 10.10.10.1 single connection
```

What does the use of the `single connection` command indicate?

    A. The TACACS+ server uses a single UDP connection.

    B. Only a single connection is allowed at any time.

    C. The TACACS+ server uses a single TCP connection.

    D. The TACACS+ server is single and seeking a connection.

17. Which is not a method of using AAA on a router?

   A. DIAMETER

   B. RADIUS

   C. LOCAL

   D. TACACS+

18. Suppose you were going to configure AAA services with local authentication on your new router. Which of the following commands would you use? (Choose all that apply.)

   A. `aaa new-model`

   B. `aaa authentication local default login`

   C. `aaa authentication default login local`

   D. `aaa authentication login default local`

   E. `username `***`username`***` password `***`password`***

19. Which ports are used within TACACS+?

   A. TCP 39

   B. UDP 49

   C. UDP 1813

   D. TCP 59

   E. UDP 101

   F. TCP 49

20. Which of the following is not a response message from a RADIUS server?

   A. ACCESS-CONTINUE

   B. ACCESS-REJECT

   C. ACCESS-ACCEPT

   D. ACCESS-REQUEST

   E. ACCESS-CHALLENGE

Answers to Review Questions

1. D. TACACS+ differs from RADIUS in respect to communications because it uses TCP instead of UDP.

2. C. The vendor-specific attribute assigned to Cisco within the IETF attributes is 26.

3. C. The command `aaa new-model` must be issued from global configuration mode. This enables AAA services globally and allows you to continue with a RADIUS, TACACS+, or LOCAL configuration.

4. B, D. Normally, ACCEPT is the correct response to someone entering the correct username and password. However, you could get a CONTINUE message that requires further authentication before you get an ACCEPT message.

5. E. Additional Tasks under the Configure tab is the correct place to set up AAA.

6. B, E. Remember that the word *method* in *method lists* refers to the type of authentication that can be done. There are five methods that can be used: local, TACACS+, RADIUS, line, and enable.

7. C. Up to four methods can be defined in a method list.

8. C. This was an example I showed in the chapter where I used PPP as an authentication method. I further defined that I used the local database. All of the other command sequences have incorrect or incomplete syntax.

9. A, C. When using the SDM, once you click on the box to enable AAA, a pop-up dialog box advises you that it will configure vty authentication and authorization as well as console authentication.

10. E. The only answer with the correct syntax is E, which implements a method list with not only TACACS+ but line and enable as a last resort. The other choices have either missing syntax or are incorrect.

11. D. AAA authentication is performed in global configuration mode because it applies to the router as a whole.

12. B. A method list is used to define what authentication methods to use and the order in which they will be used. It's always best to have more than one way of authenticating, particularly if you are using an external server such as a TACACS+ or RADIUS server. If communication goes down between the device and the server, you want a way to get in.

13. B, D. You must enable AAA before you can configure any AAA servers. Once that is complete, then you can expand AAA ➤ AAA Servers And Groups to expose the AAA Servers selection. Highlight that and then click the Add button to add an AAA server.

14. D. SSH is not a service that is offered via TACACS+ authorization. The choices for TACACS+ authorization are rlogin, PPP, SLIP, EXEC, and Telnet.

15. C. TACACS+ supports the encryption of the entire packets, excluding the TCP header. RADIUS, on the other hand, supports the encryption of the password only.

16. C. Cisco's TACACS+ server has the ability to limit the communication to a single TCP connection in order to improve performance over multiple connections every time a request is made.

17. A. DIAMETER is not one of the methods of using AAA on a router.

18. A, D, E. You need to enter `aaa new-model` to start configuring AAA services. Then you need to enter `aaa authentication login default local` because you are using AAA to log in and then the default method is the local database. Finally, you need to configure a username and password.

19. F. Recall that I said that RADIUS uses UDP ports and TACACS+ uses TCP ports. So you can eliminate all the UDP answers immediately. Then you need to remember that TCP 49 is the port used in TACACS+.

20. A. The four types of messages used within a RADIUS server are ACCESS-REQUEST, ACCESS-ACCEPT, ACCESS-REJECT, and ACCESS-CHALLENGE. In TACACS+, there is also a CONTINUE message.

Answers to Written Lab

1. aaa new-model

2. aaa authentication login default local

3. tacacs-server *ip address*

4. UDP

5. 4

6. 26

7. auth-proxy

8. commands

9. ACCESS-ACCEPT

10. DIAMETER

Chapter

5

Securing Your Router

THE FOLLOWING CCNA SECURITY EXAM OBJECTIVES ARE COVERED IN THIS CHAPTER:

- ✓ Secure Cisco routers using the SDM Security Audit feature
- ✓ Use the One-Step Lockdown feature in SDM to secure a Cisco router
- ✓ Use CLI and SDM to configure SSH on Cisco routers to enable secured management access
- ✓ Use CLI and SDM to configure Cisco routers to send Syslog messages to a Syslog server

In this chapter, we'll explore some of the ways to secure your router. Cisco has made this task easy by scripting the procedure for us. You can secure your router either from a command-line interface or in the Security Device Manager (SDM) graphical environment. There are many ways to accomplish this, but we will examine some automated methods that Cisco has included from the perspective of both a command-line interface (CLI) and the SDM. Also, we will cover configuring SNMP on a Cisco router. (This topic is not necessarily in the CCNA Security test objectives, but it is covered for completeness.)

Finally, you will learn how to implement secure management access and reporting. This includes configuring SSH from both the SDM and the CLI. We will discuss the use of the Syslog facility to send log messages to a Syslog server.

Using the Command-Line Interface to Lock Down the Router

The feature that you can use on a Cisco IOS router to automatically lock down the router is called *AutoSecure*. AutoSecure has been available in general distributions since IOS release 12.3(1). The purpose is to allow administrators who may not be familiar with all the security features of the IOS to use one simple command to lock down their router to a minimal level of security. The command is auto secure. It is issued in the privileged EXEC mode.

AutoSecure deals with two general areas of router security:

- The management plane, or specific areas that apply to administrative control of the router
- The forwarding plane, which applies to those features that deal with forwarding packets

Let's look at these in a bit more depth, shall we?

Locking Down the Management Plane

Lockdown of the management plane applies to the following five areas of concern on the router:

- Disabling unneeded global services
- Disabling per interface services that are potential attack vectors

- Enabling useful global security features
- Enabling log features that enhance security
- Securing access to the router itself

Disabling global services   When the auto secure command is issued, several global services are automatically disabled without notice to the user. Table 5.1 lists the global services that are disabled.

TABLE 5.1   Global Services Disabled by AutoSecure

Service	Function
Finger	An antiquated service that provides useful information to an attacker.
Packet Assembler and Disassembler (PAD)	Packet assembler and disassembler services that could leave the router vulnerable.
Small Servers	TCP/UDP diagnostic services that could be exploited to cause a denial of service.
BOOTP	Insecure protocol that is similar to DHCP.
HTTP Server	HTTPS is the preferred method because it is encrypted.
IDENT	An antiquated identification service specified in RFC 1413 that could provide useful information to an attacker.
Cisco Discovery Protocol (CDP)	Provides information about next-hop Cisco devices. This is useful to an attacker and vulnerable to a denial of service attack if an attacker sends many CDP packets to a router.

CDP is useful for internal management purposes, so it's better to disable it for external interfaces only than to disable it altogether, as the AutoSecure feature does. |
| Network Time Protocol (NTP) | Natively an insecure protocol. It can be made more secure with MD5 authentication and access lists. |
| Source Routing | Source routing is a bad idea in all but debugging purposes, so disabling it on a global basis is prudent. |

Disabling per interface services   After you run AutoSecure, the per interface services listed in Table 5.2 will be disabled on all interfaces, again without notice to the user.

TABLE 5.2   Disabled per Interface Services

Service	Vulnerability
ICMP Redirects	Doesn't serve a purpose on properly configured networks, but could be exploited if the network is not configured correctly.
ICMP Unreachables	Can be exploited for denial of service attacks.
ICMP Mask Reply	Mask reply messages can reveal subnet masking, which could be useful to attackers.
Proxy-arp	Proxy-arp is another service that can be exploited for denial of service attacks.
Directed Broadcast	Known to be a cause for Smurf attacks.
Maintenance Operations Protocol (MOP)	MOP is part of the DECnet protocol suite used for maintenance and could be exploited if a vulnerability is discovered.

Enabling global services   After you run AutoSecure, the following per global services will be enabled:

Service password-encryption   Encrypts all service-level passwords so that they are not visible in the configuration

Service tcp-keepalives-in   Generates keepalive packets on idle incoming network connections

Service tcp-keepalives-out   Generates keepalive packets on idle outgoing network connections

Securing access to the router   After you run AutoSecure, the following will be configured:

Banner message   If one doesn't exist, you will be prompted to provide one interactively.

Login and password   These are configured on the AUX, the console, and vty lines. The transport input and transport output are configured to allow Telnet and SSH only. The exec time-out on the console and the AUX ports are configured for 5 and 10 seconds, respectively.

Logging for security   After AutoSecure is run, the logging options listed in Table 5.3 are enabled, which allows for identification of incidents via detailed log analysis. This enhances proper incident response.

TABLE 5.3   Logging for Security Features

Feature	Function
Time stamps and sequence numbers	Essential for doing detailed log analysis of debug and log messages.
Login-related events	Can reveal attempts at login attacks.
Logging console critical	Sends logging messages to all TTY lines and limits on severity.
Logging buffered	Logs messages to an internal buffer.
Logging trap debugging	Logs messages with a severity higher than debugging and sends them to the Syslog server.

Locking Down the Forwarding Plane

There are significantly fewer features involved in locking down the forwarding plane than there are for locking down the management plane. You can secure the forwarding plane by enabling the following features:

- Cisco Express Forwarding (CEF)
- TCP Intercept, if available
- Unicast Reverse Path Forwarding (uRPF), if available
- CBAC, if available

Table 5.4 shows those features in detail.

TABLE 5.4   Features Used in Securing the Forwarding Plane

Feature	Function
Cisco Express Forwarding (CEF)	Enables CEF or distributed CEF (depending on platform) to be able to better handle SYN flood type of attacks.
TCP Intercept	When available, this is configured for connection time-out if you select it.
Unicast Reverse Path Forwarding (uRPF)	uRPF is used against IP spoofing attacks by verifying the source IP address.
Context-Based Access Control (CBAC)	CBAC is enabled when the router has firewall services in use.

Now that you know what is done when AutoSecure is enabled, let's see what it looks like when we do it.

Exercise 5.1 shows how to configure the router using AutoSecure. In the exercise, you'll see a number of prompts where the administrator needs to enter in information. An alternative option is to use the keyword no-interact. This causes the IOS to enter a default configuration without prompting the administrator for further input.

EXERCISE 5.1

Configuring with AutoSecure

You may see slightly different response messages, depending on what version of IOS you are using and what features are enabled, but here are the steps:

1. Enter **auto secure** at the router prompt:

Router1#**auto secure**

You will see text like the following:

```
        --- AutoSecure Configuration ---


*** AutoSecure configuration enhances the security of
the router, but it will not make it absolutely resistant
to all security attacks ***


AutoSecure will modify the configuration of your device.
All configuration changes will be shown. For a detailed
explanation of how the configuration changes enhance security
and any possible side effects, please refer to Cisco.com for
Autosecure documentation.
At any prompt you may enter '?' for help.
Use ctrl-c to abort this session at any prompt.


Gathering information about the router for AutoSecure
```

2. When you see the message Is this router connected to internet?, type **yes**.

3. When you see the message Enter the number of interfaces facing the internet, press the Enter key to accept the default of 1. You will then see text like the following:

Interface	IP-Address	OK?	Method	Status	Protocol
FastEthernet0/0	172.16.100.1	YES	NVRAM	up	down
FastEthernet0/1	192.168.100.1	YES	NVRAM	up	down
Serial0/0/0	unassigned	YES	NVRAM	administratively down	down

4. Next you will see the following message: Enter the interface name that is facing the internet. Enter **FastEthernet0/1**.

    You will see the following text:

    ```
    Securing Management plane services...

    Disabling service finger
    Disabling service pad
    Disabling udp & tcp small servers
    Enabling service password encryption
    Enabling service tcp-keepalives-in
    Enabling service tcp-keepalives-out
    Disabling the cdp protocol

    Disabling the bootp server
    Disabling the http server
    Disabling the finger service
    Disabling source routing
    Disabling gratuitous arp

    Here is a sample Security Banner to be shown
    at every access to device. Modify it to suit your
    enterprise requirements.

    Authorized Access only
      This system is the property of So-&-So-Enterprise.
      UNAUTHORIZED ACCESS TO THIS DEVICE IS PROHIBITED.
      You must have explicit permission to access this
      device. All activities performed on this device
      are logged. Any violations of access policy will result
      in disciplinary action.
    ```

5. When you see the following text, enter **%** as your delimiter:

    ```
    Enter the security banner {Put the banner between
    k and k, where k is any character}.
    ```

6. Enter the text you want as your security banner, for example, **WARNING: Authorized access only. Violators will be prosecuted!**

7. Enter another **%**.

8. Follow the instructions to enter an enable secret password:

```
Enable secret is either not configured or is the same as enable password
Enter the new enable secret:
```

9. Confirm the enable secret password:

```
Confirm the enable secret:
```

10. At the prompts, enter **ruser1** as the username, then enter and confirm a password:

```
Enter the username:
Enter the password:
Confirm the password:
```

You will see the following text:

```
Configuring AAA local authentication
Configuring Console, Aux and VTY lines for
local authentication, exec-timeout, and transport
Securing device against Login Attacks
Configure the following parameters
```

11. When you see the following text, enter **30**:

```
Blocking Period when Login Attack detected:
```

12. When you see the following text, enter **3**:

```
Maximum Login failures with the device:
```

13. When you see the following text, enter **10**:

```
Maximum time period for crossing the failed login attempts:
```

14. You will configure an SSH server next, so when you see the following prompt, press the Enter key to accept the default of yes:

```
Configure SSH server? [yes]:
```

15. When prompted, enter **router1** as the hostname and then enter **myrouter.com** as the domain name.

You will see text like the following:

```
Configuring interface specific AutoSecure services
Disabling the following ip services on all interfaces:
```

```
  no ip redirects
  no ip proxy-arp
  no ip unreachables
  no ip directed-broadcast
  no ip mask-reply
Disabling mop on Ethernet interfaces

Securing Forwarding plane services...

Enabling CEF (This might impact the memory requirements for your platform)
Enabling unicast rpf on all interfaces connected
to internet
Tcp intercept feature is used prevent tcp syn attack
on the servers in the network. Create autosec_tcp_intercept_list
to form the list of servers to which the tcp traffic is to
be observed
```

16. When you see the following text, enter **yes**:

```
Enable tcp intercept feature? [yes/no]:
```

AutoSecure lists the configuration that you generated:

```
This is the configuration generated:

no service finger
no service pad
no service udp-small-servers
no service tcp-small-servers
service password-encryption
service tcp-keepalives-in
service tcp-keepalives-out
no cdp run
no ip bootp server
no ip http server
no ip finger
no ip source-route
no ip gratuitous-arps
no ip identd
banner motd ^C
WARNING: Authorized access only.  Violators will be prosecuted!
^C
```

```
security passwords min-length 6
security authentication failure rate 10 log
enable secret 5 $1$u7lI$OLIOAS7.rnTRAiZICkHz91
username ruser1 password 7 15001E1F01387A
aaa new-model
aaa authentication login local_auth local
line con 0
 login authentication local_auth
 exec-timeout 5 0
 transport output telnet
line aux 0
 login authentication local_auth
 exec-timeout 10 0
 transport output telnet
line vty 0 4
 login authentication local_auth
 transport input telnet
line tty 1
 login authentication local_auth
 exec-timeout 15 0
login block-for 30 attempts 3 within 10
hostname router1
ip domain-name myrouter.com
crypto key generate rsa general-keys modulus 1024
ip ssh time-out 60
ip ssh authentication-retries 2
line vty 0 4
 transport input ssh telnet
service timestamps debug datetime msec localtime show-timezone
service timestamps log datetime msec localtime show-timezone
logging facility local2
logging trap debugging
service sequence-numbers
logging console critical
logging buffered
interface FastEthernet0/0
 no ip redirects
 no ip proxy-arp
 no ip unreachables
 no ip directed-broadcast
```

```
 no ip mask-reply
 no mop enabled
interface FastEthernet0/1
 no ip redirects
 no ip proxy-arp
 no ip unreachables
 no ip directed-broadcast
 no ip mask-reply
 no mop enabled
interface Serial0/0/0
 no ip redirects
 no ip proxy-arp
 no ip unreachables
 no ip directed-broadcast
 no ip mask-reply
ip cef
access-list 100 permit udp any any eq bootpc
interface FastEthernet0/1
 ip verify unicast source reachable-via rx allow-default 100
ip tcp intercept list autosec_tcp_intercept_list
ip tcp intercept drop-mode random
ip tcp intercept watch-timeout 15
ip tcp intercept connection-timeout 3600
ip tcp intercept max-incomplete low 450
ip tcp intercept max-incomplete high 550
!
end
```

17. When you are asked whether to apply the configuration, press Enter for the default of yes:

```
Apply this configuration to running-config? [yes]:
```

You will see text like the following:

```
Applying the config generated to running-config
The name for the keys will be: router1.myrouter.com

% The key modulus size is 1024 bits

router1#
000018: *May 15 20:40:13.071 UTC: %AUTOSEC-1-MODIFIED:
AutoSecure configuration has been Modified on this device
```

Understanding One-Step Lockdown

Most, but not all, functions that were used in the CLI AutoSecure process can be performed with Cisco SDM. The procedure is called One-Step Lockdown. First we will walk through the procedure of configuring One-Step Lockdown. Later in this section, I will outline the differences between One-Step Lockdown and AutoSecure.

Configuring One-Step Lockdown with SDM

To configure One-Step Lockdown with SDM, follow these steps:

1. Of course, the first thing in configuring One-Step Lockdown is to enter SDM. (For an introduction to SDM, see Chapter 3, "Securing Administrative Access.") The main screen is shown in Figure 5.1.

FIGURE 5.1   The Cisco Router and Security Device Manager (SDM) screen

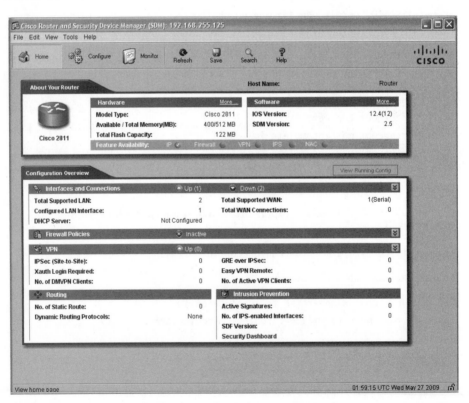

2. If you click the Configure button, a number of options appear on the left side of the screen. Select the Security Audit option and you will see the screen shown in Figure 5.2.

FIGURE 5.2 The Security Audit screen

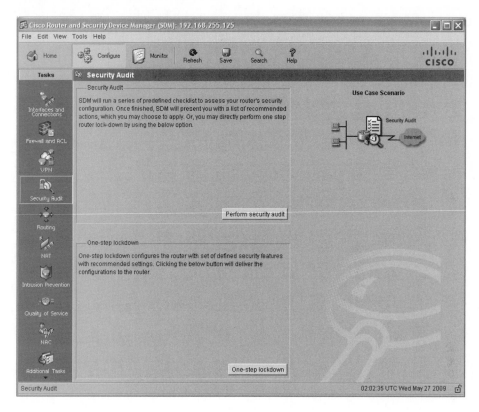

3. You will notice that you have two options on this page. For this exercise, of course, click the One-Step Lockdown button. You will see the screen shown in Figure 5.3.

FIGURE 5.3 The SDM Warning screen

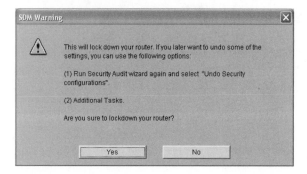

4. The SDM Warning screen explains how you can undo what you are about to perform. Then it asks if you are sure you want to lock down your router. Click the Yes button and the screen shown in Figure 5.4 appears.

FIGURE 5.4   The One-Step Lockdown screen

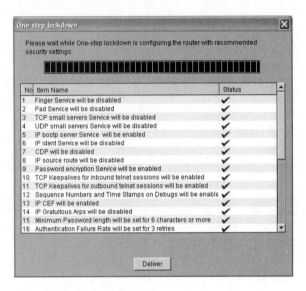

5. You are presented with all of the changes that will be performed by the one-step lockdown process. Click the Deliver button and the commands will be sent to the router. The next screen shows the status of the delivery. As you can see in Figure 5.5, there were a total of 59 commands delivered to the router.

FIGURE 5.5   The Commands Delivery Status screen

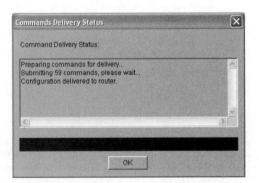

Differences between One-Step Lockdown and AutoSecure

Several features that are part of the AutoSecure feature are not used in One-Step Lockdown. Table 5.5 shows which features are configured in each method.

TABLE 5.5 Differences between One-Step Lockdown and AutoSecure

Feature	One-Step Lockdown	AutoSecure
NTP	Not disabled	Disabled
TCP Intercept	Not configured	Configured
AAA	Not configured	Configured
Anti-spoofing ACLs	Not configured	Configured
Selective Packet Discard (SPD)	Not configured	Configured
SNMP v3	Configuration not supported; disabling supported	Configuring and disabling supported

Securing Management and Logging

The ability to have secure communications for management and logging purposes is essential to the operation of the network. Administrators need and expect to have secure communication to the router without risk of exposing usernames and passwords in clear text.

In the following sections, I will cover how to configure Syslog support, how to configure SNMP, how to configure administrator access through Secure Shell or SSH, and finally, how to configure Network Time Protocol (NTP) support.

Configuring Syslog Support on a Cisco Router

Syslog messages are generally log messages from a variety of network devices and hosts. These hosts and network devices are defined as Syslog clients because they are the ones sending information to a Syslog server. These logging messages allow administrators to look at events in the past and obtain information used in identifying problems, responding to security events, and general troubleshooting. This is important in a Cisco router environment because routers have a limited amount of buffer space to hold log messages. (*Buffer space* is another term for the amount of RAM that is allocated for log messages.) Depending on what level of messages you are receiving, the buffer could fill up and be overwritten very quickly. So it is best to have one or more external Syslog servers configured to send log messages to.

In this section, you will discuss how to configure support for a Syslog server on a Cisco router. Sending log messages to an external server is not only good practice, it is often required for compliance purposes. In today's security environment, it is a must.

Table 5.6 shows examples of where log messages can be sent.

TABLE 5.6   Log message destinations

Destination	Description
Console	If you have a physical connection to the console with a terminal program, log messages can be sent directly to the console.
VTY	Virtual terminal connections (such as Telnet or SSH) can be configured to receive log messages; however, you must enter monitor mode by issuing the `terminal monitor` command.
SNMP	SNMP sends messages, in the form of traps, to an SNMP monitoring station, which can also archive the messages.
Buffer	The buffer stores messages directly on the router, but it's usually limited to a small amount of space and can be easily overwritten.
Syslog	Syslog servers are easy to set up and can hold as many messages as there is disk space available. There is usually additional intelligence required to perform correlation, archives, etc.

A good and relatively inexpensive Syslog server is Kiwi Syslog. Kiwi Syslog was recently bought by Solarwinds. You can download a free 30-day trial at www.kiwisyslog.com/kiwi-syslog-server-overview/.

In Table 5.7, I have listed the log severity levels according to Cisco and a description of them. Depending on what types of information you are interested in, you have the option of picking exactly the level you need. It should be noted that choosing a particular severity level also gives you the messages belonging to levels of greater severity. So choosing level 4 also includes levels 3, 2, 1, and 0. In times when you are trying to troubleshoot an issue, you may want to use debugging to get very detailed log messages.

TABLE 5.7 Log severity levels

Severity Level	Severity Name	Description
0	Emergencies	System is unusable—unrecoverable error.
1	Alerts	Condition requires immediate action. An example would be high temperature.
2	Critical	Hardware or software errors. An example might be memory allocation errors.
3	Errors	System is still usable, but errors exist.
4	Warnings	Warning messages. An example would be that an operation failed.
5	Notifications	Notifications are messages that are of importance but not an error. For example, an interface came up.
6	Informational	Information about normal operation of the systems, such as a packet was denied due to an ACL.
7	Debugging	Special messages that are very detailed and used for troubleshooting.

 Syslog uses UDP port 514 to communicate to the Syslog server. UDP is typically used where traffic is one way.

A Cisco log message consists of three basic components:

- Time stamp
- Severity level and message type
- Text of the message

You can see the components in the following example message:

```
May 29 23:33:48 CST: %SYS-5-CONFIG_I: Configured from console by
vty0 (192.168.1.30)
```

- `May 29 23:33:48 CST` is the time stamp.
- `SYS-5-CONFIG_I` identifies the severity level of 5 and the fact that it was generated as a configuration of an interface.
- `Configured from console by vty0 (192.168.1.30)` is the text of the message.

Using SNMP v3 to Secure Management Traffic

Simple Network Management Protocol (SNMP) is the most widely used protocol for managing network devices and hosts today. It was first introduced as version 1 in a series of RFCs in 1988. Since then, it has gone through two major iterations, with the most current being version 3. What is the difference? We will explore them in the following sections.

Basic Components of SNMP

In version 1 and version 2c, the architecture of SNMP contained three major components, as seen in Table 5.8.

TABLE 5.8   SNMP components

Component	Description
SNMP Manager	The Manager is designed to monitor and control systems that contain SNMP agents. This is also called a network management system (NMS) and it's the receiver of traps or messages from the agents.
SNMP agent	The agent is a piece of software, often built into an operating system, that supports the sending of trap messages and the receipt of control messages.
Management Information Base (MIB)	The Management Information Base is a set of objects defined by the maker of the corresponding equipment or software. An example might be usage statistics of a router interface.

There are basically three types of SNMP messages that are exchanged between agent and manager:

Trap   This is a message that is sent from the agent to the manager. It is based on some condition or threshold and is an alert of some kind.

GET   This message is designed to query an agent and retrieve data from the system.

SET   This message sends a control parameter to the agent for implementation on the device.

It's important to note that a trap is an event notification that is sent to one or more log servers automatically once it's configured. GET and SET are used by a network management system to either query data that exists on a device or actually configure one or more settings on that device.

 The default port settings that are used in SNMP are UDP 161 for general SNMP messages and UDP 162 for SNMP trap messages.

The flow of SNMP traps and messages (GET/SET) is illustrated in Figure 5.6. Traps are sent from the agent side (in this case, a Cisco switch) to the network management station. The GET/SET messages are sent from the network management station to the agent device.

FIGURE 5.6   SNMP message flow

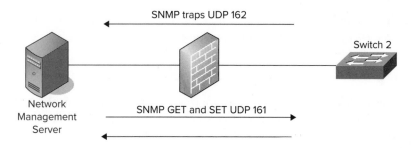

SNMP traps UDP 162

Switch 2

Network
Management
Server

SNMP GET and SET UDP 161

Since this is a book about security, you might be wondering how secure it would be to send configuration information over the wire. Turns out it really isn't. In versions 1 and 2c, there was no support for authentication and/or encryption. These versions use the concept of *community strings* to either read from or write to the agent. One community string is configured for read-only access and one community string is configured for read-write access. As you might have guessed, the GET command uses the read-only community string and the SET command uses the read-write community string. A common community string is *public* for read-only and *private* for read-write access.

This discussion of SNMP only introduces the main concepts. A couple of other types of messages are GET-NEXT messages and GET-RESPONSE messages that are used when performing a "walk" of the MIB. These are more advanced topics and not covered as an exam objective.

SNMP V3 Security Model

Unlike SNMP v1 and v2c, SNMP v3 provides for securing the communications between manager and agent. To introduce this, let's look at a couple of concepts.

The idea of a security model is one of the concepts. If we didn't have SNMP, there might be some kind of proprietary management protocol used to manage security. But that's not the case here, so SNMP is our security model. The security model should have provisions for both user and group authentications. The security model supported by SNMP has the following three levels, in order of security strength:

noAuthNoPriv   No authentication and no privacy relies on community strings alone for authentication, and there is no encryption for privacy. This is the level available in SNMP V1 and V2c.

authNoPriv   Authentication and no privacy is one of the options available within SNMP v3. It provides authentication in the form of a hash such as HMAC MD5 or HMAC SHA but no encryption for privacy.

authPriv   Authentication and privacy is the other option available within SNMP v3. Besides providing the authentication previously noted, it provide encryption such as DES, 3DES, or AES.

To summarize, SNMP v1 and v2c have no authentication other than community strings, and SNMP v3 has authentication, privacy, and integrity.

Securing Administration Using SSH

Today's security environment requires a secure way to administer your network. That's why Secure Shell (SSH) is recommended to connect to your router to monitor, configure, and troubleshoot. Although Telnet is still available as an option, its use is discouraged because the session is not encrypted and usernames and passwords can be seen in clear text.

SSH uses a client-server model. Your Cisco router is both an SSH server and an SSH client. Therefore, you can use SSH on a desktop client to connect to a router, then the router itself can be a client, allowing you to jump from one router to another securely.

 Many operating systems today do not offer an SSH client natively. There are commercial clients available such as SecureCRT from VanDyke Software. But if your budget is a bit tight, there are also open-source options like PuTTY, which is available for Windows and Unix environments and can be downloaded at http://ftp.chiark.greenend.org .uk/~sgtatham/putty/download.html.

SSH can be configured using either the command line or the SDM tool. Let's examine the steps necessary to configure it by command line first:

1. Before you can configure SSH, a domain name must be defined. Use the following syntax in global configuration mode:

    ```
    Router1(config)# ip domain-name myrouter.com
    ```

2. If this is a new router (or recently reset to default), you may not have any crypto keys configured on it. You can display any keys configured by using the following command in privileged EXEC mode (see Chapter 3 for how to get into this mode):

    ```
    Router1# show crypto key mypubkey rsa
    ```

3. If you have keys displayed after doing this command, you will need to *zeroize* them by performing the following command in privileged EXEC mode:

Router1# **crypto key zeroize rsa**

This process essentially resets the keys to zero.

The zeroize command deletes all keys. Make sure that's what you want to do.

4. Once you've reset the keys, you need to generate new ones. Enter the following command:

Router1(config)# **crypto key generate rsa general-keys modulus 1024**

Notice that I have used 1024 as the modulus size for generating the RSA keys. This is the minimum recommended size, although you can go lower with 512 or higher with 2048. (For more information on encryption keys, see Chapter 9, "Understanding Cryptographic Solutions.")

5. Next we want to limit the amount of time that it takes for the SSH connection to time out. Specify the amount of time in seconds. The following example sets the time-out limit to 120 seconds, or 2 minutes:

Router1(config)# **ip ssh timeout 120**

6. You may want to limit the number of retries for SSH authentication by using the following command in global configuration mode: **ip ssh authentication-retries** *integer*.

7. Last, you want to allow SSH as an option to be used inbound on the VTY lines. Use the following to allow only SSH:

Router1(config-line)# **transport input** *ssh*

When configuring SSH, make sure you are connected via console or maintain your active connection while you test access from another workstation. Bottom line, don't get locked out by a typo or some other misconfiguration.

Using SDM to Configure a Syslog Server, SSH, SNMP, and NTP

The SDM can be used to configure not only a Syslog server, but also SSH, SNMP, and NTP. These are found under the Additional Tasks menu on the left after you select the Configure icon at the top.

Configuring a Syslog Server Using SDM

To configure a Syslog server using SDM, follow these steps:

1. Log in to SDM and select Configure ➢ Additional Tasks.

2. Click the Router Properties tree menu, which will take you to the screen shown in Figure 5.7.

FIGURE 5.7   Viewing router properties

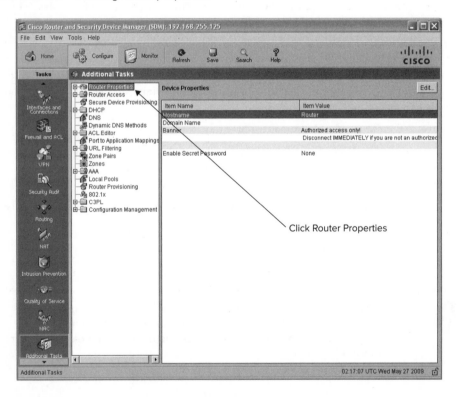

3. If you expand Router Properties, you will see several options to choose from. Select the Logging task and the screen shown in Figure 5.8 appears. As you can see, Syslog is disabled but Logging To Buffer is enabled. Both Logging Level and Host Logging Level are set to Debugging, which is severity level 7.

FIGURE 5.8   Viewing the logging settings

4.   In the upper-right corner of this screen, there is an Edit button. Click it and the screen shown in Figure 5.9 appears.

FIGURE 5.9   Editing the logging settings

As you can see, the Logging Buffer check box is already checked and Logging Level is set to Debugging.

5. Now you need to click on the Add button to add a Syslog server to the configuration. When you do so, you will see the screen shown in Figure 5.10.

FIGURE 5.10   Adding a logging host

6. You will need to add either the IP address of the host you want to use or the fully qualified hostname in the space provided. Click OK, and on the next screen, shown in Figure 5.11, you will see the server you just configured in the Add Logging Host screen.

FIGURE 5.11   The logging host has been added.

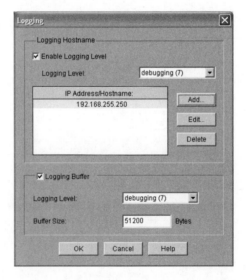

7. Once you click OK on this screen, the Commands Delivery Status screen, shown in Figure 5.12, appears and you can observe that you are submitting one command to the router for configuration.

FIGURE 5.12   The Commands Delivery Status screen

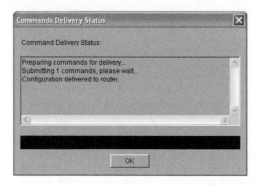

8.   Click OK on the Commands Delivery Status screen to return to the Additional Tasks
     screen, shown in Figure 5.13. You can now see that a Syslog server has been configured
     and that the IP address is shown.

FIGURE 5.13   A Syslog server added to logging settings

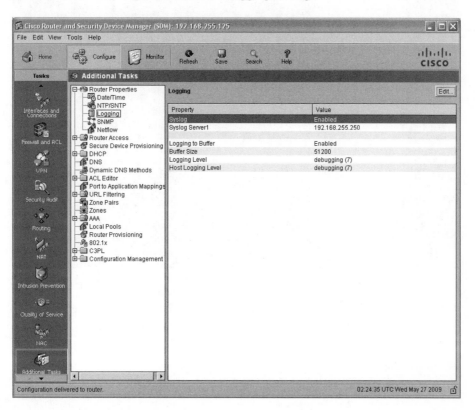

Configuring SSH Using SDM

I just showed you how to configure SSH from a command line. Now you do the same thing using the Cisco SDM:

1.   Log in to SDM and select Configure ➢ Additional Tasks.

2.   From there, click the Router Access tree item on the left side of the screen and then expand it to reveal the subtasks. Choose SSH and you will see the SSH Key Setup screen, shown in Figure 5.14.

FIGURE 5.14   The SSH Key Setup screen

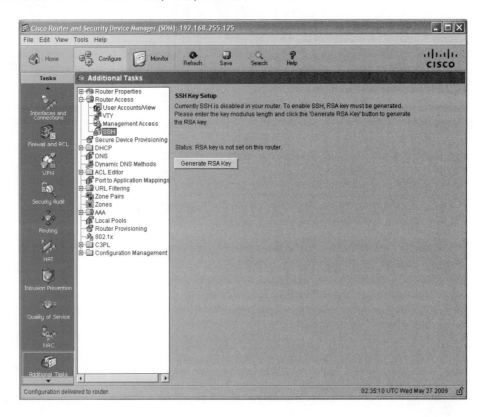

3. On this screen, click the Generate RSA Key button. In the Key Modulus Size dialog box that appears, enter the key modulus size in bits, as shown in Figure 5.15. Cisco recommends 1024 bits as a minimum. You may enter a maximum of 2048 bits.

FIGURE 5.15   Specifying the key modulus size

 You may recall from the section "Securing Administration Using SSH" earlier in this chapter that a domain name must be configured in order to generate the RSA keys. If you are in SDM and you haven't configured a domain name yet, you can go back to the Additional Tasks menu, click the Router Properties tree, and expand it to show the edit function.

4. After you enter the key modulus size, click the OK button and you will be prompted to enter in your SSH credentials, as shown in Figure 5.16. Enter your credentials and click the OK button.

FIGURE 5.16   Entering SSH credentials

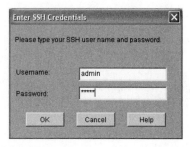

Configuring SNMP Using SDM

Configuring SNMP is also on the Additional Tasks menu of the SDM, located under the Router Properties tree. Follow these steps:

1. Log in to SDM and select Configure ➢ Additional Tasks.

2. Click the Router Properties tree menu, and expand the Router Properties tree to locate the SNMP selection, as shown in Figure 5.17.

FIGURE 5.17   SNMP tasks

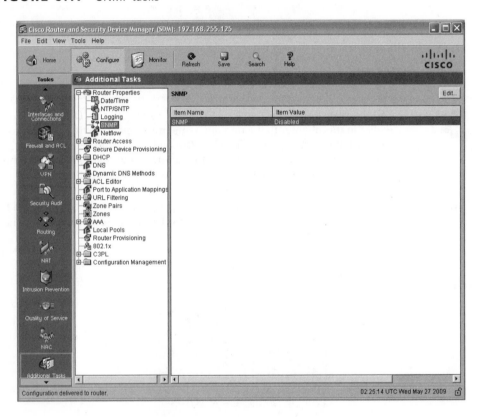

3. As you can see in Figure 5.17, SNMP is disabled. Notice the Edit button in the upper-right corner. Click it and you'll see the SNMP Properties screen, shown in Figure 5.18. On this screen, click to check the Enable SNMP box. Once SNMP is enabled, you can add a community string by clicking the Add button.

FIGURE 5.18   Setting SNMP properties

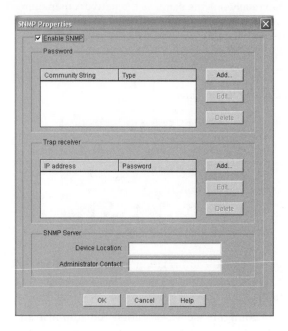

4. Click the Add button and you will be presented with the Add A Community String dialog box, shown in Figure 5.19. Add the string you want to use and select either Read-Only or Read-Write. Then click OK. You should configure a read-write string in addition to a read-only community string if you need to change any configuration settings. This means you will repeat this step.

FIGURE 5.19   Adding a community string

5. After you configure the read-only and/or read-write community strings, you'll configure the trap receiver. In the SNMP Properties screen, click the Add button in the Trap Receiver section. In the Add A Trap Receiver screen, shown in Figure 5.20, enter the IP address of the trap receiver and the password.

A trap receiver is the same as the network management system or the server that is collecting information for the network management system. An example might be a CiscoWorks server.

FIGURE 5.20   Adding a trap receiver

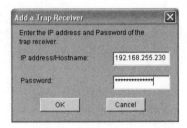

6. Clicking OK after entering the information will take you back to the SNMP Properties screen, shown in Figure 5.21. You will notice that the community strings and trap receiver are configured and you are ready to use SNMP on the router.

7. Optionally, you can configure a device location and administrative contact. In a large organization or one with many devices, this can be valuable information, so it's a good idea to go ahead and populate those fields.

FIGURE 5.21   SNMP properties have been configured.

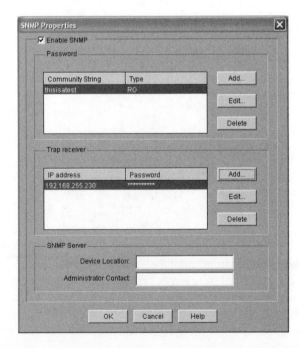

8. Click the OK button to return to the Additional Tasks menu for SNMP, shown in Figure 5.22, where you will notice that all of your configuration selections are displayed in the SNMP window.

FIGURE 5.22   The Additional Tasks window shows SNMP configured.

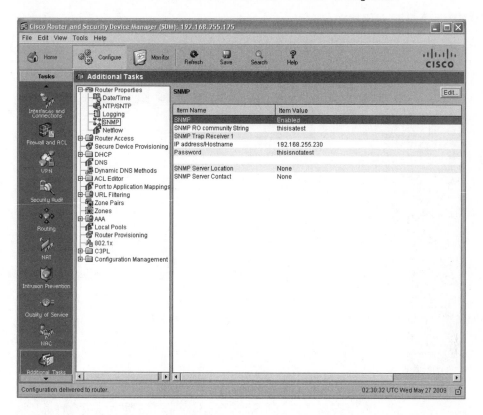

Configuring NTP Using SDM

Network Time Protocol (NTP) is used to distribute time services to network devices and hosts to ensure synchronization with authoritative time servers. NTP uses a hierarchical model that utilizes the stratum as a level of hierarchy. *Stratum* refers to the distance from the reference clock. Typically one or more servers or routers in the network have a connection to a stratum level 0 or atomic clock so that they can maintain a precise time throughout the enterprise. NTP uses UDP port 123 to communicate.

It is important from a security standpoint that all network devices maintain accurate time so that logs have an accurate time stamp and event correlation is done properly. Event correlation is discussed in Chapter 8, "Implementing Cisco IOS Intrusion Prevention."

To configure NTP using SDM, follow these steps:

1.   Log in to SDM and select Configure ➤ Additional Tasks.

2.   From the Router Properties menu, choose NTP/SNTP, as seen in Figure 5.23.

FIGURE 5.23   NTP tasks

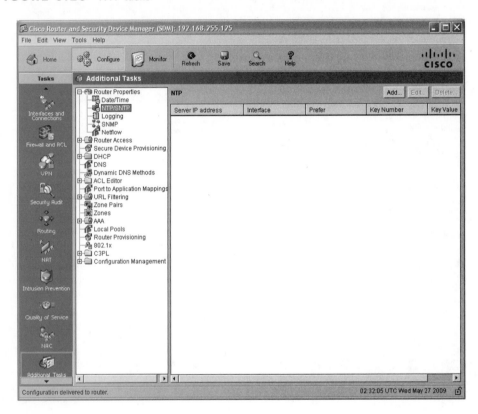

3.   Click the Add button in the upper-right corner. The Add NTP Server Details screen appears, as shown in Figure 5.24.

FIGURE 5.24   The Add NTP Server Details screen

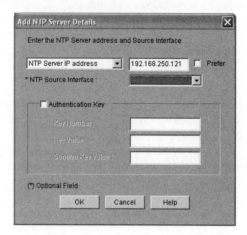

4. Add the IP address or hostname of the NTP server.

5. Indicate the source interface using the drop-down menu.

6. You have the option of configuring more than one NTP server. In that case, you may prefer the use of one over the other, so there is a Prefer check box that you can select.

7. The other option on this screen is for configuring authentication. If you want to perform authentication between the router and the NTP server, fill in the key information required. When you're finished, click OK.

 You might prefer one NTP server over another because it may be connected to a more accurate time source or it might be in a location that's closer to the server in question. One way to ensure a more secure time source is to use NTP authentication. Outside providers of a time source may require it.

Summary

In this chapter, you learned about securing Cisco routers using the SDM Security Audit feature. You also used SDM's one-step lockdown feature. Switching to the command line, you explored the use of AutoSecure and then I discussed the differences between one-step lockdown and AutoSecure.

You learned how to configure SSH on Cisco routers using both the command-line interface and SDM. Finally, you used SDM to configure NTP, SNMP, and Syslog.

Exam Essentials

Remember the differences between using one-step lockdown in SDM and using AutoSecure via the command-line interface.   The main differences are in the areas of TCP Intercept, AAA, anti-spoofing ACLs, and Selective Packet Discard. Most of these are enabled in AutoSecure and not in one-step lockdown. NTP is disabled in AutoSecure but not in one-step lockdown. Also, SNMP v3 can be disabled and configured in AutoSecure but only disabled in one-step lockdown.

Know how to configure SSH via the command-line interface and also using the SDM. Configuring SSH requires that you establish a domain name for the router as well as create RSA keys. In some cases, you will be required to zeroize the keys prior to creating new ones. You can configure an SSH time and also limit transport input to SSH on VTY lines.

Understand how to configure NTP using SDM.   Network Time Protocol (NTP) can be configured with SDM. Use the Configure button and the Additional Tasks selection from the taskbar on the left. Choose Router Properties and then configure your server(s). You can also choose to prefer one server over another and use authentication with outside time sources.

Know how to use SDM to configure Syslog messages.   SDM can be used to configure Syslog. Choose the Configure button and the Additional Tasks selection from the taskbar. Once again, you will be using the Router Properties menu. If you expand Router Properties, you will see several options from which to choose. Select the Logging task. You can enable Syslog, configure Syslog servers, change logging levels, and change properties.

Remember how to use the SDM One-Step Lockdown tool to secure a Cisco router.   The Security Audit wizard can be used within SDM to choose the One-Step Lockdown tool. The One-Step Lockdown tool will send a series of commands to the router. You can undo the lockdown after it's performed by either manually using Router Properties or selecting Undo Security Configurations using the Security Audit wizard.

Written Lab

Write the answers to the following questions:

1. When logging is used, what is the severity level of notifications?

2. What is the CLI command used to automatically lock down your router?

3. In SNMP, what is a set of objects defined by the maker of the corresponding equipment or software?

4. What port protocol and number is used by NTP?

5. Which of the global services encrypts all service-level passwords so that they are not visible in the configuration?

6. What is the name of the command to reset the crypto keys when you're configuring SSH support?

7. What is the name of the feature used by SDM to lock down the router?

8. What port and protocol are used by Syslog?

9. When you're using AutoSecure, enabling Cisco Express Forwarding (CEF) is part of securing which plane?

10. What is the command to limit access to VTY lines to only SSH?

(The answers to the written lab can be found following the answers to the review questions for this chapter.)

Hands-on Lab

This hands-on lab exercise is for practicing requirements to configure SSH via the command-line interface.

Hands-on Lab 5.1: Configuring a Router for SSH Administrative Access

In this lab, you will manually configure the router for SSH administrative access. Use the following information when configuring SSH on the VTY lines:

Domain: thisuser.com

Modulus size: 1024

SSH time out: 60

1. Log in to your router and go into privileged mode by typing **en** or **enable**.

2. Enter global configuration mode by typing **config t** or **configure terminal**.

3. Type **ip domain-name thisuser.com** to configure the domain name.

    Router#**config t**
    Enter configuration commands, one per line. End with
    CNTL/Z.
    Router(config)# **ip domain-name thisuser.com**

4. The next step is to see if there are any existing RSA crypto keys. Let's type a show command here to see: **show crypto key mypubkey rsa.**

    Router# **show crypto key mypubkey rsa**

5. If you have existing keys, you will need to *zeroize* them to remove them. Type the command **crypto key zeroize rsa.**

    Router# **crypto key zeroize rsa**

6. Now you need to generate new keys. Enter the following command, remembering that you need a modulus of 1024: **crypto key generate rsa general-keys modulus 1024.**

    Router(config)# **crypto key generate rsa general-keys modulus 1024**

7. The next step is to set a time-out. While still in global configuration mode, type **ip ssh timeout 60** to set the time-out for SSH.

    Router(config)# **ip ssh timeout 60**

8. And now the last step is to actually configure the VTY lines to use SSH as the transport. First you need to be in VTY 0 4 line config mode. Type the command **vty 0 4** to enter line configuration mode. Then type the command **transport input ssh** to limit the input transport to only SSH.

    Router(config)# **vty 0 4**
    Router(config-line)# **transport input ssh**
    Router(config-line)# **end**

    You have completed the configuration of SSH using the command-line interface.

Review Questions

1. You have been asked to secure a remote router as soon as possible. Unfortunately, the only access you have to the router is using SSH. Which of the following would you use to lock down the router?

    A. router1# **lockdown**

    B. router1# **lockdown**

    C. router1# (config)**auto secure**

    D. router1# **auto secure**

    E. router1# **autosecure**

2. Which of the following is *not* one of the global services turned off when AutoSecure is used?

    A. BOOTP

    B. ARP

    C. NTP

    D. CDP

    E. PAD

3. You are investigating the router logs from the last 24 hours. You discover a memory allocation error on one of the routers. Which log severity level can this be attributed to?

    A. Emergencies

    B. Debugging

    C. Critical

    D. Alerts

    E. Informational

4. Which of the following is *not* one of the basic messages used in SNMP v1 and v2c and exchanged between agent and manager?

    A. GET

    B. TRAP

    C. SET

    D. TRANS

5. You have been asked to configure an NTP server on a router. You have navigated to the Additional Tasks menu in the SDM. From which tree item is NTP configured?

    A. Configuration Management

    B. Router Properties

    C. Router Access

    D. Router Configuration

6. Which one of the following is the port used in NTP?

   A. TCP 160

   B. UDP 321

   C. TCP 123

   D. UDP 123

   E. UDP 161

7. You have been asked to configure SSH using the command line interface. However, you have discovered that some keys were left over on the router. What command is used to clear the RSA keys so that you can regenerate them?

   A. `router1#clear rsa keys`

   B. `Router1#(config)rsa clear keys`

   C. `Router1#(config)crypto key zeroize rsa`

   D. `Router1#crypto rsa key zeroize`

   E. `Router1#crypto key zeroize rsa`

8. Which of the following are *not* security levels used in the security model in SNMP v2c? (Choose two.)

   A. authNoPriv

   B. noAuthPriv

   C. noAuthNoPriv

   D. authPriv

9. Which of the following is not enabled in SDM one-step lockdown but is configured using AutoSecure?

   A. AAA

   B. CBAC

   C. NTP

   D. Unicast Reverse Path Forwarding

10. Which of the following is *not* one of the features that are enabled during lockdown of the forwarding plane of a router?

   A. TCP Intercept

   B. uRPF

   C. SSH

   D. CEF

   E. CBAC

11. You have selected a logging level of 4 for your Syslog messages. Which of the following are *not* also included in this level?

   A. Warnings

   B. Critical

   C. Notification

   D. Alerts

12. Which of the following are *not* types of community strings used within SNMP? (Choose three.)

   A. RW

   B. RO

   C. RS

   D. WR

   E. TO

13. Which of the following is *not* one of the destinations for log messages?

   A. Console

   B. VTY

   C. NTP

   D. SNMP

14. Which of the following services can be exploited to perform denial of service attacks?

   A. Directed Broadcast

   B. NTP

   C. Proxy-arp

   D. MOP

   E. ICMP redirects

15. Which port does SNMP use for trap messages?

   A. TCP 161

   B. UDP 162

   C. TCP 160

   D. UDP 161

16. Which one of the following is the protocol and port used with Syslog?

   A. TCP 515

   B. UDP 514

   C. TCP 123

   D. UDP 123

   E. TCP 514

17. In generating RSA keys, what is the minimum key modulus size recommended by Cisco?

   A. 512

   B. 2048

   C. 1024

   D. 4096

   E. 256

18. Which features exists in SNMP v3 but not in either of the two previous versions? (Choose three.)

   A. Encryption

   B. Integrity

   C. Authentication

   D. Authorization

19. What is the severity level of the following log message?

```
May 29 23:33:48 CST: %SYS-5-CONFIG_I: Configured from console
by vty0 (192.168.1.30)
```

   A. 5

   B. 4

   C. 3

   D. 0

20. Which of the following is disabled in AutoSecure but *not* disabled in one-step lockdown?

   A. Syslog

   B. NTP

   C. SSH

   D. HTTP

Answers to Review Questions

1. D. The AutoSecure feature is performed in privileged EXEC mode and is done by issuing the `auto secure` command.

2. B. ARP is not turned off. The router wouldn't work too well without it. However, Proxy-ARP is turned off under the interfaces, which is different.

3. C. The critical severity log level is for hardware and software errors.

4. D. The three basic messages that are sent between the SNMP agent and manager are GET, SET, and TRAP.

5. B. The Router Properties tree item, when expanded, includes configuration for NTP/SNTP.

6. D. NTP uses UDP 123 to communicate.

7. C. The keys are cleared from the global configuration menu. The correct command is `crypto key zeroize rsa`.

8. B, D. The security levels associated with SNMP v2c are authNoPriv and noAuthNoPriv. This is because there is not support for encryption until SNMP v3. There is no such level as noAuthPriv because it doesn't make sense to encrypt without authentication.

9. A. AAA is the only one in the list that is configured in AutoSecure but not SDM one-step lockdown.

10. C. The only answer that is not one of the IOS features that are enabled during lockdown of the forwarding plane is SSH. SSH is part of the management plane.

11. C. Notifications are level 5 and therefore not included in level 4 messages.

12. C, D, E. SNMP uses read-only (RO) and read-write (RW) community strings.

13. C. There are five log message destinations, including the console, buffer, VTY, SNMP, and Syslog. NTP is not a destination for log messages.

14. C. Proxy-arp can be exploited to perform denial of service attacks.

15. B. Trap messages use UDP 162.

16. B. Syslog uses UDP 514 to communicate to a Syslog server.

17. C. Cisco recommends a minimum key modulus size of 1024.

18. A, B, C. The two previous versions of SNMP before SNMP v3 supported only the community string authentication methods. SNMP v3 also supports encryption, integrity, and other forms of authentication.

19. A. If you look at the message, you will see that it is a level 5, indicated by the 5 in the middle.

20. B. NTP is disabled in AutoSecure but not in one-step lockdown.

Answers to Written Lab

1. 5

2. `auto secure`

3. MIB

4. UDP 123

5. Service password-encryption

6. `zeroize`

7. One-step lockdown

8. UDP 514

9. Forwarding

10. `transport input ssh`

Chapter

6

Layer 2 Security

THE FOLLOWING CCNA SECURITY EXAM OBJECTIVE IS COVERED IN THIS CHAPTER:

✓ Describe how to prevent layer 2 attacks by configuring basic Catalyst switch security features

In this chapter, I'll discuss layer 2 attacks and how to mitigate them. First we will look at basic prevention of attacks on the switch itself. Then we will explore VLAN attacks, how they are mounted, and what configurations can prevent their success.

We will look at Spanning-Tree Protocol (STP) attacks and how to configure your switch to prevent them. A common attack is an attempt to overflow the CAM table on the switch, and we will look at why this works and how to prevent it from happening.

Rounding out the chapter I will cover preventing MAC spoofing, configuring port security, and a few other topics such as SPAN, RSPAN, and storm control.

For up-to-the-minute updates for this chapter, please see www.sybex.com/go/ccna-security.

Basic Protection of Layer 2 Switches

Cisco Catalyst layer 2 switches are commonly used in both large and small office environments. Depending on the size of the organization, they may or may not be connected to other switches. These switches usually have multiple ports, support virtual LANs (VLANs), and can carry multiple VLANs across trunks to other switches and/or routers.

The basic switch operation is as follows: a frame is seen on a port, the MAC address is recorded in the CAM table, and forwarding decisions are based on that CAM table. If the destination MAC address is in the CAM table, then the frame is sent directly to the port associated with that MAC address. If the destination MAC address is not known or the frame is a broadcast, then the frame is flooded to all ports other than the source port in that VLAN.

For the purposes of this book, I use the term *Content Addressable Memory (CAM) table*. On some switches, the term *MAC Address Table* is used instead. Both refer to the internal table in the switch that captures the MAC address and which port it was seen on. The terms can be used interchangeably, but you may have to use different commands to display them. For more information, see www.cisco.com and search for the particular model of switch you are using.

Let's discuss some of the ways you can prevent attacks against the switch itself by looking at some of the parameters you can assign to all switches in your network:

Use SSH instead of Telnet   Telnet is supported and can be used to remotely access the switch for administration purposes. However, the Telnet program does not protect the username and password while in transit, hence they can be captured in cleartext. Secure Shell (SSH) is the preferred method of accessing your switch because it encrypts the username and password while in transit.

Use SNMP v3   Simple Network Management Protocol (SNMP) is used to generate traps to a network management station and can also be used to configure switches if the read-write option is enabled. SNMP versions 1 and 2 do not contain adequate protections for other than read-only access, so if you want to enable the read-write string, consider using SNMP v3. (SNMP v3 is covered in Chapter 5, "Securing Your Router.")

Enable logging   Logging of messages and reviewing them periodically is an important security methodology for any network device, not just switches. Logging can give you a chronological event history, which might explain what happened in the event of a security incident.

Secure port and VLAN configurations   You can also use the following security measures to protect switches:

- Turn off ports that are not used.
- Assign the ports not in use to a nonrouted VLAN in case they do get turned on by accident.
- Set trunk ports to be off instead of auto.
- Don't use native VLANs to transmit user data.
- Use private VLANs to further secure sensitive data with a VLAN.

How to Prevent VLAN Attacks

VLAN attacks are usually characterized as *VLAN hopping* because the attacker hopes to gain access by "hopping" from one VLAN to another within the switch. Usually this is not possible without being routed through a layer 3 switch or a router. However, there are a couple of attack vectors that are possible from layer 2 within the realm of VLAN attacks. One is called double tagging and the other switch spoofing. Let's look at these in a little more detail.

Double Tagging

Double tagging enlists the use of a feature of 802.1Q trunks called native VLANs. A native VLAN does not add a tag when moving between trunked switches, as shown in Figure 6.1.

FIGURE 6.1   Usual operation of a native VLAN

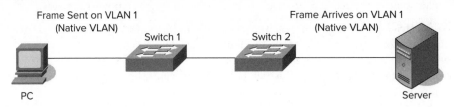

In this attack, a host that is attached to a native VLAN adds a second tag to the frame. Before the frame is transmitted to the second switch, the first tag is stripped off. Then, when arriving at the second switch, the frame has a tag that is active and available to be transmitted to a VLAN, which lives on the second switch. This is shown in Figure 6.2.

FIGURE 6.2   Double tagging on a native VLAN

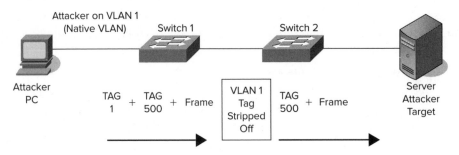

This kind of attack can be thwarted by not using the native VLAN (VLAN 1) for transmitting data. VLAN 1 is the default and is usually targeted by hackers. The following sample configuration shows a native VLAN that has been configured to be one that is not utilized:

```
Switch3(config)# interface gigabitethernet 0/14
Switch3(config-if)# switchport trunk native vlan 900
```

Switch Spoofing

Switch spoofing is an attack in which the attacker forces a connection to another switch using a trunk port. The basic idea is to connect to a switch port with another switch capable of sending Dynamic Trunk Protocol (DTP) messages. If the other side happens to be set for a trunk and in auto negotiation mode, then another switch can connect up and form a trunk with it. This is bad because a trunk carries traffic from all VLANs (if so configured), so an attacker could potentially see traffic from the entire network.

To avoid these types of attacks, you should turn off all trunk ports where you are not using them. Also, if you do have trunks, disable DTP on trunk ports to avoid switch spoofing attacks.

You can make configuration changes on the switch to mitigate switch spoofing attack vectors.

The first way to do this is to configure the port to be an access port versus a trunk port:

```
Switch3(config)# interface gigabitethernet 0/2
Switch3(config-if)# switchport mode access
```

The next method is to configure the port to disable DTP on a trunk port:

```
Switch3(config)# interface gigabitethernet 0/20
Switch3(config-if)# switchport trunk encapsulation 802.1q
Switch3(config-if)# switchport mode trunk
Switch3(config-if)# switchport trunk nonegotiate
```

Mitigating STP Attacks

Spanning-Tree Protocol (STP) is used to maintain a loop-free path, particularly when redundant links are utilized for high availability. STP provides continuous protection against layer 2 broadcast storms.

Although a CCNA should already be familiar with the details of how STP works, a brief discussion is in order here. One of the key facets of how STP does its job is the election of a *root bridge*. The root bridge is elected through the use of Bridge Protocol Data Units (BPDUs), which are exchanged with all the switches that are participating in the network. These BPDUs are exchanged to determine the bridge priority. The switch with the lowest bridge priority is elected as the root bridge. As a network administrator, you can manually manipulate the bridge priority in order to make a particular switch the root bridge.

Another parameter you will want to be familiar with is *cost*, which is used to determine the *root port*. Every other switch besides the root bridge will have a root port, which is the port closest to the root bridge, determined by the lowest cost to the root bridge.

Once the root bridge has been elected, all ports will be in either *blocking mode* or *forwarding mode*. These are the two steady states that a port can be in. When STP is enabled, the ports go through a listening phase in order to process BPDUs to determine the root bridge. In learning mode, the switch is adding frames to the switching table. As mentioned previously, then the port will be in either blocking or forwarding mode.

In an STP attack, an attacker hopes to gain access to a network by introducing a rogue switch, which has connections to two or more switches in the internetwork. The object of the attack is to get traffic to flow through the rogue switch, allowing the attacker to capture and analyze traffic.

Let's look at a typical switch network with STP, shown in Figure 6.3.

FIGURE 6.3   Typical switch network with STP

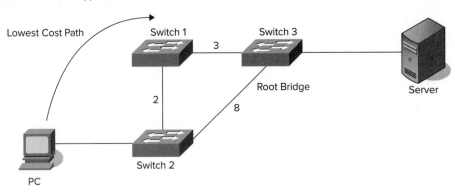

In this example, there is a total of three switches, which are interconnected. The host PC is connected to Switch 2 and is sending traffic to the server. To make the example less complex, assume that Switch 3 is the root bridge. In this example, the preferred path would be through Switch 1.

Figure 6.4 shows the attacker scenario; the attacker has inserted a rogue switch into the mix. In this scenario, the attacker has connected Switch 4 between Switch 2 and Switch 3. The wily attacker has changed the bridge priority to be lower than Switch 3 and has exchanged BPDUs with the other non-root bridges. Now the preferred path to the root bridge is through Switch 3, where the attacker can capture traffic destined for the server.

FIGURE 6.4   Rogue switch in the network

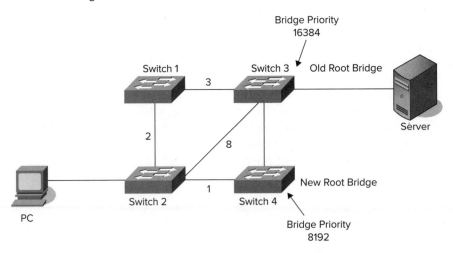

If the attacker has administrative control of the switch and can force traffic through it, then they can configure Switched Port Analyzer (SPAN) of any one of the ports on the switch or a complete VLAN, if desired.

Cisco has two security features built into its layer 2 switches that can mitigate an STP attack:

Root Guard   Root Guard is a feature that can be enabled on any non-root port on a switch. It protects the port from being changed to a root port in response to receiving a superior BPDU. If the port receives such a BPDU, then the port goes into a *root-inconsistent* state. When the port is in root-inconsistent mode, no data can be forwarded. If the BPDUs stop being sent to the port, the port will return to the forwarding state it was in before.

Here are the configuration commands for enabling Root Guard on a Cisco switch:

```
Switch3(config)# interface gigabitethernet 0/15
Switch3(config-if)# spanning-tree guard root
```

BPDU Guard   BPDU Guard is a security feature built into the switch when you enable Portfast. Portfast is a feature that puts the port into forwarding mode very quickly rather than going through the normal spanning tree algorithm. Portfast assumes that the port is connected to a PC or workstation and does not have the capability of causing loops; therefore it doesn't need to go through the full spanning tree listening and learning process.

BPDU Guard protects ports by being reactive to a BPDU message. Under normal circumstances, these user ports should not receive any BPDU messages. If they do and BPDU Guard is enabled, the port shuts down.

The following commands are used for configuring BPDU Guard:

```
Switch3(config)# interface gigabitethernet 0/17
Switch3(config-if)# spanning-tree portfast bpduguard
```

Mitigating DHCP Server Spoofing

Today's IT environment mandates use of the Dynamic Host Configuration Protocol (DHCP) to obtain IP addresses. Statically configured IP addresses are usually reserved for servers or other network devices in which it is required that the IP address not change. DHCP servers are typically found in an office LAN environment to serve IP addresses to PCs and other hosts that require them. A typical host will send out a DHCP request and the first DHCP server to respond will give that host an IP address, a default gateway, and a network mask and usually DNS information as well.

What would happen if an attacker were able to masquerade as a DHCP server? I've just outlined the type of information that is given out. Could that cause a problem? The answer is yes, it could. The attacker's goal here is to hand out a default gateway, which is usually a rogue machine—it could even be the rogue DHCP server. All that is required is for the attacker's machine to be the first to respond to a DHCP request. A fast machine and close proximity to the target is usually all that is necessary. If the attacker can force you to send all traffic through a machine he controls, the attacker can both capture your traffic and forward it to the real destination, all without your knowledge. This could go on indefinitely without detection, due to the "behind-the-scenes" nature of the attack.

 The attacker could also use the rogue DHCP server to hand out incorrect DNS information and thus could direct users to a malicious server.

Configuring DCHP Snooping

DHCP snooping is a feature on the Cisco Catalyst switches that allows you to configure protection against DHCP spoofing. It uses the concept of *trusted ports* and *untrusted ports*. A trusted port can accept DHCP messages that might be received, such as DHCPOFFER. An untrusted port is not allowed to receive DHCP messages, and if it receives one, the port is disabled.

To set up DHCP snooping, you must first enable it globally using the following command:

```
Switch1(config)# ip dhcp snooping
```

Next we go back to that concept of trusted and untrusted. Once DHCP snooping is enabled, all ports are untrusted by default. That means you have to configure all of the ports that you want to trust. To configure a port as a trusted port, use the following commands:

```
Switch1(config)# interface gigabitethernet 0/4
Switch1(config-if)# ip dhcp snooping trust
```

Another type of configuration you might want to consider is setting up DHCP snooping on particular VLANs only. This might come in handy in an office environment. You use the following command to set up DHCP snooping on a single VLAN (in this case it is VLAN 50):

```
Switch1(config)# ip dhcp snooping vlan 50
```

Last, you might want to set up *rate limiting* to limit the number of DHCP messages that you receive per second. Why, you ask? Some attackers use DHCP to perform a denial of service attack by exhausting the IP address scope and preventing anyone else from obtaining an IP address, effectively cutting them off the network. In the following example, I limit the number of messages per second to two.

```
Switch1(config)# interface gigabitethernet 0/9
Switch1(config-if)# ip dhcp snooping limit rate 2
```

Dynamic ARP Inspection

Another feature that builds upon the DHCP snooping feature is dynamic ARP inspection (DAI). This works in conjunction with the DHCP binding table to mitigate an ARP spoofing attack. An ARP spoofing attack works like this: An attacker sends Gratuitous ARP (GARP) messages, which relay incorrect IP addresses with MAC addresses. The idea, once again, is to direct traffic to an attacker-controlled machine. If the attacker can poison the ARP cache, then they can direct the traffic at will.

Enter dynamic ARP inspection. As mentioned, the feature builds upon DHCP snooping and works similarly. The same trusted and untrusted ports concept is present in DAI. The configuration also must be enabled globally before it can be used at the port level. It is necessary to configure DAI on a VLAN level. The following command enables DAI on a VLAN with the ID 10:

```
Switch1(config)# ip arp inspection vlan 10
```

Because once DAI is configured, all ports are considered untrusted, you must configure each one that you want to be a trusted port on a per-interface basis.

```
Switch1(config)# interface gigabitethernet 0/11
Switch1(config-if)# ip arp inspection trust
```

Protecting against CAM Table Attacks

A Cisco Catalyst switch uses a Content Addressable Memory (CAM) table to store MAC addresses and the port(s) where they are seen. This is how forwarding decisions are made in the switch. If the frame enters a port and the destination MAC address is known as part of the CAM table, the frame is forwarded out that corresponding port and that port only.

So let's look at a normal switch operation scenario. In Figure 6.5, Host 1 is sending a packet to Server 1. Because Server 1 is known as a destination and has an entry in the CAM table, the packet coming from Host 1 is sent to the corresponding port, in this case Port 0/9.

FIGURE 6.5 Switch operation under normal conditions

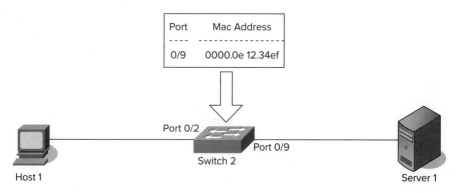

But let's examine another scenario. What happens when the CAM table is full? If the table is full, no more new MAC addresses can be learned. When that happens, the frames are flooded out through all interfaces other than the one on which it was received regardless of VLAN assignment. This creates a situation in which your intelligent switch has now been turned into a hub because that's the behavior of a hub, or multiport repeater. Why is this a problem? Now an attacker can see all the traffic and can use a packet analyzer such as Wireshark to capture all the traffic and potentially decode it, revealing valuable information for further attacks.

A collection of tools called dsniff can illustrate some of the attacks in this section, including macof, which can overflow the CAM table with MAC addresses. If you would like to examine the tools, you can find them at www.monkey.org/~dugsong/dsniff.

You will see later in the chapter why we can overcome these types of attacks with Cisco layer 2 security features such as port security, which will limit the number of MAC addresses. It is also important to note that not every switch is the same and the size of the CAM tables varies, as well as default behavior.

Preventing MAC Spoofing

Let's look at another type of attack, which is aimed squarely at the CAM table. *MAC spoofing* is an attack whereby the attacker sends out a false, or "spoofed," MAC address of a known target on the network. This is known as *packet crafting*, where the attacker alters the contents of a packet. In the MAC spoofing example in Figure 6.6, we have an attacker who has determined what the target MAC address is and is using an attack tool such as arpspoof (also a component of dsniff—see previous note).

FIGURE 6.6   Mac spoofing example

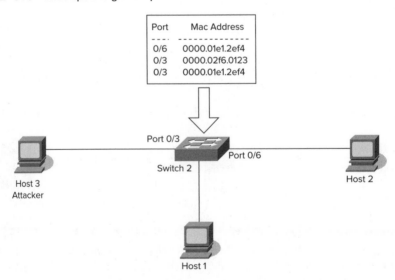

In this example, the attacker sends out frames with the MAC address of the target, in this case Host 2. This means that if Host 1 were to send any frames that were destined to go to Host 2, they now go to Host 3, the attacker's host.

Mac spoofing attacks can also be mitigated using Cisco layer 2 security features such as port security, specifically by configuring sticky secure commands. Configuring port security with sticky secure commands allows MAC addresses that initially enter a port to be allowed and no others. This would stop an attack such as MAC spoofing dead in its tracks.

Configuring Port Security

Configuring port security is one of the most simple yet effective methods of controlling who is on your network. If you take the time to configure port security before you deploy a switch, you won't have to worry about it afterward. Port security is just one of the layers of defense you can apply to a layer 2 switch.

Let's talk about the actions that can be taken automatically when you configure port security on your switch. There are three possible outcomes for a violation of port security:

Shutdown   Starting with the strictest mode first, shutdown will do just what it says and shut down a port when it perceives a security violation. It will also send an SNMP trap and a Syslog message. No traffic will flow over the port after a port security violation.

Restrict   Restrict operates with a method of notification. Each time there is a violation, a Syslog message and an SNMP trap are generated, and a violation counter is incremented.

Protect   Protect allows you to use a single MAG address (the default) and allow no others, or you can specify the number of MAC addresses you want to allow. When you get a violation of the configured number of MAC addresses, any previously allowed MAC addresses will continue to pass traffic, but any beyond that will be dropped and no notification will be sent.

It's important to note that a port security violation can be generated in situations in which no attack is occurring. What happens if you unplug your laptop at one location and plug into another switch port? A violation will occur, of course. But what determines where your MAC address is kept on the switch and for how long? You knew the answer to that one; it's a configuration option.

There are three types of configuration options when it comes to configuring secure MAC addresses:

Static secure MAC address   A static secure MAC address is configured from the command line and is saved in the running configuration and the CAM table.

Sticky secure MAC address   A sticky secure configuration is similar to a static secure except that you don't have to manually configure the MAC address. The switch learns the MAC address dynamically and then stores it in the running configuration and the CAM table.

Dynamic secure MAC address The dynamic secure option is similar to the sticky secure configuration in that the MAC address is learned; however, the difference is that it is only stored in the CAM table, not in the running configuration. It will be lost if the switch is rebooted.

Port security on a Cisco switch is not enabled by default. Once you configure port security without any other options, the default behavior is to drop packets upon violation and the maximum number of MAC addresses is set to 1.

 The switch hardware used in this section was the Cisco Catalyst 3550. The commands that you see might be slightly different on other switches, so please make sure you check the configuration guide for the switch and/or version of IOS that you are using. This is a good idea not only with the Catalyst but also with any hardware or IOS. There can be slight differences from version to version, so it's always good to be informed.

Let's examine the command-line configuration for port security.

Starting with a basic port security configuration, the following is configured on interface GigabitEthernet 0/19:

```
Switch2(config)# interface gigabitethernet 0/19
Switch2(config-if)# switchport mode access
Switch2(config-if)# switchport port-security
```

With this configuration, you would have port security in which a violation results in the port getting shut down. That means that you would have exactly one MAC address allowed on the port.

In the following example, I will use a sticky secure configuration so that I don't have to configure the MAC address manually, yet I still have a high level of control:

```
Switch2(config)# interface gigabitethernet 0/20
Switch2(config-if)# switchport mode access
Switch2(config-if)# switchport port-security mac-address sticky
```

In this example, I will use a protect configuration with a maximum number of MAC addresses:

```
Switch2(config)# interface gigabitethernet 0/21
Switch2(config-if)# switchport mode access
Switch2(config-if)# switchport port-security
Switch2(config-if)# switchport port-security maximum 3
Switch2(config-if)# switchport port-security violation protect
```

And finally, here is an illustration of manually configuring a MAC address on a switch port:

```
Switch2(config-if)# switchport port-security mac-address dead.beaf.0000
```

To additionally illustrate some of the functionality shown here, I will look at some of the show commands for switchport security. The following is an example of the show port-security command:

```
Switch2#show port-security

Secure Port  MaxSecureAddr  CurrentAddr  SecurityViolation  Security Action
             (Count)        (Count)      (Count)
-----------------------------------------------------------------------
    Gi0/19          3            1              0               Protect
-----------------------------------------------------------------------
Total Addresses in System (excluding one mac per port)    :0
Max Addresses limit in System (excluding one mac per port) :6176
```

The next option is to look at specific MAC addresses that are configured by using the show port-security address command:

```
Switch2# show port-security address
         Secure Mac Address Table
Vlan    Mac Address     Type           Ports     Remaining Age (mins)
-----------------------------------------------------------------------
10      000c.0d3f.00ae  SecureDynamic  Gi0/18    13
-----------------------------------------------------------------------
Total Addresses in System (excluding one mac per port)    :0
Max Addresses limit in System (excluding one mac per port) :6176
```

Then you might want to look at the port security settings on a specific interface. The command show port-security interface will display the configured port security settings for a given interface:

```
Switch2# show port-security interface gigabitethernet 0/21

Port Security              : Enabled
Port Status                : Secure-down
Violation Mode             : Protect
Aging Time                 : 0 mins
Aging Type                 : Absolute
SecureStatic Address Aging : Disabled
Maximum MAC Addresses      : 3
```

```
Total MAC Addresses       : 1
Configured MAC Addresses  : 1
Sticky MAC Addresses      : 0
Last Source Address:VLAN  : 0000.0000.0000:0
Security Violation Count  : 0
```

 **Real World Scenario**

Port Security Enabled

Sally is a network engineer at a large enterprise. The enterprise has many floors and available switched ports. It also has a large number of consultants and contractors at any given time. Sally's boss has asked her to implement port security to keep anyone from just plugging in and accessing the network. To keep administration to a minimum, Sally has been given the authority to statically configure MAC addresses for contractors and consultants and to implement sticky secure for employees. By establishing a baseline, Sally can ensure that new consultants and contractors would have to provide a MAC address to be granted access.

Sally implemented the following configurations, one for existing employees and one for consultants and contractors:

- Employee Configuration

```
Switch1(config)# interface gigabitethernet 0/08
Switch1(config-if)# switchport mode access
Switch1(config-if)# switchport port-security
Switch1(config-if)# switchport port-security mac-address sticky
Switch1(config-if)# switchport port-security maximum 1
```

- Contractor/Consultant Configuration

```
Switch1(config)# interface gigabitethernet 0/24
Switch1(config-if)# switchport mode access
Switch1(config-if)# switchport port-security
Switch1(config-if)# switchport port-security maximum 1
Switch1(config-if)# switchport port-security mac-address a001.ae0d.0001
Switch1(config-if)# switchport port-security violation shutdown
```

These are just examples of individual ports. There would be configurations for all ports in use to complete the exercise. In addition, you would likely configure all other ports not in use to be on a nonrouted VLAN and/or shutdown.

Recommendations for Layer 2 Security

The following are Cisco's recommendations for layer 2 security. Some are based on the principles that were discussed earlier in the chapter and others are just good security practice.

- Disable unneeded services.

- Administratively shut down any inactive ports.

- Limit management access to administrators only.

- Use SNMP v3 if network management is desired because information transmitted is encrypted.

- Don't send user data over a native VLAN using trunk ports.

- Engage Spanning-Tree Protocol protection features such as BPDU Guard and Root Guard.

- Use port security to place limitations on the number of MAC addresses allowed.

- Turn on DHCP snooping and DAI for protection against man-in-the-middle type attacks.

Configuring SPAN, RSPAN, and Storm Control

In the following sections, I discuss Switched Port Analyzer (SPAN), which allows someone to use a network analyzer to examine traffic from a specific port or VLAN. Then I further that concept to go beyond one switch with the RSPAN features. Rounding out the chapter is a discussion of storm control, which is used to inhibit LAN storms.

Configuring Switched Port Analyzer (SPAN)

Switched Port Analyzer is typically used for network analysis or potentially an IDS or IPS.

Using SPAN with a Network Analyzer

One of the biggest reasons to configure Switched Port Analyzer (SPAN) on a switch is to use a network analyzer such as Wireshark to capture traffic to assist in troubleshooting connectivity issues. Typically there will be a host or server on which you will want to see traffic entering and leaving. Configuring SPAN involves configuring both a source and a destination port to monitor. Your source port is typically the port of the traffic that you want to see. And the destination is the port where you have a traffic analyzer plugged in. Let's examine this with an example, shown in Figure 6.7.

FIGURE 6.7 Switched Port Analyzer (SPAN) example

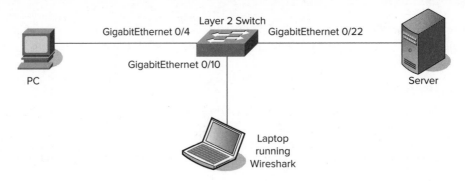

Using SPAN with an Intrusion Detection System (IDS)

Another major reason to use a SPAN port is to enable the use of an intrusion detection system (IDS). Chapter 8, "Implementing Cisco IOS Intrusion Prevention," discusses intrusion detection systems further. An IDS would typically be used to monitor connections to firewalls, critical systems, databases, and the like. Let's look at a sample configuration where I am going to configure an interface that connects to a firewall, as shown in Figure 6.8.

FIGURE 6.8 Using an IDS with SPAN

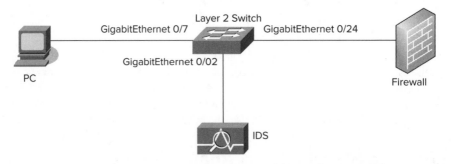

In this case I want to configure the source port (Port 0/24) to be the port that connects to the firewall and the destination port (Port 0/2) to be the one that connects to the IDS. Let's examine the configuration from a command-line perspective. The commands to set the source and destination ports and to set up monitoring are as follows:

```
Switch1(config)# monitor session 1 source interface gigabitethernet 0/24
Switch1(config)# monitor session 1 destination interface gigabitethernet 0/2
```

Configuring Remote Switched Port Analyzer (RSPAN)

SPAN is configured and applies to a single switch. There is also a method for analyzing multiple switches. The destination is on a switch that is remote to the other source ports, which are on different switches. RSPAN can be used where it is necessary to monitor multiple points on a network without spending the money to have multiple monitors in place.

The example in Figure 6.9 shows a network with three switches connected together. There is a switch on each floor of this three-story building, and each serves the employees on the floor on which it is placed. But the budget allows only one IDS sensor. The IDS is located on the third floor and connected to GigabitEthernet 0/24. There are two particular ports we are interested in monitoring. One is the router connection, which is connected to the Internet (GigabitEthernet 0/1), and the other is on the second floor, where there is a critical financial system connected to GigabitEthernet port 0/10.

FIGURE 6.9   RSPAN configuration

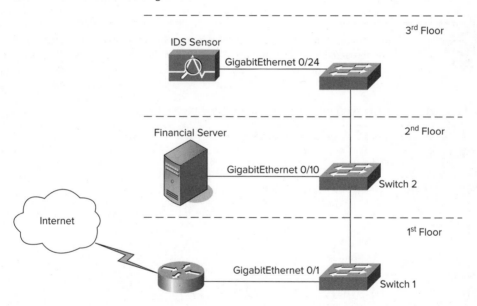

Let's walk through the configuration of an RSPAN as shown in the diagram. RSPAN requires that we create a VLAN so that we can have a destination for our monitor ports. We then have to configure the VLAN as an RSPAN VLAN. It's important to note that only RSPAN traffic traverses this VLAN. See the configuration steps listed:

```
Switch3(config)# vlan 500
Switch3(config-vlan)# remote-span
```

Now that we have the RSPAN VLAN configured, we need to specify which ports are source ports to monitor. In this case we want to monitor the router port and the financial server port, as previously mentioned. The keyword both used after the interface in this example means both transmit and receive traffic:

```
Switch1(config)# monitor session 1 source interface gigabitethernet 0/1 both
Switch2(config)# monitor session 1 source interface gigabitethernet 0/10 both
```

Next we need to configure the destination, using the VLAN that we set up earlier:

```
Switch1(config)# monitor session 1 destination remote vlan 500
Switch2(config)# monitor session 1 destination remote vlan 500
```

Last we need to configure the forwarding destination port to point to the remote VLAN to have the IDS monitor the traffic:

```
Switch3(config)# monitor session 1 source remote vlan 500
Switch3(config)# monitor session 1 destination interface gigabitethernet 0/24
```

Remember that the commands used in this chapter may be different depending on the switch hardware and on the version of the operating system. Check the configuration guide for the switch and/or version of the IOS that you are using.

Now let's verify the switch configuration for the three switches. Let's start with Switch 1:

```
Switch1# show monitor session 1 detail
Session 1
---------------
Type : Remote Source Session

Source Ports:
    RX Only:        None
    TX Only:        None
  Both:         Gi 0/1
Source VLANs:
    RX Only:        None
    TX Only:        None
    Both:           None
Source RSPAN VLAN:  None
Destination ports:  None
Filter VLANs:       None
Dest RSPAN VLAN:    500
```

Next let's look at Switch 2:

```
Switch2# show monitor session 1 detail
  Session 1
  ---------------
  Type : Remote Source Session

Source Ports:
    RX Only:        None
    TX Only:        None
    Both:Gi 0/10
Source VLANs:
    RX Only:        None
    TX Only:        None
    Both:           None
Source RSPAN VLAN:  None
Destination ports:  None
Filter VLANs:       None
Dest RSPAN VLAN:    500
```

Last, let's look at the Switch 3 configuration, which will be different than the other two switches because the destination port lives here.

```
Switch1# show monitor session 1 detail
  Session 1
  ---------------
  Type : Remote Source Session

Source Ports:
    RX Only:        None
    TX Only:        None
    Both:           None
Source VLANs:
    RX Only:        None
    TX Only:        None
    Both:500
Source RSPAN VLAN:  None
Destination ports:  Gi0/24
Filter VLANs:       None
Dest RSPAN VLAN:    None
```

Configuring Storm Control

In a LAN environment, there is always the potential for a LAN storm. If you've been in the network business for a while, it would be unusual if you have not personally experienced one. LAN storms can result from misconfigurations, denial of service attacks, broadcast storms, or users plugging in equipment where they shouldn't—the list goes on and on.

The symptoms of a LAN storm are anything from a minor delay in processing to a complete shutdown of the network, stopping traffic flow. It can be a crippling event in which drastic action needs to be taken to restore normal operations.

Fortunately, over the years, many improvements have been made in switch hardware and software to limit the crippling effects of a LAN storm. One way to control the effects of such a storm is to limit the amount of a specific type of frame after a certain threshold is reached. Indeed, this is what *storm control* does. Storm control looks at the type of frame— broadcast, multicast, or unicast—and then measures the number of frames received within a 1-second interval and compares that to preconfigured thresholds to determine action. If the traffic exceeds the threshold for a given type, then that type of traffic is blocked.

The default behavior on a Catalyst 3550 switch in a multicast storm would be to block all traffic except for control traffic. In a broadcast or unicast storm, the default behavior is to block only the type of frame that is causing the storm.

Bear in mind that you might want to change the default behavior based on your needs. Blocking activity can affect your network negatively by blocking traffic such as routing updates. Proper network configuration can help with limiting these issues in the first place.

Storm control can be configured on a per-interface basis and thresholds can be set for each type of traffic (broadcast, unicast, and multicast). Thresholds are set as a percentage of the total traffic on the port and can range from 0.00 to 100.00. Both ends of that range mean specific things: 0.00 percent means that no traffic will flow and 100.00 percent mean that no traffic will be blocked. You can also configure thresholds based on packets per second or in bits per second. The actions that can be configured are to shut down ports and to send an SNMP trap.

Let's look at some configurations for storm control:

```
Switch1(config)# interface gigabitethernet 0/4
Switch1(config-if)# storm-control unicast level 80.5
Switch1(config-if)# storm-control multicast level bps 3k 1k
Switch1(config-if)# storm-control broadcast level pps 100k
Switch1(config-if)# storm-control action shutdown
```

In this example, I set three separate levels of storm suppression, using three different types of measurements. In the first, I set the unicast storm control level to be 80.5 percent. In the second, the multicast storm control level was set to 3,000 bits per second with a falling suppression level of 1,000 bits per second. This means that the traffic must fall below 1,000 bits per second to be forwarded again. If you don't set a falling suppression level, the falling suppression level is set to 3,000 bits per second. And finally, the broadcast level of storm control was set using 100,000 packets per second.

Summary

In this chapter, you learned about basic approaches to layer 2 security, such as enabling SNMP version 3, turning trunk ports off when not in use, and turning unused ports off. Then we discussed attacks against VLANs, specifically double-tagging attacks and switch-spoofing attacks. These attacks can be mitigated by not using native VLANs to transmit data and by turning off Dynamic Trunk Protocol (DTP). Another type of attack is the Spanning-Tree Protocol (STP) attack, which takes the form of insertion of rogue switches. Two mitigating controls are used for this, Root Guard and BPDU Guard. Next we covered DHCP spoofing attacks, followed by CAM table attacks such as MAC spoofing. Then we covered the topic of port security settings and finally Switched Port Analyzer (SPAN), RSPAN, and storm control.

Exam Essentials

Remember the basic approaches to maintaining layer 2 security.   To maintain layer 2 security, you can use SSH instead of Telnet, use SNMP version 3, enable logging, and configure port and VLAN security features as follows:

- Turn off ports that are not used.
- Set trunk ports to be off instead of auto.
- Avoid using native VLANs to transmit user data.
- Use private VLANs to further secure sensitive data with a VLAN.

Know what kinds of attacks can be made against VLANs and the mitigating controls. Attacks against VLANs are usually characterized as VLAN hopping. The attacker wants to jump from the VLAN he has compromised to another higher-value VLAN. This chapter included discussions of double tagging and switch spoofing. The features to combat them include turning off DTP on trunk ports and configuring the native VLAN to not carry user data.

Understand attacks against Spanning-Tree Protocol (STP) and the features you can configure to mitigate the threat.   An attack against STP involves introducing a rogue switch to the network. The mitigation for these types of attacks is to configure Root Guard and BPDU Guard.

Be able to discuss the features that can be enabled to combat DHCP spoofing.   With DHCP spoofing, an attacker hopes to direct traffic to a rogue-controlled host by setting either a rogue default gateway or a rogue DNS server. The countermeasures are to configure DHCP snooping and dynamic ARP inspection (DAI).

Know the types of attacks that affect the CAM table and the features that can be used to deter them.   CAM table attacks are carried out by manipulating MAC address usage. The main form of attack is to attempt to overload the CAM or MAC address table. When this happens, frames get flooded to all ports except the one from which the attack is made. This enables the attacker to potentially capture traffic.

Understand the different types of port security features and how to configure them. Configuring port security is one way to combat MAC address attacks. You can utilize three outcomes in the event of a violation: shut down the port, restrict the port, or notify. There are three types of secure MAC address configurations: sticky secure, static secure, and dynamic secure ports. If you configure port security with no other options, the default is to shut down the port on violation and to allow only one MAC address on the port.

Be able to configure Switched Port Analyzer (SPAN) and know what it's used for. Switched Port Analyzer (SPAN) is used primarily for two things: capturing traffic for analysis and sending traffic to an intrusion detection system (IDS). To configure SPAN, you must specify a source port or VLAN and then a destination port and whether or not you want to capture traffic in one direction or both directions.

Know how to configure Remote Switched Port Analyzer (RSPAN). Remote SPAN, or RSPAN, is used when you want to send traffic from multiple switches to a single remote port. In the example in this chapter, we had a three-story building with three switches in it. We wanted to capture traffic on two different ports on two of the three switches. Our IDS was on the third switch. We configured a VLAN on the third switch and then set up monitoring from two different ports on Switches 1 and 2. Finally, we configured the destination port for the VLAN traffic to go to for the IDS.

Understand LAN storms and how to configure storm control. Storm control is important to configure (and it's good network design) to combat LAN storms. There are three types of packets on which you can configure storm control: unicast, multicast, and broadcast. Each can be configured with a suppression rate threshold. You can specify the threshold in terms of a percentage of traffic, bits per second, or packets per second. Responses to reaching the threshold are to shut down the port and to send an SNMP trap.

Written Lab

Write the answers to the following questions:

1. What are the two types of VLAN hopping attacks?
2. BPDU Guard protects what type of ports?
3. Switch spoofing involves what type of attack?
4. Which type of attack requires the use of native VLAN to send data?
5. What does DTP do?
6. What is the difference in SPAN and RSPAN?
7. DHCP spoofing is countered with which features?
8. What is a tool that can be used to do MAC-level attacks?
9. What is the name of the command that is used when configuring a SPAN port?
10. What are the three types of suppression rate thresholds that can be configured for storm control?

(The answers to the written lab can be found following the answers to the review questions.)

Hands-on Labs

In this section, you'll examine three of the Cisco layer 2 protection mechanisms covered earlier in the chapter. These labs were done with a Cisco 3550 switch. You can use any Cisco switch, but please note that some of the commands used here may not match your commands.

Hands-on Lab 6.1: Configuring Protection against a Spanning Tree Attack

In this exercise, you will configure protection against a spanning-tree attack by enabling Root Guard and BPDU Guard.

1. Log into your switch and enter privileged mode by typing **en** or **enable**.
2. Enter global configuration mode by typing **config t**. Then enter interface configuration mode to configure Root Guard for the GigabitEthernet port 0/24. Type the command **interface gigabitethernet 0/24** to enter interface configuration mode and then type **spanning-tree guard root** as shown here:

```
Switch# config t
Enter configuration commands, one per line.  End with CNTL/Z.
Switch(config)# interface gigabitethernet 0/24
Switch(config-if)# spanning-tree guard root
```

3.   Now that you have configured Root Guard on this interface, you'll move on to another interface so that you can configure BPDU Guard. Since you are still in interface configuration mode, you will need to type **exit** to return to global configuration mode.

4.   Type **interface gigabitethernet 0/18** to enter interface configuration mode for that port. Now type **spanning-tree portfast bpduguard** to enable the feature on the interface.

```
Switch(config-if)# exit
Switch(config)#
Switch(config)# interface gigabitethernet 0/18
Switch(config-if)# spanning-tree portfast bpduguard
```

Now you have completed the configuration of two key features to protect against spanning tree attacks.

Hands-on Lab 6.2: Configuring SPAN on a Cisco Switch to Do Troubleshooting

In this scenario, you have been asked to analyze traffic coming from a particular host and going to a particular server to perform troubleshooting. As part of this exercise, you will have to configure SPAN on the switch:

1.   Examine the diagram shown in Figure 6.10 to see where you are going to configure SPAN on the switch.

FIGURE 6.10   Example SPAN configuration

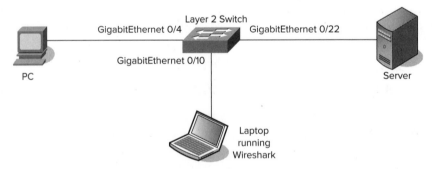

2.   Log into your router and enter privileged mode by typing **en** or **enable**.

3.   Enter global configuration mode by typing **config t**. Look at the diagram and you will see that SPAN will need to be configured on either the port with the host or the port with the server. Because you are more interested in the server traffic, you are going to configure SPAN with the source of GigabitEthernet 0/22 because you want to

see all the traffic entering and exiting that port. Enter the command **monitor session 1 source interface gigabitethernet 0/22**.

```
Switch# config t
Enter configuration commands, one per line.  End with CNTL/Z.
Switch(config)# monitor session 1 source interface gigabitethernet 0/22
```

4. Next you will configure the destination to which your SPAN traffic will go. Because you are using a laptop with Wireshark plugged into port GigabitEthernet 0/10, that's where you want to configure the destination. Type **monitor session 1 destination interface gigabitethernet 0/10** at the configuration prompt. Then type **exit** to get out of configuration mode.

```
Switch(config)#monitor session 1 destination interface gigabitethernet 0/10
Switch(config)# exit
```

5. At this point, you can begin analyzing traffic because the traffic is now mirrored on the port to which your laptop is connected.

Hands-on Lab 6.3: Configuring Port Security on a Cisco Switch

In this scenario, you have been asked to configure port security on two ports on Switch 5. You will be configuring one port to have a maximum limit of three MAC addresses. You will configure the same port to be in protect mode. Additionally, you will configure the port to be sticky secure. You have been told that there is a highly sensitive server connected to the second port, so you will configure the port to shut down in the event of a violation. Further, you will configure a static MAC address and specify that this MAC address is the only one allowed. Follow these steps:

1. Log into your router and enter privileged mode by typing **en** or **enable**.

2. Enter global configuration mode by typing **config t**, and then you will have to enter interface configuration mode for the first port, which is GigabitEthernet port 0/14. Type **interface gigabitethernet 0/14** to enter interface configuration mode.

```
Switch5# config t
Enter configuration commands, one per line.  End with CNTL/Z.
Switch5(config)# interface gigabitethernet 0/14
Switch5(config-if)#
```

3. Next configure port security on the port by first typing **switchport mode access** to make sure it is an access port and not a trunk port. The next command to configure is **switchport port-security**. This turns on port security. Next type **switchport port-security maximum 3**. Finally, configure sticky secure by typing **switchport-security mac-address sticky**.

```
Switch5(config-if)# switchport mode access
Switch5(config-if)# switchport port-security
```

```
Switch5(config-if)# switchport port-security maximum 3
Switch5(config-if)# switchport port-security mac-address sticky
```

4. That's one port down. Repeat part of the process by typing **exit** at the prompt and returning to global configuration mode. Now you will configure port 0/18. Type **interface gigabitethernet 0/18** at the prompt to enter interface configuration mode. Then type **switchport mode access** as you did in the previous step to make it an access port. The next command to type is **switchport port-security**. Finally, type **switchport port-security mac-address 0000.021e.2f36** to complete the configuration that allows only the listed MAC address to be used on this port.

```
Switch5(config-if)# exit
Switch5(config)# interface gigabitethernet 0/18
Switch5(config-if)# switchport mode access
Switch5(config-if)# switchport port-security
Switch5(config-if)# switchport port-security mac-address 0000.021e.2f36
Switch5(config-if)# end
```

Review Questions

1. Which of the following is *not* a correct configuration option when configuring port security?

   A. Shutdown

   B. Err-disable

   C. Protect

   D. Restrict

2. What feature would you configure if you had to do some troubleshooting with a network analyzer such as Wireshark?

   A. DAI

   B. BPDU Guard

   C. SPAN

   D. DHCP snooping

3. Which two methods are primarily used when an attacker attempts a VLAN hopping attack? (Choose two.)

   A. Double switching

   B. Double tagging

   C. Switch spoofing

   D. MAC spoofing

4. Which type of port security method can be described by learning a MAC address and *not* adding it to the running config?

   A. Secure MAC

   B. Sticky secure MAC

   C. Dynamic secure

   D. MAC secure

5. If a non-root port on a switch receives a BPDU that is superior and Root Guard is enabled, what happens?

   A. The port becomes a root port.

   B. The port is disabled.

   C. Frames are forwarded as usual.

   D. The port goes into root-inconsistent mode.

6. RSPAN requires the use of which of the following to make it work?

   A. VLAN

   B. Port aggregation

   C. Port security

   D. DAI

7. Which of the following is *not* a method of basic layer 2 security?

    A. Use of SNMP v3

    B. Logging

    C. Use of Telnet

    D. Use of SSH

8. If you were an attacker and you wanted to capture packets on a switch but you were armed with a PC with access to only a single port on the switch, which attack might you attempt?

    A. CAM table attack

    B. VLAN attack

    C. DHCP spoofing

    D. MAC spoofing

    E. All of the above

9. What layer 2 feature of a Cisco Catalyst switch would allow two hosts in the same VLAN to be unable to communicate with each other?

    A. ACLs

    B. Private VLAN

    C. DAI

    D. STP

10. A double-tagging attack uses which feature of the Catalyst switch to facilitate the attack?

    A. Private VLAN

    B. ISL tagging

    C. Console port

    D. Native VLAN

11. Which of the following is a correct secure port configuration option?

    A. Sticky secure

    B. Secure sticky

    C. Secure static

    D. Dynamic sticky

12. When dynamic ARP inspection is used, which of the following correctly identifies the response to an ARP reply entering an untrusted port if it does not match an entry in the DHCP binding table? (Choose two.)

    A. Reply is dropped.

    B. SNMP trap is sent.

    C. Port security is enabled.

    D. Port is disabled.

13. What happens when an attacker is able to send enough MAC addresses to max out the CAM table?

A. The port is shut down.

B. Frames are flooded to all ports.

C. It results in a denial of service.

D. The switch functions as normal.

14. Which two of the following can be configured for storm control?

A. Broadcast

B. IP

C. Multicast

D. TCP

15. Which of the following commands is needed to enable DHCP snooping on a switch port? (Choose two.)

A. Switch(config-if)# `ip dhcp snooping trust`

B. Switch(config)# `ip dhcp snooping trust`

C. Switch(config)# `ip dhcp snooping`

D. Switch(config-if)# `ip dhcp snooping`

16. Which of the following is not a basic approach to maintaining layer 2 security?

A. Turn off unused ports.

B. Use private VLANs.

C. Do not configure trunk ports.

D. Avoid using native VLANs to transmit data.

17. Which of the following is not an option to use when configuring RSPAN?

A. RX only

B. TX only

C. Layer 3

D. VLAN

18. Which of the following is the correct command for enabling root guard on a switch port?

A. Switch(config-if)# `spanning-tree guard root`

B. Switch(config)# `stp root guard`

C. Switch(config)# `spanning-tree rootguard`

D. Switch(config-if)# `stp guard root`

19. Which of the following commands would show the status of port security on an interface?

   A. Switch# `show port-security`

   B. Switch# `show port security`

   C. Switch# `show port security interface`

   D. Switch# `show port-security interface`

20. Depending on which type of switch you are on, there are two different terms for dynamically learned MAC addresses on a switch that mean the same thing. Which two are they?

   A. TCAM

   B. MAC table

   C. CAM

   D. MAC address table

Answers to Review Questions

1. B. The three modes that you can configure are to shut down the port, restrict the port, and protect the port.

2. C. Switch Port Analyzer (SPAN) is the feature you might use to copy a port's traffic flow and send it to another port. This is useful when using a traffic analyzer.

3. B, C. Double tagging is one method for attempting to do VLAN hopping. In double tagging, an additional tag is added to an already tagged packet in order to traverse the VLAN. The second method is called switch spoofing; the goal is to insert a rogue switch into an infrastructure by attempting to force a trunk connection with an existing switch.

4. C. Dynamic secure is the method that learns MAC addresses but doesn't add them to the running configuration. It places a copy in the CAM table only.

5. D. When a non-root port receives a superior BPDU and Root Guard is enabled, the port goes into root-inconsistent mode and no data is passed through the port.

6. A. The one thing that RSPAN requires that SPAN does not is the configuration of a VLAN so that traffic can traverse multiple switches.

7. C. Telnet use is discouraged because usernames and passwords are transmitted in cleartext.

8. E. The fact is, a PC with access to a single port could execute any or all of these attacks if the attacker had the right tools on the PC. Some of these attacks would require some other conditions to be present, but since the question didn't list any caveats, you could assume the worst case (or the best case, if you are the attacker).

9. B. A private VLAN can establish a VLAN within a VLAN, so even though two hosts might be in the same VLAN, a private VLAN can isolate one host from another.

10. D. Double tagging utilizes the native VLAN to get traffic to traverse from one switch to another.

11. A. Sticky secure is one of the options for configuring port security. It puts a copy of the MAC address learned on the port into the running configuration.

12. A, D. If an ARP reply enters an untrusted port *and* it doesn't match an entry in the DHCP binding table, the ARP reply is dropped and the port is disabled.

13. B. Assuming the switch is in a fail-open mode, a loaded CAM table or MAC address table would result in the frames being flooded to all ports. This would allow an attacker to capture packets on that switch.

14. A, C. Storm control can be configured for unicast, broadcast, and multicast traffic. Since we are talking about layer 2 traffic in this chapter, the other two options do not apply.

15. A, C. The command `ip dhcp snooping` must be done in global configuration mode to enable DHCP snooping for the entire switch. Then if you want to trust a single port you must issue the `ip dhcp snooping trust` command under interface configuration mode.

16. C. The other choice as a basic approach to maintaining layer 2 security would be to set trunk ports to be off instead of auto, not to avoid using them.

17. C. RSPAN can use a VLAN, RX only, TX only, or both.

18. A. The correct command is `spanning-tree guard root`, issued from the interface configuration mode.

19. D. The proper command is `show port-security interface`. If you use the `show port-security` command by itself, you will display port security for the whole switch.

20. C, D. The terms CAM and MAC address table mean the same thing.

Answers to Written Lab

1. Double-tagging and switch spoofing

2. Non-root ports

3. VLAN hopping

4. Double tagging

5. Dynamic Trunk Protocol allows a trunk port to configure itself automatically. This is discouraged because it allows an attacker access if he can connect a rogue switch.

6. RSPAN works on multiple switches, whereas SPAN is used on a single switch.

7. DHCP snooping and DAI

8. Dsniff

9. `monitor`

10. Percentage of traffic, bits per second, and packets per second

Chapter 7

Implementing Cisco IOS Firewall

THE FOLLOWING CCNA SECURITY EXAM OBJECTIVES ARE COVERED IN THIS CHAPTER:

✓ **Implement the Cisco IOS firewall feature set using SDM**

- Describe the operational strengths and weaknesses of the different firewall technologies

- Explain stateful firewall operations and the function of the state table

- Implement Zone Based Firewall using SDM

✓ **Mitigate threats to Cisco routers and networks using ACLs**

- Explain the functionality of standard, extended, and named IP ACLs used by routers to filter packets

- Configure and verify IP ACLs to mitigate given threats (filter IP traffic destined for Telnet, SNMP, and DDoS attacks) in a network using CLI

- Configure IP ACLs to prevent IP address spoofing using CLI

- Discuss the caveats to be considered when building ACLs

In this chapter, I'm going to discuss why you might use a firewall and how firewalls have evolved over time. There are a number of different technologies that have been deployed and we will discuss those in some detail.

Then we will examine the firewall feature set that is in Cisco IOS and how it can be used to secure your data. We will look at the operation of the firewall and how to configure it from a command-line interface (CLI) and also how to configure Zone Based Firewall using the Cisco Security Device Manager (SDM).

Firewall Basics

If you're new to security, you might be wondering what constitutes a firewall. I guess the answer depends on when you asked the question and in what context. The term *firewall* comes from the automobile vernacular and is used to describe that piece of the car that separates the engine from the inside of the car. Open up the hood of your car and you will see what I mean. The firewall is in theory supposed to keep a fire from spreading from the engine to the inside of the car. Funny, in every movie I've seen, there's no stopping a fire once it starts in a car.

But let's get back to the network security aspect of a firewall. The basic firewall is supposed to do two things: allow the traffic desired and reject all the traffic that is not desired. Over the years it has grown to do more things, as you will see.

The evolution of firewalls started back in the mid to late 1980s. In chronological order, these are the types of firewalls that were developed.

Packet-filtering technology   *Packet filters* "allow" traffic based on rules pertaining to layer 3 or IP addresses and/or TCP or UDP ports. These are still in use today. So what's the issue with them? The rules are limited. They allow or deny packets strictly on the basis of an IP address and/or a port. This is akin to something being either black or white—it either matches or it doesn't. If it matches a permit, then the traffic is passed. If it doesn't, then it is denied. Unfortunately, the world isn't just black or white; it's gray. What does that mean? Sometimes traffic that technically matches rules still might contain packets that are nefarious. We will talk about these a bit later.

Circuit-level firewall   The *circuit-level firewall* operates at the transport and session levels where it validates TCP and UDP port traffic prior to allowing the connection. Then, once the connection is established, it monitors traffic to see if it's part of the already allowed conversation.

Application-layer firewall   The *Application-layer firewall* can control various aspects of the application. The main drawback to an Application-layer firewall is slow performance. While very effective, the level of detail that is required doesn't allow for the performance that might be required.

Stateful firewall   The *stateful firewall* is today's standard. It tracks state at the lower layers of the OSI model, as opposed to the Application layer, which works only at layer 7. The advantage is that you are inspecting the Network and Transport layers, among others, to see if the traffic is part of an existing conversation or is attempting to start a new conversation.

A summary of the evolution of firewalls is shown in Table 7.1. We will get into more detail on some of the aspects of packet filtering and what *state* is all about in the following sections.

TABLE 7.1   Firewall Technologies

Type	Description
Packet filter firewall	The first type of firewall. A packet filter performs its duties based on packet rules. Packet rules are usually applied at layer 3, using a source and/or destination address. They can also be applied at layer 4, using ports as a discriminator. These packet filter rules can be applied into or out of an interface.
Circuit-level firewall	A second generation of firewall that uses intelligence to determine if traffic matches a connection request or if it belongs to existing flows. This is called a circuit-level firewall because the connection is sometimes called a virtual circuit.
Application-layer firewall or proxy server	The third-generation firewall. It operates at the Application layer. It keeps track of the state of connections, sequence numbers, username/password requests, basically anything that is done at the application level. This type of firewall is also called a proxy. Many organizations use some kind of proxy for their outbound web traffic, as an example.
Stateful firewall	The fourth and current generation of firewall. The stateful firewall keeps track of state information at a much lower level than the Application-layer firewall.

Packet Filtering Firewall

Packet filtering has been a feature of routers for some time now, operating at layer 3, or the network layer. Packet filters typically use *access control lists (ACLs)* to permit or deny traffic. Access lists in a Cisco router can be used for more than just packet filtering. They can be used to control traffic on many different levels, depending on how they are used.

You can also designate TCP or UDP ports to allow or deny traffic. Ports are a transport layer designation associated with a service that is operating on a host. For example, a web server generally operates on TCP port 80. Combining this with a source and/or a destination network address, such as an IP address, you can get fairly granular in your filtering.

Let's look at an example of basic packet-level filtering on a Cisco router. In Figure 7.1, you see a router with a connection to the Internet and also a connection to an internal LAN. In this basic configuration, there is no DMZ segment, just an internal and an external network. We have a host on the inside that wants to get to the Internet and we are providing a mail server on the inside that needs to receive mail from the Internet. If we look at Access-list 101, it is applied inbound from the Internet and then Access-list 102 is applied outbound toward the Internet.

FIGURE 7.1 Basic packet-level filtering

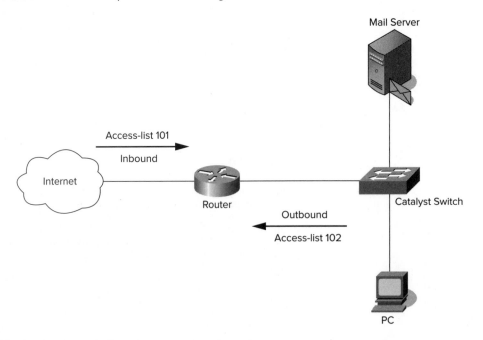

This is a basic packet filter. If traffic matches a specific pattern inbound, that is, port 25 (SMTP) destined for the mail server, then it would be permitted. On the outbound side, traffic that is destined for the Internet, that is, port 80 (HTTP), would be permitted. All other traffic would be denied implicitly.

Application-Layer Firewall

An Application-layer firewall is unique in that it can inspect layers 3, 4, 5, and 7 of the OSI model, and therefore it can prevent attacks on applications and services. Sometimes this type of firewall is called a proxy or an *application gateway*. A common use of this kind of firewall is to filter traffic to the Internet. One reason this is used is to control what websites an organization's users are allowed to visit and what types of applications they can use.

Application-layer firewalls offer the following advantages:

- User-level authentication
- Control of application use
- Detailed logging
- Protection against denial of service attacks

There can also be disadvantages in using an Application layer firewall. Some of them are listed here:

- Slow performance.
- Packets are switched in software, not hardware. That means instead of using specific hardware Application Specific Integrated Circuits (ASICs) to switch packets, they are switched in software, which is a slower process.
- Sometimes special client software is required.
- Application support is limited.

Stateful Firewall

Today the networking world is run by stateful firewalls. What does that mean exactly? A stateful firewall can dynamically monitor connections and inspect information in the packet header to determine if the packet is part of an existing connection or not.

Stateful firewalls keep their information about the state in a *state table*, which exists on the firewall. The state table contains information about various communication threads. It keeps track of all sessions and inspects packets traversing the firewall. If a packet matches a session that's already in the state table, then the packet will be allowed to pass.

So what are the advantages and disadvantages of using a stateful firewall? Let's look at both, starting with the advantages:

- Important first line and primary means of defense. Most organizations have a stateful firewall protecting their network from the Internet or from other organizations if they are working within a shared infrastructure.

- Much improvement over packet filters. As mentioned previously, there is no intelligence to packet filters; they either match or they don't.

- Better performance than other types of firewalls. Because of the level of intelligence— i.e., the state table—performance is much improved over ACL lookups, to name one advantage.

- Line of defense against spoofing and denial of service attacks. The firewall can identify anomalous traffic and prevent such attacks from being effective.

Now some of the disadvantages:

- Can't stop an application attack. Because the stateful firewall doesn't interpret layer 7 information, attackers can use embedded commands within the HTTP header, for example, to conduct attacks against the application.

- Can protect only those protocols that are stateful. UDP and ICMP have limited support in stateful firewalls.

- Stateful firewalls in and of themselves don't provide user authentication.

Access Control Lists

In the following sections, we will examine the basics of access control lists and how to construct static packet filters. I'll also cover how to use standard, extended, and named access lists to filter packets. Then we will explore filtering traffic that's directed to the router as well as filtering to protect against IP spoofing. Finally, I'll cover some caveats of using ACLs.

Basic ACLs

Access control lists (ACLs) are used for packet filtering on a Cisco router. They can also be used for selecting traffic for particular reasons (you will see in Chapter 12, "Implementing Site-to-Site IPSec VPN Solutions," that we use them to determine what traffic should flow over a VPN tunnel).

Access lists are scanned in order from top to bottom to look for a match that specifies whether a particular form of traffic is a permit or deny. If the access list is applied to an interface, it is applied to either the inbound direction or the outbound direction, as defined by the interface.

Because they can impact performance, much thought must be given to the construction and application of access lists.

There are two types of numbered access lists: standard and extended. You can also apply names instead of numbers to the access list, which may make more sense when working with a large number of them:

Standard access list   A standard access list uses only source addresses to filter traffic. It doesn't specify destination or port, only addresses.

In the following example, I am allowing all traffic from 172.16.100.0 through 172.16.100.255:

```
access-list 50 permit 172.16.100.0
```

Extended access list   An extended access list allows you to exert much finer control on the packets that you allow or deny. An extended access list can use IP address, protocol, port, source, and destination to make decisions on the disposition of the packet.

In the following example, I am allowing all traffic from host 10.1.1.40 to host 192.168.230.3, using TCP port 80 (which is for HTTP traffic):

```
access-list 101 permit tcp host 10.1.1.40 host 192.168.230.3 eq 80
```

Named access list   Before IOS version 11.2, you could use only numbers to designate access lists. Beginning in 11.2, you can use names to designate access lists. However, you can only use named lists for packet and route filters.

In the following example, I go back to the extended access list that I just configured. Now I am going to assign a name of HTTP_IN to designate the access list:

```
access-list HTTP_IN permit tcp host 10.1.1.40 host 192.168.230.3 eq 80
```

In today's world, it is rare to use something other than IP on your network, but there are still plenty of legacy applications that use other protocols. In Table 7.2, you can see all the ACL numbering schemes used in the Cisco IOS. If you have large numbers of IP ACLs, you may have to use the extended ranges of standard and extended IP ACLs, which are shown at the end of the table.

TABLE 7.2   ACL Numbering Scheme

ACL Number Range	Type of ACL
1 to 99	IP standard ACL
100 to 199	IP extended ACL
200 to 299	Protocol type-code ACL
300 to 399	DECnet ACL
400 to 499	XNS standard ACL

TABLE 7.2 ACL Numbering Scheme *(continued)*

ACL Number Range	Type of ACL
500 to 599	XNS extended ACL
600 to 699	Appletalk ACL
700 to 799	MAC address ACL
800 to 899	IPX standard ACL
900 to 999	IPX extended ACL
1000 to 1099	IPX SAP ACL
1100 to 1199	Extended MAC address ACL
1200 to 1299	IPX summary address ACL
1300 to 1999	IP standard ACL (extended range)
2000 to 2699	IP extended ACL (extended range)

Turbo ACLs

If you have one of the following models of routers, you can make use of turbo ACLs:

- Cisco 7200 series router
- Cisco 7500 series router
- Cisco 12000 series router

A turbo ACL processes a regular ACL into a lookup table for greater efficiency. One of the requirements of a turbo ACL is that it has more than three entries. The turbo ACL reduces the CPU utilization and, accordingly, the latency involved with large access lists. In this fashion, you can be fairly certain of the processing time associated with adding another entry to a large access list.

To use the turbo ACL feature, you must compile the access list that you wish to convert. You use the command access-list compiled in global configuration mode to use the turbo ACL features:

```
Router(config)# access-list compiled
```

To show the status of the turbo ACLs, use the command show access-list compiled:

```
Router# show access-list compiled
```

How to Develop ACLs

There are a few guidelines that you want to consider when developing ACLs. Table 7.3 lists those considerations.

TABLE 7.3 ACL development guidelines

Guideline	Description
Use your security policy to guide your ACL development.	You should always consult your security policy to ensure that your ACL development complies and achieves the desired result.
Write out your ACLs.	Getting your thoughts on paper before you start enhances your chances of achieving your goal.
Use a development system.	Have a place to store and develop your ACLs and have a library of previously used ACLs to refer to.
Test your ACLs.	It's always best if you can test your ACLs on a lab system before you put them into production.

Applying ACLs to Router Interfaces

You can create ACLs all day, but they don't mean a thing until you apply them to an interface. Figure 7.2 shows the directions in which ACLs are applied to the router interfaces. The inbound, or in, direction means traffic being sent toward the router interface from the local LAN or WAN interface. Outbound, or out, means traffic outbound from the router to the local LAN or WAN.

FIGURE 7.2 ACL directions

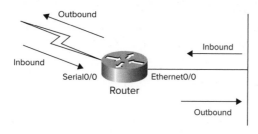

The way you apply an ACL is very important, so make sure you are accomplishing your goals when you apply it. You apply your access list through the `ip access-group` command:

```
Router(config-if)# ip access-group 101 in
```

Filtering Traffic with ACLs

The first thing you want to filter are addresses that could be spoofed. If you don't let these in or out of the network in the first place, your risk is much lower. So let's start with IP spoofing filters.

We want to filter IP spoofing attacks from both directions:

- IP address spoofing – inside
- IP address spoofing – outside

Let's examine the example in Figure 7.3.

FIGURE 7.3   Filtering IP spoofing attacks

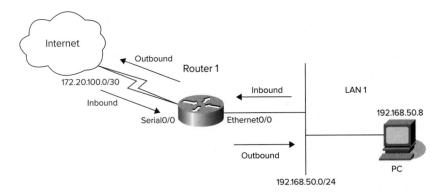

In this example, I do not want internal addresses that reside on LAN 1 to be able to come into that LAN interface from other locations. Also, I don't want the following other addresses to come into the LAN interface.

- RFC 1918 addresses
- Local host addresses (127.0.0.0/8)
- IP multicast address range (224.0.0.0/4)
- Internal addresses (192.168.50.0/24)

Access Control Lists

Here's an access list that would deny access to the addresses just used:

```
Router1(config)# access-list 101 deny 192.168.0.0 0.0.255.255 any log
Router1(config)# access-list 101 deny 172.16.0.0 0.15.255.255 any log
Router1(config)# access-list 101 deny 10.0.0.0 0.255.255.255 any log
Router1(config)# access-list 101 deny 127.0.0.0 0.255.255.255 any log
Router1(config)# access-list 101 deny 192.168.50.0 0.0.0.255 any log
```

But where to apply it?

In this case, you would want these addresses to be filtered going into the Serial0/0 address:

```
Router1(config)# interface serial0/0
Router1(config-if)# access-group 101 in
```

And that covers spoofing from outside. But what about from the inside?

From the inside you want to permit all the inside addresses, but no others. The following access list 110 accomplishes that:

```
Router1(config)# access-list 110 permit 192.168.50.0 0.0.0.255 any log
Router1(config)# access-list 110 deny ip any any log
Router1(config)# interface ethernet0/0
Router1(config-if)# access-group 110 in
```

Now we move on to attack vectors such as denial of service (DoS). ICMP (ping) can be used to cause DoS attacks, so you may want to filter that from coming in to the router:

```
Router1(config)# access-list 120 deny icmp any any echo log
Router1(config)# access-list 120 deny icmp any any redirect log
Router1(config)# access-list 120 deny icmp any any mask-request log
Router1(config)# access-list 120 permit icmp any 192.168.50.0 0.0.0.255
```

The following instructions allow any ping destined for the local LAN to flow to that network but block all the rest:

```
Router1(config)# access-list 130 permit icmp 192.168.50.0 0.0.0.255 any echo
Router1(config)# access-list 130 permit icmp 192.168.50.0 0.0.0.255 any
parameter-problem
Router1(config)# access-list 130 permit icmp 192.168.50.0 0.0.0.255 any
packet-too-big
Router1(config)# access-list 130 permit icmp 192.168.50.0 0.0.0.255 any
source-quench
Router1(config)# access-list 130 deny icmp any any log
Router1(config)# interface e0/0
Router1(config-if)# ip access-group 130 out
```

ICMP is now blocked in both directions. Let's look at our last ACL topic, which is service filtering. You will want to filter access to the following services:

- VTY filtering
- SNMP filtering
- Route filtering

A VTY filter is used to permit only the traffic you'd like to have access via either Telnet or SSH.

```
Router1(config)# access-list 70 permit host 192.168.50.8 log
Router1(config)# access-list 70 deny any log
Router1(config)# line vty 0 4
Router1(config-line)# transport input telnet
Router1(config-line)# login
Router1(config-line)# password p4ssw0rd
Router1(config-line)# access-class 70 in
```

An SNMP filter list works the same way, with a slight difference in syntax due to SNMP configuration. In this case, I am designating that packets matching access list 80 have read-only access, indicated by ro in the following example:

```
Router1(config)# access-list 80 permit host 192.168.50.8
Router1(config)# snmp-server access-list 80 ro
```

Last, but not least, is a distribute list. Distribute lists are used to filter routing information. In this case, I am denying one network, but then permitting everything else. The distribute list is used under the router rip command here, but it applies to any routing protocol:

```
Router1(config)# access-list 14 deny 172.20.100.0 0.0.0.3
Router1(config)# access-list 14 permit any
Router1(config)# router rip
Router1(config-router)# distribute-list 14 out
```

Logical and Performance Considerations for ACLs

When developing your ACLs, there are a number of logical and performance considerations to consider. They are listed in Table 7.4.

TABLE 7.4 Logical and Performance Considerations for ACLs

Consideration	Description
Implicit deny	There is an implicit deny ip any any command at the end of every access list. You do not see it listed in the configuration, but it is there, so it's good to keep this in mind. That means every list needs at least one permit command in it.
Limitation of standard ACLs	Standard ACLs are not effective for most applications because they can filter only the source address(es). Consider using extended ACLs to gain more granularity.
Evaluation order	An access list is scanned and evaluated in sequential order, so it is important to consider where an ACL statement should exist in a given list.
Statement order	Place the most specific ACL statements toward the top of the list, taking care to see that you don't negate a statement later in the ACL.
Directional filtering	Make sure you have the right direction for your ACL. Inbound means toward the router interface. Outbound means away from the interface.
ACL placement	When placing ACLs in a network, you want to place the extended ACLs close to the source and standard ACLs close to the destination.
Router-generated packets	When you place an ACL on an interface, it filters traffic passing through the router; however, packets generated by the router going outbound are not filtered.
Modifying numbered ACLs	In Cisco IOS 12.3, you can use numeric sequence numbers to edit your ACLs. Prior to this release, you had to copy the list offline, edit it, remove the old one, and paste in the new one. In 12.3 and above, you can paste in a statement at the particular sequence number that you desire. You can also delete individual line(s) from an ACL.

The Cisco IOS Firewall

The Cisco IOS Firewall feature set provides a stateful security software component to the traditional IOS router software. It allows you to provide a firewall to a router environment, where a separate, hardware firewall is not feasible from either a cost or design perspective.

The Cisco IOS Firewall feature set includes the following functions:

- Authentication proxy to control access to resources
- Transparent firewall support
- Stateful packet inspection for true firewall function
- Application inspection for protection of common protocols and applications
- Protection against distributed denial of service (DDoS) attacks
- Logging of transactions and support for audit and alerts

The following sections provide an overview.

Authentication Proxy

Authentication proxy is a method by which you can restrict access to certain resources by requiring users to authenticate. This support is usually tied to sending authentication requests to servers elsewhere in the network. It commonly uses AAA services on the router to do so. AAA-supported servers include RADIUS and TACACS, as well as others. A typical application would grant outbound access to the Internet. Users who try to access the Internet using a browser are prompted for a username and password to gain access. The username and password are sent to the authentication server to determine whether the user has access to the resource requested.

Transparent Firewall

The transparent firewall is a new feature that was first introduced in IOS 12.3(7)T on limited platforms and is now in mainline release starting in 12.4(1). A *transparent firewall* can be used when you want to have a firewall in between network segments where introducing a layer 3 firewall is impractical for whatever reason. Transparent firewall utilizes layer 2 bridging and applies the IOS firewall between those segments that are bridged.

Stateful Packet Inspection

Context-Based Access Control (CBAC) was the first implementation of *stateful packet inspection (SPI)* based in Cisco's IOS software. Prior to the introduction of CBAC, static layer 3 ACLs were the norm, and there was no tracking of the state of a connection. CBAC introduced a way to do more than just permit or deny, based on IP address or port usage. This functionality was introduced in IOS version 11.2p.

Context-Based Access Control

CBAC, also referred to as stateful packet inspection, is the core component in Cisco's stateful firewall in IOS. The inspection uses ACLs to determine traffic to filter but is augmented with the ability to monitor several attributes in TCP, UDP, and ICMP packets to ensure that traffic permitted is legitimate return traffic from connections originating on the inside or secure side of the firewall.

Context-Based Access Control

Let's talk a bit about the process for CBAC and how it works. Figure 7.4 shows the basic components.

FIGURE 7.4   Cisco IOS CBAC components

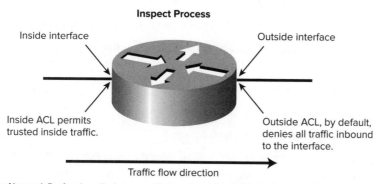

Inspect Process

Inside interface

Outside interface

Inside ACL permits trusted inside traffic.

Outside ACL, by default, denies all traffic inbound to the interface.

Traffic flow direction

Source: *Cisco Network Professional's Advanced Internetworking Guide* by Patrick J. Conlan.

 Real World Scenario

Remote Office Security

A fictitious retail company we will call OutiTech Furniture has many folks who work out of their home offices. Each home office has a broadband connection and a Cisco ISR router. The router supplies a VPN connection back to company headquarters and provides for Internet access. Let's examine one such home office. The user of this home office is a buyer for the company. In particular, he buys rare furniture for the company to sell in its boutique furniture stores. In this case, the buyer is in Denver and is searching on the Internet for sales to attend for the purpose of buying more rare furniture. He is scouring the Internet looking for some Victorian pieces. CBAC is in place on the Internet connection. Let's take a look and examine what happens when a packet leaves the buyer's PC and heads out to the Internet.

The buyer opens his favorite browser, intending to search for those Victorian pieces. He likes using Bing to search. As soon as he types `http://www.bing.com` and presses Enter, a packet leaves the PC headed toward the router and then the Internet. The packet will first be checked against an outgoing access list, it will be inspected, and state information will be saved. Because the state information is saved, a temporary inbound access list is configured to allow that return traffic to come back from Bing's servers. The packet is then allowed out at this point. On the return trip, the packet will be evaluated against the inbound access list. Because CBAC added the temporary inbound list, the packet is allowed back in. And that's a quick look at a CBAC scenario. The step-by-step process is outlined below:

1. Packet is sent from a workstation toward the Internet.

2. Packet is checked against outgoing access list.

3. Packet is inspected and state information is saved as a new state table entry.

4. State information is used to create a temporary access list that allows return traffic back in.

5. Packet is allowed out to the Internet.

6. Return traffic comes back to the outside interface.

7. Packet is checked against the inbound access list.

8. Because the packet is part of the original outbound conversation and therefore matches the inbound access list, the packet is allowed back to original host.

9. Packet is inspected again.

10. When the conversation is terminated or times out, the temporary access list is removed.

Figure 7.5 shows how TCP packets are handled; Figure 7.6 shows the process for UDP handling.

FIGURE 7.5   Cisco IOS firewall TCP handling

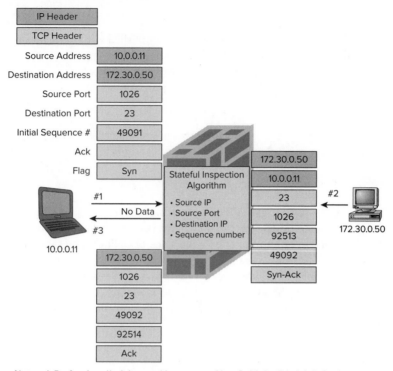

Source: *Cisco Network Professional's Advanced Internetworking Guide* by Patrick J. Conlan.

FIGURE 7.6   Cisco IOS firewall UDP handling

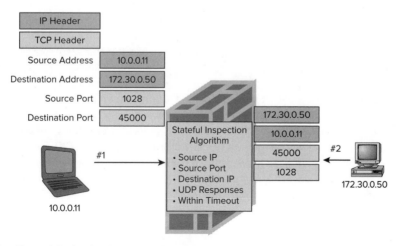

Source: *Cisco Network Professional's Advanced Internetworking Guide* by Patrick J. Conlan.

DDoS Protection

Distributed denial of service (DDoS) is a very real attack vector in today's Internet environment. DDoS attacks are used to deny resources for political purposes, extortion attempts, and just to show you it can be done. The attack is usually accomplished with *botnets*—hundreds and even thousands of disparate computers that have been taken over by malware and are under the control remotely of a command and control computer, usually run by hackers or criminal organizations.

 Real World Scenario

Online Ticket Outlet under Attack

A new online ticket outlet called OnlineTix has been steadily winning market share from the competition, who has reigned over the market for years. A misguided employee of the competition has decided to attempt to cripple the sales of OnlineTix by renting a botnet from a Russian hacker. That employee launches a distributed denial of service using the botnet during the peak sales time when tickets for the new teen star Jenna Nevada's new-world tour went on sale. The data center where OnlineTix's servers are housed are behind a group of Cisco routers. Lucky for them, the IOS Firewall DDoS protections were configured before the attack started.

The Cisco IOS Firewall feature set includes protections against DDoS attacks with some default settings that are activated when an inspection rule is applied. These monitor and regulate TCP SYN half-open connections.

Half-Open Connections

Whenever someone sends a packet to a service that is listening on a specific TCP port, a *half-open connection* can occur. Initially, a SYN packet is sent to the TCP port, which responds with a SYN-ACK. Because DDoS packets are generated artificially, there is no way to complete the TCP three-way handshake with an acknowledgement (ACK). The connection remains open because the firewall is expecting a completion that never happens. Generate enough of these and you start chewing up valuable resources on the firewall and legitimate connections cannot be made.

When the default inspect settings are in place, some finite thresholds are set for half-open connections. When these are met, you can send a reset or just kill the connection. Once the connection is reset or killed, another can take its place.

Configure Cisco IOS Firewall with SDM

You can configure an IOS firewall using the Cisco Security Device Manager (SDM). You should be familiar with the basic operation of SDM now, after using it in previous chapters. However, you will use a different tab for this configuration. As in the past, click the Configure tab at the top of the screen. Next, click on the Firewall and ACL selection on the left side of the screen in the Taskbar, as shown in Figure 7.7.

FIGURE 7.7   Cisco Router and Security Device Manager Firewall and ACL settings

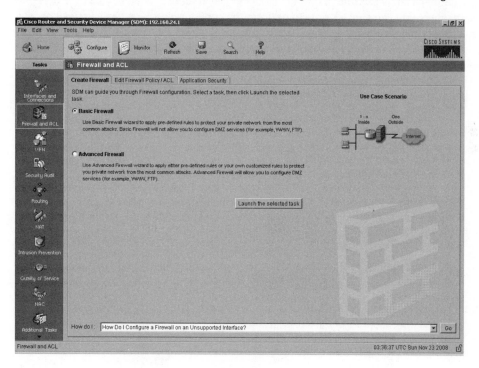

There are three tabs on this screen, but you will start with the first one (default), which is Create Firewall.

Basic Firewall

There are two options for creating a firewall using the SDM. The first and default selection is Basic Firewall. Basic Firewall is used when you don't have a demilitarized zone (DMZ) in place and are not offering services externally. The basic firewall uses predefined rules and provides basic protection against common attacks. A common use for this configuration would be a remote office that has a single Internet connection.

 Real World Scenario

Protecting OutiTech Remote Offices

Going back to the example from earlier in the chapter, let's examine OutiTech's small remote office in Tysons Corner, Virginia. It's a four-person office that performs sales for the Atlantic seaboard. This office is certainly not large enough to warrant an investment in a fixed hardware firewall, but it still needs the functionality. So the two-person IT department decided that a small ISR router with the IOS Firewall feature set would be just the ticket. Here's where you come in; it's time to perform the configuration for a basic firewall because this office is connected to only the Internet and has the aforementioned four persons on the local LAN. This is a fairly simple configuration, but it still requires a high level of security. Let's jump right in and use SDM to configure a basic firewall that allows the work to be done and also allows Internet access but still protects the resources on the local LAN. The following illustration shows the Internet connection.

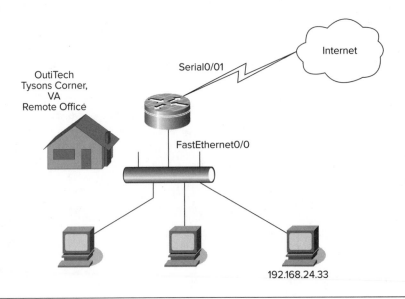

Take a look at Cisco's use case scenario shown in Figure 7.5. This gives you a idea of what I was just describing. I'll come back to the advanced firewall configuration later on in the chapter.

The next screen presented by the wizard (shown in Figure 7.8) outlines exactly what will happen when you configure a basic firewall. As you can see, default rules are applied both inbound and outbound, default inspection rules are deployed, and IP unicast reverse-path forwarding is enabled on the outside interface.

FIGURE 7.8   Cisco Router and Security Device Manager Basic Firewall Configuration Wizard

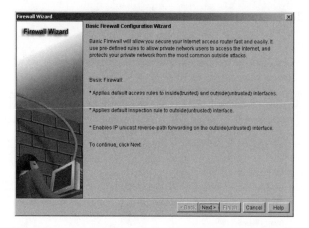

IP Unicast Reverse-Path Forwarding

Without getting into detail, *IP unicast reverse-path forwarding* is a method of having the router verify the reachability of the source IP address. This is important when trying to limit malicious traffic from entering your network. Many options are available with this feature, so be aware: If you use the default as the wizard does, the least restrictive functionality is enabled.

The next screen, shown in Figure 7.9, is the interface configuration screen. As would be expected, you have to select an outside or untrusted interface (usually facing the Internet) and an inside interface that is usually not facing the Internet (typically a LAN interface) and therefore is a trusted interface.

FIGURE 7.9   Basic Firewall Interface Configuration screen

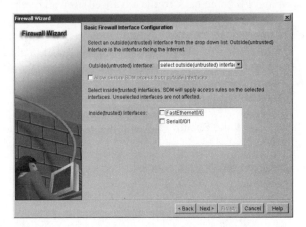

For the Tyson's Corner firewall, the outside interface is Serial0/0/1, which goes to the Internet. The inside interface is FastEthernet0/0. Figure 7.10 shows selections.

FIGURE 7.10   Selecting the outside and inside interfaces in the Basic Firewall Interface Configuration screen

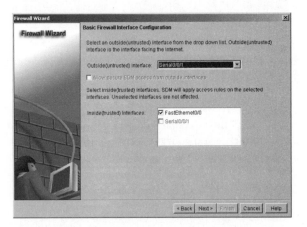

Once you've selected the inside and outside interfaces, click Next to configure the firewall. The configuration summary (Figure 7.11) shows what actions were taken on which interface.

FIGURE 7.11   Internet Firewall Configuration Summary screen

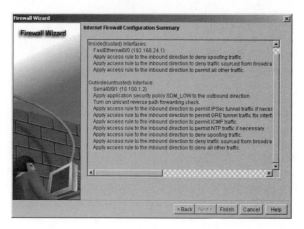

I'll show you how to configure this from an IOS command line a little bit later in the chapter. For now, remember that all of these actions are canned, so to speak, and the only customization available in the basic firewall is the inside and outside interface selection. Later in the chapter, I'll show you other options that are available using SDM.

And, of course, we must deliver the configuration to the router. If you're using the wizard, click Finish to perform this task. Figure 7.12 shows the commands delivery status message. By now this should be routine. As you can see, 49 command entries were delivered to the router by the wizard.

FIGURE 7.12   Commands Delivery Status dialog box

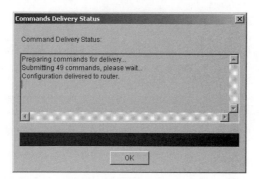

To complete the whole experience, take a look at Figure 7.13. If you see this message, it's obvious that you successfully completed this configuration task.

FIGURE 7.13   Successful configuration message

Once the configuration is complete, you can see graphically which commands have been delivered to the router and which policies are in place on the Edit Firewall Policy/ACL tab (Figure 7.14). You now have the option to edit what was delivered as needed. The default view shows you the rules as they apply to outbound packets.

FIGURE 7.14   Cisco Router and Security Device Manager Edit Firewall Policy/ ACL settings

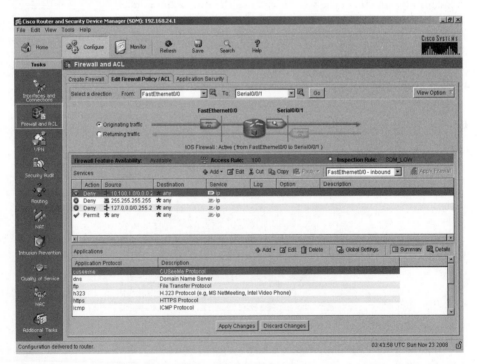

If you click the drop-down list for the From direction, you can change the packet direction and look at the rules and policies that are applied to packets traveling from Serial0/0/1 to FastEthernet0/0, as shown in Figure 7.15.

FIGURE 7.15   Selecting a packet direction in the Edit Firewall Policy/ACL tab

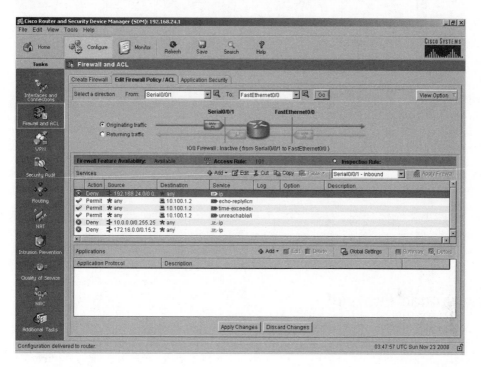

Click the Application Security tab to review application security policies that were put in place. The initial view, Figure 7.16, shows you what the SDM_LOW policy has set as far as inspection. The initial view is of the E-mail section, where you can see which applications will be inspected. (A checked box indicates that an inspection policy is in place for that application.) Each checked item is converted to an inspect statement in the command line. By default, ESMTP, IMAP, and POP3 email applications are inspected. Inspection policies can also be put in place for email, instant messaging, and peer-to-peer networks. URL, HTTP, and application/protocol filtering is also available. Click a task button to view the settings that were put in place by the wizard and edit the selections to fit your operations.

FIGURE 7.16 Cisco Router and Security Device Manager Application Security tab

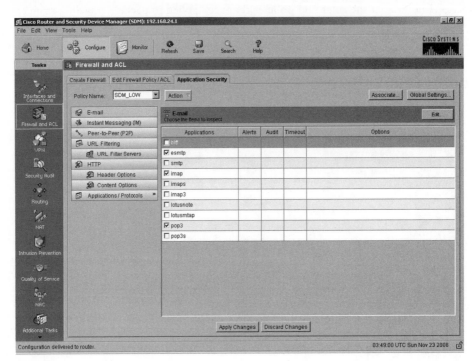

Advanced Firewall

Next we will move on to the Advanced Firewall configuration.

Let's suppose that OutiTech Furniture's regional salesperson on the West Coast works at a home office and has decided to offer up her own website for the purposes of doing online order taking. Since this is a small operation, she doesn't expect it to be a high-volume business.

But, before OutiTech will allow her to offer a website online, it requires a DMZ segment on her firewall. Her router has an unused FastEthernet interface that would be perfect for the DMZ, as shown in Figure 7.17. You've already activated the interface and it is available for use. Now that an interface for the DMZ is available, you must set rules to allow access inbound from the Internet for HTTP, in this case. So let's jump right into the configuration of the advanced firewall.

In SDM, go back to the Create Firewall tab. Select Advanced Firewall and then click Launch The Selected Task. Figure 7.18 shows the Create Firewall tab with Advanced Firewall selected.

FIGURE 7.17   OutiTech regional sales home office Internet connection

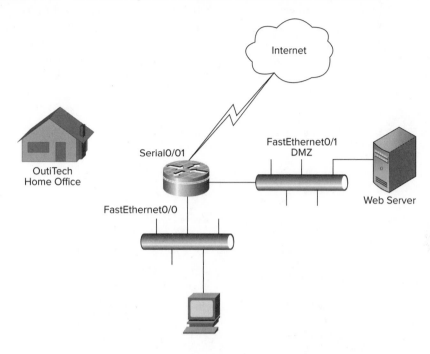

FIGURE 7.18   Cisco Router and Security Device Manager Create Firewall tab

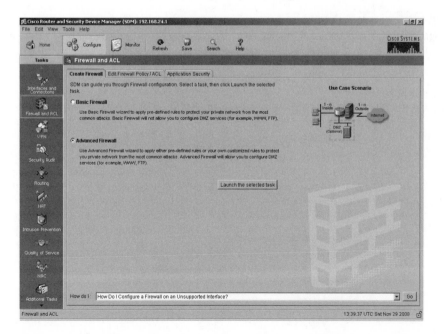

Again, as shown in Figure 7.19, the wizard gives you a summary of the tasks required to configure the firewall. Compared to the basic firewall wizard, the major difference is that the Advanced Firewall Configuration Wizard offers the option to configure a DMZ interface. You would set up a DMZ when you have services exposed to the Internet, such as a publicly available web server or an externally available Outlook Web Access email server. You can also use a DMZ to separate network segments. For instance, marketing might not need access to finance and vice versa.

FIGURE 7.19 Cisco Router and Security Device Manager Advanced Firewall Configuration Wizard

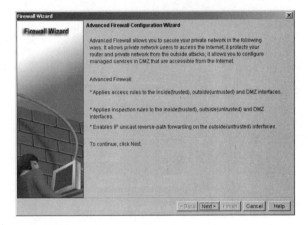

Click Next to move on to the Advanced Firewall Interface Configuration screen, shown in Figure 7.20. Again, it's pretty much the same screen as before, with the notable addition of a DMZ interface selection.

FIGURE 7.20 Advanced Firewall Interface Configuration screen

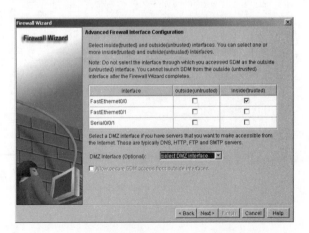

Choose FastEthernet0/1 to serve as the DMZ interface, Serial0/0/1 for the outside interface, and FastEthernet0/0 for the inside interface. Once you've made your selections, your screen should look like Figure 7.21. Notice that the new Ethernet interface, FastEthernet0/1, now shows up as the DMZ interface. As before, Serial0/0/1 is the outside interface and FastEthernet0/0 the inside interface. Click Next to continue.

FIGURE 7.21   Choosing the inside and outside interfaces in the Advanced Firewall Interface Configuration screen

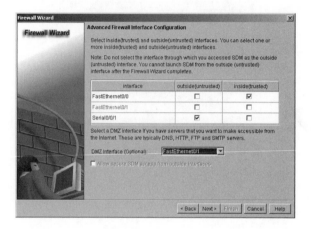

Your next step will be to set up your DMZ. Figure 7.22 shows the Advanced Firewall DMZ Service Configuration screen. A typical scenario might have SMTP, HTTP, and HTTPS services deployed in a DMZ. Click the Add button and move on to the creation of some services.

FIGURE 7.22   Advanced Firewall DMZ Service Configuration screen

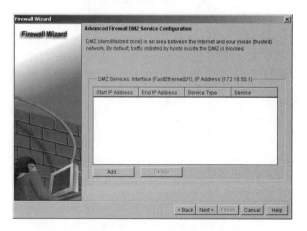

Figure 7.23 shows the DMZ Service Configuration dialog box. This is where you start to configure the host for the bid website. Then, you can select either TCP or UDP and the port number of the service. When you've finished, you can use this dialog box to configure another host. Simply choose Add again.

FIGURE 7.23 DMZ Service Configuration dialog box

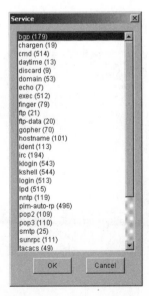

If you click the button with the dots (next to the service box), it brings up the list of services shown in Figure 7.24.

FIGURE 7.24 Service list

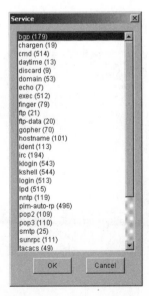

I have configured the web server, shown in Figure 7.25. If you have multiple servers to configure, you will have the opportunity to add more when you get back to the Service Configuration dialog box.

FIGURE 7.25   Web server configured in the DMZ Service Configuration dialog box

Figure 7.26 shows Advanced Firewall DMZ Service Configuration screen with the first service in place. As previously mentioned, you can click Add to configure as many more services as required. By the way, since it is not unusual to have more than one service on a server, the SDM allows you to configure more than one service. You simply configure each one individually.

FIGURE 7.26   Advanced Firewall DMZ Service Configuration screen with one service configured

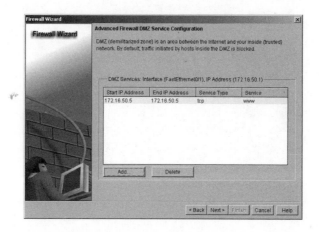

As with the basic firewall wizard, the advanced firewall wizard allows you to review the configuration commands that are going to be sent to the router. These are the inspect commands that are going to be delivered. Figure 7.27 shows the preview screen. When you've finished reviewing the inspect commands, click Close.

FIGURE 7.27 Preview SDM Application Security Policy dialog box

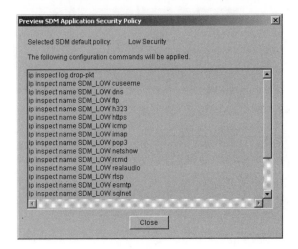

Now that you have configured the application security policy, you can move on to the firewall configuration. Here you have the option to use a default security policy or a custom one that you have defined. For this exercise, let's move forward with a default Low security policy, as shown in Figure 7.28.

FIGURE 7.28 Advanced Firewall Security Configuration screen

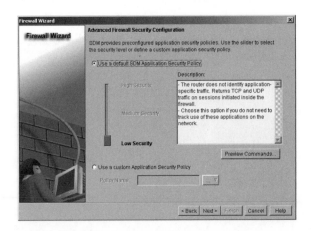

When you click Next, the wizard again, as shown in Figure 7.29, provides a summary of the commands that are going to be delivered to the router. Take particular notice that Context-Based Access Control (CBAC) is going to be activated on the DMZ interface. This is because you configured a service that is to be inspected. Remember that there has to be an access list and an inspect policy; a policy by itself or an access list by itself is useless.

FIGURE 7.29   Internet Firewall Configuration Summary screen box

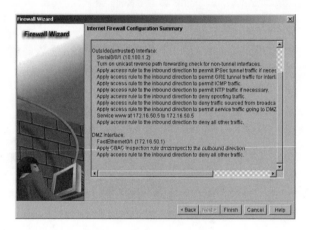

Next, as shown in Figure 7.30, you see the familiar delivery status screen. Note that the number of commands to be delivered is larger because the office now has a DMZ interface and this makes the configuration more complex.

FIGURE 7.30   Commands Delivery Status dialog box

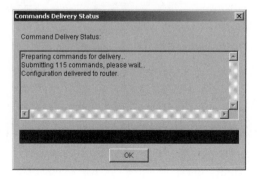

And finally, as shown in Figure 7.31, you are back to the Edit Firewall Policy/ACL tab. Here you can see all of the things that have been configured for the router. And, as before, you can review rules and policies for the reverse direction by clicking the appropriate buttons.

FIGURE 7.31   Cisco Router and Security Device Manager Edit Firewall Policy/ACL tab showing advanced firewall settings

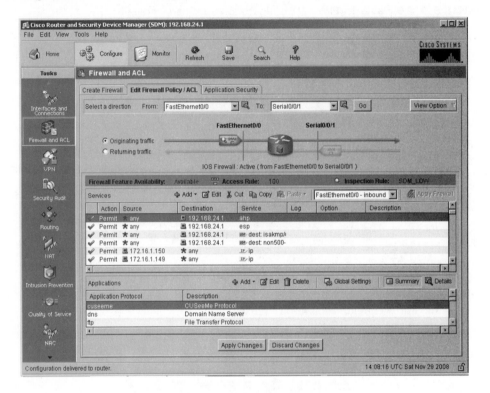

That completes your configuration with the advanced firewall wizard. I'll review the configuration with you from a command-line perspective in the next section so you can get a more detailed look at what was sent to the router.

Verify Cisco IOS Firewall Configurations

Now that you have seen the various configurations using the SDM, I'll show you what was configured from a command-line perspective and discuss those configurations in a bit more detail.

Basic Firewall

Starting with the access list section, we'll go through the configurations for a basic firewall. As you will recall, the basic firewall didn't give you a lot of options for configuring things; it just put some defaults out there. Actually, the basic firewall wizard gave you no options. So, let's take a look at some snippets of the configuration using the command-line interface.

Inspection Commands for the Basic Firewall

Let's have a look at the command-line interface code that shows the inspection process that you configured for the basic firewall. Because the default preconfigured selection was used, the inspect name is SDM_LOW. The inspection policy that is put in place when you select the defaults is what Cisco has designated as the minimum inspection level policy.

```
ip inspect name SDM_LOW cuseeme
ip inspect name SDM_LOW dns
ip inspect name SDM_LOW ftp
ip inspect name SDM_LOW h323
ip inspect name SDM_LOW https
ip inspect name SDM_LOW icmp
ip inspect name SDM_LOW imap
ip inspect name SDM_LOW pop3
ip inspect name SDM_LOW netshow
ip inspect name SDM_LOW rcmd
ip inspect name SDM_LOW realaudio
ip inspect name SDM_LOW rtsp
ip inspect name SDM_LOW esmtp
ip inspect name SDM_LOW sqlnet
ip inspect name SDM_LOW streamworks
ip inspect name SDM_LOW tftp
ip inspect name SDM_LOW tcp
ip inspect name SDM_LOW udp
ip inspect name SDM_LOW vdolive
```

As you can see, the SDM_LOW is set up for applications that might be used from inside the network to go out to the Internet.

HTTP Commands for the Basic Firewall

Let's take a look at a common application that is used, HTTP. HTTP is the HyperText Transfer Protocol but is also commonly referred to as web traffic or port 80, because it is the protocol used in web browsing. To have a web session with a website on the Internet, an outgoing access list would have to exist. A temporary inbound access list would be installed for the duration of the session. This is provided as the CBAC function monitors the state of the connection.

Inside Interface and Outbound ACL Commands for the Basic Firewall

Moving right along, here is the interface FastEthernet0/0, which is designated as the inside interface for the firewall. The only command that is applied here is the access list inbound. The wizard applied that access list using the statement `ip access-group 100 in`.

```
interface FastEthernet0/0
description $FW_INSIDE$
ip address 192.168.24.1 255.255.255.0
ip access-group 100 in
duplex auto
speed auto
!
```

Outside Interface and Inbound ACL Commands for the Basic Firewall

Next, take a look at the outside interface for the firewall, Serial0/0/1. The wizard applied three commands to this interface. The command `access -list 101` was set in the inbound direction. Also, because this is an external-facing interface, the `ip verify unicast reverse-path` command is placed here. Remember that this command attempts to verify the path to avoid spoofing. Last, the inspect rule is applied to the outside, or external-facing, interface. The wizard implemented the default `SDM_LOW` rule set.

```
!
interface Serial0/0/1
description $FW_OUTSIDE$
ip address 10.100.1.2 255.255.255.0
ip access-group 101 in
ip verify unicast reverse-path
ip inspect SDM_LOW out
```

Access Lists Commands for the Basic Firewall

Two access lists were applied to the interfaces. Let's start with access list 100, which was applied inbound to the FastEthernet0/0 interface. First, traffic that would be identified as from the Serial0/0/1 interface is denied access to prevent spoofing. Because the command is applied inbound to the interface, only spoofing traffic would ever be inbound here. This command is followed by a couple of antispoofing statements that disallow the Internet loopback space and an IANA-reserved block.

```
access-list 100 remark auto generated by SDM firewall configuration
access-list 100 remark SDM_ACL Category=1
access-list 100 deny ip 10.100.1.0 0.0.0.255 any
access-list 100 deny ip host 255.255.255.255 any
access-list 100 deny ip 127.0.0.0 0.255.255.255 any
access-list 100 permit ip any any
access-list 101 remark auto generated by SDM firewall configuration
access-list 101 remark SDM_ACL Category=1
access-list 101 deny ip 192.168.24.0 0.0.0.255 any
access-list 101 permit icmp any host 10.100.1.2 echo-reply
access-list 101 permit icmp any host 10.100.1.2 time-exceeded
access-list 101 permit icmp any host 10.100.1.2 unreachable
access-list 101 deny ip 10.0.0.0 0.255.255.255 any
access-list 101 deny ip 172.16.0.0 0.15.255.255 any
access-list 101 deny ip 192.168.0.0 0.0.255.255 any
access-list 101 deny ip 127.0.0.0 0.255.255.255 any
access-list 101 deny ip host 255.255.255.255 any
access-list 101 deny ip host 0.0.0.0 any
access-list 101 deny ip any any log
!
```

 If you want to get into more detail on these special antispoofing addresses, check out RFC 3330 and RFC 3704.

The wizard allows all the rest of the legitimate traffic. The permit ip any any statement does just that. So much for the inside interface.

Now, take a look at the access list for the outside interface, access list 101. As with the previous access list, the first thing the wizard did was prevent traffic from the other interface's address space—again, any such traffic is not legitimate. Next, because this is an external interface, the wizard allowed specific ICMP statements. The first one allows a ping reply. The next statement allows the firewall to respond with a time-exceeded message. This can be important in troubleshooting. And last, unreachable messages are allowed.

The next set of statements basically deny everything inbound. The first set denies RFC 1918 addresses inbound. The assumption here is that the RFC 1918 addresses are prohibited from being routed on the Internet. The Internet is connected on the outside interface.

 You might run into some problems if you used the wizard to create an internal firewall and you used RFC 1918 addresses in your internal network. But don't get hung up on that right now.

Moving down to the last statement, you find a deny ip any any log statement. You might be asking yourself, "Why not just use the one line and be done with it?" The key here is that the keyword log is used on the end of the deny statement. Basically, that's saying you aren't interested in any of the previous statements from a logging perspective but you are interested in everything else. That essentially finishes off the configuration of the basic firewall. It's very basic, but it makes it easy to implement the minimum for a router that isn't offering services to the Internet but does have an interface on the Internet.

Putting It All Together

So, let's take this a step further and follow the path of a packet. We'll examine both directions that it might take in our scenario. Looking back at Figure 7.9, you can see that the rules, such that they are, have been applied in the outbound direction from FastEthernet0/0 to Serial0/0/1.

 Real World Scenario

Remote Office—Crisis Averted

One of OutiTech's home office remote buyers mentioned earlier has been searching for a very specific piece of antique French furniture that is needed for a special order by a customer. The buyer's PC is a host on the inside interface of this network with an IP address of 192.168.24.33. The agent comes across a site that purports to have many rare pieces of antique French furniture for sale. But when he clicks the link, there isn't any furniture listed and the website launches a series of attempts to download Trojan horses to the buyer's PC. Because you have set up CBAC on the router, all the attempts are denied because they were not part of the conversation originated by the buyer's PC. CBAC has averted the crisis!

It's important to note that while this is a legitimate example, no one technology is foolproof and it pays to have multiple levels of defense to combat the threat. With that in mind, let's examine what took place.

If we examine the rules that are applied, the incoming packets first face three deny statements. These are the IP spoofing addresses that I discussed earlier. This means any packet or sender matching those rules would be denied from entering the router on interface FastEthernet0/0.

The next statement is a permit any any, and since the packet didn't match any of the deny statements, it is allowed into the router. So any IP that exists on the FastEthernet0/0 interface will be allowed into the router so long as it doesn't match any of the deny rules you put in place.

Now let's look at the reverse direction. Take a look back at Figure 7.14 and you will see that the originating traffic is now coming in on the Serial0/0/1 interface. A packet faces a few more rules here. First and foremost is the rule denying any traffic from the 192.168.24.0 network. This is an antispoofing rule. Rules are processed in order, so the next three lines are permits that allow some types of ICMP traffic to the outside interface.

The next two lines deny any addresses from the RFC 1918 address space since this address space shouldn't appear on the Internet. And then there are some more antispoofing rules followed by a deny any any statement. So, other than permitting the ICMP traffic to the outside interface, you haven't allowed any traffic into the router.

Advanced Firewall

Now, I want to take you through the advanced firewall configuration. I'll show you a snippet from the configuration that includes all of the relevant sections. Remember that the primary difference in the basic and the advanced firewall configurations is in the use of a DMZ interface.

Inspection Commands for the Advanced Firewall

Here is an excerpt from the show running-configuration output showing all of the relevant sections pertaining to the firewall configuration.

```
ip inspect name SDM_LOW cuseeme
ip inspect name SDM_LOW dns
ip inspect name SDM_LOW ftp
ip inspect name SDM_LOW h323
ip inspect name SDM_LOW https
ip inspect name SDM_LOW icmp
ip inspect name SDM_LOW imap
ip inspect name SDM_LOW pop3
ip inspect name SDM_LOW netshow
ip inspect name SDM_LOW rcmd
ip inspect name SDM_LOW realaudio
ip inspect name SDM_LOW rtsp
ip inspect name SDM_LOW esmtp
ip inspect name SDM_LOW sqlnet
ip inspect name SDM_LOW streamworks
ip inspect name SDM_LOW tftp
ip inspect name SDM_LOW tcp
ip inspect name SDM_LOW udp
ip inspect name SDM_LOW vdolive
ip inspect name dmzinspect tcp
ip inspect name dmzinspect udp
```

Right away you will notice a slight difference in the inspect statements in that some inspection is occurring on that DMZ interface. Other than those last two statements that set up the DMZ inspections, the configuration is the same as you saw for the basic firewall.

Inside Interface and Outbound ACL Commands for the Advanced Firewall

Next, we have the same access list inbound on the inside interface. No change here except that now we have an `ip inspect` statement on this interface.

```
interface FastEthernet0/0
description $FW_INSIDE$
ip address 192.168.24.1 255.255.255.0
ip access-group 100 in
ip inspect SDM_LOW in
duplex auto
speed auto
crypto map SDM_CMAP_1
!
```

DMZ Interface and ACL Commands for the Advanced Firewall

Here is a look at the DMZ interface. It looks similar to the outside interface on a basic firewall, but notice that we have the inspect statement in the outbound direction.

```
interface FastEthernet0/1
description $ETH-LAN$$FW_DMZ$
ip address 172.16.50.1 255.255.255.0
ip access-group 101 in
ip inspect dmzinspect out
duplex auto
speed auto
!
```

Outside Interface and Inbound ACL Commands for the Advanced Firewall

Taking a look at the outside interface, you can see a typical configuration with an access list and, as before, a verify unicast reverse-path statement.

```
interface Serial0/0/1
description $FW_OUTSIDE$
ip address 10.100.1.2 255.255.255.0
ip access-group 102 in
ip verify unicast reverse-path
```

So now, let's look at the actual access lists and see what is different here from the basic firewall.

```
!
ip local pool SDM_POOL_1 172.16.1.100 172.16.1.150
!
```

Okay, this line is here for a reason. Obviously, a local pool of addresses is defined. It is a holdover from a previous remote access VPN connection. Why is it relevant? When you look at the following access lists, you will notice that the SDM took note of this and created an access list that reflects the addresses that are part of the pool. The wizard takes into account all local addresses, not just those assigned to a specific interface. For instance, if the remote VPN access was enabled, then those connecting would get a local address from the local pool configured. They would be treated just like someone connected on the local LAN.

```
!
access-list 100 remark auto generated by SDM firewall configuration
access-list 100 remark SDM_ACL Category=1
access-list 100 permit ahp any host 192.168.24.1
access-list 100 permit esp any host 192.168.24.1
access-list 100 permit udp any host 192.168.24.1 eq isakmp
access-list 100 permit udp any host 192.168.24.1 eq non500-isakmp
access-list 100 permit ip host 172.16.1.150 any
access-list 100 permit ip host 172.16.1.149 any
access-list 100 permit ip host 172.16.1.148 any
access-list 100 permit ip host 172.16.1.147 any
access-list 100 permit ip host 172.16.1.146 any
access-list 100 permit ip host 172.16.1.145 any
access-list 100 permit ip host 172.16.1.144 any
access-list 100 permit ip host 172.16.1.143 any
access-list 100 permit ip host 172.16.1.142 any
access-list 100 permit ip host 172.16.1.141 any
access-list 100 permit ip host 172.16.1.140 any
access-list 100 permit ip host 172.16.1.139 any
access-list 100 permit ip host 172.16.1.138 any
access-list 100 permit ip host 172.16.1.137 any
access-list 100 permit ip host 172.16.1.136 any
access-list 100 permit ip host 172.16.1.135 any
access-list 100 permit ip host 172.16.1.134 any
access-list 100 permit ip host 172.16.1.133 any
access-list 100 permit ip host 172.16.1.132 any
access-list 100 permit ip host 172.16.1.131 any
```

```
access-list 100 permit ip host 172.16.1.130 any
access-list 100 permit ip host 172.16.1.129 any
access-list 100 permit ip host 172.16.1.128 any
access-list 100 permit ip host 172.16.1.127 any
access-list 100 permit ip host 172.16.1.126 any
access-list 100 permit ip host 172.16.1.125 any
access-list 100 permit ip host 172.16.1.124 any
access-list 100 permit ip host 172.16.1.123 any
access-list 100 permit ip host 172.16.1.122 any
access-list 100 permit ip host 172.16.1.121 any
access-list 100 permit ip host 172.16.1.120 any
access-list 100 permit ip host 172.16.1.119 any
access-list 100 permit ip host 172.16.1.118 any
access-list 100 permit ip host 172.16.1.117 any
access-list 100 permit ip host 172.16.1.116 any
access-list 100 permit ip host 172.16.1.115 any
access-list 100 permit ip host 172.16.1.114 any
access-list 100 permit ip host 172.16.1.113 any
access-list 100 permit ip host 172.16.1.112 any
access-list 100 permit ip host 172.16.1.111 any
access-list 100 permit ip host 172.16.1.110 any
access-list 100 permit ip host 172.16.1.109 any
access-list 100 permit ip host 172.16.1.108 any
access-list 100 permit ip host 172.16.1.107 any
access-list 100 permit ip host 172.16.1.106 any
access-list 100 permit ip host 172.16.1.105 any
access-list 100 permit ip host 172.16.1.104 any
access-list 100 permit ip host 172.16.1.103 any
access-list 100 permit ip host 172.16.1.102 any
access-list 100 permit ip host 172.16.1.101 any
access-list 100 permit ip host 172.16.1.100 any
access-list 100 deny ip 10.100.1.0 0.0.0.255 any
access-list 100 deny ip 172.16.50.0 0.0.0.255 any
access-list 100 deny ip host 255.255.255.255 any
access-list 100 deny ip 127.0.0.0 0.255.255.255 any
access-list 100 permit ip any any
access-list 101 remark auto generated by SDM firewall configuration
access-list 101 remark SDM_ACL Category=1
access-list 101 deny ip any any log
access-list 102 remark auto generated by SDM firewall configuration
```

```
access-list 102 remark SDM_ACL Category=1
access-list 102 deny ip 172.16.50.0 0.0.0.255 any
access-list 102 deny ip 192.168.24.0 0.0.0.255 any
access-list 102 permit icmp any host 10.100.1.2 echo-reply
access-list 102 permit icmp any host 10.100.1.2 time-exceeded
access-list 102 permit icmp any host 10.100.1.2 unreachable
access-list 102 permit tcp any host 172.16.50.5 eq www
access-list 102 deny ip 10.0.0.0 0.255.255.255 any
```

The next to the last line is where the wizard configured the web server. Notice that the outside interface is allowing any host on the Internet to access the web server IP on port 80. Other than that, it's pretty much the same configuration as a basic firewall, with the notable exception of the DMZ.

Implementing Zone-Based Firewall

The Zone-Based Firewall feature approaches security from a slightly different perspective than the traditional line-by-line access list. In this feature, first found in version 12.4(6)T, you define zones that reflect the way you work rather than defining individual rules for interfaces. The Zone-Based Firewall implements virtually all of the features of the classic firewall, combined with some new features to create a "zone defense."

The traditional access-list firewall was and is interface driven. That is, you must apply traditional source/destination pairs to an interface to permit or deny the traffic desired. But what if you could state default behavior for traffic flowing from one zone to another? Wouldn't that make your life a little easier? For example, what if you had a DMZ segment in which traffic came in from the Internet and was destined for servers that lived in that DMZ segment? Rather than list each and every server, what about using an Internet zone that allows web traffic into the DMZ zone? Sounds like it would save a lot of time and make it easier to administer, doesn't it? Well, that's just a taste of what zone-based firewalls are all about.

Let's look at some of the rules that are in place to govern how interfaces are placed into zones and interaction between zones.

- Before you can put an interface into a zone, you must first define and configure the zone.

- Interfaces may belong to only one security zone.

- Once you assign the interface to a zone, certain rules apply; all interfaces in the same zone can converse, but anything to or from any other zone is implicitly denied, with the notable exception of traffic that is allowed to all router interfaces.

- The way you allow traffic to or from a zone is to configure a policy to do so.

- If an interface does not belong to a zone, then you cannot configure a policy that allows traffic to/from it.

- You may have to configure a policy to pass all traffic to or from specific zones, even if you don't require that an interface be part of a policy.

- As mentioned, traffic is allowed to and from the router by default. However, you can configure a policy that can deny this traffic.

Let's look at a traditional case in which you can apply a zone-based model. Figure 7.32 shows a router with two interfaces: a public one that faces and is connected to the Internet and then a second, internal, private interface for users at the site.

FIGURE 7.32   Basic zone setup

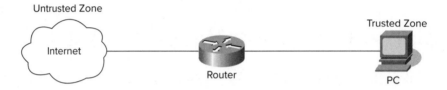

In the example earlier in the chapter, you configured a basic firewall using the wizard inside of SDM. What you created was a zone-based firewall using presets built within SDM. You chose the SDM_LOW policy set and applied it.

When implementing a zone-based policy using Cisco SDM, there are only three actions available:

- Inspect—This action is equivalent to configuring stateful packet inspection.

- Drop—Dropping packets is the same as applying the traditional deny statement.

- Pass—Pass is the equivalent to a simple permit. There is not a stateful component to this because it is implemented in the inspect function.

Summary

In this chapter, you learned about the evolution of firewalls and the different kinds of firewalls over the years. I discussed the stateful firewall as well as the Cisco IOS Firewall feature set and how it can be used. You also learned about and configured both the basic firewall and advanced firewall using the Cisco Security Device Manager. You then learned about the configuration from a command-line perspective and looked more closely at the options the firewall wizard used. The IOS Firewall feature set is a powerful tool to have available for any Internet-facing router. The Zone-Based Firewall adds yet another dimension to your firewall toolset.

Exam Essentials

Remember the evolution of firewalls and the kinds that were discussed.   The four kinds of firewalls are as follows: The first generation was the packet filter firewall, based on access lists or rules. Next came the circuit-level firewall, which mimicked a virtual circuit. The Application-layer firewall, or proxy, was considered the third generation, and finally, the stateful packet inspection firewall or stateful firewall is the current generation.

Know what a stateful firewall is and why it's different than the other types of firewalls.   A stateful firewall is one that uses an internal state table to monitor traffic that is part of an existing connection. It can also inspect packet headers and determine whether traffic is being initiated.

Understand the Cisco SDM for deploying the firewall feature set.   The Cisco SDM can assist with configuring firewall services by using two built-in wizards, one for setting up a basic firewall and one for setting up an advanced firewall. The primary difference in using an advanced firewall is the option to configure a DMZ interface.

Be able to name the features that can be implemented with the Cisco IOS Firewall feature set.   The IOS Firewall feature set includes stateful packet inspection, transparent firewall support, application inspection, and an authentication proxy.

Know the steps in CBAC or stateful packet inspection.   When stateful packet inspection is utilized, a packet is inspected to make sure that first it matches an existing access list. If so, the packet is permitted in the direction noted. Then, when the packet returns, it is inspected again and a temporary access list is put into place to allow that return traffic that was part of the original conversation.

Written Lab

Write the answers to the following questions:

1. If you log in to a router and encounter an access list in the configuration that is numbered access list 101, what type of access list is it?

2. Write the command to apply access list 100 to an interface inbound to the interface.

3. CBAC is also known as what?

4. An Application-layer firewall protects what layer?

5. Which component of Zone-Based Firewall is the same as stateful packet inspection?

6. Which type of firewall was the first generation of firewall?

7. How many kinds of firewalls can you configure with wizards in Cisco SDM?

8. What is meant by implicit deny?

9. What is another name for an Application-layer firewall?

10. At what configuration mode is an access list applied?

(The answers to the written lab can be found following the answers to the review questions.)

Hands-on Lab

In this lab you can use any Cisco router that you have available. You can configure an access list on almost any model, if not every model. This was done on a 2800 series.

Hands-on Lab 7.1: Configuring an Access List

In this lab you will configure an extended access list using the command-line interface.

1. Log into your router and go into privileged mode by typing **en** or **enable**.

2. Enter global configuration mode by typing **config t** or **configure terminal**.

3. Configure an access list 100 that allows traffic to flow from a source IP of 192.168.100.53 to a destination IP of 10.40.1.101 using port 80 as shown here:

```
Router# config t
Enter configuration commands, one per line.  End with
  CNTL/Z.
Router(config)# access-list 100 permit tcp host 192.168.100.53 host 10.40.1.101
eq 80
```

> The router will convert certain well-known ports to keywords that match the ports. For instance, in the preceding code, you typed 80 for web services. But when you finish the exercise and go back to look at what is in the access list, you will see the following code, in which the 80 is replaced with *www*:
>
> access-list 100 permit tcp host 192.168.100.53 host 10.40.1.101 eq www

4. Now you need to apply the access list to an interface, and in this case, you will apply it inbound to the interface.

5. Enter interface configuration mode by typing the following:

```
Router(config)# interface FastEthernet1/0
Router(config-if)# ip access-group 100 in
```

You have completed the configuration of an access list and applied it to an interface.

Review Questions

1. Which function is not an IOS Firewall feature?

   A. Antivirus

   B. DDoS protection

   C. Stateful packet inspection

   D. Access lists

2. What is another name for CBAC?

   A. Protection policy

   B. Stateful packet inspection

   C. Access control

   D. None of the above

3. What is a command that is used to specify inspection?

   A. `policy map`

   B. `access-list`

   C. `transform-set`

   D. `tunnel-list`

4. If you configured an authentication proxy on your firewall, what type of server is supported as an authentication server?

   A. RADIUS

   B. TACACS

   C. All of the above

   D. None of the above

5. What is the primary difference between a basic firewall and an advanced firewall configuration?

   A. A loopback interface

   B. Stateful packet inspection

   C. More access lists

   D. DMZ interface configuration

6. True or false? The `ip unicast verify reverse-path` feature allows specific packets to traverse the firewall.

   A. True

   B. False

7. Which one of the following is not a basic firewall default inspect service?

    A. cuseeme

    B. realaudio

    C. rtmp

    D. https

8. Why would you log your deny statements on the firewall? (Choose all that apply.)

    A. To see who is trying to traverse your network

    B. Audit requirements

    C. Increased performance

    D. Reduced log files

9. True or false? Access lists provide better protection than CBAC for inbound attacks from the Internet.

    A. True

    B. False

10. The transparent firewall takes advantage of which feature in order to provide this service?

    A. IP routing

    B. Virtual access lists

    C. Bridging

    D. Hot Standby Routing Protocol

11. True or false? An IP extended access list uses the range 100 to 200.

    A. True

    B. False

12. What of the following is a correct standard access list?

    A. access-list 200 permit 192.168.10.0

    B. access-list 100 deny 10.1.2.0

    C. access-list 10 permit 192.168.10.0

    D. access-list 10 permit 192.168.10.0 10.1.100.0

13. What is a command used to filter routing updates?

    A. access-list

    B. distribute-list

    C. route-list

    D. access-group

14. Which is *not* one of the guidelines for developing ACLs?

  A. Write them out.

  B. Use a development system.

  C. Test your ACLs.

  D. Send them to a peer.

15. Starting with what version of IOS can you add individual lines to an access list without deleting and replacing the access list?

  A. 12.2

  B. 12.3

  C. 11.3

  D. 12.1

16. True or false? In a standard access list, the source and destination are both present.

  A. True

  B. False

17. What is the command to perform inspection on a particular protocol or service?

  A. `ip inspect`

  B. `inspect`

  C. `inspection`

  D. `ip inspection`

18. What are the best practices for placement of your ACLs? (Choose two.)

  A. Place an extended list close to the source.

  B. Place an extended list close to the destination.

  C. Place a standard list close to the destination.

  D. Place a standard list close to the source.

19. What is at the end of every access list but not displayed?

  A. `end`

  B. `permit ip any any`

  C. Implicit `deny`

  D. Implicit `permit`

20. What is the command to display the status of a turbo ACL?

  A. `show access-list compiled`

  B. `show turbo-acl`

  C. `show access-list turbo`

  D. `show turbo compiled`

Answers to Review Questions

1. **A.** Antivirus capability is not one of the features of the IOS Firewall feature set.

2. **B.** Stateful packet inspection did what CBAC does today.

3. **B.** An access list is used to activate CBAC.

4. **C.** Both RADIUS and TACACS servers are supported.

5. **D.** An advanced firewall configuration includes a DMZ interface.

6. **B.** False. The `ip unicast verify reverse-path` is an antispoofing feature that requires the verification of the reachability of the source address.

7. **C.** RTMP is not one of the services under the basic firewall inspect settings.

8. **A, B.** When you log your deny statements on the firewall, you can monitor those log messages to see who is trying to get into your network. Some auditors also like to see this as a preventative security measure.

9. **B.** False. Access lists are actually part of the CBAC solution, and prior to the implementation of CBAC, static access lists provided less protection than the current CBAC solution.

10. **C.** Bridging is used in the transparent firewall configuration because it might be used where there isn't a possibility to insert new IP ranges.

11. **B.** Almost, but not quite. An IP extended access list uses the range 100 to 199 or 2000 to 2699.

12. **C.** A standard access list uses numbering from 1 to 99 and only source address.

13. **B.** A distribute list is used under the routing configuration to filter routing updates.

14. **D.** When you develop ACLs, you should write them out, use a development system, and test them. There is no guideline about sending them to a peer. You should also make sure your ACL development adheres to your security policy.

15. **B.** In IOS version 12.3, you can add or delete an individual line number within an access list.

16. **B.** False. A standard access list uses only the source address.

17. **A.** The command to perform inspection on certain protocols or services is `ip inspect`.

18. **A, C.** An extended access list should be close to the source and a standard access list should be close to the destination.

19. **C.** An implicit deny is at the end of every access list, even though it doesn't show in the configuration.

20. **A.** The command to display the status of a turbo ACL is `show access-list compiled`. The other options are fictitious.

Answers to Written Lab

1.   Extended access list

2.   `ip access-group 100 in`

3.   Stateful packet inspection

4.   Layers 3, 4, 5, and 7

5.   Inspect

6.   Packet filter firewall

7.   Two, via the basic firewall wizard and the advanced firewall wizard

8.   Implicit deny means that because there isn't a specific rule to allow a packet, it is denied by default.

9.   Proxy is another name for an Application-layer firewall.

10. Global configuration mode and interface configuration mode. The access list is created in global configuration mode and applied within the interface configuration mode.

Chapter

8

Implementing Cisco IOS Intrusion Prevention

THE FOLLOWING CCNA-SECURITY EXAM TOPICS ARE COVERED IN THIS CHAPTER:

✓ Define network based vs. host based intrusion detection and prevention

✓ Explain IPS technologies, attack responses, and monitoring options

✓ Enable and verify Cisco IPS operations using SDM

In this chapter we are going to discuss an important component of any security arsenal, the Intrusion Prevention System (IPS), also discussed in this section is the Intrusion Detection System (IDS). We will cover the differences in the two terms. The reason this topic is important is that you need to have a view into what is happening both inside your network and outside it and be able to take action, sometimes automatically, to thwart a threat.

We will explore the technologies in use with Intrusion Prevention and Detection as well as look at the monitoring options.

In the final section, we will walk through configuring the Cisco IOS IPS using Cisco SDM.

IDS and IPS

Intrusion Detection System (IDS) and *Intrusion Prevention System (IPS)* sensors can help protect your network from malicious traffic. The two systems are deployed differently and work in different ways. Each system has particular strengths and weaknesses when deployed separately, but when used together, IDS and IPS can provide a more robust level of security. In the sections that follow, we will look at each type of system individually and then together to see how to provide a better defense by layering the two technologies.

Introducing the Intrusion Detection System

An IDS is usually defined as a system that is detecting or listening to traffic and sending alerts about it. An IDS usually has no functionality to perform any action (such as dropping a packet); however, some systems may be able to send TCP resets. An IDS typically sees a copy of the traffic sent to a SPAN port (see Chapter 6, "Layer 2 Security," for more on SPAN), in which the IDS is placed.

The active response that the IDS can take is limited because it is primarily a passive device. You can configure the IDS to block malicious traffic using other network devices, but only after it has detected the traffic. The original malicious traffic has already passed through the network to its destination and could not be blocked. The other network devices (for example, security appliances such as the Cisco PIX firewall, Cisco ASA firewall, or routers) can be configured in response to malicious traffic detection to prevent further intrusion. Subsequent traffic in the flow will be blocked by the security device. The IDS is also capable of sending a TCP reset to the end or source host and terminating any malicious TCP connections.

To recap, the functions that the IDS sensor can take when malicious traffic is detected are as follows:

- Send an alert to a management station
- Configure a network device to block traffic
- Send a TCP reset to the traffic source

Basic Functions of the Intrusion Prevention System

The Intrusion Prevention System is characterized as an active device. This is because the device is implemented as an inline sensor and can take action based on the alert type. The IPS requires the use of more than one physical interface or the use of virtual interfaces, and all network traffic must pass through the sensor. Network traffic enters through one interface and exits through another.

 Real World Scenario

PCI Protection for a Remote Office

A remote sales office for the XYZ Corporation has begun taking credit cards for orders placed over the phone. The orders are entered into computers at the remote office, using an application at the corporate headquarters. A recent PCI audit has determined that additional protections need to be in place for the remote office, even though the application is hosted at the corporate office. Your boss has tasked you with solving their problem. You have proposed deploying a Cisco IDS sensor at the remote office. The illustration shows the proposed location of the IDS sensor at the remote office network.

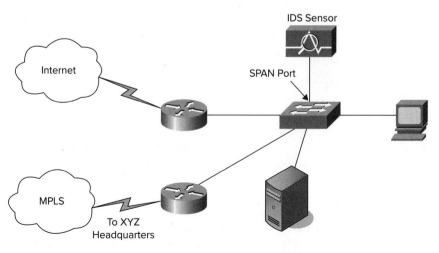

In this configuration, the sensor must be able to see the traffic, so the IDS is placed on a SPAN port on the switch. When an IDS sensor sees a packet that matches a signature for suspicious traffic, it will send an alert to the syslog server. Administrators must then determine if further actions are needed on the firewall.

Adding IPS to the XYZ Corporate Office Network

Based on the success at the XYZ remote office, your boss now wants you to install an IPS in the XYZ corporate office network. This time we are talking about an IPS, which implies that it will be inline. The illustration shows where this device might be placed on the network. Now the IPS can protect the network by taking action on an alert. All traffic headed for the XYZ corporate office network must pass through it.

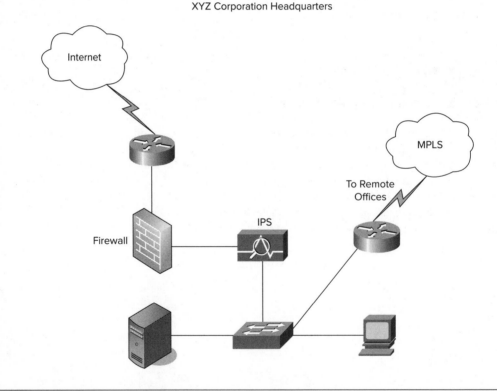

XYZ Corporation Headquarters

An IPS differs from an IDS in that it has the ability to take action. When an IPS detects malicious traffic, it can send an alert to the management station, just like an IDS. But, more importantly, it can immediately block the malicious traffic. The traffic is blocked by the IPS, not by another device, so both the original traffic and subsequent traffic are blocked proactively. IPS prevents the attacks before the traffic enters the network.

The IPS is capable of responding in real time, before network security can be compromised. The most common action for many events is to send an alert and log the event to a syslog or

Security Device Event Exchange (SDEE). You can configure the IPS to perform other actions, as appropriate for a given threat. The IPS can drop the packet, reset the connection, block traffic from a specific source IP address, or block traffic for a specific connection.

The specific actions that an IPS can take are explained here:

Send an alarm The IPS can send an alarm to a syslog server or a centralized management interface. This action is typically combined with other preventive actions.

Drop the packet The IPS can drop the packet. This action is effective for all Internet protocols and prevents malicious packets from reaching the intended target.

Reset the connection The IPS is capable of sending a TCP reset to the end or source host and terminating any malicious TCP connections. This action works only for TCP sessions.

Block traffic The IPS can block traffic from the source IP address of the attacker for a specified amount of time. The IPS can also block traffic on a connection for which an attack signature was seen for a specified amount of time.

Because network attack vectors are becoming more sophisticated, the proactive approach of an IPS is required to protect against network viruses, worms, malicious applications, and vulnerability exploits.

Using IDS and IPS Together

When you consider having one or the other of these sensors on your network, think about the benefits you would get from having both. An IPS sensor is much like a firewall; it can block traffic that is malicious or threatening. It should block only traffic that is known to be a threat, though. IPS should not block legitimate traffic or you could suffer a disruption in connectivity and find that applications are unable to perform their tasks. In some cases, that could mean the company is losing money—never a good thing for an IT person to have caused!

As you design and configure your IPS, you also have to think about the processing overhead and the latency that can be introduced into the traffic path if the IPS sensor is trying to scan for too many things as the traffic passes through. This basically means that you are going to have to tune the IPS device so that it scans only for things that are known to be malicious. This can leave an open or grey area that is not being totally secured.

Enter the IDS sensor. You can place the IDS device into the network so that it verifies or checks on the IPS device. You must tune the IPS so that all of the good traffic is allowed into the network. Anything that may slip in under the radar could then be further scanned by the IDS device. The IDS device can scan for everything. You do not have to worry about IDS dropping something that is legitimate or taking too long and causing delay. A word of caution though; if too little traffic is being filtered on the IPS, then the IDS may see too much and cause performance issues or miss traffic. It's a bit of a balancing act.

In addition to that, you can look at the data between the two devices and see what improvements you might be able to make to the IPS setup if the IDS device keeps detecting threats. It is a great way to stay on top of what is getting into or, even worse, being generated on your network. Also, this might be a good time to verify the security policies on your security devices.

Benefits and Drawbacks of IPS/IDS Sensors

A network-based monitoring system offers the benefit of easily seeing attacks that are occurring across the entire network. Seeing the attacks against the entire network gives a clear indication of the extent to which the network is being attacked. Furthermore, because the monitoring system is examining only traffic from the network, it does not have to support every operating system used on the network.

On the drawbacks side, encryption of the network traffic stream can effectively blind the sensor. Reconstructing fragmented traffic can also be a difficult issue. Possibly the biggest drawback to network-based monitoring is that, as networks become increasingly larger (with respect to bandwidth), it becomes more difficult to place the sensor at a single location in the network and successfully capture all the traffic. Capturing all the traffic requires the use of more sensors throughout the network. However, having multiple sensors increases costs.

Types of IDS and IPS Sensors

Intrusion sensors can be categorized into a few different types or groups based on the approach they use to identify malicious traffic. The second criterion for grouping the sensors is by scope; this means how many systems or what part of the network the sensor is capable of protecting. Scope-based classification is the next topic we will cover.

Sensor Scope

IDS and IPS sensors can be broken into two different scopes of use:

- A network-based sensor is a device placed on the network and is intended to protect many hosts.

- A host-based sensor is generally software, placed on a single system, that protects that single host from attack.

You will generally see acronyms like NIDS, NIPS, HIDS, and HIPS for network-based or host-based IDS or IPS.

In this chapter, we will mostly focus on IPS sensors. IPS is the primary function built into the Cisco IOS for a router, and IPS provides more functionality than IDS.

Network-Based Intrusion Prevention System

Network-based sensors examine packets and traffic that are traversing through the network for known signs of malicious activity. Because these systems are watching network traffic, they will notice attack signatures but they will not be able to determine if the attacks succeed or fail. It is usually difficult, if not impossible, for network-based monitoring systems to assess the success or failure of the actual attacks. They only indicate the presence of intrusive activity.

A network-based Intrusion Prevention System (NIPS) can detect malicious packets that are designed to slip past the simplistic filtering rules of a firewall. NIPS devices are placed in the network to verify traffic (or at least the critical areas of traffic). NIPS is good at preventing lower-layer (meaning Layers 1–3 in the OSI model) attacks, but unfortunately it can't detect threats in encrypted traffic that passes through the sensor. A NIPS device for the most part only sees traffic as it is passing through (not as a flow or sequence of packets). This severely limits the device's ability to correlate traffic with its threat vector.

Host-Based Intrusion Prevention System

A host-based sensor examines information at the local host or operating system. The host-based Intrusion Prevention System (HIPS) has full access to the internal operating system of the workstation, and it can detect changes to things like memory, configuration files, Registry settings (for Windows boxes), and the like. Host-based sensors can be implemented at a couple of different complexity levels. HIPS can be more aggressive and complex when the system is configured to examine actual system calls, or the implementation can be much simpler, just examining system log files. In VPN environments, where encrypted traffic flows through the network, the HIPS is the only option to examine traffic in clear text.

Some host-based monitoring systems can halt attacks before they start, whereas others types of systems only report what has already happened. Cisco has a solution in the host-based Intrusion Prevention System market called Cisco Security Agent (CSA). The Cisco Security Agent is a *shim* (a piece of code that sits between the operating system and the application) that monitors all changes to the operating system of a host computer. The Cisco Security Agent can be deployed on both servers and desktops. The various server and desktop platforms for CSA 6.*x* (latest at the time of this writing) are shown in Table 8.1.

TABLE 8.1 Platforms Supported by Cisco Security Agent 6.*x*

Type of Agent	Platform Support
Server agent	Windows Server 2003
	Windows 2000 Server
	Windows 2000 Advanced Server
	Red Hat Enterprise Linux 4.0 ES and AS
	Red Hat Enterprise Linux 3.0 ES and AS
	Solaris 9 SPARC (64-bit)
	Solaris 8 SPARC (64-bit)
	VMware ESX 3.2
	VMware GSX 3.0 and 2.5
	VMware Server
Desktop agent	Windows Vista
	Windows Embedded
	Windows XP Professional
	Windows XP Tablet
	Windows 2000 Professional
	Red Hat Enterprise Linux 4.0 WS
	Red Hat Enterprise Linux 3.0 WS
	VMware WS 5.x
	VMware Player

As you might have guessed by now, the Cisco Security Agent needs a manager to control and monitor all of those agents. This product is called Cisco Secure Agent Management Center (CSAMC).

However, HIPS is usually made for a specific operating system and does not protect against attacks targeting the lower layers (1–3) of the OSI model. Another disadvantage is that an attacker could, with enough reconnaissance, detect that the host is still there and possibly even figure out that the host has HIPS protecting it. All this really means is that no security technology or protection is foolproof. That's why we use multiple layers of defense to protect our information assets. In Figure 8.1, we show where the different technologies might be used.

FIGURE 8.1   IDS/IPS Placement

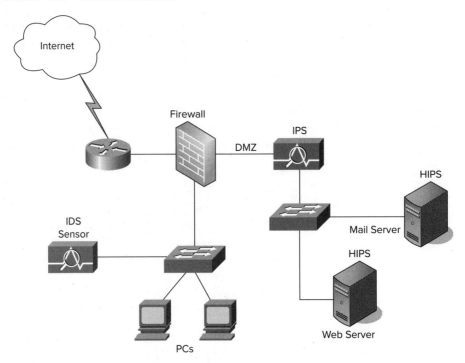

IDS and IPS Approaches

IDS and IPS sensors have a few different approaches they can use to scan for and identify offending traffic. Each of the approaches has benefits and drawbacks, but by using a mix of approaches, you can get very good results. The approaches that the sensors can use include these:

- Signature based
- Policy based
- Anomaly based
- Honeypot

Signature-Based Approach

The signature-based approach is simply pattern matching. The device (IPS or IDS) looks for a specific sequence of bits in a packet or content that is known to be a malicious attack. In some cases this might be a single packet and in others it could be multiple packets. A device using signature-based scanning requires the use of a signature database for data comparison. This type of approach is pretty easy to employ, but (as I am sure you can guess) it doesn't leave any room for dynamic learning.

Typically the system will scan for a signature only if a packet is associated with a particular service (a destination port is usually used). This method can process packets quickly. The inspection process can be made more robust for systems that need to recognize traffic with protocols that do not use well-known ports. For applications such as Trojan horses and their associated traffic, the malicious traffic may be next to impossible to identify using a destination port, because the application changes ports dynamically.

Tuning an IPS sensor can take a bit of doing in that you will likely receive numerous alerts in the time immediately following a new installation. These are called false positives, and they occur when a signature fires on traffic that is not malicious. After the system is tuned and adjusted to the specific network parameters, there will be fewer false alerts than with a policy-based approach (discussed next).

Policy-Based Approach

A policy-based approach to intrusion detection uses an algorithm to make decisions. For example, let's say that a sensor on the XYZ network scans for port sweeps on all of the systems for a given subnet. A policy-based sensor has been implemented that detects a port sweep. The policy can be set to look for the presence of a unique port or set of ports that are being scanned on a particular machine. When a specific threshold of ports or packets probing the ports is reached, the policy sends an alarm. The policy could be further restricted or filtered to look for specific types of packets that are of interest. You can set the policy for multiple requirements as well—something like all the probe packets originating from a single source. You have countless ways to configure the policy to look for traffic or scans.

Policy-based approaches require you to perform some tuning so that the security measures conform to your overall security policy for the network and your company. Also, you will want to make sure the sensor is checking for unauthorized patterns on the specific network it is monitoring. Policy-based approaches can be used to look for a very simple statistical event or complex relationships.

Anomaly-Based Approach

The anomaly-based approach looks for network traffic that is outside a definition of what is considered normal. The most difficult task that an administrator faces with this type of monitoring is to effectively define normal traffic.

Some scanning systems have hard-coded definitions of normal traffic patterns. Other systems are deployed for a test period of a couple of weeks to learn what normal network patterns are by observation. After the test period is over, administrators should analyze what is and is not normal traffic. In either case, it can be very difficult to maintain the definition of normal. You want to reduce, and hopefully eliminate, the chances of improperly classifying abnormal traffic as normal traffic.

Anomaly-based scanning can be much easier to implement in small networks where there are likely to be fewer variables to define. Using the anomaly-based approach in a large network with a huge number of traffic types, applications, changes, accesses, and variables to define can be a daunting task.

There are two types of anomaly-based IDS and IPS: statistical and nonstatistical.

Statistical anomaly detection   A statistical anomaly-based system learns the profile of the monitored network (traffic patterns) from the network itself over a period of time. After that period, the system can detect when statistical properties of the network traffic deviate enough from the usual pattern, and when they do, the system triggers an alarm.

Nonstatistical anomaly detection   A nonstatistical anomaly-based system has a predefined definition of known good behavior (usually coded by the vendor). An alarm triggers when an event outside the profile occurs. Examples of events that can be considered malicious by nonstatistical anomaly IPS or IDS systems include the following:

- A communication between two devices using the non-IP-based protocol in a network where only the IP is to be used
- A routing protocol update that originated from a user device
- A broadcast storm or a network sweep
- An anomalous packet, such as a Christmas tree packet (in which all TCP flags are set)
- A TCP segment where the source and destination IP addresses are the same and the TCP source and destination ports are the same

Honeypot Approach

Honeypot systems are used by security professionals to lure attackers for the purpose of watching and learning about attack methods hackers use. There are programs that imitate a network-attached host with a backdoor so that the attackers can be watched. One of the original ideas behind the honeypot approach was to distract attacks from the real network devices, but today's honeypot is largely for analyzing incoming attacks and malicious traffic. The honeypot approach allows you to prepare for malicious traffic and attacks before they attack the real network.

When you implement a honeypot, you must dedicate a server or virtual machine that can be sacrificed and compromised. Once it has been deployed in an area that can be attacked, it cannot be used for normal network activity unless it has been wiped completely clean and a new operating system has been loaded.

Many operating systems have been modified to act specifically as honeypots. These operating systems offer both an internal system (the system that gets attacked) and an external system (used to monitor and watch what happens to the internal system).

IPS Signatures

Let's look at what a signature does. *Signatures* are the primary means for a sensor to identify traffic and take action on it. The actual process within an IPS sensor that matches traffic to a signature is called a microengine or a *signature microengine (SME)*. A signature microengine is a kind of preprocessor that handles specific groups of signatures. A sensor has multiple microengines; each of the microengines is responsible for a group of signatures. The signatures are grouped by protocol or other similar characteristics.

Table 8.2 provides a list of SMEs that are supported by the IOS IPS both before and after version 12.4(11)T, when SME and signature versions were substantially upgraded. I will explain more about this in the section titled "Signature Files," later in this chapter.

TABLE 8.2   SMEs Supported by IOS IPS

SME before 12.4(11)T	SME after 12.4(11)T	Description
ATOMIC.IP	ATOMIC.IP	Provides simple Layer 3 IP alarms
ATOMIC.ICMP	ATOMIC.IP	Provides simple Internet Control Message Protocol (ICMP) alarms based on the following parameters: type, code, sequence, and ID
ATOMIC.IPOPTIONS	ATOMIC.IP	Provides simple alarms based on the decoding of Layer 3 options
ATOMIC.UDP	ATOMIC.IP	Provides simple User Datagram Protocol (UDP) packet alarms based on the following parameters: port, direction, and data length
ATOMIC.TCP	ATOMIC.IP	Provides simple TCP packet alarms based on the following parameters: port, destination, and flags
SERVICE.DNS	SERVICE.DNS	Analyzes the Domain Name System (DNS) service
SERVICE.RPC	SERVICE.RPC	Analyzes the remote procedure call (RPC) service
SERVICE.SMTP	STATE	Inspects the Simple Mail Transfer Protocol (SMTP)
SERVICE.HTTP	SERVICE.HTTP	Provides an HTTP decode-based string engine that includes anti-evasive URL de-obfuscation
SERVICE.FTP	SERVICE.FTP	Provides FTP service special decode alarms
STRING.TCP	STRING.TCP	Offers TCP regular expression–based pattern inspection engine services
STRING.UDP	STRING.UDP	Offers UDP regular expression–based pattern inspection engine services
STRING.ICMP	STRING.ICMP	Provides ICMP regular expression–based pattern inspection engine services

TABLE 8.2   SMEs Supported by IOS IPS *(continued)*

SME before 12.4(11)T	SME after 12.4(11)T	Description
MULTI-STRING	MULTI-STRING	Supports flexible pattern matching and Trend Labs signatures
OTHER	OTHER	Provides an internal engine to handle miscellaneous signatures

Signature Types

Generally, four categories of signatures are defined:

- Exploit signatures
- Connection signatures
- String signatures
- DoS signatures

Exploit signatures   Exploit signatures typically identify a traffic pattern unique to a specific exploit. Therefore, each exploit variant may require its own signature. Attackers may be able to bypass detection by slightly modifying the attack payload. It is often necessary to produce an exploit signature for each attack tool variant.

Connection signatures   Connection signatures generate an alarm based on conformity to and validity of the network connections and protocols. For example, an alarm might be generated if something is found that does not meet the specification of HTTP, in other words, something that is not in the RFC.

String signatures   The string signature engines support regular expression pattern matching and alarm functionality. An example of a regular expression might be foo.*bar, which would indicate the text foo and the text bar on the same line with any single character (except a newline) between them.

DoS signatures   DoS signatures contain behavior descriptions that are considered characteristic of a DoS attack. The purpose of a denial of service attack is to consume the resources of a host. For example, an attack might attempt to create many TCP half-open connections.

To understand how traffic is scanned by the sensor and which components are used, you have to think about the microengines and categories of signatures just described. The process works like this:

1. Traffic passes through the sensor.

2. The sensor decides which microengine to activate, so the traffic can be scanned with the right signatures to determine whether the traffic is malicious.

3. The sensor activates one or more sensor microengines.

4. Once activated, the microengine inspects the data.

The sensor bases its microengine selection on the following:

- The network protocol of the traversing traffic
- The type of operating system associated with a signature
- The session port
- The type of attack

Signature Files

The signatures that an IPS sensor uses are loaded into the system with a signature definition file (SDF). The SDFs must be downloaded from cisco.com. You must have a login for the Software Download Center and a support agreement on the device that uses the SDF in order to access the downloads. If you have all of that in place, you can download updated SDFs from the site and load them onto your router in flash. How and where you can load the files are discussed in "Configuring IOS IPS," later in this chapter.

The SDFs are based on the different versions of operating systems for the mainline IPS sensor platforms. The current version of SDFs is 5. Version 5 first became available in Cisco IOS version 12.4(11)T.

For IPS sensor platforms like the Cisco IPS 4200 Series, almost 2,000 signatures are available. For the IOS IPS, there are about 1,700 signatures. The total number of signatures available isn't as important as the number that your device can support. Cisco IOS IPS uses SDFs that contain signature descriptions for the most relevant attacks; Cisco updates these on a regular basis. You can download the files from Cisco's website in different sizes, based on the amount of RAM your router has in typical default configurations. You can download the file named 128MB.sdf, which is called the basic signature set, or you can get the 256MB.sdf file, which is called the advanced signature set. With the default amount of RAM, an 1800 Series router would use the 128MB.sdf and a 3800 Series would use the 256MB.sdf.

WARNING   Your IDS/IPS is only as good as your last update, so make sure you keep up with signatures as they are released. Today's threats are rapidly changing, and you can't protect against something unless you know about it. Old signatures are unlikely to protect against a similar but newer attack vector.

One last thing before I move on to IPS alarms. Prior to the IOS 12.4(11)T release, IOS IPS had 132 built-in signatures available. The built-in signatures are included in the image for backward compatibility. Starting in IOS release 12.4(11)T and later, there are no built-in (hard-coded) signatures within the IOS.

IPS Alarms

An IPS sensor can react in real time when a signature is matched. This allows the sensor to act before network security has been compromised. The sensor can act and then log the event with a syslog message, or it can send alerts using Security Device Event Exchange.

IPS Reporting

An IPS can send alerts using syslog or SDEE. SDEE is recommended because it is the newer, more secure feature for sending the alert data. SDEE uses HTTPS to exchange the alerts with the IPS and a monitoring station.

When using IOS IPS on a router, SDEE is used to report events to the SDM. However, the SDM is limited by the fact that it can't do real-time monitoring or correlate the events from multiple sensors. In order to have these advanced features, you will have to deploy Cisco Security Monitoring, Analysis, and Response System (CS-MARS) or Cisco Works.

For those of you who have a smaller-scale implementation of IPS or can't afford to use the MARS or Cisco Works solution, Cisco has an alternative. You can download the Cisco IPS Event Viewer (IEV) software. The download requires a CCO login and, to get signature updates, you must have a valid maintenance contract for each of the sensors you are using.

As previously stated, you can configure IPS to choose a response to the threats it detects. The following are the response actions that the IPS can take when packets in a session match a signature:

Send an alarm   IPS can send an alarm to a syslog server or a centralized management interface. This action is typically combined with other preventive actions.

Drop the packet   This action is effective for all Internet protocols and does not affect any legitimate user if the source IP address was spoofed.

Reset the connection   This action works only for TCP sessions. The IPS can send a TCP RST message to the source and destination of the session. To do this, it spoofs the IP address of each device, making the source believe it is the destination and the destination believe it is the source.

Block the traffic   The sensor has the ability to block traffic, either from a specific IP address or from a connection.

> **Source IP address**   Blocking the source IP address of an attacker blocks the traffic for a specified amount of time. Take care when using the IP address option, because the attacker could be spoofing the IP address they are using. If the attacker is spoofing the IP address, you could inadvertently block a legitimate user's IP. Furthermore, if an IP address is being spoofed, the attack could continue to enter the network disguised as a different source, since you blocked only the previous, spoofed IP.

> **Connection**   When you block a connection that a signature matched, that connection is blocked for only a specified amount of time. You can use this approach to deny the attacker's session. This reduces the chance of being spoofed.

Configuring IOS IPS

In this section we will look at the configuration of Cisco IOS IPS. We will use the graphical interface of Cisco SDM to configure the IOS IPS. The SDM gives you an abundance of options to configure for the Cisco IOS IPS. You can configure every option through the IPS Edit menu.

SDM also uses the IPS Policies Wizard, which makes the deployment much faster on a new router. The wizard allows you to set interface and traffic flow, SDF location, and signature deployment. The wizard will also check to make sure the router has enough memory and resources before it actually configures the router. The IPS Policies Wizard configures IPS using default signature descriptions, as defined in the SDF files provided by Cisco or the built-in signatures included in Cisco IOS.

If you want to customize the signatures after the wizard deploys the default settings, you can use the IPS Edit menu available in SDM. Using the IPS Edit menu allows you to modify, disable, or delete a signature parameter.

1. Start off by opening the SDM interface on a router with no configuration. The router needs an IP address on one of its interfaces so that you can get to the SDM, but other than that, leave it blank.

Figure 8.2 shows the SDM Home screen.

FIGURE 8.2   SDM Home screen

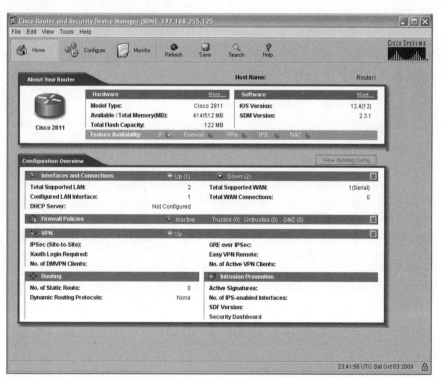

2. Next, click the Configure button in the main toolbar at the top of the screen. When the Configuration screen, shown in Figure 8.3, opens, the Interfaces And Connections screen is displayed.

FIGURE 8.3   Interfaces And Connections screen

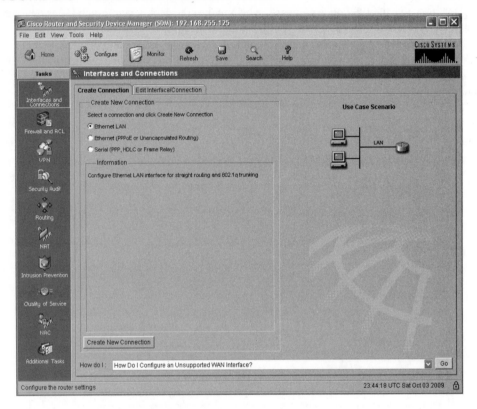

3. Click the Intrusion Prevention button in the Tasks bar. When the Intrusion Prevention System (IPS) page opens, as shown in Figure 8.4, click the Create IPS tab. Notice the Launch IPS Rule Wizard button toward the bottom of the screen.

4. Click the Launch IPS Rule Wizard button to start the wizard. After you start the wizard, if your router hasn't been previously configured, you will get a notification like the one shown in Figure 8.5. The wizard is going to enable SDEE for you so that the SDM can receive alerts from the IPS when an event takes place. Click OK to continue.

FIGURE 8.4   Intrusion Prevention System (IPS) screen

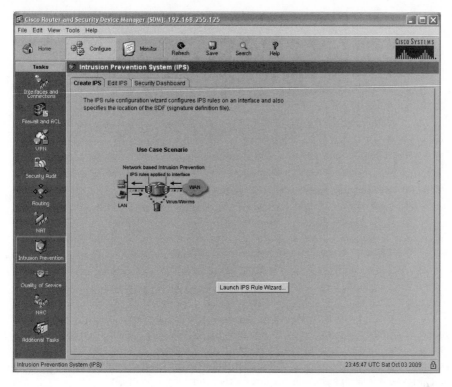

FIGURE 8.5   SDEE enable notification

5.   The Welcome screen of the IPS Policies Wizard, shown in Figure 8.6, goes over the basic configuration steps. You can see that you will have to choose the interface where the IPS rule is going to be set. Then you will determine the direction in which traffic is going to flow. Finally, you will specify the location of the SDF that the sensor is going to use for its signature database. Click Next to continue.

FIGURE 8.6   IPS Policies Wizard Welcome screen

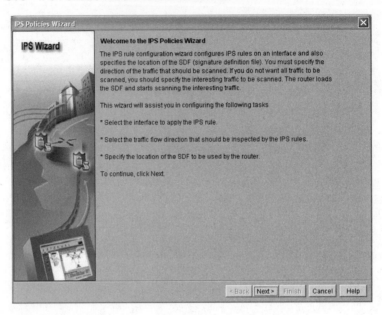

6. The first thing to determine in an IPS setup is the interface where the rule is to be located and the direction in which the traffic should be flowing through the router. We will configure the inbound Serial0/0/0 interface first by clicking the appropriate check box. Figure 8.7 shows the selection for this Internet connection.

FIGURE 8.7   Select Interfaces screen of the IPS Policies Wizard

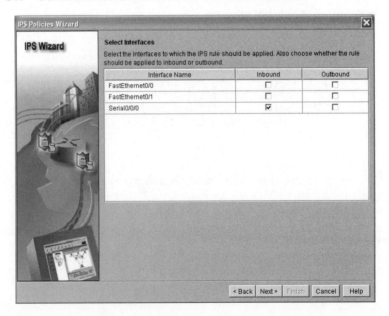

The inbound interface is the interface that comes in from the Internet. Let's assume that the office network we are configuring has a T1 that is connected to an Internet service provider (ISP). That T1 is connected to the Serial0/0/0 interface on the router, so that means we need to select interface Serial0/0/0 as the inbound interface. The rule is also going to be applied to this interface. The wizard will do that for you automatically.

In our example office, the internal network is connected to the FastEthernet0/0 interface, so you would select FastEthernet0/0 as the outbound interface. (If you are configuring your test network, you can select the two interfaces that are appropriate for your setup.) Click Next to continue.

7. When the SDF Locations page, shown in Figure 8.8, opens, you will be able to set the location of the SDF for the router. By default most routers have an SDF loaded on them. As discussed previously, the file that is loaded on the router is based on the capacity of your router. The router we are using here uses the 128MB.sdf file.

FIGURE 8.8   SDF Locations screen of the IPS Policies Wizard

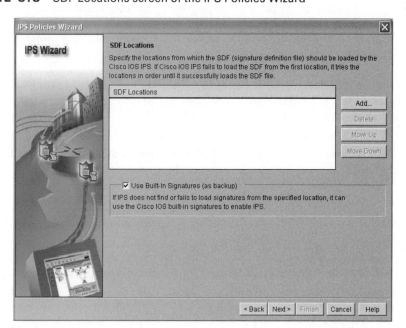

By default the Use Built-In Signatures (As Backup) check box is checked. Keep in mind that, as I mentioned earlier, it is not recommended to use these signatures on their own; they don't provide up-to-date threat signatures.

Click the Add button on the top right of the screen. The Add A Signature Location dialog box, shown in Figure 8.9, will allow you to specify the location of the SDF file for the wizard.

FIGURE 8.9   Add A Signature Location dialog box

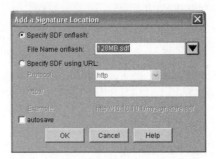

> There should be an SDF on the flash on your router if you bought the router with the license for IPS services. If you are upgrading a router to an IOS that supports IPS or upgrading the SDM version to support IPS, there will be a default file in both of those upgrades. Otherwise, you can purchase the appropriate software and load it onto your router. Flash is the recommended location for storing the file.

8. In the Add A Signature Location dialog box, by default, the Specify SDF Onflash radio button is selected. Click the down-arrow button, and if there is a file in flash, you can choose it from the list.

   There could also be a file stored on an external server, such as an HTTP server. To use an SDF stored on an external server, click the Specify SDF Using URL radio button and then specify the protocol and location of the server and the file for the wizard. When you have finished, click OK to continue to the next step.

9. If you look at Figure 8.10, you can see that the `flash://128MB.sdf` file is now the SDF location specified for the IPS. You can configure more than one file; click Add again and specify the next SDF location.

   Additional files are typically specified as a backup measure. The next file will be added to the bottom of the list. Once the configuration is in place, the router will try to load the files in order, top to bottom, until one loads. So, if you are putting more than one location in the list, make sure that each file is up to date and the file you want loaded is at the top of the list. When you have specified all the file locations you want, click Next to move on.

10. When the Summary page for the wizard opens, you can review the settings that you have configured. Figure 8.11 shows the Summary page. You can see the rules that will be applied for setting the traffic flow direction as well as the location of the SDF that you specified. Click Finish to apply the settings.

FIGURE 8.10   SDF Locations screen with file added

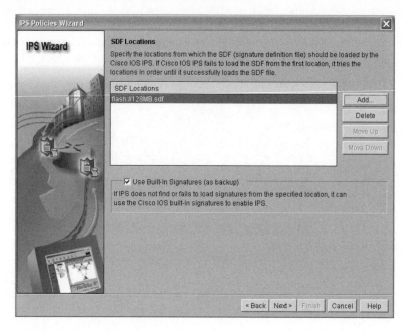

FIGURE 8.11   IPS Policies Wizard Summary page

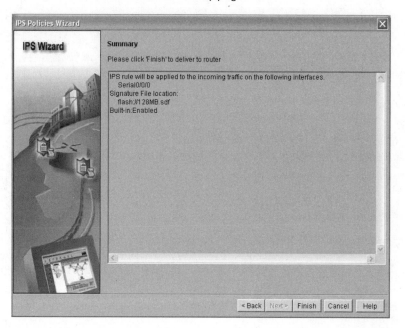

11. The Commands Delivery Status information box, shown in Figure 8.12, shows you the status of the commands that SDM is sending to the router. Before sending the commands, the wizard verifies that the router has adequate resources for the configuration. Once the configuration has been delivered to the router, click OK.

FIGURE 8.12 Commands Delivery Status dialog box

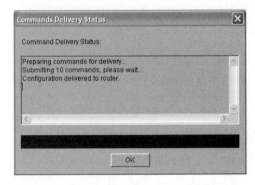

12. After the wizard is complete, the Edit IPS tab on the Intrusion Prevention System (IPS) page opens, as shown in Figure 8.13. Make sure that you have the Edit IPS tab selected.

FIGURE 8.13 Intrusion Prevention System (IPS) Edit IPS window

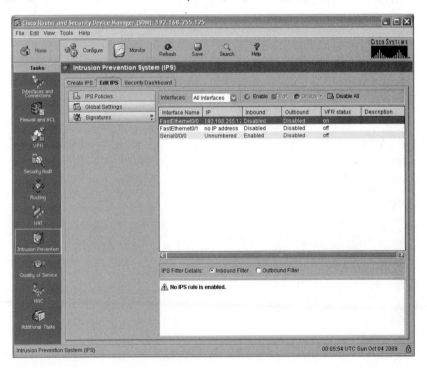

You can select and configure three sections from this screen. Right below the tabs is a column of buttons. The first one is IPS Policies, which should be selected at this time. From this screen, you can see which interfaces have an inbound or outbound policy enabled. You can also disable or edit the policy using the buttons along the top of the screen.

13. Figure 8.14 shows the Global Settings page. To get to this screen, click the Global Settings button on the left side of the screen. You can get quite a bit of information from this screen. You can change any of the options by clicking the Edit button on the top right of the screen. You can also see if syslog and SDEE are enabled and what the alert thresholds are.

FIGURE 8.14   Global Settings screen

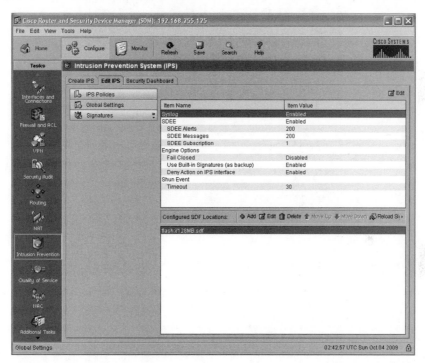

The Engine Options information is very useful. You can see what the default security stance of the IPS is; notice that in our example, Fail Closed is disabled. This means that if any of the SMEs don't operate, the IPS will allow traffic to pass without being scanned. If you want the IPS to drop traffic when it can't scan it, then you must change the Fail Closed option to Enabled.

You can use the CLI global command `ip ips fail closed` to enable the Fail Closed option. If you want to disable the option, then use the no form of the command, like this: `no ip ips fail closed`.

You will remember that we left the Use Built-In Signatures check box checked, so the Use Built-In Signatures (As Backup) option is enabled. The default setting for the IPS is to drop traffic; you can see that with the Deny Action On IPS Interface option listed as Enabled.

14. The two tabs of the Global Settings screen are the Syslog And SDEE tab and the Global Engine tab. To see these tabs, click the Edit button toward the top right of the screen. These are shown in Figure 8.15 and Figure 8.16, respectively.

FIGURE 8.15   Syslog and SDEE tab of the Edit Global Settings dialog box

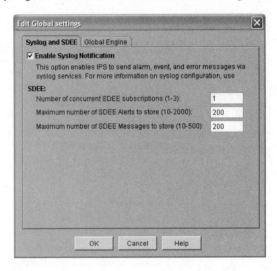

FIGURE 8.16   Global Engine tab of the Edit Global Settings dialog box

15. Finally, you can access the last of the three editing features on the Edit IPS tab by clicking the Signatures button. Figure 8.17 shows the Signatures screen. If you are responsible for running the IPS, you will most likely spend most of your time in this screen. This is where you can configure, enable, or disable signatures that are in the database. You can filter or look at just a specific group of signatures by selecting a folder from the Signatures drop-down list on the left side of the screen.

FIGURE 8.17   Signatures screen

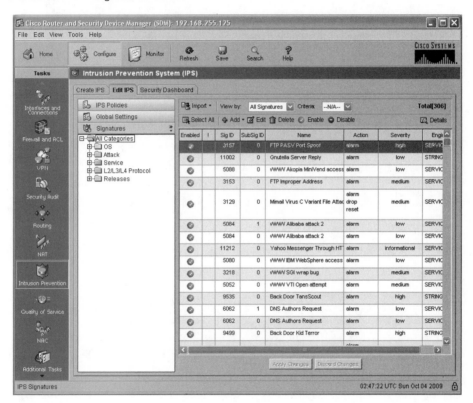

16. To edit a signature, select it and click the Edit button just above the signatures table.

In the example I will edit Signature ID 3157, the FTP PASV Port Spoof signature.

17. Figure 8.18 shows the top half of the Edit Signature screen. Scroll down to see the rest of the editable options in Figure 8.19.

FIGURE 8.18 Top half of Edit Signature screen

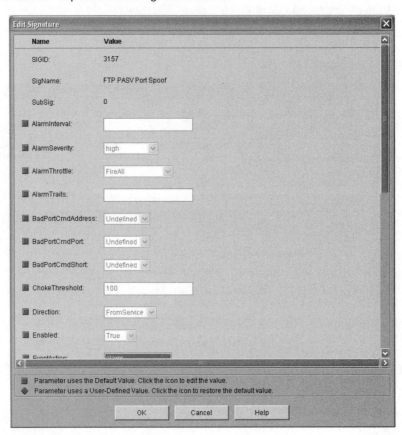

FIGURE 8.19   Edit Signature screen continued

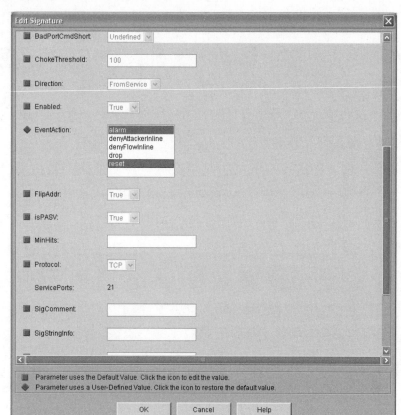

A green square next to a grayed-out option indicates that the default settings are being used. If you click the green box, the icon changes to a red diamond, and you can change the setting. If you want to revert the setting to the default, simply click the red diamond.

18. Close the Edit Signature screen and select the Security Dashboard tab from the Intrusion Prevention System (IPS) page. This screen is shown in Figure 8.20.

FIGURE 8.20 Security Dashboard

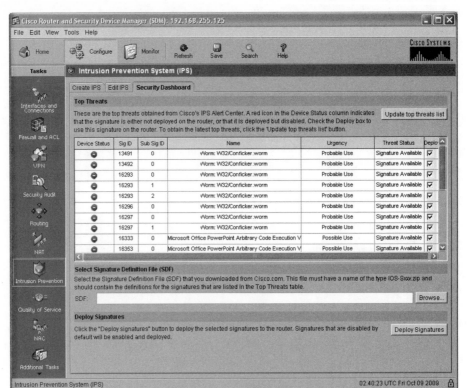

The Security Dashboard is useful because it has a semi-automated way to keep up to date with the newest threats. It is a lot of work to stay up with the newest threats and make sure that all the appropriate signatures are on your router; the Top Threats field on the Dashboard makes that process easier. The Top Threats listed on the screen are pulled from Cisco CCO to keep you up to date. The red circle in the Device Status column indicates that the current SDF file running on this router doesn't have the signatures for these threats.

19. Click the Browse button next to the Select Signature Definition File (SDF) field to locate a SDF that has all of the signatures in it. You can download the file from Cisco, and it will have a filename such as IOS-S252.zip. The SDM will go to that file and get the signatures needed for the new threats.

20. Click the Deploy Signatures button, and the new signatures will be added to the signature database currently on the router.

Summary

In this chapter you learned the differences between IDS and IPS technologies. You learned that you can use both types of sensors in your network and that they can complement each other. We looked at the different types of IDS and IPS, based on what they are protecting (network-based and host-based sensors). Each of these types has different strengths depending on the type of threats they are best at defending against. Using both technologies together gives you a more secure, layered defense.

You learned about the different approaches that can be employed when a sensor is scanning traffic. We dove into signature-based scanning and had a look at the signatures themselves. We looked at the actions that a sensor can take when malicious traffic is detected.

Finally, we walked through the configuration of IOS IPS on a Cisco ISR router. We used the Cisco SDM to set up the IPS and then edit and refine the configuration.

Exam Essentials

Remember the difference between intrusion prevention and intrusion detection.   The difference between intrusion detection and intrusion prevention is the difference between a passive system and an active system. Because the IPS is an active system, it can take action based on an alert, such as dropping the packet. The actions an IDS can take are more limited.

Understand the differences between network-based and host-based IPS and IDS.   Network IDS and IPS are installed on the network and protect multiple hosts (for example, they may protect a DMZ or a server farm). A host detection system is installed on an individual host and protects only that host.

Know the different approaches to IDS and IPS systems.   The four approaches to IDS and IPS systems are signature-based, policy-based, anomaly-based, and honeypot systems.

Understand IPS signatures, signature microengines, and the various types of signatures. The two types of signature files that can be loaded are the basic signature definition file and the advanced signature definition file. They are labeled `128MB.sdf` and `256MB.sdf`, respectively. Signature microengines (SMEs) are preprocessors that combine like signatures and process them.

Know how to enable IOS IPS using the Cisco SDM.   Recall the steps in enabling the IOS IPS using the SDM. Click the Configure button at the top of the screen and then choose Intrusion Prevention on the lower-left side. Once there, you can implemented the IDS Policy Wizard, edit the IPS, or use the Security Dashboard.

Written Lab

Write the answers to the following questions:

1. What is the primary difference between IPS and IDS?

2. What kind of IPS would be deployed on a Unix workstation?

3. What does a signature definition filename end in?

4. What is the name of the advanced signature definition file?

5. A passive system is what kind of a system?

6. What is the command-line interface command to enable the IPS to fail closed?

7. What is the name of a system that is used to collect information on how a hacker attacks a host?

8. Top Threats is a feature displayed on what screen?

9. Cisco Security Agent (CSA) is what kind of Intrusion Prevention System?

10. What type of anomaly-based system has a predefined definition of known good behavior?

Hands-on Lab

Hands-on Lab 8.1: Configuring an IPS Policy Using Cisco SDM

In this lab, you will need a Cisco router that supports SDM and also has an IOS version that supports IPS.

1. Launch SDM and log in to your router.

2. Click the Configure tab at the top of the screen. Then choose Intrusion Prevention at the bottom left-hand side of the screen. This will open the Create IPS tab; from there choose the Create IPS Policy Wizard.

3. Enable SDEE if it is not already enabled.

4. Choose the interface that you want to configure for IPS and in what direction you want to watch traffic.

5. Add a signature location. Now you have completed the basic configuration of an IPS.

6. Review the screenshots in Figures 8.8 through 8.16 to make sure you have completed the steps correctly.

Review Questions

1. What type of sensor has the ability to block traffic before it enters the network?

   A. IDS

   B. HIDS

   C. IPS

   D. SDEE

2. Which type of sensor listens to traffic in promiscuous mode as it enters the network?

   A. IDS

   B. HIPS

   C. IPS

   D. SDEE

3. Which scope of sensor is made for a specific computer operating system?

   A. HIPS

   B. NIDS

   C. NIPS

   D. SDEE

4. Which type of sensor is best at blocking DoS attacks for the whole network segment?

   A. HIPS

   B. NIDS

   C. NIPS

   D. SDEE

5. A honeypot is best at doing what?

   A. Defending the network from attack.

   B. Getting attacked so you can learn.

   C. Allowing you to put up an SMTP relay.

   D. A honeypot has no purpose for the network.

6. What is the most common type of IDS/IPS that scans traffic?

   A. Honeypot

   B. Signature

   C. Policy

   D. Anomaly

7. Which component in the IPS matches the traffic to a signature?

A. Signature microengine (SME)

B. Subject matter expert (SME)

C. Policy generator

D. Policy engine

8. Which type of file is downloaded from Cisco and updated on the router to give you the newest signatures?

A. Image

B. Signature policy

C. SFD

D. SDF

9. True or false? The Cisco IOS IPS has a built-in set of signatures in the IOS.

A. True

B. False

10. An IPS sensor can block traffic as one of its actions; true or false?

A. True

B. False

11. Which one of the following is *not* a response to an alert on an IPS?

A. Send an alarm.

B. Reset the connection.

C. Drop the packet.

D. Send ICMP redirect.

E. Block the packet.

12. Which type of sensor is used inline in a network?

A. IDS

B. HIDS

C. IPS

D. HIPS

13. When using the SDM to edit IPS settings, which of the following is *not* an option under the Global Engine tab of the Edit Global Settings option?

A. Enable Engine Fail Open

B. Enable Engine Fail Closed

C. Use Built-In Signatures (As Backup)

D. Enable Deny Action On IPS Interface

14. What are the three option tabs when using the SDM to configure Intrusion Prevention? (Choose all that apply.)

A. Create IPS

B. Security Dashboard

C. Edit IPS

D. Signature settings

15. Which two options are valid responses to an IPS event?

A. UDP reset

B. Drop packet

C. Send alert

D. Modify an access list dynamically

16. After you launch the IPS Policies Wizard, what is the first thing that you do when configuring IPS?

A. Select signatures

B. Apply rules

C. Select interface

D. Select location of the signature files

17. Which protocol is used when you want to have secure logging of IPS events?

A. Syslog

B. SSH

C. SDEE

D. SSL

18. Which type of anomaly detection uses "learned normal behavior" as its basis to detect anomalies?

A. Hybrid

B. Nonstatistical

C. Stochastic

D. Statistical

19. The advanced signature set for a Cisco IOS IPS uses which signature file?

A. `128MB.sdf`

B. `64MB.sdf`

C. `256MB.sdf`

D. `192MB.sdf`

20. If an IPS sensor is set to block traffic, what are the two types of blocking it can perform?

A. Destination address

B. TCP sequence number

C. Source address

D. Connection

Answers to Review Questions

1. C. Because it is inline, an IPS sensor has the ability to block traffic entering the network.

2. A. An IDS performs a deep packet inspection of traffic passing through the network.

3. A. A host-based sensor must be designed specifically for the operating system it is deployed on.

4. C. A network Intrusion Protection System (IPS) is deployed inline; therefore it can block traffic.

5. B. A honeypot is put into place so that you can learn what types of attacks are being run. This way you can learn from the attacks and better defend your network.

6. B. The most common type of scanning is a signature-based sensor.

7. A. A signature microengine (SME) is used to scan the traffic against a signature and determine if it matches.

8. D. The SDF is downloaded from Cisco CCO in order to get the most up-to-date signatures.

9. A. The IOS IPS has roughly 100 built-in signatures, but they are largely out of date.

10. A. Only the IPS sensor can block traffic coming into the network.

11. D. An IPS sensor cannot send an ICMP redirect, but it can send an alarm, reset the connection, drop the packet, or block the packet.

12. C. An IPS is used primarily inline in a network environment. An IDS is typically connected to a SPAN port on a Cisco switch.

13. A. You can set the engine to fail open, but you do this by making sure the Enable Engine Fail Closed check box is not checked. Therefore, there is no option labeled Enable Engine Fail Open.

14. A, B, C. The three tabs when you initially configure Intrusion Prevention are Create IPS, Edit IPS, and Security Dashboard. Signature settings are an option under the Edit IPS tab.

15. B, C. Two of the options that are valid responses to an IPS event are to send an alert and to drop packets. Other options available are to reset the connection (TCP only) and block the packet.

16. C. The first task that you perform when using the IPS Policies Wizard is to select an interface to apply the IPS rule to.

17. C. SDEE provides a secure channel to communicate IPS events and logs.

18. D. Statistical anomaly detection "learns" the network behavior for a given time to create a baseline. After that, if the traffic deviates from the baseline enough, an alert is generated.

19. C. The Cisco IOS IPS has two signature sets, the basic and advanced sets. The basic is `128MB.sdf` and the advanced is `256MB.sdf`.

20. C, D. The two types of blocking are source address blocking and connection blocking. Both of these are blocked for a specified time only.

Answers to Written Lab

1. Active (IPS) versus passive (IDS)

2. Host-based Intrusion Prevention System (HIPS)

3. `.sdf`

4. `256MB.sdf`

5. IDS

6. `ip ips fail closed`

7. Honeypot

8. Security Dashboard

9. HIPS

10. Non-statistical

Chapter
9

Understanding Cryptographic Solutions

THE FOLLOWING CCNA-SECURITY EXAM TOPICS ARE COVERED IN THIS CHAPTER:

✓ **Implement site-to-site VPNs on Cisco routers using SDM**

   ▪ Explain the different methods used in cryptography

In Chapter 9 we are going to discuss cryptographic solutions. We will look at an introduction to cryptography, paying attention to the history of cryptography and how some of the ciphers evolved over the years. Then we will examine symmetric encryption in detail.

In the last section of this chapter, we will look at encryption algorithms and how to make a selection based on your criteria.

Introduction to Cryptography

Cryptography is defined many ways, but the main point to get across is that we are talking about the encryption of a message, file, and so on. We will get into other facets of the study of encryption, but let's look at the basics first.

You may have heard the term *cryptology*, which some use interchangeably with *cryptography*. In reality, the term *cryptology* encompasses the study of *cryptography*, which is the encoding of something, and *cryptanalysis*, which is the breaking of a code. Much as we see in the technology and military sectors today, there is a constant struggle between those trying to keep thing secrets and those trying to discern those secrets. No cipher can be considered unbreakable because there's always someone with the ability or resources to eventually break the code.

We trace the roots of cryptography back to ancient Rome, where Caesar used a form of cryptography, which we now call the *Caesar cipher*, to encode messages to his commanders in the field. Following that, the Hundred Years' War in France and England brought us the Vigenère cipher, which is known as a polyalphabetic cipher. The mathematician Babbage later showed us that a polyalphabetic cipher such as Vigenère's was vulnerable to frequency-analysis techniques. Later, electromechanical devices were used to encrypt messages, such as the infamous Enigma machine, used by the Germans during World War II. The British and Polish were able to break the Enigma machine encryption and decrypt many messages, which aided the Allies during the war. Fast-forward to the 1970s, when modern computing got started and the need for encrypted data traffic was born. The first U.S. government standard, Data Encryption Standard (DES), was brought forth in 1976. Today, the Advanced Encryption Standard (AES) is the standard algorithm.

We will look at some of these algorithms in depth and discuss some of the various types of encryption.

Caesar's Cipher

As previously mentioned, Caesar used a simple cipher to get encrypted messages to his commanders. This is known as a substitution cipher, or shift cipher. That is because Caesar used the alphabet and shifted each letter three places in order to make his cipher. Figure 9.1 shows the basis of how this cipher worked.

FIGURE 9.1   Caesar cipher

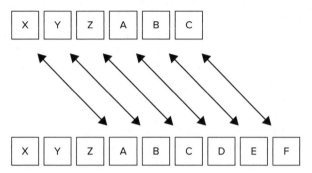

In the illustration, you can see that for every letter of the alphabet, the substituted letter is three places away. It is very simplistic but was likely effective for the times. In Figure 9.2, you can see what the phrase "the quick brown fox" looks like after the Caesar cipher has been used on it.

FIGURE 9.2   Caesar cipher example

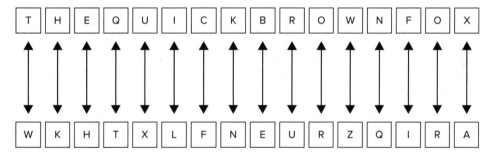

The Caesar cipher is also known as ROT3, or rotation of 3 places. Fast forward to the 1980s, and members of the Unix community were very active in an online community called Usenet. In the net.jokes newsgroup, ROT13, or rotation of 13 places, was used to hide offensive jokes, answers to riddles, and the like. The number 13 was used because the same number is used to encrypt or decrypt (add 13 or subtract 13).

Over the years, the substitution cipher has been found in everything from kids' decoder rings all the way up to gangsters' messages. In 2006, a mafia boss in Sicily was captured because he used a variation of a substitution cipher. On a humorous note, in 1999, Netscape Communicator was found to have used ROT13 as a way of encrypting its email passwords.

Substitution ciphers are very easy to crack, especially if you use frequency analysis to determine where the patterns are. Simple ciphers can be spied with the native eye, without the use of computers.

Vigenère Cipher

We can see the weaknesses of the substitution cipher, presented in the previous section. The next evolution of the cipher was the polyalphabetic cipher. In the 1900s this cipher was attributed to Blaise de Vigenère, a French cryptographer; however, the cipher has been traced back to a book written in the 1500s by Giovanni Batista Belaso, an Italian. Vigenère had merely published an updated version of this cipher, but his name has been widely attached to this type of cipher.

The Vigenère cipher takes a number of substitution ciphers and a keyword that is used between them, making frequency analysis difficult if not impossible. But that doesn't mean the cipher is unbreakable. Indeed, it was initially cracked by Charles Babbage, but he did not publish the solution. The solution was published in the 1900s by Friedrich Kasiski, a German cryptographer.

The Vigenère cipher basically uses the 26 letters of the alphabet together with a secret key to encrypt the text. Let's look at an example using the Vigenère cipher. In this example, we will use a secret key called newkey to encrypt our message, which is "meet me in paris." Refer to the Vigenère table in Figure 9.3.

FIGURE 9.3   Vigenère table

A	B	C	D	E	F	G	H	I	J	K	L	M	N	O	P	Q	R	S	T	U	V	W	X	Y	Z
B	C	D	E	F	G	H	I	J	K	L	M	N	O	P	Q	R	S	T	U	V	W	X	Y	Z	A
C	D	E	F	G	H	I	J	K	L	M	N	O	P	Q	R	S	T	U	V	W	X	Y	Z	A	B
D	E	F	G	H	I	J	K	L	M	N	O	P	Q	R	S	T	U	V	W	X	Y	Z	A	B	C
E	F	G	H	I	J	K	L	M	N	O	P	Q	R	S	T	U	V	W	X	Y	Z	A	B	C	D
F	G	H	I	J	K	L	M	N	O	P	Q	R	S	T	U	V	W	X	Y	Z	A	B	C	D	E
G	H	I	J	K	L	M	N	O	P	Q	R	S	T	U	V	W	X	Y	Z	A	B	C	D	E	F
H	I	J	K	L	M	N	O	P	Q	R	S	T	U	V	W	X	Y	Z	A	B	C	D	E	F	G
I	J	K	L	M	N	O	P	Q	R	S	T	U	V	W	X	Y	Z	A	B	C	D	E	F	G	H
J	K	L	M	N	O	P	Q	R	S	T	U	V	W	X	Y	Z	A	B	C	D	E	F	G	H	I
K	L	M	N	O	P	Q	R	S	T	U	V	W	X	Y	Z	A	B	C	D	E	F	G	H	I	J
L	M	N	O	P	Q	R	S	T	U	V	W	X	Y	Z	A	B	C	D	E	F	G	H	I	J	K
M	N	O	P	Q	R	S	T	U	V	W	X	Y	Z	A	B	C	D	E	F	G	H	I	J	K	L
N	O	P	Q	R	S	T	U	V	W	X	Y	Z	A	B	C	D	E	F	G	H	I	J	K	L	M
O	P	Q	R	S	T	U	V	W	X	Y	Z	A	B	C	D	E	F	G	H	I	J	K	L	M	N
P	Q	R	S	T	U	V	W	X	Y	Z	A	B	C	D	E	F	G	H	I	J	K	L	M	N	O
Q	R	S	T	U	V	W	X	Y	Z	A	B	C	D	E	F	G	H	I	J	K	L	M	N	O	P
R	S	T	U	V	W	X	Y	Z	A	B	C	D	E	F	G	H	I	J	K	L	M	N	O	P	Q
S	T	U	V	W	X	Y	Z	A	B	C	D	E	F	G	H	I	J	K	L	M	N	O	P	Q	R
T	U	V	W	X	Y	Z	A	B	C	D	E	F	G	H	I	J	K	L	M	N	O	P	Q	R	S
U	V	W	X	Y	Z	A	B	C	D	E	F	G	H	I	J	K	L	M	N	O	P	Q	R	S	T
V	W	X	Y	Z	A	B	C	D	E	F	G	H	I	J	K	L	M	N	O	P	Q	R	S	T	U
W	X	Y	Z	A	B	C	D	E	F	G	H	I	J	K	L	M	N	O	P	Q	R	S	T	U	V
X	Y	Z	A	B	C	D	E	F	G	H	I	J	K	L	M	N	O	P	Q	R	S	T	U	V	W
Y	Z	A	B	C	D	E	F	G	H	I	J	K	L	M	N	O	P	Q	R	S	T	U	V	W	X
Z	A	B	C	D	E	F	G	H	I	J	K	L	M	N	O	P	Q	R	S	T	U	V	W	X	Y

Starting with the *m* from our message, we encode this by using the row starting with *n* for the letter in the *m* column. In this case, the letter is *z*. The next letter would look for the row starting with *e*, using the letter in the *e* column, which would be *i*. Continuing further, the first two words of the message, "meet me," would be encoded as "ziad qc."

One-Time Pads

A one-time pad is also known as a Vernam cipher, which was created by and then patented by Gilbert Vernam in 1917, while employed by AT&T. The Vernam cipher was a stream cipher that used an exclusive OR (XOR) against plaintext with a key. Another cryptographer in the U.S. Army Signal Corps expanded on this idea by using random data as the key.

The idea behind using a Vernam cipher is that the cipher is unbreakable, assuming that the key is used only once (hence the name one-time pad, because they are generally used only one time).

The problems come in when you have to deliver the key to the recipient and then store it. These challenges usually limit the use of Vernam ciphers to only extremely secure communications.

Transposition Ciphers

A transposition cipher is just like it sounds. Letters are transposed so that they no longer exist in the original format. An example might be the original plaintext "SEE YOU IN ST LOUIS." If we engaged a transposition cipher, we might have a result such as "NSETUIYEOIULSSO." Nothing has been changed, just the position of the letter moved or transposed. The transposition cipher is also called permutation.

A form of transposition cipher is the rail fence cipher. In this cipher the words are read like a rail fence. In the example below, we have the words "PICK UP THE PACKAGE AT THE USUAL PLACE," using a three-place key.

```
P....U....E....K....A....E....A....A
.I.K..P..H..P.C.A.E..T..H..U.U.L..L.C
..C.....T....A...G.....T....S....P...E
```

Reading the letters up and down, you see that the letters spell out the phrase.

Transposition is still a part of some modern algorithms, such as Data Encryption Standard (DES) and Triple Data Encryption Standard (3DES).

Symmetric Encryption

Symmetric encryption algorithms are probably the most commonly used encryption algorithms. One of the main advantages of symmetric encryption is speed. Because you are using the same key to encrypt and decrypt, the mathematics behind the calculation is much simpler. This allows the key lengths to be shorter. Examples of symmetric encryption algorithms are DES, 3DES, AES, Blowfish, RC4, and SEAL.

> **Symmetric vs. Asymmetric Encryption**
>
> What's the difference between symmetric and asymmetric encryption? With symmetric encryption, you use the same key to encrypt and decrypt. With asymmetric encryption, you use a key pair. The keys are different; one key is public and the other is private. Symmetric encryption is faster, but asymmetric encryption is better for communication between parties who are not known to each other, because there is no need to share a secret key with an unknown person. For more information, see Chapter 11, "Using Asymmetric Encryption and PKI."

Symmetric Encryption Keys

Symmetric encryption keys can range in length from 40 bits to 256 bits. As you might expect, the shorter the key length, the less protection you might be afforded. There are some generally accepted protection principles for various key lengths. As you can see in Table 9.1, a 256-bit key provides protection against quantum computing, whereas at the other end of the spectrum, 40 bits can be broken very easily with a brute-force attack. Key lengths in between those can be expected to provide protection for a certain number of years, as shown in Table 9.1.

TABLE 9.1   Key-length Protection for Various Algorithms

Approximate Level of Protection	Symmetric Key	Asymmetric Key	Hash
3 years' protection	80	1248	160
10 years' protection	96	1776	192
20 years' protection	112	2432	224
30 years' protection	128	3248	256
Quantum computing protection	256	15424	512

DES Encryption Algorithm

The Data Encryption Standard (DES) has now been in use for over 35 years and still has not been found to have a significant flaw. However, because its key length is relatively short, it can be susceptible to brute-force attacks.

DES uses a 64-bit key, but only 56 of the bits are used for encryption. Unfortunately, 16 of those remaining 56 bits are known and 40 bits are unknown. The other 8 bits are used for parity. What that means, essentially, is that DES has a 40-bit key strength.

DES has two operating modes, stream cipher and block cipher. Further, each of these two modes has two types within it. The following list shows the modes and types.

Block cipher modes

- Electronic Code Book (ECB) mode creates the same cipher text from plaintext each time. This mode is susceptible to replay attacks, among others.
- Cipher Block Chaining (CBC) mode uses XOR of the previous ciphertext and then encrypts with the DES key.

Stream cipher modes

- Cipher Feedback (CFB) mode turns a block cipher into a stream cipher and operates similarly to CBC.
- Output Feedback (OFB) mode generates keystream blocks that are XORed with the plaintext to create ciphertext.

Of all of these modes, CBC mode is the most prevalent, because it is used with IPSec. In fact, Cisco's implementation of IPSec using DES (and 3DES) operates in CBC mode.

The following are suggested guidelines for DES usage:

- Change the key frequently because of its susceptibility to brute-force attacks.
- Use a secure channel to transmit keys.
- Use CBC mode, because it is the most secure within DES.

3DES Encryption Algorithm

Triple DES, as the 3DES encryption algorithm has become known, essentially strengthens the original DES algorithm by applying it three times. Because the original DES algorithm is cryptographically strong, it can be made much stronger by encrypting the data three times. This triple encryption makes a brute-force attack unfeasible. The effective key strength can be either 112 bit or 168 bit, which is what Cisco uses. Let's examine how the 3DES algorithm works.

1. A first 56-bit key is used to encrypt the plaintext.
2. A second 56-bit key is used to decrypt the data.
3. A third 56-bit key is used to encrypt the data again.

If you use different first and third keys, you get an effective key strength of 168 bits, which is what Cisco does. If you use the same key in steps 1 and 3, then you have an effective key strength of 112 bits.

The encrypt-decrypt-encrypt sequence creates a much stronger key strength than using three different keys encrypted three times. That method would yield an effective 58-bit key strength, instead of the 168-bit key strength that is 3DES.

3DES is very much in use in today's environment and is still very secure. It's been around a long time without anyone finding a weakness.

Advanced Encryption Algorithm

Advanced Encryption Algorithm (AES) came about after the federal government decided that it needed to create a new standard that would replace DES as the official government encryption cipher. A bake-off of sorts was initiated in 1997. The winner, selected in 2000, was the Rijndael cipher, a mixture of the last names of the two creators, Joan Daemen and Vincent Rijmen. This cipher became an official government standard in 2002.

The Rijndael cipher uses a variable key length and block size in the implementation of the cipher. There are potentially nine different combinations of key length and block size. You may use a key length of 256 bits, 192 bits, or 128 bits to encrypt block sizes of 128 bits, 192 bits, or 256 bits.

The Rijndael cipher operates as an iterated block cipher. It uses multiple transformation cycles on its way to an end output. The Rijndael cipher uses only the original key lengths and block sizes; however, one of the key features of this cipher is that it can be expanded on 32-bit borders for the block size and/or the key length.

AES runs much faster than its predecessor, 3DES. This allows it to run in software more effectively and can be better suited for those applications that require low-latency and/or high throughput.

Because AES is a relatively new algorithm, it has been employed by Cisco for just a few years. The following devices and software versions support AES used in IPSec VPN.

- PIX Firewall Software versions 6.3 and above

- ASA Software versions 7.0 and above

- Cisco IOS 12.2(13)T and above

- Cisco VPN 3000 Concentrator Software versions 3.6 and above

SEAL

The Software-Optimized Encryption Algorithm (SEAL) is an alternative to the more traditional DES, 3DES, or AES algorithms. SEAL uses a 160-bit key and is less processor intensive than some of the other alternatives. SEAL is supported in Cisco IOS 12.3(7) but not with routers that have a hardware encryption card, meaning that it's used only in software. SEAL is available only from Cisco and has the following restrictions:

- SEAL is supported only in the K9 subsystem.

- IPSec must be supported by your router and the peer router.

- No hardware IPSec encryption can be used.

Rivest Ciphers

The Rivest ciphers are also known as the RC ciphers. Ron Rivest is a well-known cryptographer and professor at MIT. He is the author of the Rivest ciphers known as RC2, RC4, and RC5 and coauthor of RC6. Table 9.2 briefly describes the algorithms.

TABLE 9.2   Rivest Ciphers

RC Algorithm	Description
RC2	Variable-length key-block cipher, designed to be an alternative to DES.
RC4	Variable key-length stream cipher used frequently in file encryption products, as well as in Secure Sockets Layer (SSL).
RC5	RC5 has a variable-length key and variable-length block size.
RC6	Block cipher meant to compete for the AES standard.

Of all of these, RC4 is used most prevalently. It is used frequently within SSL to secure web transactions.

Encryption Algorithms

Encryption algorithms are used in security all the time, for purposes ranging from encrypting a laptop to securing a VPN tunnel. Some categorize these two uses as securing the data at rest, such as in a database, and securing the data in transit, such as using it with SSL or a VPN tunnel. In this section we will look briefly at hashes. We will also look at how to choose the correct encryption algorithm for your particular needs.

 Real World Scenario

B2B VPN IPSec Tunnel

Your company has signed an agreement to do business with a partner. As part of the agreement, you will need to set up a VPN tunnel with the partner company. You have been told that the business with the partner will involve confidential information. The requirements are that you must use encryption and that it must be fast. Your business partner uses Cisco equipment, as do you. What would be the best choice for an encryption standard for your VPN tunnel?

Providing that the business partner's equipment could support it, the best choice would be AES, which is supported in recent versions of Cisco equipment and software. If the partner's equipment is a bit older, 3DES would be the next choice. Both of those standards are relatively fast compared to other types of algorithms and are secure.

Choosing the Right Encryption Algorithm

An important task when you look at securing your data is to choose the correct encryption algorithm. Generally two criteria are considered essential when discussing an encryption algorithm.

Choose a trustworthy algorithm.   A trustworthy encryption algorithm is one that has been vetted through the security community. That is to say, it has been around for many years and has proven to be resistant to attacks.

Protect against brute-force attacks.   An encryption algorithm must have sufficient key length to protect the data for the level of confidentiality required. For example, a key length of 40 might not be enough for your application.

The following is a list of trustworthy encryption algorithms:

- DES
- 3DES
- AES
- RC4

You might be questioning why DES would be considered a trustworthy encryption algorithm when it is only 40 bits and can be brute-forced. If you only need to protect some data for a brief time, DES might be a good choice for that particular application. 3DES is good when a higher level of security is needed. AES might be a better choice when you need a high level of security, but low latency and/or high throughput. The point to be made here is that each algorithm has its place.

Hashing Functions

Hashing functions are used to ensure integrity of the data you are trying to protect. Hashes are one-way mathematical functions that are virtually impossible to reverse. Therefore, when you create a hash, it is highly unlikely that a hash value that matches the original would have been tampered with.

A hash means that you are combining an arbitrary bunch of data with the hash function. You get a fixed-length hash value or sum. This hash value or sum is used to verify that the data you sent is the data that was received. Many pieces of software are distributed over the Internet, so in order to verify that they are not tampered with, you need to compare the hash value that was provided by the distributor with the hash value that you get once you receive the software.

A number of open-source and commercial software packages use Message Digest 5 (MD5) as their choice for a hash function. One way to verify a software package that has been hashed with MD5 is to use an application like md5sum on Unix platforms or Winmd5sum, which is a third-party open-source program available for the Windows platform.

You may be familiar with cyclic redundancy check (CRC) checksums. Hashes are similar to this but are much more cryptographically secure. A hash is strong enough that any two separate sets of data are virtually assured not to create the same hash value.

Hashing functions are covered in more detail in Chapter 10, "Using Digital Signatures."

Summary

In this chapter you learned about the history of cryptography and the difference between cryptography and cryptanalysis. You also learned about the differences in encryption algorithms.

We explored the different types of symmetric encryption algorithms that can be employed.

Finally, we looked at criteria on how to choose the algorithm that you want to suit your application.

Exam Essentials

Remember the historical evolution of cryptography and the differences between cryptology, cryptography, and cryptanalysis.   One of the original works of cryptography was the Caesar cipher, or substitution cipher. A Vigenère cipher is a polyalphabetic cipher. A transposition cipher doesn't change the plaintext but merely rearranges it.

Understand the differences in asymmetric and symmetric encryption and then be able to discuss the various symmetric encryption algorithms.   The main differences in symmetric and asymmetric encryption are that in symmetric encryption, the same key is used. Symmetric encryption keys range in length from 40 bits to 256 bits.

Know the different types of symmetric encryption algorithms.   The most common types of symmetric encryption algorithm are the DES, 3DES, AES, and SEAL algorithms.

Know the different types of encryption algorithms and how to make a choice that fits your application.   The two primary criteria for choosing your encryption algorithm are trustworthiness and protection against brute-force attacks, which is really about key strength.

Written Lab

Write the answers to the following questions:

1. What is the current government standard for encryption?
2. What type of encryption algorithm uses a single key to encrypt/decrypt?
3. What type of cryptography does not change the text but rather changes the position of the text?
4. What is the name of the cipher that uses a polyalphabetic scheme?
5. Which alternative algorithm to 3DES uses a 160-bit key?
6. Which block cipher mode use XOR as part of its algorithm?
7. Which cipher is also called a one-time pad?
8. What is the name of the cipher used in AES?
9. What is the name of the task someone who breaks ciphers performs?
10. Which type of symmetric encryption is not supported in IPSec hardware?

Hands-on Lab

Hands-on Lab 9.1: Creating a Substitution Cipher

1. Using the regular alphabet, create a four-position substitution cipher.
2. Refer to the alphabet shown here to create a four-position substitution cipher:
    ABCDEFGHIJKLMNOPQRSTUVWXYZ
3. The phrase you will be encoding is "IS THIS THING ON."
4. Starting with the word *IS*, count down four places for each letter, so the *I* will become *M* and the *S* will become *W*.
5. Complete the rest of the words in the phrase.
6. Review the completed encoded phase that follows and see if yours matches up:
    MW XLMW XLMRK SR

Review Questions

1. Which type of cipher substitutes letters of the alphabet, based on a position offset from the original letter?

    A.   Block cipher

    B.   Substitution cipher

    C.   Vigenere cipher

    D.   Polyalphabetic cipher

2. Which type of cipher is a rail fence cipher?

    A.   Substitution

    B.   Block

    C.   Streaming

    D.   Transposition

3. What is the minimum level of IOS that supports AES for IPSec encryption?

    A.   12.1(3)

    B.   12.3(1)

    C.   12.2(13)T

    D.   12.2(1)T

4. What IPSec protocol would you choose if you had an application that was sensitive to latency but required high security?

    A.   3DES

    B.   AES

    C.   SEAL

    D.   RC4

5. What is the name of the attack method that can be used to defeat all cryptography methods?

    A.   Brute force

    B.   Spoofing

    C.   Honeypot

    D.   Fuzzing

6. Which type of encryption algorithm uses an encryption, decryption, and encryption scheme to achieve a 168-bit key strength?

    A.   SEAL

    B.   RC4

    C.   RC2

    D.   3DES

7. Which current encryption algorithm key strength that follows is considered inadequate, subject to brute-force attacks?

   A. 30 bit

   B. 40 bit

   C. 56 bit

   D. 64 bit

8. What type of encryption algorithm uses a 160-bit key?

   A. SEAL

   B. RC4

   C. DES

   D. CBC

9. Which algorithm is frequently used in file-encryption software?

   A. 3DES

   B. RC4

   C. RC2

   D. SEAL

10. What function does a hash perform?

   A. Confidentiality

   B. Compression

   C. Availability

   D. Integrity

11. True or false: the Rijndael cipher is *not* supported on the Cisco VPN 3000 Concentrator.

12. Which of the following key lengths for symmetric encryption provides protection against quantum computing?

   A. 128

   B. 112

   C. 256

   D. 212

13. Using the same key in both of the 3DES encrypt cycles of the process would yield a key strength of ____ bits.

   A. 112

   B. 116

   C. 168

   D. 132

14. Which of the following is *not* a key length option when using AES?

    A. 256

    B. 192

    C. 128

    D. 112

15. What is the name of the software used on Unix systems that can determine hash values?

    A. Hashsum

    B. Md5sum

    C. Winmd5sum

    D. Md5value

16. Which of the following is not considered a trustworthy symmetric encryption algorithm?

    A. IDEA

    B. RC2

    C. RC4

    D. 3DES

17. True or false: a hash can be used to provide confidentiality of data.

18. Which of the following types of encryption algorithm is *not* a symmetric encryption algorithm?

    A. DES

    B. RSA

    C. RC4

    D. AES

19. How many possible combinations of AES key length and block size are there?

    A. 6

    B. 8

    C. 9

    D. 10

20. If you have to use DES because of compatibility purposes with a business partner, what can you do to mitigate the risk? Choose all that apply.

    A. Rotate keys frequently.

    B. Use DES twice.

    C. Protect your communications regarding keys.

    D. Use OFB mode.

Answers to Review Questions

1. B. In a substitution cipher, a different letter that is some number of places away from the original letter of the alphabet is substituted for the original letter. This is also referred to as a Caesar cipher.

2. D. A rail fence cipher is a type of transposition cipher, where the letters of the message aren't changed, just moved.

3. C. The minimum level of IOS that supports AES as an encryption algorithm is 12.2(13)T.

4. B. AES, which is the latest government standard, also runs very fast, so it is beneficial to use in a low-latency application situation.

5. A. Brute-force attacks can be used to defeat all cryptography methods, assuming there are enough time and resources. No one method can be considered unbreakable.

6. D. Triple DES, or 3DES, takes the DES encryption scheme and performs an encryption, decryption, and encryption with three different keys to achieve a 168-bit key strength.

7. B. A 40-bit key strength is considered inadequate because of brute-force attack vulnerability. However, it is adequate if you only need to protect some data for a brief time.

8. A. SEAL uses a 160-bit key for encryption.

9. B. RC4 is frequently used in file-encryption software.

10. D. A hash is used to perform data integrity.

11. False. The Cisco VPN 3000 Concentrator supports AES on version 3.6 and above.

12. C. In symmetric encryption, a key length of 256 is considered to provide protection against quantum computing.

13. A. Using the same key in both encrypt cycles yields a key strength of 112 bits. If different keys are used during the two encrypt cycles, then the key strength is 168 bits.

14. D. The three options for key lengths when using AES as your encryption scheme are 128, 192, and 256 bits.

15. B. The md5sum program is typically part of the Unix distribution and can be used to determine MD5 hash values.

16. B. Of the encryption algorithms listed, only RC2 is not considered a trustworthy algorithm.

17. False. A hash can be used only for data integrity.

18. B. DES, RC4, and AES are all symmetric encryption algorithms. RSA is an asymmetric encryption algorithm, covered in Chapter 11, "Using Asymmetric Encryption and PKI."

19. C. There are three possible key lengths and three possible block sizes in AES as it is today, which equates to nine possible combinations.

20. A, C. The two items on this list that can be done to mitigate the risk of using DES are to rotate the keys frequently and protect your communications regarding keys.

Answers to Written Lab

1. AES

2. Symmetric

3. Transposition

4. Vigenère

5. SEAL

6. CBC

7. Vernam

8. Rijndael

9. Cryptanalysis

10. SEAL

Chapter

10

Using Digital Signatures

**THE FOLLOWING CCNA-SECURITY EXAM
TOPICS ARE COVERED IN THIS CHAPTER:**

- ✓ Hashing overview
- ✓ Explain hash function and values
- ✓ Explain hashing algorithms
- ✓ Explain digital signatures

In Chapter 10 we are going to discuss hashing functions. The hashing function will lay the groundwork for hashing values. To generate the hashing values, we will look at two primary hashing algorithms, MD5 and SHA-1.

Once you have an understanding of hashing and its components, we will discuss digital signatures. We will look at the features that make up digital signatures and the algorithms that generate them.

Hashing Overview

What is hashing? Simply put, hashing is taking some type of input data and generating some sort of value. This value is typically a fixed-length integer. The process of taking input data and generating the value is called a *hash function*. The output of the hash function is called the *hash value*.

There are a couple of other terms for hash value. One is *fingerprint*, because the value is supposed to be unique for any data, the same way a fingerprint is unique to a person. The other is *message digest*, or simply *digest*. The name of one popular hashing algorithm, Message Digest 5 (MD5), is based on this term.

We'll discuss the terminology and hashing process in greater detail throughout this chapter.

Hashing is used for many things within technology. It is used in file integrity, database indexing, and security features, to name a few. Hashing starts with data. The data can be as small as a one-page document or as large as a single program that is a gigabyte in size. A hashing program takes the data and runs it through a mathematical algorithm. The output of the mathematical algorithm is the hash value. In summary, hashing takes variable-length data and generates a fixed-length value.

To help explain hashing, we will look at a few types of hashing not specific to security. Have you ever downloaded a file from the Internet? Have you seen an SHA-1 or MD5 value next to the download? These SHA-1 and/or MD5 values are examples of *file integrity hashing*. The website hosting the download has taken the file you wish to download and run it through a hashing program. The output is the hash value. It is listed on the website so that once you have completed your download, you can run it through your own hashing program and compare the hash values. If the value from your hashing program is the same as the hash value listed on the website, you know the program has not been altered or corrupted. Another thing you may have noticed is that the length of the value is always the same. This is called a *fixed-length output*.

 HashCalc (www.slavasoft.com/hashcalc/) is a freeware program that allows you to calculate the hash values of a file.

Hashing is also used to improve search efficiency in databases. Table 10.1 is a list of names and addresses of people. Such a list inside a database is called a *data array*. Immediately you will notice that the names and addresses are not the same length. When data fields are different lengths, a search has to look at every field. This takes a long time in a large database.

TABLE 10.1   Data Array without Indexing

Name	Address
Teresa Von	123 Best Ave
Daniel Smith	4567 Sunset Lane
Robert Ramsalbottom	89101 Annapolis Circle

Now if we used a hashing algorithm against each line of data, it would generate a unique identifier. This process would be called database indexing via hashing.

- Teresa Von + 123 Best Ave = 7463
- Daniel Smith + 4567 Sunset Lane = 8374
- Robert Ramsalbottom + 89101 Annapolis Circle = 1923

Table 10.2 shows the result of hashing. To search, you take the search data and run it through the hashing program. This generates a unique identifier like the four-digit numbers shown in the Index column of the table. (Most hashing algorithms will produce a large identifier, but for this example and simplicity we are using a four-digit number.) Once the program knows the unique identifier, it can search a single field in the database—the index or search field—for a matching four-digit number. This is much more efficient than searching multiple fields of variable length.

TABLE 10.2 Data Array with Indexing

Index (Search Field)	Name	Address
7463	Teresa Von	123 Best Ave
8374	Daniel Smith	4567 Sunset Lane
1923	Robert Ramsalbottom	89101 Annapolis Circle

Now let us expand on the two examples. We saw in the first example how hashing was used for *integrity* and in the second example how it was used for *efficiency*. In security we can use both of these methods. Say we want to transmit data between two parties over the Internet. We want to guarantee the data has not been altered (integrity), and we want to transfer the data as efficiently as possible. A hashing algorithm is what we need. The sender will hash the data that needs to be sent. The sender will then send the data and in a separate transmission send the hash value. The receiver will receive the data and hash value. It will then run the data through its own hash algorithm and generate a hash value. Then it will compare the generated hash value with the hash value that was sent by the sender. If the values are equal, the receiver knows the data was not altered. This process is very efficient because only the original data and a small hash value are sent to verify the integrity.

 Real World Scenario

Verifying the Integrity of Downloaded Software

The remote sales office for the XYZ Corporation is hosting a web server for software downloads. Customers access the web server from the Internet and download the software for installation on their computer. Customers have been complaining that the software is not installing correctly. It was determined that the software file on the web server was corrupted. Your boss has tasked you with providing a solution to guarantee that the software being downloaded is not corrupt.

You decide to provide hashing values on the website for all software downloads. Customers will be able to use these hashing values to verify that the downloaded software is not corrupt.

Before any software is provided on the web server, it will be run through a hashing program to generate a hash value. The software will be listed on the website with the hash value displayed in a hexadecimal format next to the download link. Once the customers download the software, they can run the software file through a hashing program to generate the hash value. If the hash values the customers generate match the hash values listed on the website, the customers know the software is not corrupt.

Features of Hash Functions and Values

A hash function is a mathematical program that takes variable-length data and produces a fixed-length value. The process that takes place to generate the value from the data is called the *hash function*. Figure 10.1 shows the hash function process.

FIGURE 10.1   Hash function process

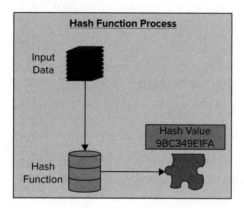

We start with the data. We need some type of data in order to hash. Once we have data to hash, the data then moves into the hash function. Each hashing algorithm computes the data differently.

Explaining the actual hashing algorithm computations is outside the scope of this book. The RFCs for the hashing algorithms would be a great place to view the mathematical computations. The RFCs for the common hashing algorithms are discussed in "Hashing Algorithms," later in this chapter.

Once the hash function has completed, it produces a hash value. The hash value is used to verify the integrity of the data after transfer.

We looked at the hash function from a logical view. Now we will look at the hash function from a simple equation perspective. Let's put some variables around each component in the hash function.

- d = Data to be hashed

- F = Hash function

- h = Hash value

As always, we will start with the data d. We put the data in the hash function $F(d)$. The output of $F(d)$ will provide h. In simple equation terms $F(d) = h$.

In security applications, one of the essential features of a hash function is that the equation works only one way. So $h = F(d)$ cannot be true. You cannot take the h and determine the d. This is called a *one-way hash*.

Also, the hash function must not take a different d and generate the same h. If a different d generates an identical h, this is called a collision.

Now that you know how a hash function works, we need to look at what makes up a hash function. A hash function has five main features:

- Easily compute the hash value for any message
- Must never create the same hash value from two different sets of data
- Cannot modify the message without altering the hash value
- Cannot determine the message from the hash value
- Take variable-length data and produce a fixed-length value

Let us look at each of these features in greater detail. Table 10.3 will take the hash function features and turn them into simple terms.

TABLE 10.3   Hash Function Terms

Hash Function Features	Simple Terms
Easily compute the hash value for any message	Fast and efficient
Must never create the same hash value from two different sets of data	Collision resistant
Cannot modify the message without altering the hash value	Manipulation resistant
Cannot determine the message from the hash value	One-way hash
Take variable-length data and produce a fixed-length value	Fixed-length hash value

Fast and Efficient

A hash function must be fast and efficient, especially if it is used in cryptography. For example, a sender wants to start a communication with a receiver. If that communication is going to be hashed when sent and also when received, the hash function has to work as fast as possible so as not to delay the communication. This is especially important for digital signatures (see "Digital Signatures," later in this chapter, for more information).

Collision Resistant

Collisions are usually undesirable, and in the world of hashing this holds true as well. A collision occurs when the hashing algorithm produces the same hash value for two different sets of data. Because hashing is used for integrity, it is very important that the hashing algorithm does not produce duplicate hashes for different data. Newer hashing algorithms are being created and deployed because of the collision issues seen in some of the most prominent algorithms like MD5 and SHA-1. Collisions may happen in everyday use of hashing but may go unseen by the average administrator.

 Just to clarify, the collision is not physical in nature—two hashes are not bouncing around on the wire and hitting each other. The term means the algorithm produced the same hash value on two different types of data.

Collisions do not go unnoticed by hackers, however. If a hacker can make a hashing algorithm cause a collision, they can start to reverse engineer the algorithm. This is particularly important to hackers when they try to crack passwords. If a hacker knows how to manipulate the hash, they can create a table of known hashes. These tables are called *rainbow tables*. With a list of rainbow tables, a hacker can reverse engineer the hash and gain access to the data, in this case the password.

Manipulation Resistant

Just as two different data sets need to produce different hashes, it is important that changes to a data set produce a different hash. If there is any change in the data, no matter how minimal, the hash must change. If a hacker could modify the data and the hash stayed the same, the hashing function would be useless.

To demonstrate this feature, we will put a simple phrase through two different hashing functions, MD5 and SHA-1 (discussed in more detail in "Hashing Algorithms," later in this chapter). Then we will alter the phrase by one character and see how the hashing values change.

- "I will pass the Cisco CCNA Security Test!"
  - MD5 = f3fe82c8a8059137a9d65669f76bffe6
  - SHA-1 = b81fc23a64c6478d3738c58ff3d2f9e669da80c5
- "I will pass the Cisco CCNA Security Pest!"
  - MD5 = 89fc1190eeaa0ca0bbff176fc9f218ea
  - SHA-1 = 90fff0bff553ddd534e41f1f71a4b2f59930d296

All we did was change "Test" to "Pest." A simple letter change completely modified the hash value. This is manipulation resistance at work.

One-Way Hashing

A one-way hash takes data and creates a hash that cannot be used to re-create the data (although in some cases a one-way hash can be reverse engineered by a hacker). Two-way hashes also exist but are less common. With a two-way hash, you can re-create the data from the hash. In this chapter we are concerned only with one-way hashing.

Fixed-Length Hashing Values

Most hash values are of fixed length—that is, the hash value generated by the hashing algorithm is always the same length, no matter how much data is computed.

The two most common hashing algorithms are the MD5 and SHA-1 algorithms. The MD5 algorithm produces a 128-bit or 32-character hexadecimal hash value. The SHA-1 algorithm produces a 160-bit or 40-character hexadecimal hash value. Here are sample hash values of the same input data.

- MD5 = d41d8cd98f00b204e9800998ecf8427e

- SHA-1 = a9993e364706816aba3e25717850c26c9cd0d89d

Hash Message Authentication Code

Hash Message Authentication Code (HMAC) is a way to further secure a hash. HMAC is not a hash function requirement but has its place when we talk about securing the hash function. Because some popular hash algorithms have been shown not to be completely collision resistant, it is important to add newer techniques to validate the integrity of a hash. HMAC accomplishes this by adding another layer of data into the hashing mix. This layer is called a *secret key*. The secret key is known only by the sender and receiver, and it provides authentication to HMAC.

In the HMAC process, the input data is taken and a secret key is added. Both the input data and secret key are put through the hashing algorithm. This produces an *HMAC hash*. The size of the HMAC hash is the same as that of the corresponding hashing algorithm. (The two main types of HMAC hashes are HMAC-MD5, which produces a 128-bit hash, and HMAC-SHA-1, which produces a 160-bit hash.) Figure 10.2 shows the HMAC process.

FIGURE 10.2   HMAC process

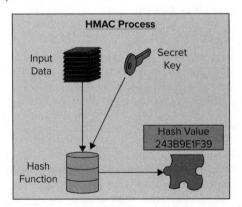

The receiver verifies the data by taking the received data and running it through its own hashing algorithm and adding the secret key. It then compares the hash values. If the hash values are equal, then the message has integrity and simple authentication. The authentication is gained by the secret key shared between the sender and receiver. As long as no one else gains access to the secret key, the HMAC hash is secure. As with any secret key or password, you must safeguard it to prevent unauthorized usage.

To expand on HMAC we will use our equation from the hash function section. We will add a variable s for the secret key.

- d = Data to be hashed
- F = Hash function
- h = Hash value
- s = Secret key

We will start with the data d. We put the data and secret key in the hash function $F(d + s)$. The output of $F(d + s)$ will provide h. In simple equation terms $F(d + s) = h$. This too is a one-way hash, so $h = F(d + s)$ is not true (you cannot generate the original data from the hash value). The receiver takes the data, adds a secret key, and computes the hash. As long as the data and secret keys are the same, the hash values should be equal.

Hashing Algorithms

In this section we will talk about the mathematical computations used to create the hashing algorithms. The two specific hashing algorithms we will discuss are Message Digest 5 (MD5) and Secure Hash Algorithm (SHA-1).

MD5 Algorithm

In this section we will discuss the MD5 hashing algorithm. We will start with the creation and evolution of the algorithm. We will move into the features and finally the advantages and disadvantages of using MD5.

The MD5 algorithm was invented in 1991 by Ronald Rivest of MIT.

> **NOTE** Ronald Rivest is the same Rivest who helped create the RSA algorithm. He is the *R* in RSA.

MD5 is based on an older hashing algorithm called MD4. The best-known use of MD4 is with Microsoft Windows NT-Hash, which is used in NT, XP, and Vista operating systems. The MD4 hashing algorithm was cracked in the late nineties. MD5 fixed the weakness in MD4 and was ratified in 1992 in RFC 1321. MD5 was designed to run efficiently on 32-bit processors.

The MD5 algorithm produces a fixed-length hash value, 128 bits in length. For binary people that is four times the length of an IPv4 address, or the same size as an IPv6 address. For the non-binary people it is a 32-character hexadecimal number. You may see this number when you download a file from the Internet.

MD5 is very collision resistant. The algorithm was designed to generate unique hash values for each unique input. However, lately there have been rumblings in the security community about the weaknesses in MD5. Many government agencies will be required to move to a stronger algorithm in a few years.

The following list describes the advantages and disadvantages of MD5.

- Advantages of MD5
  - Utilizes a fast computation algorithm
  - Provides collision resistance
  - Is in widespread use
  - Provides a one-way hash
- Disadvantages of MD5
  - Has known security flaws and vulnerabilities
  - Is less secure than the SHA-1 algorithm

SHA-1 Algorithm

In this section we will discuss the Secure Hash Algorithm version 1 (SHA-1). We will look at the birth of SHA-1 and then move to the features and functions. We will finish this section with the advantages and disadvantages of SHA-1.

SHA was created in 1993 by the National Institute of Standards and Technology (NIST). Soon after its creation a flaw was uncovered. The original version with the flaw was named SHA-0 and withdrawn from use. The revised version, SHA-1, came out in 1995. SHA-1 is the most widely used version. For further details on SHA-1 refer to RFC 3174.

 There are two newer versions of SHA. SHA-2 is available for use and has options for the digest lengths. SHA-3 is in development to fix known issues in SHA-1 and SHA-2. SHA-2 and SHA-3 are outside the realm of this chapter.

SHA-1 produces a fixed-length hash value of 160 bits, or 40 hexadecimal characters. SHA-1 is able to process only input data with a maximum length of $(2^{64} - 1)$ bits. SHA-1 is based on the MD4 and MD5 hashing algorithms. SHA-1 produces a larger hash value (160 bits) than MD5 (128 bits), thus making it harder to crack with brute force or reverse engineering. However, the computation time for this longer hash value makes SHA-1 slower than MD5.

The following list describes the advantages and disadvantages of SHA-1.

- Advantages of SHA-1
  - Produces a longer hash value than MD5
  - Is collision resistant
  - Is in widespread use
  - Provides a one-way hash
- Disadvantages of SHA-1
  - Is a slower computational algorithm than the MD5 algorithm
  - Has known security vulnerabilities

MD5 and SHA-1 Comparison Chart

Table 10.4 provides a high-level comparison between the MD5 and SHA-1 hashing algorithms.

TABLE 10.4   Comparing MD5 to SHA-1

	MD5	SHA-1
Hashing Type	One-way	One-way
Input Data Size	Unlimited	$(2^{64} - 1)$
Hash Value	128-bit	160-bit
Computation Speed	Faster	Slower
Attack Protection	Weaker	Stronger
Hashing Collisions	Resistant	Resistant
RFC	1321	3174

Most of the time it is best practice to use SHA-1 over MD5. MD5 is a little faster than SHA-1, but the weaker security in MD5 should be a driving force to use SHA-1.

Digital Signatures

In the following sections we will discuss digital signatures. We will start with an overview, which includes a description and the features of digital signatures. We will move into the digital signature process by looking at the two main algorithms, DSA and RSA. Finally, we will compare the DSA and RSA algorithms.

Digital Signatures Overview

A digital signature is an electronic means to validate the authenticity and integrity of a message, software, or document. Most digital signatures use asymmetric cryptography to accomplish the authenticity.

You know that your signature on paper proves you validated and received a document. Likewise, a digital signature can validate an electronic document, message, or even a software program. It is probably easier to forge your personal signature than it is to forge a digital signature. We will get into the reasons why throughout this section.

Digital signatures provide three main features.

- Integrity
- Authentication
- Non-repudiation

We will look at each of these features in more detail.

Integrity

In the first part of this chapter we discussed hashing and how hashing provides integrity. Hashing also provides integrity to digital signatures. To create a digital signature the data is hashed. We will get into the actual process in the next section.

Authentication

We first talked about authentication when we discussed HMAC. The drawback for HMAC is that both parties have to know the secret key. This does not work well when the parties do not know each other. Digital signatures provide a different type of authentication feature, while still ensuring as efficiently as possible that the party one is dealing with is who they say they are.

Non-repudiation

What is non-repudiation? Let us first look at repudiation. Repudiation is the ability to refute something. It is simply being able to say "I did not say that" with no proof that you did. Non-repudiation is the ability to prove that someone *did* say something. If we can prove something came from someone or someone said something, they cannot deny the fact. Just like a real signature, a digital signature may be used to prove that you communicated something or that you saw a document.

Digital Signature Process

In today's world there are two main digital signature processes—Digital Signature Standard (DSS) and the RSA algorithm. We will review the two standards in the follow sections. Figure 10.3 shows the digital signature process.

FIGURE 10.3   Digital signature process

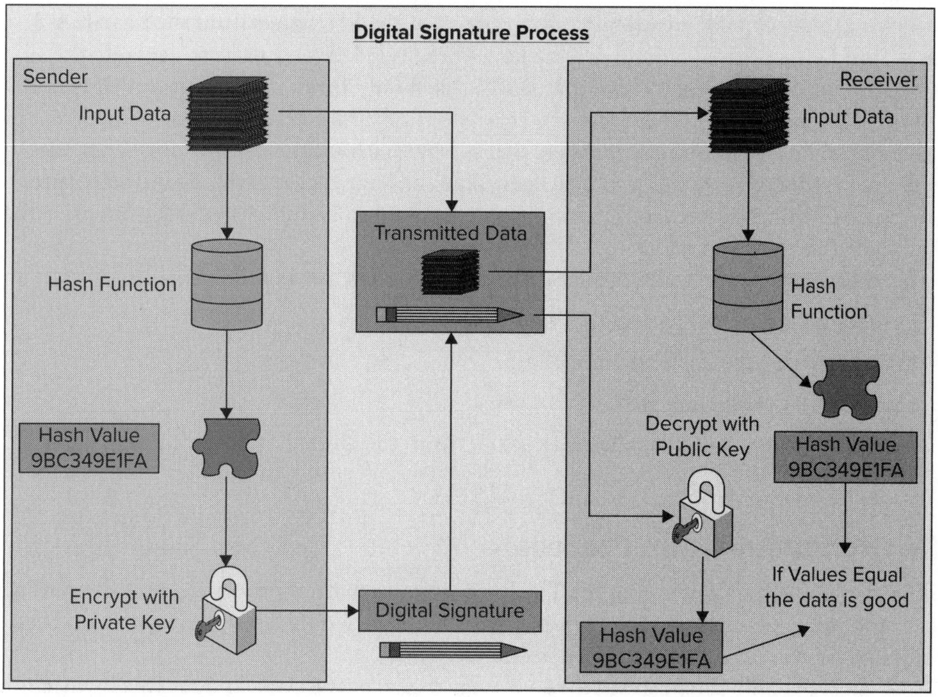

Digital Signature Process

Sender   Receiver

Input Data

Input Data

Transmitted Data

Hash Function

Hash
Function

Hash Value
9BC349E1FA

Decrypt with
Public Key

Hash Value
9BC349E1FA

If Values Equal
the data is good

Encrypt with
Private Key

Digital Signature

Hash Value
9BC349E1FA

Digital Signature Standard

In 1994, the National Institute of Standards and Technology (NIST) issued a Federal
Information Processing Standards (FIPS) publication for Digital Signature Standard (DSS).
This standard is outlined in FIPS Publication 186.

You can view the actual standard on the NIST website at
www.itl.nist.gov/fipspubs/fip186.htm.

The DSS outlines a specific algorithm to be used in creating the digital signature. This
algorithm is the Digital Signature Algorithm (DSA). In the next section we will look at the
DSA process.

DSA Digital Signature Process

DSA is considered to be *public key cryptography (PKC)*. Public key cryptography is different
from secret key cryptography like that used in HMAC. Public key cryptography utilizes
both private and public keys. The public key is assumed to be known by all of the public.

DSA utilizes two keys for generating the digital signature. The first key comes from the hashing function. The original hashing function used with DSA was SHA-1. The current version of DSA is capable of using newer versions of the SHA algorithm such as SHA-2. The second key is created from a private key. These two keys are used to generate the digital signature. It is good to note that DSA is used only for digital signatures. It is not used for encryption.

Once DSA has generated the message digest from hashing the data, it uses its private key to encrypt the message digest. The encrypted message digest is the digital signature. Because DSA utilizes a two-key system, it is considered to be more processor intensive than other algorithms such as RSA.

The main features of the DSA digital signature process are as follows:

- Utilizes multiple keys to generate the digital signature.
- Uses SHA-1 as the hashing algorithm.
- Considered slower than RSA.
- The DSA software can legally be exported from the United States because it lacks encryption.

RSA Digital Signature Process

RSA is also public-key cryptography. The RSA digital signature process is more streamlined, faster, and more flexible than the DSA process. But some would argue that with the speed and flexibility comes a decrease in security.

RSA encrypts only the hash value or message digest of the data. It does this by using the private key. The encrypted message digest is the digital signature. The digital signature is added to the original data. This is sent to the recipient.

The recipient then generates its own message digest from the data that was sent. The recipient decrypts the digital signature with the sender's public key. If the generated message digest and the decrypted message digest are equal, the data has integrity and is authenticated. Integrity is proven when the two hash values are the same. Authentication is proven because the public key will decrypt only messages created by the sender's private key.

The main features of the RSA digital signature process are as follows:

- Considered faster and more flexible than DSA.
- Encrypts only the message digest.
- Uses private key to encrypt and public key to decrypt.
- It typically cannot be exported from the United States because of the encryption laws.

The Department of Commerce controls the export law on encryption software. The law restricts the export of encryption software, components, and hardware. If you have ever downloaded software or bought hardware with encryption capabilities, you probably had to agree not to export the item.

DSA and RSA Comparison Chart

Table 10.5 provides a high-level comparison between the DSA and RSA digital signature algorithms.

TABLE 10.5   Comparing DSA to RSA

	DSA	RSA
Key Type	Public key	Public key
Encryption	No	Yes
Computation Speed	Slower	Faster
Security Strength	Strong	Strong

Summary

In this chapter you learned about the overall function of hashing. We addressed how hashing can be used for file integrity checking, database indexing, and ultimately security functionality. We showed you examples of these functions ranging from integrity checking a file to the efficiency of database indexing and brought it all together with security. With integrity checking and efficiency, we laid the groundwork for the rest of the chapter.

You learned about the features and functions of the hash function. The hash function is the main process of hashing. It takes in data and spits out a hash value. Important things to know about the hash function are the features needed to provide a good hash. The value section of this chapter outlined different types of values that can be generated from the hash function. We focused on the one-way hash and the fixed-length hash value.

We discussed hashing algorithms, which compute the data and create the hash value. The two types of hashing algorithms we reviewed are MD5 and SHA-1. These are the two primary hashing algorithms in existence today.

Finally, we looked at digital signatures. Digital signatures employ the use of hashing to generate a unique signature for each document. We looked at the DSS and how it is processed. We also focused on two digital signature processes, DSA and RSA. We then compared the DSA and RSA processes.

Exam Essentials

Understand what a hashing function does.   A hash function is a mathematical program that takes variable-length data and produces a fixed-length value. It is simply the process, function, and/or algorithm that takes the data and generates the hash.

Understand the features of a hashing function.   Hashing functions need to be fast and efficient. A hashing function needs to be collision resistant to provide unique output for all data. Manipulation resistance ensures that changes in the data change the output of the hash value. A one-way hash ensures that the hash value cannot reproduce the original data. The hashing function produces a fixed-length hash value from variable-length inputs.

Know the two primary hashing algorithms.   The two algorithms are MD5 and SHA-1. The MD5 algorithm generates a 128-bit hash value output. The SHA-1 algorithm generates a 160-bit hash value output. The MD5 algorithm computes faster than the SHA-1 algorithm, but the SHA-1 algorithm is more secure than the MD5 algorithm. You should use the SHA-1 algorithm instead of the MD5 algorithm when speed is not an issue.

Understand what a digital signature is and its features.   A digital signature is a way to sign a document, message, or software to prove who it came from and that it has not been altered. A digital signature provides three main features: integrity, authentication, and non-repudiation.

Know the different digital signature processes and features.   The two digital signature processes discussed in this chapter are DSA and RSA. DSA utilizes multiple keys to generate the digital signature. It uses SHA-1 as the hashing algorithm. DSA can be exported from the United States because it lacks encryption. RSA encrypts only the message digest, not all of the data (encrypting all of the data would double the amount of data that is transferred). RSA is considered faster and more flexible than DSA, but RSA cannot be exported from the United States because of the encryption laws.

Written Lab

Write the answers to the following questions:

1. What functionality does hashing provide: confidentiality, integrity, or availability?
2. HMAC adds what to the hashing equation?
3. Which hashing algorithm is considered faster?
4. Which hashing algorithm produces a 160-bit hash?

5. What is the term when a hashing function produces the same hash from different data?

6. What are other names for hash value?

7. Which digital signature process is considered faster?

8. What does DSS stand for?

9. What does the RSA encrypt in digital signatures?

10. Which key is used to generate the digital signature?

Hands-on Lab

Hands-on Lab 10.1: Generate a Hash Value from a File

In this hands-on lab you will need a text editor such as Notepad (any text editor will work) and a hashing program such as HashCalc. The hashing program will need to provide either an MD5 or SHA-1 output value to complete this lab.

1. Open your favorite text program, such as Notepad.

2. Generate simple text within a file.

3. Save the file.

4. Open a hashing program, such as HashCalc.

5. Choose the text file you just created. Select the MD5 and/or SHA-1 hash.

6. Generate and view the hash value for the file.

7. Open the text file and modify the text.

8. Run the file through the hash program again.

9. View the difference in the hash values.

Review Questions

1. MD5 generates what length of hash value?

    A. 168 bit

    B. 128 bit

    C. Variable length

    D. 160 bit

2. What are two common hashing algorithms? (Choose two.)

    A. RSA

    B. SHA-1

    C. Diffie-Hellman

    D. MD5

3. Which hashing algorithm is considered faster?

    A. SHA-1

    B. AES

    C. MD5

    D. All algorithms are the same speed.

4. Which hashing algorithm's maximum input data is $(2^{64} - 1)$?

    A. SHA-1

    B. SHA-1 and MD5

    C. MD5

    D. None of the above

5. Which of the following is not a main feature of a hashing function?

    A. Unable to modify the message without altering the hash value

    B. Take variable-length data and produce a fixed-length value

    C. Determine the message from the hash value

    D. Easily compute the hash value for any message

6. Which hashing algorithm is considered more secure?

    A. MD5

    B. RSA

    C. SHA-1

    D. DSS

7. Which hashing algorithm has a longer hash value?

   A. DSA

   B. ROIBCE

   C. ABC

   D. SHA-1

8. HMAC uses what additional feature for authentication in hashing?

   A. Public key

   B. Secret key

   C. Private key

   D. Car key

9. Who invented the MD5 algorithm?

   A. Ronald Rivest

   B. Adi Shamir

   C. Len Ableman

   D. Michael Dedorf

10. When a hash value is written out, it is typically displayed in what format?

   A. Binary

   B. PHP

   C. ASP

   D. Hexadecimal

11. How much does the hash value typically change when a simple change is made to the data?

   A. One character

   B. Two characters

   C. No characters

   D. Many characters

12. What processor speed was MD5 designed for?

   A. 128 bit

   B. 32 bit

   C. 8 bit

   D. 64 bit

13. What was the original algorithm used in DSS?

   A. RSA

   B. DSA

   C. DSP

   D. MD5

14. Which of the following is *not* a feature of a digital signature?

    A. Providing authentication

    B. Providing integrity

    C. Providing repudiation

    D. Providing non-repudiation

15. Which hashing algorithm does DSA utilize?

    A. MD4

    B. SHA-1

    C. DSS

    D. RSA

16. Which digital signature algorithm is considered faster?

    A. RSA

    B. DSA

    C. DSS

    D. DSP

17. Which part of the message does RSA encrypt?

    A. Entire message

    B. Message header

    C. Message digest

    D. RSA does not encrypt.

18. Which algorithms are considered public key cryptography? (Choose all that apply.)

    A. RSA

    B. DSA

    C. HMAC

    D. CA

19. How does a digital signature provide authentication?

    A. A message digest can be decrypted only with a public key generated by a private key.

    B. A message digest can be decrypted only with a private key generated by a public key.

    C. With the use of a secret key.

    D. Only integrity is provided with digital signatures.

20. What part of the message does DSA encrypt?

    A. Entire message

    B. Message header

    C. Message digest

    D. None of it

Answers to Review Questions

1. B. MD5 generates a fixed-length 128-bit output value.

2. B, D. SHA-1 and MD5 are the two common hashing algorithms. RSA and Diffie-Hellman are public-key cryptography protocols.

3. C. MD5 is faster than SHA-1, but it is commonly thought of as less secure than SHA-1. AES is an encryption algorithm.

4. A. SHA-1 has a maximum input data limit of (2^{64} – 1). MD5 does not have a limit.

5. C. A hashing function should generate a hash value but is unable to determine the message from the hash.

6. C. SHA-1 is considered more secure than MD5. RSA is a digital signature process and DSS is a standard.

7. D. SHA-1 is the only hashing algorithm listed, and it generates a 160-bit hash value compared to MD5's 128-bit, which is not listed.

8. B. A secret key is added in the hash for HMAC. Only the sender and receiver know the secret key. Public and private keys are used in digital signatures, not hashing.

9. A. Ronald Rivest invented MD5 and MD4. Adi Shamir and Len Ableman are the *S* and the *A* in RSA. Michael Dedorf is fictitious.

10. D. Most of the time you see a hash value in print it will be in hexadecimal. Binary would be very long if it was typed out. PHP and ASP are programming languages.

11. D. It is hard to say how many changes will be made to the hash value. The best answer is many characters. If you change one character in the data, it doesn't change just one character in the hash value.

12. B. MD5 was designed for 32-bit processors; 8-bit processors were out but much slower. In the early nineties 64-bit and 128-bit processors did not exist.

13. B. Digital Signature Algorithm (DSA) was the original algorithm used in DSS. RSA is available now. DSP stands for digital signal processor, and MD5 is a hashing algorithm.

14. C. Repudiation—the ability to deny that you did something—is not wanted with digital signatures. We use digital signatures to be able to prove who *did* do something.

15. B. SHA-1 is the correct answer. RSA is an alternative to DSA. MD4 is an older hashing algorithm. DSS is the standard outlining DSA.

16. A. RSA is considered faster, but some would argue that it is less secure than DSA. DSS and DSP are not digital signature algorithms.

17. C. RSA encrypts only the message digest. This limits the amount of data that needs to be transmitted.

18. A, B. The only two that apply are RSA and DSA. HMAC is secret key, and CA is part of Public Key Infrastructure (PKI), not PKC.

19. A. If the message digest is decrypted with the public key and it matches the hash sent by the sender, it is considered authenticated.

20. D. Technically DSA does not encrypt anything. It requires other protocols to accomplish this.

Answers to Written Lab

1. Integrity

2. Secret key

3. MD5

4. SHA-1

5. Collision

6. Message digest, fingerprint

7. RSA

8. Digital Signature Standard

9. Message digest

10. Private key

Chapter

11

Using Asymmetric Encryption and PKI

THE FOLLOWING CCNA-SECURITY EXAM TOPICS ARE COVERED IN THIS CHAPTER:

✓ Asymmetric encryption usage

✓ Asymmetric algorithms and the computations behind them

✓ The components of a PKI

✓ Certificate authorities and their structures

✓ Digital certificates creation, information and usage

✓ PKI standards

In this chapter we are going to continue our discussion from previous chapters on encryption. We will discuss asymmetric encryption and the uses of the technology. Once you understand asymmetric encryption, we will take a deep dive into the workings of two of the primary algorithms, including the mathematics behind the algorithms and the benefits and drawbacks for each solution.

We will then move into the Public Key Infrastructure (PKI), looking at the components of a PKI and how these components work together. Our discussion will then shift to digital certificates. We will outline the enrollment, usage, and information fields for digital certificates.

In the last section, we will look at some of the common PKI standards that provide the foundation of the PKI environment.

Asymmetric Encryption

Asymmetric encryption, also called *public key cryptography (PKC),* is an encryption technique that utilizes a key pair. The key pair includes a public key and a private key. The public key is just that—available to the public. It is made available to anyone who needs to use it. The private key is to be used by a single entity and has to remain private to maintain its integrity.

As with our discussions of symmetric encryption and secret key cryptography in previous chapters, we know that one of the drawbacks of symmetric encryption is the difficulty of sharing a secret key. How do you distribute the secret key, how often should you change the secret key, and what happens if the secret key is compromised? Because of these issues, *asymmetric encryption* was created. Asymmetric encryption allows two parties to create a secure communication channel without any prior knowledge of each other; that is, they don't have to share a secret key. It accomplishes this by using the public key cryptography process.

One drawback of asymmetric encryption over symmetric encryption is processing time. Asymmetric encryption is much slower than symmetric encryption because of the massive computational mathematics involved, which is what makes the technology secure. But the slow performance of this encryption method makes asymmetric encryption impractical for many applications. The main use for asymmetric encryption is to provide a means for creating secret keys for symmetric encryption.

With asymmetric encryption, both the public and private keys can be used for encryption and decryption. Within a single message exchange, though, each key can provide only encryption *or* decryption. If the public key is used to encrypt the message, the private key is used to decrypt, and vice-versa. Different security features are achieved depending on which key is used to encrypt the message. These security features include confidentiality and authentication.

Confidentiality provides a means to keep data private. When information travels over an insecure medium such as the Internet, confidentiality is a necessity. Asymmetric encryption provides confidentiality with the use of the public key.

Authentication provides a means to prove the origin of the data. Knowing where the data comes from is very important. Without authentication, a hacker could impersonate a source and deliver compromised data. Asymmetric encryption utilizes the private key to prove that the source of the data is valid.

Public Key Cryptography Process

In this section we will discuss the components, features, and usage of asymmetric encryption. The components include the public and private key exchange. We will discuss confidentiality and authentication in the features section. Finally, we will provide practical usage information for asymmetric encryption. Figure 11.1 shows the public key cryptography process.

FIGURE 11.1   Public key cryptography process

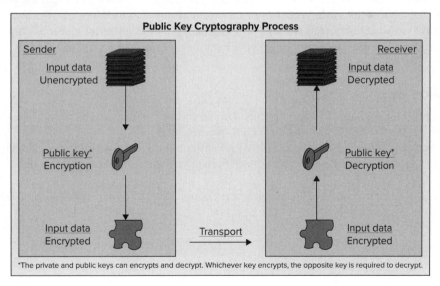

Key Pairs

The public key cryptography process revolves around two keys, one available to the public and the other private, belonging to a single entity. The public and private keys must have different values to be effective. You cannot take the public key and determine the private key, at least not in any time frame that would be relevant.

Key Size

The key size for asymmetric algorithms varies. For most asymmetric algorithms, the key sizes range from 512 bits and 4096 bits. Typically the key size is a multiple of 512 (for example, 512, 1024, 2048, or 4096). Most asymmetric algorithms can utilize variable-length keys.

As with any encryption technique, the longer the key is, the more secure the output will be. This security, of course, is at a cost of computing time. The most common recommendation is to use an algorithm of 2048 or higher for asymmetric encryption.

Private Key

The private key can be calculated multiple ways depending on the algorithm. Some algorithms determine the private key after the public key process has finished. Other algorithms pick a random number and use that as the private key.

On Windows systems, the private keys can be stored in multiple places. They are typically stored in the Registry but can be stored as files in the file system.

The private key can be used to encrypt or decrypt data. In most cases it is used to decrypt data that has been encrypted with the public key. The reason for this is that many asymmetric algorithms are used on the Internet for secure communication to websites. Because most people do not have their own keys, they will request the public key of the website. They will use the public key to encrypt the traffic, which means that the website will have to use its private key to decrypt the traffic.

Public Key

The public key is meant to be used by anyone. No security is given to the public key. It is presumed to be in the public domain with other eyes on it.

Asymmetric algorithms generate public keys differently. Some algorithms pick random numbers, whereas other algorithms create the private key first and then calculate the public key.

The asymmetric algorithm has to be strong enough that the public key cannot be used to determine the private key.

Features

Asymmetric encryption provides two major features: confidentiality and authentication. It accomplishes each of these features in different ways depending on the use of the public or private key.

Confidentiality is achieved by the use of the public key. When the public key is used for encryption, the private key has to be used for decryption. The private key is on one system. When the data is encrypted with the public key, only the system with the private key can decrypt it. Thus we are confident that the data is being decrypted by the right system and only by that system. This preserves the confidentiality of the data.

Authentication is achieved when the private key is used to encrypt the data. We know that only the public key can decrypt data that is encrypted by the private key. We also assume that the public key is known by everyone. If we receive data and can decrypt the data with the public key, we know that the data came from the owner of the private key and no one else. This is authentication because we proved that the system that sent us the data is what it claims to be.

Drawbacks

The main drawback of asymmetric algorithms is the time it takes the algorithms to calculate the keys. The structure of asymmetric algorithms is to use large numbers, which make it secure. These numbers can be hundreds of bits long. Asymmetric algorithms have complex mathematics behind them to generate these keys. Because of the complex mathematics, it takes the processor more time to compute all of these keys—many seconds in some cases compared to milliseconds for some symmetric algorithms.

Another important drawback is the asymmetric algorithm strength compared to the strength of symmetric algorithms. There is no concrete data that proves the ratio between symmetric and asymmetric strengths, but it is important to know that asymmetric algorithms are considered weaker than their symmetric counterparts. An asymmetric algorithm with a 1024-bit key can be 50–90 percent weaker than the same 1024-bit key for symmetric algorithms. This will come into play when you use an asymmetric algorithm to generate a key for a symmetric algorithm. New symmetric algorithms like Advanced Encryption Standard (AES) have variable length strengths and require large secret keys. To generate a secret key via asymmetric encryption, the algorithm will have to generate a larger key and may have to use an asymmetric algorithm of 6144 bits to match the 256-bit or 512-bit key of the symmetric algorithm.

Usage

The main use of asymmetric algorithms is to generate secret keys for symmetric algorithms. Because of the drawbacks we just discussed, asymmetric algorithms are not suited for large data encryption. But they are the best solution when it comes to creating secret keys between two unknown devices. These two devices can be a web server and a PC or two Virtual Private Networks (VPN) connections with limited knowledge of each other.

Hybrid Encryption

A hybrid cryptosystem utilizes both asymmetric and symmetric encryption techniques. There are two main types of encryption with a hybrid encryption solution:

- Key exchange encryption—Encrypt the keys with asymmetric encryption.
- Data encryption—Encrypt the data with symmetric encryption.

Because asymmetric encryption is slow and requires more computing power, it is best suited for small amounts of data. Asymmetric encryption is perfect for encrypting keys. Symmetric encryption is much faster and capable of encrypting large amounts of data efficiently. This makes symmetric encryption perfect for data confidentiality.

The following process is used in hybrid encryption:

1. Encryption from sender
   a. Sender obtains the public key of the receiver.
   b. Sender creates a symmetric secret key with the public key and asymmetric encryption.
   c. Sender encrypts the data using the newly created secret key and symmetric encryption.
   d. Sender encrypts the symmetric secret key with the public key and asymmetric encryption.
   e. Sender transmits both the encrypted secret key and data to the receiver.

2. Decryption from receiver

   a. Receiver uses their private key to decrypt the symmetric secret key.

   b. Receiver uses the symmetric secret key to decrypt the data.

   Figure 11.2 shows the hybrid encryption process.

FIGURE 11.2   Hybrid encryption process

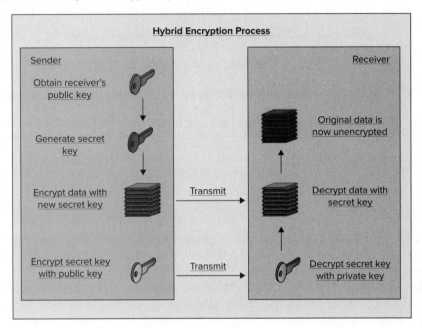

 An example of a hybrid encryption solution is *Secure Shell (SSH)*. SSH utilizes PKC to authenticate the remote PC when connecting. If you have ever used SSH, you should have noticed a message about the SSH signature. You have to accept the signature before making a connection to the SSH-enabled device. Most SSH clients require only this during the first connection and save the signature for subsequent connections. Once the connection is authenticated, symmetric encryption is used to secure the data between the PC and the device.

Asymmetric Encryption Algorithms

The asymmetric encryption algorithm is the heart of asymmetric encryption. The algorithm is the mathematical engine that crunches the numbers to compute the public and private keys. There are multiple asymmetric encryption algorithms, and each algorithm determines the keys differently.

Table 11.1 lists a few sample asymmetric algorithms.

TABLE 11.1 Sample Asymmetric Algorithms

Acronym	Full Name and Description
RSA	Rivest, Shamir, and Adleman. Most widely used PKC in e-commerce transactions.
DH	Diffie-Hellman. Creates secret keys for symmetric encryption.
DSA	Digital Signature Algorithm. Used to create digital signatures.
ECC	Elliptic Curve Cryptography. Utilizes an algebraic structure for key creation.
ElGamal	ElGamal Encryption System. Based on the Diffie-Hellman Key Exchange.

We will discuss two of these algorithms in the following section: RSA and Diffie-Hellman.

RSA Algorithm

We started discussing the features of RSA in Chapter 10, "Using Digital Signatures." In this section we will take a deeper look at how RSA works. The RSA encryption algorithm was invented in 1977 by Ron Rivest, Adi Shamir, and Leonard Adleman of MIT. A patent was filed in 1977 and issued in 1983. The three inventors of the RSA algorithm formed a company called RSA Security, which released the RSA algorithm into the public domain in 2000, three years before the patent would have expired.

The RSA algorithm is one of the most widely used asymmetric algorithms. It is built into Microsoft Internet Explorer and a host of other browsers. It is also used in SSH, IPSec, PGP, and TLS. The RSA algorithm has been in existence for many years and is a proven technology.

The security of the RSA algorithm is simple to explain and simple to generate. Two prime numbers are used, and multiplying these numbers is easy. But determining the original prime numbers from the total is infeasible because of the time it would take to compute the numbers with modern computers.

The RSA algorithm is capable of using variable key lengths between 512 and 2048 bits. It is recommended that you use 2048 bits when possible. The shorter numbers have proven vulnerable because of increased computing power and the use of distributed computing employing hundreds of computers to guess the key.

The three main functions in the RSA algorithm are key creation, encryption, and decryption. We will look at these three functions in greater detail.

RSA Key Table

Table 11.2 lists the variables we will use in the "RSA Key Creation," "RSA Encryption Example," and "RSA Decryption Example" sections that follow.

TABLE 11.2 RSA Key Chart

Key	Description	Public or Private
p	Prime number	Public
q	Prime number	Public
e	Public key	Public
m	Multiplier to determine d	Private
d	Private key	Private
n	Remainder	Public
s	Secret key	Private

RSA Key Creation

In the RSA algorithm, key creation starts with two different large prime numbers, p and q, and a number e, which is not divisible by p or q. To determine the public key you need to know the values of $p * q$ and the number e. The numbers for p and q are randomly generated numbers. The number e is typically a small integer of 3, 17, or 65537. A small integer is used for e to help with computational speed.

- [$e, p * q$] equals the public key.

To obtain the private key we have to find d. The number d is a number that when multiplied by e equals $(p - 1) * (q - 1) + 1$. Or d needs to equal some multiplier m of $(p - 1) * (q - 1) + 1 = m * ((p - 1) * (q - 1)) + 1$. The number d plus $p * q$ equals the private key.

- [$d, p * q$] equals the private key.
- Always keep the value of d secret.

Determining the value of d is typically accomplished by the Euclidean algorithm. The Euclidean algorithm is an effective way of calculating the *greatest common divisor (GCD)*. Find the GCD using the following equation:

$$e * GCD = m * ((p - 1) * (q - 1)) + 1$$

In this case, the GCD will equal d.

These equations are secure because determining the original prime numbers from the result of the equations is infeasible. You could probably determine the prime numbers and ultimately *d* or *e* if you had enough time. But with large enough prime numbers, it would take thousands of years. It is assumed that by the time you calculated the numbers, the decrypted information would be of no use.

Let's assume a person lives 100 years and obtains a social security number when they are born. This would mean that the social security number should remain private for 100 years. If a 50-year-old person transmitted their social security number over the Internet and someone captured the encrypted data, the hacker would have only 50 years to decrypt the data to gain something useful. If the data were encrypted using the RSA algorithm, it would take thousands of years to compute the prime numbers used to encrypt it. Therefore, it is very unlikely that someone could break the encryption and gain access to the encrypted data.

RSA Encryption Example

We described how to compute both the public and private keys. Now let's put some practical numbers around them. We will use small prime numbers for simplicity's sake. With small prime numbers the equation will get large. Just imagine if we were to use large prime numbers.

We will create the public key using the following numbers. These numbers can be picked at random as long as they meet the criteria.

$p = 3$

$q = 5$

$e = 11$

As you can see with these numbers, *p* and *q* are prime numbers and *e* is not divisible by *p* or *q*. Now we need to determine the value of *d*.

$e * GCD = m * ((p - 1) * (q - 1)) + 1$

Let's start by breaking down the equation with known values.

$((p - 1) * (q - 1)) = ((3 - 1) * (5 - 1)) = ((2) * (4)) = 8$

$11 * GCD = m * 8 + 1$

We need to figure out what number times 11 will equal some number times 8 + 1. For our purposes this is just trial and error. Typically, the Euclidean algorithm would be used to find the GCD. So we will start with 1.

$11 * 1 \neq 1 * 8 + 1$

As you can see, 1 did not work. Let's try the number 11 for the GCD and 15 for *m*.

$11 * 11 = 15 * 8 + 1 = 121$

$m = 15 =$ any number to make the equation work, *m* is not needed after *d* is determined

$d = 11$

This works. Yes, it took some time to find the right numbers, and we used only single-digit prime numbers for p and q and a small value for e. Now we have all the numbers to compute the public and private keys.

Say we want to share a secret key that we determined by other means. We need to send this secret key to the recipient. For simplicity's sake, let's use the number 3 for the secret key.

First we need to take the secret key of 3 to the power of e modulus $p * q$.

3^{11} mod $p * q = 3^{11}$ mod $3 * 5$

3^{11} mod $15 = 177147$ mod 15

Now that we know that $3^{11} = 177147$, we need to divide 15 into 177147.

$177147 \div 15 = 11809$ *remainder* 12

In this equation it is the remainder that we need. In this case the remainder of 12 is sent to the recipient.

RSA Decryption Example

We will continue the equation from the encryption section. We just received the value of 12 from the sender. Being the recipient and the holder of the private key, we already know a few things.

$p * q = 15$

$d = 11$

$n = 12$

To determine the original secret key that was encrypted, we will take n to the power of d mod 15. Remember that $p * q$ never changes.

12^{11} mod $15 = 743008370688$ mod 15

Now we need to determine how many times the large number is divisible by 15.

$743008370688 \div 15 = 49533891379$ *remainder* 3

$15 * 49533891379 + 3 = 3$ mod 15

$3 = s =$ secret key

If you look at the previous equations you will notice that the remainder is 3. This remainder will be the same value as the original value, encrypted s. In our case it is our secret key.

Summary of the RSA Algorithm

Table 11.3 shows the main topics to remember about the RSA algorithm.

TABLE 11.3 Summary of the RSA Algorithm

Topic	Description
Usage	Widespread and the primary algorithm used in e-commerce.
Speed	Very slow and typically used for key creation only.
Patent	Released in the public domain in 2000.
Key length	Variable, between 512 and 2048.
Keys	Public and private keys are used.
Security	Strong when using large keys (e.g., 2048-bit key lengths).

Diffie-Hellman Algorithm

Diffie-Hellman (DH) is an asymmetric algorithm used to create shared secret keys over insecure channels like the Internet. Whitfield Diffie and Martin Hellman invented the algorithm in 1976. It was later uncovered that the same techniques were invented earlier by a government entity but kept classified. Diffie-Hellman is described in RFC 2631.

Diffie-Hellman can utilize variable-length keys for the security. Diffie-Hellman calls these different key lengths *groups*. The original DH group was 1 with a key length of 768 bits. The strength of this key length is weak today because of greater computing power and distributed computing techniques. DH Group 2 is a 1024-bit key and is the standard key length for Cisco VPN solutions. DH Group 5 is becoming the new standard and has a key length of 1536 bits.

> RFC 3526 describes the Diffie-Hellman group types and key lengths. There are larger groups than Group 5 to deal with the larger symmetric key requirements of AES and some of the newer symmetric algorithms.

DH Key Table

Table 11.4 lists the variables we will use in the "DH Key Creation" and "DH Key Exchange Example" sections that follow.

TABLE 11.4   Diffie-Hellman Key Chart

Key	Description	Public or Private
p	Prime number	Public
g	Primitive root	Public
a	Party A's private key	Private
b	Party B's private key	Private
g^a or A	Party A's public key	Public
g^b or B	Party B's public key	Public
As or $(g^b)^a$	Party A's shared secret key	Private
Bs or $(g^a)^b$	Party B's shared secret key	Private

DH Key Creation

The goal of the Diffie-Hellman algorithm is to create a secret key shared between two parties. It accomplishes this by generating a public key and a private key.

Diffie-Hellman requires two numbers to start the process. In Diffie-Hellman only one of the numbers (p) is prime, whereas RSA uses two prime numbers. In DH, the other number g is a primitive root g mod p. Typically, g is a small number, either 2 or 5. Both p and g are public numbers that are agreed on by both parties. Usually one party will generate p and g and then send the numbers to the other party. The receiving party either accepts or refuses the numbers.

Once both parties agree on p and g, each party needs to determine their private key (a and b, for party A and B, respectively). The private key can be any random natural number. As the name suggests, this number needs to remain private and is never transmitted over the insecure network.

Now that each party has chosen a private key, these numbers are used to generate the public keys for each party. If you remember, in RSA the public key generates the private key, but in Diffie-Hellman the private key is used to generate the public key. The equation to accomplish this is g^a mod p for party A and g^b mod p for party B. Remember that a and b are each party's chosen private keys. The results from the equation that follows will generate the public key and will be represented with an A or B.

Party A: g^a mod $p = A$

Party B: g^b mod $p = B$

Once the computation is complete, the public keys are known for each party. So far p, g, g^a, g^b, A, and B are publicly known and sent to each party in the clear.

Now that the corresponding parties know each other's public key, they can compute the shared secret key. The following equation is used to determine the shared secret key, represented by As or Bs.

Party A: B^a mod p = As

Party B: A^b mod p = Bs

Once the shared secret key is determined, it is typically used with a symmetric algorithm as the secret key. This allows the symmetric algorithm to generate a secret key without prior knowledge and over an insecure network.

All these equations come down to one simple equation to determine the shared secret key.

Party A: $(g^b)^a$ = As

Party B: $(g^a)^b$ = Bs

Because $(g^b)^a$ and $(g^a)^b$ are capable of generating the shared secret keys, these equations and corresponding numbers need to remain private. These numbers are never transmitted over the insecure network.

DH Key Exchange Example

Parties A and B want to exchange a shared secret key. Parties A and B agree on the following prime and primitive root numbers:

p = 7

g = 2

So far we know g mod p is 2 mod 7. Next, each party needs to pick a private key. Party A and B choose the following:

Party A: a = 4

Party B: b = 5

Once the parties have decided on their private keys, they need to compute the equation and send the results to the other party. The result of this is called the public key:

Party A: A = g^a mod p = 2^4 mod 7 = 2

Party B: B = g^b mod p = 2^5 mod 7 = 4

In this example the actual math is not shown. Refer to the RSA section to review the math to determine the final answer, or use a scientific calculator to perform the math.

Now Party A will send Party B the findings of A = 2 and Party B will send Party A the findings of B = 4. For each party to compute the shared secret key s, they will use the following equation:

Party A: $As = B^a \bmod p = 4^4 \bmod 7 = 4$

Party B: $Bs = A^b \bmod p = 2^5 \bmod 7 = 4$

As you can see by these equations, both parties determined the same shared secret key of 4. Normally this algorithm would use much larger numbers to compute the shared secret key.

Summary of the Diffie-Hellman Algorithm

Table 11.5 shows the main topics to remember about the Diffie-Hellman algorithm.

TABLE 11.5   Summary of the Diffie-Hellman Algorithm

Topic	Description
Usage	Establish shared secret key between two parties over an insecure network.
Speed	Much slower than symmetric algorithms.
RFC	RFC 2631 was released in 1999.
Key length	Variable, Group 1 = 768-bit, Group 2 = 1024-bit, Group 5 = 1536-bit.
Keys	Public and private keys are used.
Security	Strong when using large keys like 1024 and 1536.

Public Key Infrastructure

The Public Key Infrastructure (PKI) is a framework that includes servers, workstations, users, networks, corporations, policies, and software. The PKI framework facilitates the means to distribute, administer, verify, and revoke digital identities.

PKI environments are primarily used over insecure networks utilizing public key cryptography. Over these insecure networks a means had to be created to verify the identity of a party and generate a secure channel for communications. PKI is one way to accomplish this.

There are other ways to verify identities and create secure channels. One way is called a web of trust, where there is no centralized authority. This technique is used with Pretty Good Privacy (PGP). We have discussed some other methods in previous chapters. Those methods are not scalable. PKI is typically used for large environments where administration efforts need to be kept to a minimum.

PKI Overview

PKI uses a centralized method to administrate digital identities. Two main technologies allow for this:

- Certificate authorities
- Digital certificates

The first technology involved in administering digital identities is certificate authorities (CA). As with any type of authority, an assumption of power is required. This assumption of power can be either given or taken. For example, a government might take power from the people by using force, or the people might give power to the government by utilizing government health services. The point being made is that the assumption of power can move people, minds, and countries. The assumption of power is the foundation of the PKI framework. Without the assumption of power and authority, the PKI framework would not survive.

PKI is based on power and authority that is given. In other words, the people using the PKI give authority and power to the administrators of the CA. The CA is a company that provides the services needed to manage the PKI. Because the CA is typically a third-party entity, we call this a trusted third party (TTP).

TTPs are entities that people look to as the authority. For the TTP to work, all members within the PKI must accept the authority of the TTP. If the TTP is not authoritative, then the rules, regulations, and punishment are of no value.

Another technology of managing digital identities is digital certificates. A digital certificate is an electronic ID that can be used to identify people, computers, servers, routers, and software, to name a few.

As the Internet has grown over the years, the need to provide virtual identities has grown. There has to be a good and efficient way to prove who is who over this insecure network. A digital certificate does just that. It is proof that you are who you say you are.

Let's look at these two areas more closely. We will first look at TTPs by means of certificate authorities. Then we will look at digital certificates and the IDs they are today.

Certificate Authorities

Certificate authorities are the TTPs that provide the power and authority in a PKI. A CA is similar to a DMV or the Social Security Administration. All these entities have the power and authority to provide you with (or revoke) a form of identification. The DMV provides a driver's license and the SSA provides a social security card. The CA has the power and authority to provide you with a digital certificate, verify a certificate, or revoke one.

What is a CA? Is it a group of people in suits and sunglasses driving Crown Vic's? Not exactly. Most CAs are companies that provide a service. This trusted service is to help people identify each other over insecure networks virtually. If you have ever heard of VeriSign, you have heard of a PKI and CA provider. One thing to note about CAs is that not all CAs are service companies. A CA can be private, associated with a single company, or it can be public. VeriSign is an example of a public CA service. A CA at your workplace that supplies digital certificates only to the Active Directory (AD) domain PCs is considered a private CA.

Now that you have a little background on certificate authorities, let's dig a little deeper. The first thing we should talk about is that a CA is really a service on a server. Although in one of its definitions CA means all the things that encompass the certificate authority, when we get right down to it, the CA is a server or multiple servers.

A CA server provides multiple services. These services include the root public key, certificate requests, creations, revocations, and queries. The first CA created in a CA environment is considered the Root CA and provides the root public key. A CA will process certificate requests by creating new certificates. The CA server can also revoke bad certificates and then provide a list of bad certificates in response to queries from users and computers. Depending on the size of the CA environment, all of these services may be on one server. Most of the time you will see these services spread over multiple servers for redundancy and efficiency.

In a CA environment there is probably more than one CA server unless it is a purpose-built CA. Some VPN implementations install a single CA just to serve the VPN users.

There are four main types of CA server:

- Root CA
- Intermediate CA
- Registration authority (RA)
- Certificate revocation list (CRL)

Root CA As the name suggests, the Root CA is the foundation of the CA environment. The Root CA is the first CA server installed in a CA environment. There can be only one Root CA server. Any other CAs or certificates will ultimately have to be verified against the Root CA. A CA environment can be as simple as a single Root CA. If the environment is small enough, it may be practical to have only one CA server.

Intermediate CA Most of the time you want to have more than one CA server. A CA manages, verifies, and distributes digital certificates. What if the Root CA server is offline? The CA environment does not work, and your organization can't verify its identity to others or verify the identity of entities it communicates with. So it is good practice to have more than one CA server. If we add a CA server to an existing environment, we call that CA an intermediate CA. There can be an unlimited number of intermediate CA servers.

Many private CA implementations take the Root CA offline to protect it. If the Root CA private key gets compromised, the entire PKI environment is compromised. As long as there are intermediate CA servers online, the PKI will work. The Root CA server is periodically brought back online to manage the CA environment and certificates. In most cases it's best to keep it offline.

In large CA environments, the intermediate CA servers may be purpose built to take the load off the Root CA server. The CA environment is typically a hierarchy with the Root CA at the top. The main thing to remember about the intermediate CA servers is that they are the workhorses carrying most of the load.

Registration Authority   The RA server is a purpose-built server that handles certificate requests. You will see RA servers in large CA environments to take the load off the root and intermediate CA servers. The RA server cannot issue or revoke certificates, but it can verify the user's identity, passwords, and policies and determine the validity of a request. Once the RA has processed the certificate request, it will forward it to the root or intermediate CA. Sometimes the term *RA* also refers to the staff who manages certificates.

Certificate Revocation List   When a certificate needs to be revoked, it is done through a CRL server. The CRL server holds a list of revoked certificates. This list is not for expired certificates but for certificates that have been compromised or deemed unnecessary. For the CRL to work, the end device has to receive the list or query the CRL to verify that the certificate is not revoked. The CRL is an important part of a PKI. Without the CRL, compromised certificates could never be removed from the infrastructure. For small environments the Root CA performs double duty and acts as the CRL server. In larger environments a dedicated CRL server is used for performance improvements.

CA Structures

In this section we will discuss and diagram the different CA structures. The two main CA structures are

- Single CA structure
- Hierarchical structure—includes a Root CA and intermediate CAs

Single CA Structure

The single CA structure consists of one CA server, which is also the Root CA. In this structure, a single server provides all the CA services. We will review some of the benefits and drawbacks to the Single CA structure.

- Benefits
    - Simple to manage
    - Perfect for small environments or purpose-built scenarios
    - Centralized
- Drawbacks
    - Single point of failure
    - Not scalable
    - Affects entire PKI if the single CA is compromised

As you can see, there are some major drawbacks to a single CA structure. A single CA structure should only be used in small environments on applications that are not mission critical. Figure 11.3 displays a single CA structure.

FIGURE 11.3 Single CA structure

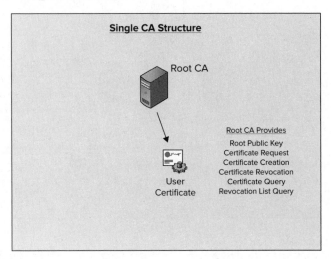

Hierarchical CA Structure

The hierarchical CA structure is the most common. It involves multiple CA servers, with the Root CA server at the top. Each server in the hierarchy specializes in providing certain services. Now we will look at the benefits and drawbacks of the hierarchical CA structure.

- Benefits
  - Distribution of the load
  - No single point of failure
  - Scalability
  - More secure (ability to take the Root CA offline)
- Drawbacks
  - Difficult to implement and manage
  - Certificate chain, determining the path of a certificate

From these benefits and drawbacks you can see that a hierarchical structure is a best practice but requires more effort. Figure 11.4 displays a hierarchical CA structure.

FIGURE 11.4 Hierarchical CA structure

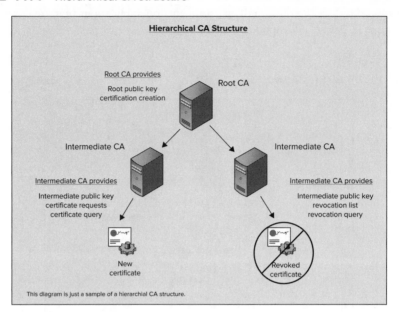

Cross-Certify CA Structure

The cross-certify CA structure is a proposed implementation that does not exist yet. The idea is to allow two or more PKIs to share information and verify each other's certificates. This would allow you to obtain one certificate and be verified by other PKIs. Here are a few benefits and drawbacks of cross-certify CA structures.

- Benefits
  - Cross-certify CAs are able to use certificates outside a single PKI. Root CA servers from other PKI structures are able to verify digital certificates that were not generated within their own PKI.
- Drawbacks
  - Cross-certify CA collaboration is limited. For cross-certify CA structures to work, collaboration between PKI owners is required. Many PKI owners have not opened their PKI infrastructure to other PKI owners.
  - Usage between private and public PKIs is administratively difficult. For cross-certify CA structures to work, they have to communicate with each PKI. Many private PKIs do not have a public interface, which is a security best practice. You would have to make the private PKI public for it to communicate with other public PKIs. This would defeat the purpose of a private PKI.

Digital Certificates

A digital certificate is a way to create electronic identities. These certificates are pieces of digital information that provide a way to verify who each entity is. For this to be possible there has to be an authority that controls, distributes, and verifies the identities. One of the most widely used authorities to accomplish this is a certificate authority (CA). There are many CA providers. During a normal day on the Internet you could use a dozen different CAs and not even know it. If you open your web browser options and find your certificates settings, you will see in the Root Certification Authorities section companies providing certificate authority. The only time you really get to choose a CA is when you enroll for a certificate. The CA can be public or private. VeriSign and Thawte are public CAs. Private CAs are those created in private organizations for internal use. A host of products allow for private CAs. Microsoft CA and OpenSSL are types of private CA servers.

Now that you've had a quick refresher on the CA server's role, let's see how to actually get a certificate.

Certificate Enrollment

The process for certificate enrollment depends on the device on which you are creating the certificate request. If the device is a Microsoft workstation, the procedure may be as simple as going to a website and filling in some information. Requesting a certificate on a VPN device may be a command-line request. And perhaps on a load balancer you have to use both a graphical user interface and a command-line interface for the request. You will have to know every command to input to get the request created.

Because there are so many different front ends to a certificate request, we will look at the common factors required for all certificate requests. You will need to input this information into the request no matter what the front end of the device looks like.

Certificate Request

One of the first questions you have to answer is what type of certificate you need. Some devices will not require you to answer this question because the type of certificate needed will be built into the certificate-request front end. But in other cases this is not so. At any rate, it is always good to understand that there are different types of certificates, including

- User certificate
- Server certificate
- CA certificate
- Software signing certificate

Each type of certificate may require some additional information in order to request the certificate. We will use the common server certificate request for the rest of this section.

The main area in a certificate request contains the distinguished name fields. All certificate requests require this information in some format. We will look at it in the standard Distinguished Name (DN) format.

- Organization: O = the legal name of the business. For our running case study this would be XYZ Corporation.

- Organizational Unit: OU = this field is optional. For large companies or any company that has multiple divisions or departments that want to differentiate the certificates, this is the field to use.

- Common Name: CN = fully qualified domain name (FQDN) of the site for this certificate. Remember that mail.xyzcorporationtest.com is different from www.xyzcorporationtest .com. The CN will have to match the FQDN of the site. You do not need to worry about anything after the root like .com or .net; www.xyzcorporationtest.com is the same as www.xyzcorporationtest.com/news from the CN perspective.

- Country: C = two-letter abbreviation for the country the business is registered in.

- State/Providence: ST = the state or providence for the business. Do not abbreviate this field because the certificate may be used around the world and other countries may not know what the abbreviation means.

- City/Locality: L = the city or locality of the business. Once again, do not abbreviate this field.

An important part of every certificate is the key size. In today's world we recommend that the key size be at least 2048 bits. The key size is typically a multiple of 512. With any key, the larger the key, the stronger the security but the longer it takes to process data with the key.

Another field that you may have to fill in is the hash algorithm. The type of application you will be using will determine the hash algorithm. Hash algorithms were discussed extensively in Chapter 10. In most server certificates on the Web, the SHA-1 hash is used.

Finally, you need to decide the format the request will be in. Depending on your CA, you may have to choose a specific format type. A couple of format types are

- Certificate management messages over CMS (CMC), described in RFC 5272

- PKCS #10, part of the PKCS standard, described later in this chapter

Certificate Classes

We have discussed the information needed to generate a certificate request. There may be other information needed that is not included in the digital request. This information may be an email address, government ID, company letterhead, or an in-person verification with the CA. The necessity for further verification of an individual or entity is determined by the certificate class.

There is no real standard for certificate classes yet. VeriSign was the originator of the concept and has created six classes for digital certificates.

- Class 0 = No verification

- Class 1 = Individual Certificate, meant for digital signing of email

- Class 2 = Business Certificate, proves the certificate belongs to the company
- Class 3 = Server and Software Signing, used to verify that a server or software program is provided by a verified source
- Class 4 = Business to Business, specific certificates for communication between two known businesses
- Class 5 = Private or Government, for use in private or government PKI environments

Each of these classes has different verification requirements. For example, Class 1 certificates require email verification to be sent and replied to. A Class 3 certificate may require multiple verifications to prove a company's name, address, and ownership.

Certificate Enrollment Process

Once we have all this information gathered, we can move forward with the actual certificate request. We will take the information and fill in the request from the device. As previously mentioned, the device could be a website, GUI, or command-line interface.

When we request a certificate, we are generating both a private and a public key. The reason we need to perform the request from the device is to protect the private key. If we request the certificate directly from the device, we will not have to copy or move around the private key and expose it to unnecessary risk.

Some devices have a means to automatically send the certificate request to a CA. This is possible, for example, in some AD environments. Other devices have an option to save the certificate request so you can manually import into a CA system. And still other devices such as routers give you the option of copying the request from the command line so you can paste it into a CA system.

Once we have created the request and sent it to a CA, we need to wait for the actual certificate. Depending on the CA, the certificate may be automatically issued or it may require further verification. Some CAs may require physical verification, as previously mentioned in the "Certificate Classes" section.

Once the CA has issued the certificate, it typically sits in a repository until it is retrieved. Most CAs have a website where you can download your certificate. Some devices and protocols offer the ability for the device to occasionally check the repository for the certificate. In this case, if the certificate is available, the device will download it and install it for use.

Digital Certificates Exposed

What does the digital certificate contain, and what does it look like? In this section we will explore the contents of a digital certificate and show you screen shots of a digital certificate. One thing to understand is that we will view the certificate in a few different formats. For this section we are using the Windows built-in viewer to examine the certificates.

The first thing we will look at is the content of a digital certificate. We will explain and provide images of each of these fields:

- Certificate Information
- Details

- Version
- Serial Number
- Signature Algorithm
- Issuer
- Validity
  - Valid From
  - Valid To
- Subject
- Public Key
- Extensions
- Certification Path

Certificate Information

When we open the certificate to view its contents, the first thing we see is the Certificate Information screen of the General tab, as shown in Figure 11.5. Our example certificate is a Root CA certificate built into Microsoft Internet Explorer.

FIGURE 11.5   Certificate General tab

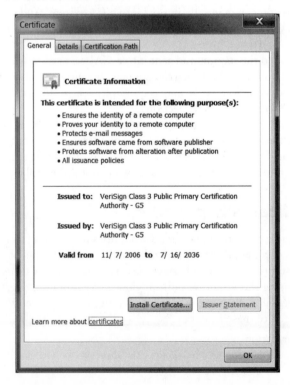

At the top of the screen is the purpose(s) of the certificate. This certificate has multiple purposes, including to ensure identity, protect email, and ensure software. Below this area is the Issued To and Issued By information. Finally, we see the Valid From and To dates. Some of this information is available in the Details section also, but it is provided on the main page for summarization.

Version Field

On the Details tab, look at the Version field (Figure 11.6), which specifies which version of digital certificate formatting was used in the creation of the certificate. Currently there are three versions: 1, 2, and 3. V3, shown in the figure, is the most common.

FIGURE 11.6   Certificate Version field

Serial Number Field

The Serial Number field is a way to identify a specific certificate. If the certificate is in question, you can use the serial number to verify that you have the proper certificate. Figure 11.7 displays the Serial Number field.

FIGURE 11.7   Certificate Serial Number field

The signature is a hexadecimal value of 32 characters. Each CA uses different values for the serial number. Serial numbers may be as short as 6 hexadecimal characters.

Signature Algorithm and Signature Hash Algorithm Fields

The Signature Algorithm field specifies which algorithm is to be used when using this certificate. Figure 11.8 displays the Signature Algorithm field.

FIGURE 11.8   Certificate Signature Algorithm field

The Signature Algorithm field in our example shows the value sha1RSA. This means that the hash is SHA-1 and the public key cryptography is RSA. Also note that below the Signature Algorithm field is a Signature Hash Algorithm field. This lists sha1.

Issuer Field

The issuer is the creator of the certificate. Figure 11.9 displays the Issuer field.

One thing you will notice in the Issuer field is some letters followed by the = sign. These letters are called distinguished names (DN), and they are used in the creation of digital certificates. It is important that you get to know what the DNs are. DNs are used not only in digital certificates but in LDAP and AD as well.

FIGURE 11.9   Certificate Issuer field

 It is good to know that different protocols such as LDAP and AD may have different meanings for DNs. I have seen tools that query with DNs and require different DNs than the corresponding protocol they are querying.

Here are a few of the most common DNs used:

- CN = Common name
- OU = Organizational unit
- O = Organization
- C = Country

Validity Fields

The validity fields determine the time period during which the certificate is valid. The Valid From field displays the start date of the certificate. Most of the time, it will be when the certificate was created. The Valid To field shows how long the certificate can be used. This can be any amount of time from 1 day to 100 years. Most certificates are valid for 1 year to 10 years. Figure 11.10 displays the Valid To field.

FIGURE 11.10   Certificate Valid To field

The certificate displayed is a Root CA certificate. It is valid from Tuesday, November 07, 2006, to Wednesday, July 16, 2036. The example certificate is valid for almost 30 years—a little long if you ask me. (The longer the certificate is valid, the more time a hacker has to compromise the certificate.)

Subject Field

The Subject field describes the entity that is associated with the public key store. Figure 11.11 displays the Subject field.

In our example, the Subject field is identical to the Issuer field. This is because the certificate is a Root CA certificate. With other kinds of certificates, the Subject field will display information specific to the company that requested the certificate. Figure 11.12 displays the Subject field of a certificate requested by Cisco. In this example, the Subject field is different from the Issuer field. Most certificates you come across will be this way.

FIGURE 11.11 Certificate Subject field—Root CA

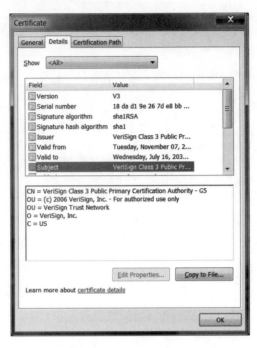

FIGURE 11.12 Certificate Subject field—server CA

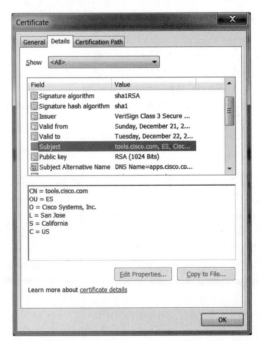

Public Key Field

One of the most important fields of a digital certificate is the Public Key field. The Public Key field, as its name suggests, holds the public key. Figure 11.13 displays the Public Key field.

FIGURE 11.13   Certificate Public Key field

The public key for this certificate is a 2048-bit key. You can copy the public key to a file if you wish.

Extension Fields

Extension fields are available only in X.509 version 3. The extension fields provide a way to add more data to the certificates. There are two types of extensions:

- **Standard extensions** include Subject Key Identifier, Key Usage, and Basic Constraints.

- **Private Internet extensions** include the Authority Information Access and Subject Information Access extensions.

Figure 11.14 displays some extension fields. You will notice the Subject Key Identifier, Basic Constraints, and Key Usage extension fields, among others. The icon next to the extension fields is white rather than orange and brown for the primary fields. Details about these fields are outside the scope of this book, but it is good to know of their existence.

FIGURE 11.14   Certificate extension fields

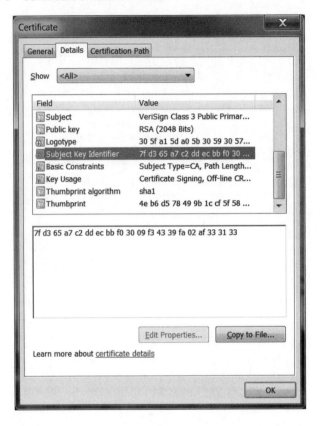

 RFC 5280 is a good place to view all the available extension fields and their descriptions.

Certification Path

The Certification Path tab displays the hierarchy of the certificate. Figure 11.15 displays the certification path information for a Root CA certificate.

Notice that a Root CA certificate has only one certificate in its certification path.

Now let's look at the certificate from Cisco again. Figure 11.16 displays the certification path for the tools.cisco.com certificate.

FIGURE 11.15   Certification path of a Root CA

FIGURE 11.16   Certification path from the server

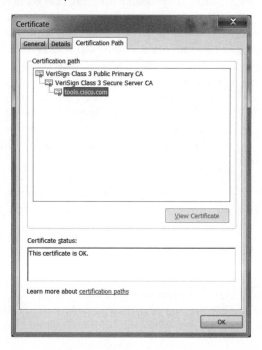

Now we have three certificates in the Certification Path section. The hierarchy is from top to bottom. The Root CA certificate is on top; this means it is the authority. The certificate in the middle is an intermediate CA certificate. Finally, the tools.cisco.com certificate is listed.

 These images are taken from a Windows PC. If you click one of the certificates in the Certification Path field, you can view the actual certificate in another window by clicking the View Certificate button.

Certificate Usage

You know what a certificate is and how you can obtain one. Now you need to know what to use it for. Certificates can be used for many things, including secure web transactions, device administration, user authentication, secure email, and even virtual dating.

We will discuss three uses for digital certificates:

- Identity
- Secure communication
- User authentication

Identity

What if you made some copies of your driver's license and carried them around with you? Anytime you wanted to do business with someone or a company, you would give them a copy of your driver's license. You are probably thinking that is crazy. Well is it, really? We do this all the time; the only difference is that we typically do not make the copies ourselves. Let's say you want to withdraw money from your bank and you have mislaid your ATM card. You go inside and fill out a withdrawal slip. You then proceed to a teller. If it is a decent bank, one of the first things the teller will do is ask you for your ID. If there were a good way to make a photocopy tamper proof, we could just give the teller a copy of our ID. When you test-drive a car, they typically make a copy of your license.

A digital certificate is like a tamper-proof photocopy. When we want to do business online with either a corporation or person, we can hand them our certificate. They take our certificate and verify it with the public key that is contained within the certificate and the public keys of the CA servers contained within their certificates.

Thus, we can use a certificate to verify an entity's identity virtually. Think of virtual dating and how people may alter the truth about themselves. A digital certificate that had to be verified against a person's driver's license and credit card before it was issued would be better than no certificate.

Secure Communication

Now that we know we can use a certificate to verify identity, let's take it one step further. We want to buy another Wiley book from our favorite website. We open our web browser and enter the address for the site. We find our next book and add it to our shopping chart. We finish shopping and want to check out. When we click the checkout button we are redirected to a secure website. If your favorite website is a reputable one, this should have been somewhat transparent to you. But in the background a digital certificate was acquired and verified. Your browser has verified the identity of the website. Once the verification is completed, the web browser has a trust relationship with the website. Now your browser takes the public key in the certificate and encrypts a message to the website. The communication between the website and your browser is secured using the public and private key exchange we discussed earlier in this chapter. If the certificate was created with the RSA algorithm, then the RSA process will be used for the communication between the two parties. Once you have finished purchasing your book, you can close your web browser and terminate the connection to the website.

User Authentication

We have discussed identity verification and secure communication with certificates. Another use for digital certificates is user authentication. You may see this with VPN solutions, both remote-access and site-to-site VPNs. Without using a digital certificate for authentication, the VPN connection will require a shared secret key. We have discussed the limitations of a manual shared secret key throughout this chapter and in Chapter 10. In a large deployment, a shared secret key is not flexible. If it is compromised, it may take days or weeks to change the shared secret keys on all the devices.

To get around the shared secret-key issue, we can use digital certificates. We will use the certificates to verify the identity of each party. We will then use the keys in the certificates to calculate a temporary shared secret key that is used for the symmetric algorithm. Figure 11.17 shows the process for user authentication with digital certificates.

FIGURE 11.17   User authentication process

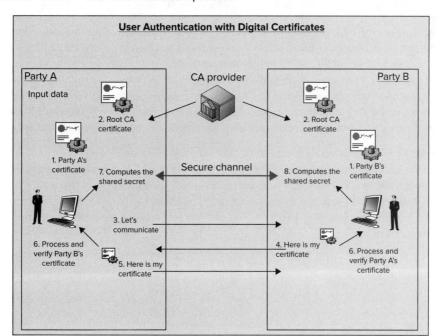

We will look at this process a little deeper.

1. Party A and Party B both have certificates issued from the same CA.

2. Party A and Party B both have the Root CA certificate installed locally.

3. Party A sends a request for communication to Party B.

4. Party B sends Party A its certificate.

5. Party A sends Party B its certificate.

6. Each party will process the other's certificate with the stored Root CA certificate's public key.

7. Party A computes a shared secret between the two parties.

8. Party B computes a shared secret between the two parties.

Many times two different communication sessions will be created—one channel from Party A to Party B and one channel from Party B to Party A. The reason for the two secure channels is that Party A will use the public key from Party B for encryption, and vice-versa. It is more secure to decrypt with a private key than it is with a public key. Only one entity has the private key. Anyone can obtain the public key. This could allow anyone to feasibly decrypt the information if it was encrypted with the private key.

 Real World Scenario

Digital Certificates as Part of a Two-Factor Authentication Solution

The XYZ Corporation has had security and management issues with their remote-access VPN solution. Your boss has tasked you with providing a solution for more than 500 remote users. You decide it would be best to implement a private PKI environment dedicated to the VPN users. The XYZ Corporation has a Microsoft infrastructure and is running AD. You decide to install and configure Microsoft CA to provide digital certificates for all the remote VPN users and the VPN appliance they will terminate to. This solution will require the users to authenticate via an individual certificate instead of a secret key shared by all 500 users.

As a security professional, you understand that with any security control, a single layer of protection is never enough. Digital certificates in a remote-access VPN environment provide one type of protection, but two-factor authentication—a way to require at least two means of authentication—should be used with any remote authentication. You might decide to accomplish this with a one-time password (OTP) that expires in a few seconds or a hardware key that is plugged into the device.

Certificate Limitations

You may have already picked up on some of the limitations of digital certificates throughout the chapter. The three main limitations of digital certificates are the following:

- They require a CRL server for revoked certificates.
- The private key is the heart of the security.
- Human interaction is necessary to administer certificate requests.

We will look at these three limitations briefly.

They require a CRL server for revoked certificates.   The certificate must have a CRL, and the CA must have a CRL server available. The device must be able to obtain a new CRL periodically to ensure that certificates have not been revoked. Many times you will see PKI implementations without a CRL server or the CRL is offline. Without a CRL server, there is no way to verify that a certificate is still good.

The private key is the heart of the security.   If the private key is compromised, all corresponding certificates are compromised. If the compromised private key is from a server certificate, a new certificate is required from the CA. If the compromised private key is from a CA, the CA and all corresponding certificates generated with that private key have to be replaced. You can see the pattern, right? If the private key to the Root CA is compromised—you guessed it—the entire PKI environment is compromised, and all certificates have to be replaced. Wow! Protect those private keys.

Human interaction is necessary to administer certificate requests.   When we discussed the certification classes, we stated that some certificates require further verification from an individual or corporation. We also mentioned that some CA servers require an administrator to approve the certificate request and revocation.

A busy IT department may overlook revoking certificates and delay approving certificate requests. A staff member at the CA may have a bad day and process a certification without verifying a company's information. Because humans are involved, the human factor is a limitation of the PKI solution.

PKI Standards

There are many standards, vendors, protocols, and technologies within a PKI. We will look at a few standards that help define some of the most-used technologies in the PKI environment. These standards include the Public Key Cryptography Standards (PKCS), X.509, and the Simple Certificate Enrollment Protocol (SCEP).

Public Key Cryptography Standards

The Public Key Cryptography Standards is a set of standards developed and administered by RSA Security. If you remember from our earlier discussions on the RSA algorithm,

RSA Security was founded by the three inventors of the RSA algorithm. RSA Security was purchased by EMC in 2004 and is now called RSA, The Security Division of EMC Corporation.

The PKCS is a set of standards that was first published in 1991. It was originally developed to deal with the growing technology of public key cryptography. The PKCS was originally comprised 15 different standards. There are currently 13 standards, as two of the standards have been deprecated. Each standard represents a different technology specific to public key cryptography. The names of the 15 standards all start with the letters *PKCS* and end with the corresponding number, such as PKCS #1 and PKCS #3. Table 11.6 lists the 13 active standards. The most important standards are in bold.

TABLE 11.6   PKCS Standards

Standard Number	Standard Name
PKCS #1	RSA Cryptography Standard
PKCS #3	Diffie-Hellman Key Agreement Standard
PKCS #5	Password-Based Cryptography
PKCS #6	Extended-Certificate Syntax Standard
PKCS #7	Cryptographic Message Syntax Standard
PKCS #8	Private-Key Information Syntax Standard
PKCS #9	Selected Attribute Types
PKCS #10	Certification Request Syntax Standard
PKCS #11	Cryptographic Token Interface Standard
PKCS #12	Personal Information Exchange Syntax Standard
PKCS #13	Elliptic Curve Cryptography Standard
PKCS #14	Pseudo-Random Number Generation (under development)
PKCS #15	Cryptographic Token Information Format Standard

PKCS #2 and #4 have been withdrawn. They are incorporated in PKCS #1. If you wish to read more on the PKCS standards, please visit http://www.rsa.com.

After looking at the table of PKCS standards, you should be able to identify some of the standards by the descriptions. RSA and Diffie-Hellman, were discussed in Chapter 10 and at the beginning of this chapter. We will take a closer look at some of the widely used PKCS standards—PKCS #1, #10, and #7.

PKCS #1 Standard

The PKCS #1 standard defines RSA cryptography standards that should be followed when the RSA algorithm is used. The standard is also described in RFC 3447 for version 2.1, published in 2003.

The PKCS #1 standard covers four main topics:

- Cryptographic primitives
- Encryption schemes
- Signature schemes with appendix
- ASN.1 syntax for representing keys and for identifying the schemes

We touched on most of these topics at the beginning of this chapter. The main thing we want to look at from these topics is the ASN.1 topic.

You need to first understand what ASN.1 is. ASN.1 is a standard that defines data structures, coding, and transmission of data. It is a standard to follow when creating information, in this case keys for RSA. An example of this is the description of the private key structure taken from RFC 3447.

The following copyright statement is on the document:

This document and translations of it may be copied and furnished to others provided that the above copyright notice and this paragraph are included on all such copies. However, this document itself may not be modified in any way, such as by removing the copyright notice or references to the Internet Society or other Internet organizations, except as required to translate it into languages other than English.

An RSA private key should be represented with the ASN.1 type RSAPrivateKey:

```
RSAPrivateKey ::= SEQUENCE {
        version          Version,
        modulus          INTEGER,  -- n
        publicExponent   INTEGER,  -- e
        privateExponent  INTEGER,  -- d
        prime1           INTEGER,  -- p
        prime2           INTEGER,  -- q
        exponent1        INTEGER,  -- d mod (p-1)
        exponent2        INTEGER,  -- d mod (q-1)
        coefficient      INTEGER,  -- (inverse of q) mod p
        otherPrimeInfos  OtherPrimeInfos OPTIONAL
    }
```

You should notice some very similar names and letters in this structure, namely, *p*, *q*, and *d*. If you go back to the "RSA Algorithm" section earlier in this chapter, you will see the same letters. This PKCS standard outlines how to create the data structure so the information for *p*, *q*, and *d* can be transmitted consistently.

PKCS #10 Standard

The PKCS #10 standard defines the Certification Request Syntax Standard. This standard is also specified in RFC 2986. The main purpose of PKCS #10 is to create a standard for digital certificate requests. When a party requests to create a digital certificate, it may be created in the PKCS #10 format. The PKCS #10 standard uses ASN.1 to structure the request.

Most of the time when you deal with a digital certificate request it will be displayed in a Base64 encoding. Following is an example:

```
-----BEGIN CERTIFICATE REQUEST-----
kdaf24928akasdf92axks2kdkoISODK9
etc...
-----END CERTIFICATE REQUEST-----
```

PKCS #10 specifies in the standard what the ANS.1 structure should follow. A sample of that structure comes from RFC 2986.

The following copyright statement is on the document:

Copyright © The Internet Society 2000. All Rights Reserved.

This document and translations of it may be copied and furnished to others provided that the above copyright notice and this paragraph are included on all such copies. However, this document itself may not be modified in any way, such as by removing the copyright notice or references to the Internet Society or other Internet organizations, except as required to translate it into languages other than English.

```
Attribute { ATTRIBUTE:IOSet } ::= SEQUENCE {
     type    ATTRIBUTE.&id({IOSet}),
     values SET SIZE(1..MAX) OF ATTRIBUTE.&Type({IOSet}{@type})
   }
```

As you can see, again the structure is very specific. If you took the Base64 certificate request and turned it into the ASN.1 format, you would see the previous data in the output.

PKCS #7 Standard

The PKCS #7 standard defines the Cryptographic Message Syntax Standard. This standard is also specified in RFC 2315. One of the main purposes of PKCS #7 is to describe a standard for transferring certificates. One example of that is that the response to a PKCS #10 request will follow the PKCS #7 standard. The actual PKCS # 10 request will be enveloped in PKCS #7 and sent to the CA.

PKCS #7 was also the basic format used in the Secure/Multipurpose Internet Mail Extensions (S/MIME). S/MIME is a PKC for signing and encapsulating e-mail.

X.509 Standard

The X.509 standard originated in the X.500 standards by the International Telecommunication Union (ITU-T). X.509 describes standards for digital certificates, certificate revocation lists (CRLs), and the certification path validation algorithm.

The current version of X.509 is version 3 and is specified in RFC 5280.

X.509 Specification of Digital Certificates

The first thing we will look at in X.509 is digital certificates. The following are the basic fields for a digital certificate following the X.509 v3 standard:

- Version
- Serial Number
- Signature Algorithm
- Issuer
- Validity
    - Valid From
    - Valid To
- Subject
- Public Key
- Extensions (X.509 v3)

We covered these fields in the "Digital Certificates Exposed" section earlier in this chapter.

X.509 Specification of CRLs

Now we will look at X.509 and how the standard affects CRLs. The main thing to understand about the CRL standard in X.509 is that it outlines the data structure for the CRL communications and messages. This structure uses ASN.1 and is much like the PKCS standard structures discussed earlier.

X.509 Specification of the Certification Path Validation Algorithm

Lastly, we will look at X.509 and the certification path validation algorithm. Certification path validation is a means to verify the certificate hierarchy. Most certificates have a Root CA, intermediate CA, and device/user certificate associated with them. The certification path validation procedures are used to verify that the path between the device/user certificate and the Root CA certificate is valid. Figure 11.18 shows a certification path for the tools.cisco.com certificate.

FIGURE 11.18   Certification path of the server

Certification path validation works by means of a *trust anchor*. The trust anchor is a CA that is part of the CA PKI environment. The top CA that issued the certificate or a dedicated intermediate CA can be used for path validation. The CA's public key, name, and any constraints are used for the validation process. Name, policy, and basic constraint fields are verified to ensure the validation does not violate any of the constraint field requirements.

The certification path validation process is linear. It starts with the device/user certificate and verifies it against the trust anchor. It then moves up to the next certificate in the path until it reaches the certificate at the top of the hierarchy, which should be a Root CA.

X.509 Specification of File Extensions

Another important thing to understand about X.509 is the file extensions. When you deal with digital certificates, you will come across different file extensions. Many times these file extensions are confusing. This section will shed some light on the common file extensions associated with X.509. Table 11.7 describes X.509 file extension types.

TABLE 11.7 X.509 File Extension Types

File Extension	Description
`.CER, .DER`	Defined in the ITU-T x.690 standard. Formatting uses ASN.1 structures. CER stands for Canonical Encoding Rules, and DER stands for Distinguished Encoding Rules. Both are based on BER (Basic Encoding Rules).

`.PEM`	Privacy Enhanced Mail (PEM) was invented by the IETF for securing email. It uses Base64 encoding. The PEM file starts and ends with
	`----BEGIN CERTIFICATE-----`
	`-----END CERTIFICATE-----`

`.P7B, P7C`	Encoding is similar to Base64. Files with these extensions contain PKCS #7 certificates. They do not contain data.
`.P12, PFX`	These files contain PKCS #12 certificates and keys. PFX is the predecessor to P12.

Figure 11.19 shows a sample certificate request in Base64 formatting. Depending on whether the file is a certificate request or a completed certificate, the beginning and ending tags may be different. In a certificate request the tags will state "`BEGIN NEW CERTIFICATE REQUEST`" and "`END NEW CERTIFICATE REQUEST`".

FIGURE 11.19 Certificate request


```
-----BEGIN NEW CERTIFICATE REQUEST-----
MIIETDCCAzQCAQAwbDELMAkGA1UEBhMCVVMxCzAJBgNVBAgTAlRYMQ8wDQYDVQQH
EwZGcmlzY28xFDASBgNVBAoTC0V0aGljYWwgSW5jMQswCQYDVQQLEwJJVDEcMBoG
A1UEAxMTZXRoaWNhbG5ldHdvcmtzLmNvbTCCASIwDQYJKoZIhvcNAQEBBQADggEP
ADCCAQoCggEBALQvs7IB5qBBYsF5sH9hpGeKa6C5uKrpN6DOrRaGXQQX9vKVj6gM
KK0tIuB60JqdWdQpNbnG4U5KvgumLu+WJbVAI6BDmQlj8FfYCOV5fTMMoqSDa7Av
CnJem3YS7EHAwB+vCuoFrTMc9YPAxcecTrYdUfFOLPYqDO6N9nVQ1Y8MpVG5jzAb
Nyj40XpoYV+2KT4JLdN5DGnJp1i5e52Jgt08nK3CKPGwIPvA67tlV/T3LHKbsiP+
lQpObOaOubim958m9w+voDpapqpndpFdVIEJJw2BoAhcRVJzxPEsTPZxvIQaV73l
SnDRTYue4X+p3KjDJ7kywR52gjc3Ci2BgxMCAwEAAaCCAZkwGgYKKwYBBAGCNwOC
AzEMFgo1LjIuMzc5MC4yMHsGCisGAQQBgjcCAQ4xbTBrMA4GA1UdDwEB/wQEAwIE
8DBEBgkqhkiG9w0BCQ8ENzA1MA4GCCqGSIb3DQMCAgIAgDAOBggqhkiG9w0DBAIC
AIAwBwYFKw4DAgcwCgYIKoZIhvcNAwcwEwYDVR0lBAwwCgYIKwYBBQUHAwEwgf0G
CisGAQQBgjcNAgIxge4wgesCAQEeWgBNAGkAYwByAG8AcwBvAGYAdAAgAFIAUwBB
ACAAUwBDAGgAYQBuAG4AZQBsACAAQwByAHkAcAB0AG8AZwByAGEAcABoAGkAYwAg
AFAAcgBvAHYAaQBkAGUAcgBiQAAAAAAAAAAAAAAAAAAAAAAAAAAAAAAAAAAAA
AAAAAAAAAAAAAAAAAAAAAAAAAAAAAAAAAAAAAAAAAAAAAAAAAAAAAAAAAAAAAAAA
AAAAAAAAAAAAAAAAAAAAAAAAAAAAAAAAAAAAAAAAAAAAAAAAAAAAAAAAAAAAAAAA
AAAAAAAAAAAAAAAAMA0GCSqGSIb3DQEBBQUAA4IBAQA/Z2LJuh7v0xeVJrhscU4F
wrTzCJ/CEsS4yLhnX/yKwb9IcsgevA5CQD7yDgfgOw4QOQTI7w8HnJFDikdiTF7i
R9LXeefLzr5Yrez4gn9Jov4rrigEet7+ghRjwSORg5n1X2/PLDGVre8GEXrAf/Td
qv519dH9D0EAfUi1W48UPaRjiP3DQ/fMZ/4F51/MzMK1KPFezvUyKJoi2yo8MTNp
SjjqvUeDliuWPcQjCj9bn3vTsD9rRKk33hVITzEJ3xYwT/9VR6RgtWs7FKj/q3rM
NJPYivoJwB484jInalHiAQdd5nTArebhkGvGEXyfM+JoDMKJby97/oXbFRhgL+kF
-----END NEW CERTIFICATE REQUEST-----
```


SCEP Standard

Simple Certificate Enrollment Protocol (SCEP) is a standard that Cisco invented as a means to issue certificates to network devices. This process is automatic and is intended for a large number of devices. The specifications for SCEP are outlined in IETF draft-nourse-scep-19.

SCEP supports four main functions:

- Certificate enrollment
- Public key distribution
- Certificate query
- CRL query

Certificate Enrollment

As the name implies, the SCEP certificate enrollment process is supposed to be simple. The device creates a certificate request via PKCS #10. The device sends the request in a PKCS #7 package. Depending on how the CA server is set up, it may automatically issue a certificate. If not, an administrator will have to issue the certificate manually. Some SCEP systems require a password. This is configurable in the requesting device.

Once a certificate is issued, it is sent back to the device in a PKCS #7 package. The device will receive the certificate and install it into the system.

 Microsoft CA has an add-on for IIS to enable SCEP. Once SCEP is enabled, devices can register for a certificate over HTTP. You point the device to the HTTP address of the CA server. The devices will automatically request a certificate. If a certificate is issued, it will be sent back to the device. Administrators can control whether the certificate is automatically sent or an approval is needed before releasing the certificate.

Public Key Distribution

Public key distribution is used to transfer public keys to devices that have not already received a public key from the CA. This allows the device to gain access to CA and RA root public keys.

Certificate Query

A certificate query is a request for a certificate from either a CA or an LDAP server. If the request is to a CA server, the device sends a request to the CA server with the issuer name and serial number of the certificate. This assumes that the devices previously had the issuer name and serial number. If not, the device is unable to query the CA for the certificate.

CRL Query

The CRL query allows the device to query for a current CRL list. SCEP does not allow for a push of the CRL. The device has to query for a new CRL. The CRL query mechanism does not scale well and is not typically used. CRL Distributed Points (CDP) is typically used when possible.

Summary

In this chapter you learned the foundation of asymmetric encryption. We discussed that asymmetric encryptions have a place in the encryption world. You also learned the limitations of asymmetric algorithms because of the large computations required to process the request. You learned how asymmetric algorithms arrive at a given output via the mathematics behind the algorithm.

After asymmetric encryption you learned about the PKI. You learned that a PKI has to have authority for it to work properly. Components of a PKI include the CA, RA, CRL, and intermediate CA servers. The first CA server is called a Root CA.

You learned that digital certificates are similar to personal IDs such as driver's licenses and social security cards. You learned how to request a certificate and what to do with the certificate once you receive it. You learned the fields within a certificate and why certain fields are important.

Finally, we discussed the PKI standards that govern the PKI and digital certificates. These standards included the Public Key Cryptography Standards, X.509, and the Simple Certificate Enrollment Protocol.

Exam Essentials

Understand the differences between asymmetric and symmetric encryption.   Asymmetric encryption utilizes a public key and a private key, and symmetric encryption utilizes a shared secret key. Asymmetric encryption is much slower than symmetric encryption.

Remember the differences between a public key and a private key.   The private key is generated during the certificate request and has to remain secure to provide security. The public key is assumed to be available to everyone and has no security.

Understand the two features public key cryptography provides.   The two features are confidentiality and authentication. These features are provided by the key used to start the encryption. The public key provides authentication, whereas the private key provides confidentiality.

Understand the RSA and Diffie-Hellman algorithms and how they determine the public and private keys.   With the RSA algorithm, the main thing to remember is the makeup of the public and private keys: p and q are the prime numbers, e is public, and d is private. With the Diffie-Hellman algorithm, one prime number is used with one primitive number. The primitive number is typically 2 or 5. Remember that p is prime and g is primitive.

Remember the components of a PKI.   The two components of a PKI are certificate authorities and digital certificates. The certificate authorities provide digital certificates for virtual identification.

Understand the certificate enrollment process and different classes available for each certificate.   Be sure you understand how to obtain a certificate. Remember that there are automatic ways and manual ways to obtain a certificate. Now that there are different types of classes for each certificate, you should focus on classes 1 and 3.

Understand the different fields present in a digital certificate.   Make sure you understand what the main certificate fields consist of. The main fields include issuer, subject, validity, and public key. Understand that the public key is part of the digital certificate.

Remember the PKCS standards and what each standard represents.   It would be good to remember all 13 active standards, but the major standards are #1, #7, and #10. #1 is for RSA, #7 is for sending certificates, and # 10 is for requesting certificates.

Remember that the main standard that governs digital certificates is X.509.   The X.509 standard governs the digital certificate's process, structure, exchange, certificate path validation, and revocation.

Written Lab

Write the answers to the following questions:

1. What are the key lengths for DH?
2. Can the public key encrypt or decrypt data?
3. What type of number(s) does the RSA algorithm use to start the key process?
4. What type of CA server is needed to guarantee that bad certificates are removed from use?
5. Which PKCS standard is used in the transmission of digital certificates?
6. What does PKI stand for? What is the purpose of PKI?
7. What is the most common digital certificate class?
8. What is the latest version for digital certificates in the X.509 standard?
9. What are the two common values for g in the DH algorithm?
10. Which encryption technique is considered stronger, asymmetric or symmetric?

Hands-on Lab

Hands-on Lab 11.1: View the Content of Root CA Certificates

1. Open your web browser, either Internet Explorer or Firefox.

2. Find the digital certificates.

   From Internet Explorer:

   A. Find the Internet Options settings: Tools ➢ Internet Options.

   B. From the General tab move to the Content tab: General ➢ Content.

   C. Click the Certificates tab.

   D. You will notice a few tabs under the Certificates window. We want to look at the Trusted Root Certification Authorities. Click the Trusted Root tab.

   From Firefox:

   A. Open your Firefox web browser.

   B. Find the Options settings: Tools ➢ Options.

   C. From the Main tab click the Advanced tab: Main ➢ Advanced.

   D. Click the View Certificates tab.

   E. Click the Authorities tab.

3. You should see several Root CA certificates. Click any of the certificates.

   This should look very similar to the figures we discussed in the "Digital Certificates" section. This is a good way to get familiar with digital certificates.

4. Browse through the other Certificate tabs to see if you have other certificates loaded on your computer.

Review Questions

1. What minimum key length is recommended when implementing asymmetric encryption?

   A. 768

   B. 1024

   C. 2048

   D. 4096

2. Who has possession of the private key?

   A. Everyone

   B. Generator of the certificate

   C. CA

   D. Requestor of the certificate

3. What are the drawbacks of asymmetric encryption? (Choose two.)

   A. Speed

   B. Key length weakness

   C. Expense

   D. Lack of use

4. What is the main use for asymmetric encryption?

   A. Encrypting large amounts of data

   B. Generating shared secret keys

   C. Encrypting images

   D. VPN data

5. Who and what possess the public key?

   A. Digital certificate

   B. Holder of the private key

   C. Anyone who requests it

   D. All of the above

6. Which are examples of asymmetric encryption algorithms? (Choose two.)

   A. AES

   B. CIA

   C. DH

   D. RSA

7. What are some uses for digital certificates? (Choose two.)
   A. Provide a degree
   B. Verify identity
   C. User authentication
   D. Generate images

8. What protocol allows for the automatic enrollment of a digital certificate request?
   A. Simple Certificate Enrollment Protocol
   B. Simple Request Enrollment Protocol
   C. Safe Certificate Enrollment Protocol
   D. Same Certificate Enroll Plan

9. What is the most widely used standard for digital certificates?
   A. X.500
   B. PKCS
   C. X.509
   D. SCEP

10. If the private key on the Root CA is compromised, what devices have to have their certificate replaced? (Choose all that apply.)
    A. Root CA server
    B. PC with user certificate
    C. Cross-Certify CA
    D. Intermediate CA
    E. CRL server

11. How many certificates are involved in the user authentication process?
    A. One
    B. Two
    C. Three
    D. Four
    E. It depends

12. How many prime numbers are used in the Diffie-Hellman algorithm?
    A. One
    B. Two
    C. None
    D. Five

13. What is the key length of Diffie-Hellman Group 2?

    A. 1024-bit

    B. 1536-bit

    C. 2048-bit

    D. Variable

14. What components are required for a PKI to be successful? (Choose all that apply.)

    A. Army

    B. Trusted third party

    C. Authority

    D. Secrecy

15. What are some drawbacks to a single server CA structure? (Choose two.)

    A. Single point of failure

    B. Ease of administration

    C. Not scalable

    D. None of the above

16. What two technologies make up a PKI?

    A. Digital certificates

    B. Certificate authorities

    C. Digital signatures

    D. Certificate authenticators

17. What fields in a certificate request should not be abbreviated? (Choose all that apply.)

    A. State

    B. Address

    C. City

    D. Country

18. The Subject field of a certificate contains what information?

    A. Company information

    B. Usage information

    C. Website name

    D. RA information

19. What protocol is considered a hybrid encryption protocol?

   A. SSE

   B. SNMP

   C. SMTP

   D. SSH

20. What are some types of CA servers in a PKI environment? (Choose all that apply.)

   A. Root CA

   B. CRL

   C. RA

   D. ABL

Answers to Review Questions

1. C. 2048 should be the minimum key length used. 1024 is considered too weak for computing power today.

2. D. The requestor is ultimately the holder of the private key. A CA does have a private key but would have to request it. The best answer is D.

3. A, B. The two main drawbacks to asymmetric encryption are the slowness to compute and the weakness in the key length compared to symmetric encryption.

4. B. Because of its speed, asymmetric encryption is used for small amounts of data for short periods of time. Generating a shared secret key for symmetric encryption is the main use.

5. D. The public key is part of the digital certificate. The holder of the private key also knows the public key, and anyone who requests a certificate is provided with the public key.

6. C, D. Diffie-Hellman (DH) and RSA are two examples of asymmetric encryption.

7. B, C. The three main uses for digital certificates are identity, secure communications, and user authentication.

8. A. Cisco devices use Simple Certificate Enrollment Protocol (SCEP) to request a certificate automatically.

9. C. X.509 is the most widely used standard. It originated in the X.500 class but is not considered part of the class anymore.

10. A, B, D, E. Any device in the actual PKI will have to obtain a new certificate from a new Root CA server certificate. The Root CA will either have to generate a new private key or be rebuilt, depending on how it was compromised. The Cross-Certify CA is not part of the same PKI.

11. E. This answer depends on how many CAs are in the certificate path. If there is only a Root CA in the path, there are three certificates. If there are intermediate CAs in the path, there are more. In the example we presented in the chapter there were three certificates in the path.

12. A. Diffie-Hellman utilizes only one prime number at the beginning process of the algorithm.

13. A. Group 2 is 1024-bit. Group 1 is 768-bit, and Group 3 is 1536-bit.

14. B, C. A trusted third party (TTP) that is given authority is necessary in a PKI. Secrecy is incorrect because PKI stands for Public Key Infrastructure. The public key is assumed to be known to everyone.

15. A, C. The CA structure is unavailable with a single server failure. The computing power of a single server will not scale for a larger environment.

16. A, B. Digital certificates provide the ID and certificate authorities provide the digital certificates. Digital signatures are not directly associated with a PKI but may be used in a PKI.

17. A, C. The city and state should not be abbreviated because certificates are used around the world, and local users may not understand the abbreviation.

18. A. The Subject field will hold the company information of the certificate. This information may be the company of the CA if the certificate is a CA certificate.

19. D. In this chapter we used SSH as the hybrid example.

20. A, B, C. Root CA, intermediate CA, CRL, and RA are the types of servers included in a PKI.

Answers to Written Lab

1. 768, 1024, 1536

2. The public key can encrypt and decrypt.

3. Two prime numbers

4. Certificate Revocation List (CRL) server

5. PKCS #7

6. PKI stands for public key infrastructure. PKI provides a means to generate, administer, and revoke digital certificates.

7. Class 3 is most commonly seen on the Internet.

8. Version 3

9. 2 or 5

10. Symmetric is considered strong when comparing key length to key length.

Chapter
12

Implementing Site-to-Site IPsec VPN Solutions

THE FOLLOWING CCNA SECURITY EXAM OBJECTIVES ARE COVERED IN THIS CHAPTER:

- ✓ Describe the building blocks of IPsec and the security functions it provides

- ✓ Configure and verify an IPsec site-to-site VPN with pre-shared key authentication using SDM

In this chapter, I'm going to discuss virtual private networks (VPNs) and also a newer technology, Cisco Easy VPN. You will use the Cisco Security Device Manager (SDM) to configure a site-to-site VPN. We will also explore what this looks like from a command-line interface (CLI) perspective and have a brief look at troubleshooting, tips, and information.

Introduction to Virtual Private Networks and IPsec

Virtual private networks have been around for some time now, and today they are frequently used for both remote access and site-to-site solutions. VPN means different things to different people, but in general it is a method for connecting two disparate networks, generally over the Internet. For the purposes of this chapter, we are going to focus on an encrypted tunnel.

We can't learn about VPNs without learning about IPsec. IP Security (IPsec) is the standard that you will be using in this chapter. IPsec is based on a series of Requests for Comments (RFCs) that were first issued during the mid to late 1990s. This specification has been continually updated and is in use around the world.

Entire books have been written on IPsec. In this book I'll try to convey just a few of the most important topics.

Today's IPsec is largely derived from the 1998 RFC 2401, which outlines an IPv4 implementation of IP Security. While a number of RFCs make up the suite as it is implemented, the following list is generally considered to include the most important and typically used features (this is not meant to be an exhaustive list):

- Authentication Header (AH)
- Encapsulating Security Payload (ESP)
- Internet Key Exchange (IKE)
- Internet Security Association and Key Management Protocol (ISAKMP)
- Hash Message Authentication Code (HMAC)
- Secure Hash Algorithm (SHA-1)
- Message Digest 5 (MD5)

- Triple Data Encryption Standard (3DES)
- Advanced Encryption Standard (AES)

For starters, let's talk about where the primary IPsec protocols live. By primary, I mean Authentication Header (AH) and Encapsulating Security Payload (ESP). If you look at the IP header diagram shown in Figure 12.1, you can see the highlighted protocol field. This is typically where you might see ICMP or TCP.

FIGURE 12.1 IP header diagram

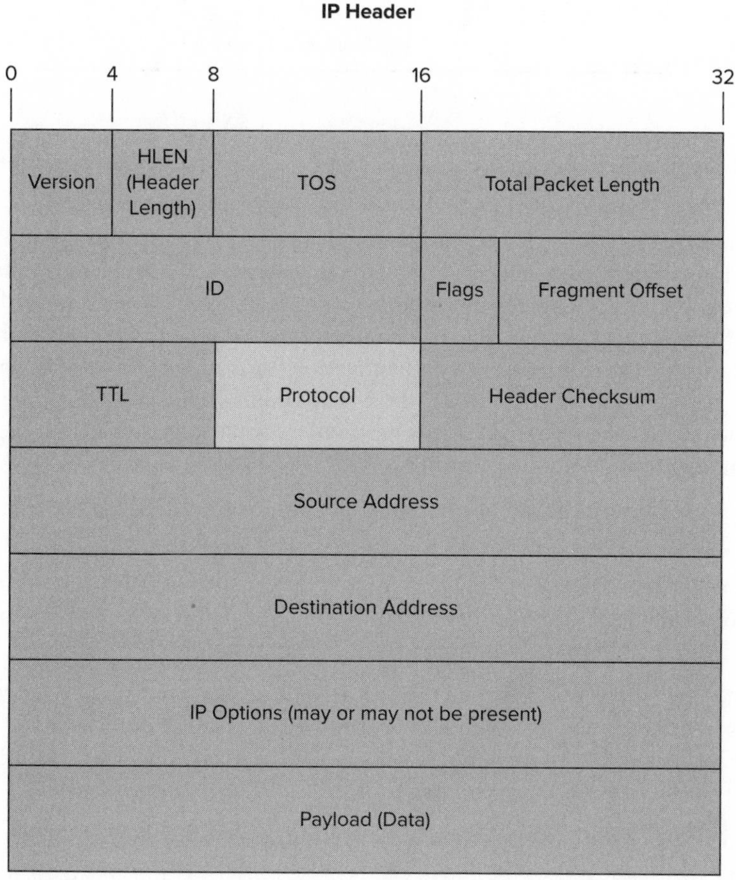

IP Header

0	4	8	16	32

Version	HLEN (Header Length)	TOS	Total Packet Length	
ID			Flags	Fragment Offset
TTL		Protocol	Header Checksum	
Source Address				
Destination Address				
IP Options (may or may not be present)				
Payload (Data)				

But there are other options for this field, and that's where IPsec fits in. The more common IP types are listed in Table 12.1.

TABLE 12.1   Common IP Types

Designation	Type
ICMP	Protocol Type 1
TCP	Protocol Type 6
UDP	Protocol Type 17
ESP	Protocol Type 50
AH	Protocol Type 51

Let me give you a bit of background on the last two, AH and ESP, because they are the essence of IPsec.

Authentication Header   The IP Authentication Header (AH) protocol is used to provide integrity and data origin authentication for IP datagrams. It can also include optional, anti-replay capability. The anti-replay protection is available only if the receiver has the ability to perform a check on the sequence number (which was incremented by the sender). The authentication header provides an authentication for those fields in the IP header that don't typically change. For example, the AH would not know what the time-to-live (TTL) field would be when it arrives at the destination because that value changes; therefore, that field would not be protected.

While there is still value in using the AH, there are limits on what it can do. The AH can be used by itself or in conjunction with ESP, which I will cover next.

Encapsulating Security Payload   Encapsulating Security Payload (ESP) can perform the same function as the AH, with the differences being in the fields that can be protected. Specifically, using ESP in tunnel mode can fully protect the entire IP header.

The ESP is unique in that it is designed to work with both IPv4 and IPv6. As mentioned earlier, it may be used in tandem with AH or deployed in a stand-alone fashion. ESP is largely used in stand-alone mode in today's IPsec VPN tunnels. The reason is that ESP can provide multiple services with just a single protocol.

ESP can provide confidentiality using data encryption, authentication via a hash function, and a form of anti-replay capability.

ESP provides two methods of operation, tunnel mode and transport mode. Remember that I said that AH had some limitations? One of the ways that ESP overcomes this limitation is using tunnel mode. In tunnel mode, the ESP header is placed just before a completely encapsulated (encrypted) IP header. In transport mode, the ESP header is inserted after the IP header and before any upper-layer-protocol header.

Although you can select encryption (confidentiality) without authentication, this leaves the service open to certain vulnerabilities that would otherwise be closed if authentication were selected. This is the reason that most ESP implementations make use of both services.

 Real World Scenario

Troubleshooting a VPN Outage

When troubleshooting VPNs, it can be very important to have a good knowledge of routing and switching. This is evidenced by the following true story. One time in a past life, the company that I was working for had a very stable VPN connection with a customer using an IPsec site-to-site VPN tunnel. Whenever we would have problems, inevitably it would be because some change had occurred on one side or another that prevented traffic from flowing through the tunnel.

Generally speaking, when a VPN tunnel goes down, it's from a lack of traffic, causing a time-out condition. With this customer, traffic was constantly flowing, so that was never a consideration. One day we got an alarm that the tunnel was not staying up. Digging in to find the problem was not easy. You could watch the tunnel come up, and then after a few minutes of being up, it would suddenly go down again. Turning on debug would show a normal connection and then a teardown.

Here's where our networking skills came in handy. Because the Internet is made up of many connections among different providers and peering points, there is always a possibility for routing issues. Once it appeared that we were having problems routing over the Internet, we started to really dig into the problem. Running a continuous ping from the two endpoints toward each other revealed that we would intermittently lose connectivity.

No surprise there, but where was the problem occurring? Both ends of the VPN tunnel had multiple ISPs. Here's where traceroute was able to help out. By launching traceroute from one VPN endpoint to the other, we could determine where the traceroute ended. Comparing that to a traceroute when you aren't having a problem leads you to see which ISP was the culprit. As it turns out, there was a single ISP that was having routing problems within its BGP autonomous system. This was causing route flapping, which in turn was causing the VPN to drop.

The fix, you might ask? Because the remote end had multiple ISPs, they were able to shut down the one with the problem and force the traffic down a different provider until the problems were resolved with the other ISP.

Moral of the story? It's hard to keep a VPN tunnel up if you can't get there from here. If the VPN is critical to your business, it's always wise to have ISP diversity with multiple connections from multiple carriers.

VPN Operation

Now you know about the components of IPsec and types of VPNs, so let's jump into how it all works. First, I'll discuss generic operation and then get more specifically into how it works in the Cisco environment.

Obviously, you've read about a lot of different technology, but to make this a little more palatable, I can generically describe IPsec in just a few tasks. Assuming you have an existing configuration, let's summarize what those tasks involve:

1. An IPsec process is started when traffic that is defined as interesting matches an existing policy.

   The interesting traffic is usually defined in terms of a source IP host or network and a destination IP host or network. This begins the IKE process.

2. IKE Phase 1 is initiated.

   What happens here is that the peers are authenticated and the IKE security associations (SAs) are negotiated. This, in turn, prepares for Phase 2 by setting up a secure channel. Phase 1 has two distinct modes that it uses: main mode and aggressive mode. The primary difference is that aggressive mode is faster. However, that speed comes with a cost. Aggressive mode is less secure because it uses only half of the key exchanges that main mode requires and some of those exchanges reveal information in cleartext.

3. In Phase 2, IPsec SAs are negotiated.

   At this point, you are able to transfer data. As long as data keeps flowing, the VPN will stay up.

A VPN Tunnel Goes Down

When a VPN tunnel goes does, usually one of two things is the cause. Either the SA has been deleted or the SA times out because it has reached a previously configured time-out threshold. Use the troubleshooting command **show crypto isakmp sa** to look at the status of the tunnel. An example of the output is shown here:

```
dst             src             state         conn-id slot status
10.100.120.1    172.16.200.1    QM_IDLE             5   0 ACTIVE
```

A look at the state field will tell you a lot about what is going on with the tunnel. The following list describes some of the state messages and what they mean. These are all main mode state messages:

- MM_NO_STATE: The ISAKMP SA has been created but there is no state at this point.

- MM_SA_SETUP: The VPN peers have agreed on parameters for the security association.

- MM_KEY_EXCH: The peers have exchanged public keys and then generated a secret key but have not yet been authenticated.

- MM_KEY_AUTH: The ISAKMP SA has been authenticated here, and if this particular router initiated the connection, it will transition to a quick mode and you should see the QM_IDLE message, indicating a QM exchange has begun.

Cisco-Specific Operation

Defining interesting traffic is one of the first steps in bringing up a VPN tunnel. Let's take a look at that from a Cisco perspective. If you have a Cisco router, you would have defined a specific access list that would determine source and destination traffic and would match a specific policy. When you defined the crypto map policy, you assigned the access list. Here's an example of what that access list might look like:

```
access-list 100 permit ip 192.168.23.0 0.0.0.255 192.168.24.0 0.0.0.255
```

And here's the entry in the crypto map that applies that access list:

```
match address 100
```

A crypto map is a Cisco IOS software configuration element that selects data flows that need security processing and secondly, defines the policy for the flows and the peer IP address that traffic should be sent to.

A transform-set defines a security protocol (usually ESP) and the associated encryption and authentication protocols that go with it, for example 3DES and SHA1-HMAC.

IKE Phase 1

Remember that I said the purpose of IKE Phase 1 is to authenticate the IPsec peers and to set up a secure channel between the peers to enable IKE exchanges. The IKE parameters used are part of a policy. Here is an example policy:

```
crypto isakmp policy 1
encr 3des
authentication pre-share
group 2
```

IKE Phase 2

During Phase 2, you have a protected IKE SA to use to negotiate an IPsec SA using parameters that were provided in the configuration. Those configuration parameters are listed next:

```
crypto ipsec transform-set ESP-3DES-SHA esp-3des esp-sha-hmac
crypto map SDM_CMAP_1 1 ipsec-isakmp
description Tunnel t010.100.1.1
set peer 10.100.1.1
set transform-set ESP-3DES-SHA
match address 100
```

Summing It Up

I've already talked about matching the access list, which gives you the interesting traffic. The only thing left is to send and receive data and to tear down the tunnel when finished (time-out).

So let's summarize the activity using Figure 12.2.

FIGURE 12.2   Cisco IPsec operation

Does traffic match interesting traffic defined by Access-List?

Have IPsec SAs been established?

If IPsec is established, encrypt traffic based on policy and transmit

If IKE SA is not established, check for IKE policies and proceed with negotiation

If IKE SA is established, negotiation of the IPsec SA is carried out as specified in policy, then packet is encrypted and transmitted

Configuring a Site-to-Site VPN

Site-to-site VPN configuration is easily accomplished using the Cisco Security Device Manager (SDM). Once I show you how easy it is, you will get a look at configuring a site-to-site VPN from a command-line perspective as well.

The Cisco SDM simplifies things greatly in terms of doing the configuration, but there are many things to consider when you use SDM solely. So let's jump right in and get started.

SDM Home

Figure 12.3 shows the Home screen. The Home screen opens whenever you bring up SDM. You have a toolbar across the top for the operation you're going to perform, and then within each menu item, you have choices along the left side of the screen. Looking at the About Your Router tab, you can see the type of router you're working with. In this case, a Cisco 2811 router is being used. On the Configuration Overview tab, you will find the number of interfaces on the router and their types as well as which interfaces are actually configured. On this tab, you can also get information about the state of the firewall policies, VPNs, routing, intrusion protection, interfaces and connections, and the like.

FIGURE 12.3 Cisco Router and Security Device Manager Home

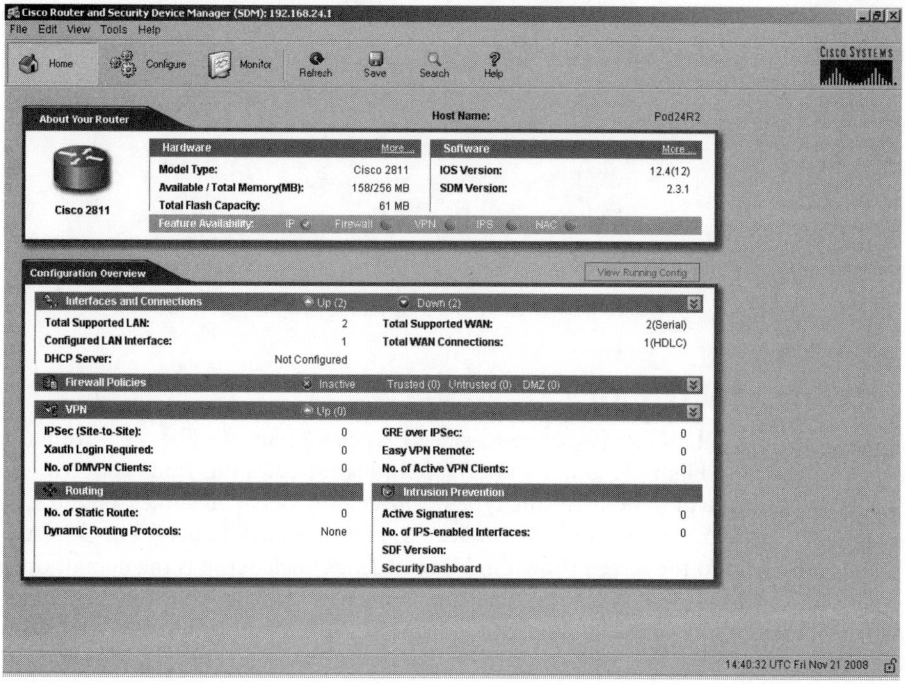

SDM Configure Tool

Now, let me introduce the Configure tool. When you click the Configure button, you will notice that the Tasks pane appears on the left side of the screen. To configure VPN, obviously you want to choose the VPN button. Once the VPN task is selected, you see the screen shown in Figure 12.4. Notice the way the configuration tasks are broken down by technologies.

FIGURE 12.4 Cisco Router and Security Device Manager Configure VPN task

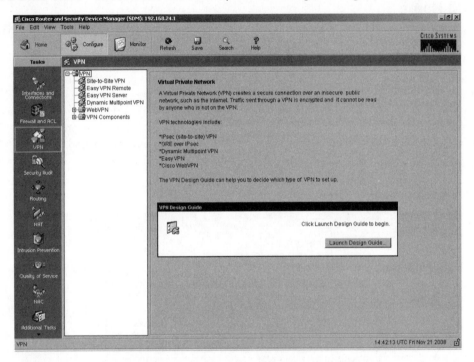

Site-to-Site VPN Wizard

Since you are going to build an IPsec site-to-site VPN, choose Site-To-Site VPN from the task tree, as shown in Figure 12.5. As you can see in Figure 12.6, this leads you to a wizard that gives you a couple of options for the type of site-to-site VPN you'd like to build.

Make sure Create A Site To Site VPN is selected, and then click Launch The Selected Task. This takes you to the screen shown in Figure 12.6. Quick Setup is the default option. It works well for this application, so go ahead and choose it. When you want to manually configure all the options yourself, choose Step By Step Wizard. On this screen, you can also click a button to view the default settings.

FIGURE 12.5   Cisco Router and Security Device Manager Create Site To Site VPN tab

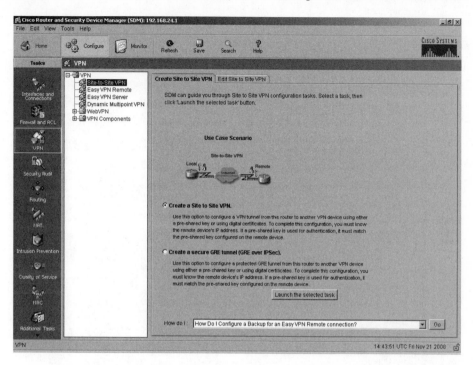

FIGURE 12.6   Cisco Router and Security Device Manager Site-To-Site VPN Wizard

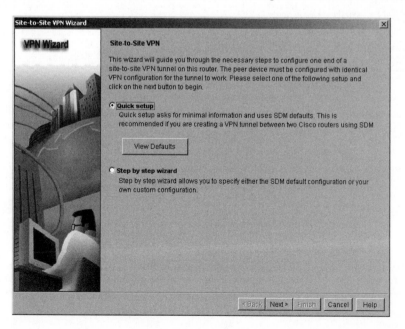

Selecting the Next button takes you to the screen shown in Figure 12.7, where you have a number of choices.

FIGURE 12.7 Cisco Router and Security Device Manager Site-To-Site VPN Wizard—VPN Connection Information screen

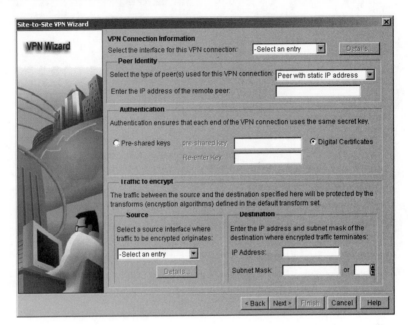

Table 12.2 describes the options.

TABLE 12.2 VPN connection information options

Option	Setting
Select The Interface For This VPN Connection	You can select which interface you want to use to terminate your VPN tunnel. The drop-down menu is limited to those interfaces that are configured and in an "up" status.
Peer Identity	This option selects the peer type, and this is where you enter the remote peer IP address.
Authentication	This option is where you select either pre-shared keys or digital certificates as an authentication method. For this exercise, select the Pre-Shared Keys option.
Traffic To Encrypt	Select the interface you will use to originate VPN traffic and which host/network will be passing through the VPN tunnel.

Figure 12.8 shows the choices I made. Notice that I used the Serial0/0/1 interface as the local peer. This interface is the entry point into the Multiprotocol Label Switching (MPLS) cloud. The local Ethernet port, FastEthernet0/0, is the point at which I chose to encrypt traffic locally destined for the remote network.

FIGURE 12.8   Example VPN connection settings

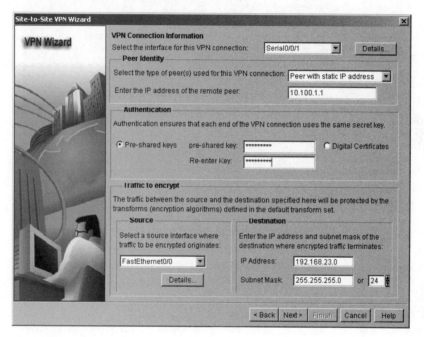

Now that you've entered your connection information, click the Next button and take a moment to review to the summary page, which will look similar to the one shown in Figure 12.9.

FIGURE 12.9 Cisco Router and Security Device Manager Site-To-Site VPN Wizard summary of the configuration

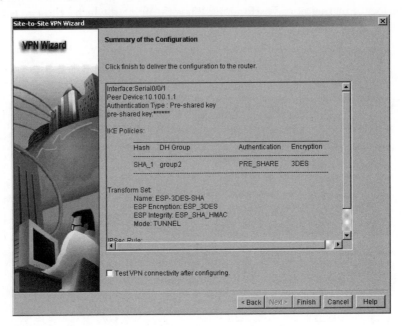

When you click the Finish button, SDM sends the finished configuration to the router. The information you entered through the wizard equates to 26 commands for the router, as you can see in Figure 12.10.

FIGURE 12.10 Cisco Router and Security Device Manager commands delivery status message

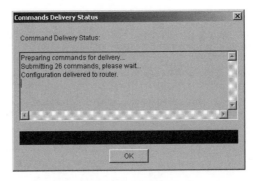

And that's the configuration using SDM. Depending on your situation, you may have to configure a remote router as the other end of this VPN tunnel. But many times, the other end of the VPN tunnel is a business partner and you have no control over the

configuration. That's why I show you some troubleshooting later on—to see some of the issues that come up when you deal with that kind of situation. In the next section, you'll explore what those same commands look like in the Cisco IOS command line on the router.

Verifying VPN

Now that you've configured a VPN using the SDM, let's have a look at what the configurations look like in IOS command-line interface. This verification process is useful when you configure a VPN so you understand what commands the router received. For the purpose of this exercise, I'll show you one end of the VPN tunnel that I configured in the previous section. First, let's look at the ISAKMP policy:

```
crypto isakmp policy 1
encr 3des
authentication pre-share
group 2
```

First, you can see that the wizard has created a policy with the numeric identifier of 1. The identifier could be any number, but the first one configured through the SDM wizard will be numbered 1. Next, the wizard specified 3DES as the encryption type. This is the default. The next step is to choose the preshared key method of authentication. Last, the wizard specified group 2. This indicates that Diffie-Hellman Group 2 is being used. Diffie-Hellman Group 2 is 1024 bits, as opposed to the default, which is Diffie-Hellman Group 1 and 768 bits.

Moving right along, the next piece of the configuration is where you specified the preshared key and the remote side peer that you need to match up to. The preshared key is starred out here and when you used SDM as well. Note that preshared keys must match on both ends of the tunnel:

```
crypto isakmp key ********* address 10.100.1.1
```

Now, look at the transform set. The transform set is where the wizard designated the type of authentication and encryption you will be using. The transform set can be named virtually anything, but in this case, SDM named it ESP-3DES-SHA. ESP-3DES-SHA tells us what is in the transform set. If you are using one device to set up VPN IPsec tunnels with multiple other sites, it is common to have multiple transform sets defined. Some of them are defined by the site that uses them. Of course, you can use any naming scheme you like. As I mentioned, in this case the transform set defines 3DES as the encryption scheme used and SHA-HMAC as the authentication used:

```
crypto ipsec transform-set ESP-3DES-SHA esp-3des esp-sha-hmac
```

Next, the wizard defines the crypto map. The first line of the configuration defines the type of crypto tunnel and names it. The name shown later in the configuration is the name defined by the SDM. Notice the optional description field shown, where the SDM took the remote IP and wrote a somewhat useful description. If you don't take the default, you can provide a description specific to your needs. For instance, if FutureTech was setting up a tunnel from the HQ to Chicago, then you might call it TunneltoChicago or something like that. Next, the peer remote IP address is set.

The next line is used to determine which transform set was actually used. Bear in mind, you could have multiple tunnels on the same router and, therefore, potentially multiple transform sets. Last, the wizard is going to specify your interesting traffic (the traffic that is allowed to traverse the tunnel) via an existing access list. I'll show the access list in a bit. In the crypto map, the wizard used a match statement to specify the access list to use:

```
crypto map SDM_CMAP_1 1 ipsec-isakmp
description Tunnel t010.100.1.1
set peer 10.100.1.1
set transform-set ESP-3DES-SHA
match address 100
```

And now take a look at the `access-list` 100 that is used to show the local-to-remote traffic that can traverse the tunnel:

```
access-list 100 permit ip 192.168.23.0 0.0.0.255 192.168.24.0 0.0.0.255
```

But hold on a minute! Is there something missing? What about the tunnel endpoint—don't we have to specify where the crypto map is applied? Indeed we do. If you will recall in the crypto map earlier, it was named SDM_CMAP_1. The wizard used that name to apply the crypto map to the appropriate interface, which in this case is Serial0/0/1. Since this is a serial line, there is a clock rate configured and also the IP address and mask of the interface:

```
interface Serial0/0/1
ip address 10.100.1.2 255.255.255.0
clock rate 2000000
crypto map SDM_CMAP_1
```

Okay, now you have seen a couple of things that the SDM can do for you. SDM automates a good bit of the work involved in creating an IPsec VPN. But you may want to use the command-line interface to change the options that are available. The choice is up to you.

Troubleshooting VPN

As you might imagine, a number of issues can come up when trying to ascertain the trouble with a VPN that doesn't work correctly. In the following sections, I'll cover a number of the commands used when troubleshooting.

Checking the Crypto Map

To verify the crypto map, use a show command. (You can also show the running configuration.) Looking at your RND1 router, issue the show crypto map command. The example shows the crypto map generated from the example set up in the previous two sections:

```
RND1#show crypto map
Crypto Map "SDM_CMAP_1" 1 ipsec-isakmp
Description: Tunnel t010.100.1.1
Peer = 10.100.1.1
Extended IP access list 100
access-list 100 permit ip 192.168.23.0 0.0.0.255 192.168.24.0 0.0.0.255
Current peer: 10.100.1.1
Security association lifetime: 4608000 kilobytes/3600 seconds
PFS (Y/N): N
Transform sets={
ESP-3DES-SHA,
}
Interfaces using crypto map SDM_CMAP_1:
Serial0/0/1
```

The result tells you everything that is contained in the running configuration.

Checking Security Associations

Now let's move on to some other show commands. When using the command-line interface, one of the primary ways to see what is happening with the VPN tunnel is to look at the ISAKMP security associations, or SAs. See the following output from issuing the show crypto isakmp sa command. Note the MM_NO_STATE output. This is not the normal state of a functioning VPN tunnel. The normal state is QM_IDLE.

```
RND1#sh crypto isakmp sa
dst src state conn-id slot status
10.100.1.1 10.100.1.2 MM_NO_STATE 0 0 ACTIVE
```

So let's explore this particular issue in depth. The usual issues that cause an MM_NO_STATE message are that the preshared keys don't match or that the interesting traffic doesn't match on both sides.

Using Debug

Besides doing a comparison of configurations, you will find that debug commands are your best friends. So, let's take a look at the issue at hand and try to do some troubleshooting using the debug commands.

WARNING   Debug should be used with caution. Issuing too many debug commands in combination with lots of traffic causes bad things to happen. I know many people—this author included—who at one time or another have turned on too many debug commands and crashed the router they were working on. Great stuff if you are working in a lab; resume-generating event if you did it to the main production router in the middle of the day. ☺

First, turn on the crypto ipsec and isakmp debugs:

```
RND1# debug crypto isakmp
Crypto ISAKMP debugging is on
RND1# debug crypto ipsec
Crypto IPSEC debugging is on
```

To verify which debugging commands you have turned on, issue the show debug command, as shown in the code that follows:

```
RND1# show debug
Cryptographic Subsystem:
Crypto ISAKMP debugging is on
Crypto IPSEC debugging is on
```

NOTE   If you have used telnet or ssh to gain access to the router you are working on, you might want to issue the command term mon prior to issuing the debug commands. Term mon is short for terminal monitor. This allows you to see the debug messages on your screen.

Now that you have verified that debugging is turned on, let's get into some troubleshooting. In the previous section, I noted that there is an MM_NO_STATE in the state field, so I am looking for some debug output that will give me an idea of the cause of the problem.

Let's assume the SA has completely timed out and there's nothing displayed when you do a show crypto ipsec sa command.

Now, source a ping command from one end of the tunnel to the other and watch what is displayed from a debug perspective. The results might look something like this:

```
*Nov 4 01:11:52.127: ISAKMP: New peer created peer = 0x45CE4878 peer_handle
 = 0x80000002
*Nov 4 01:11:52.127: ISAKMP: Locking peer struct 0x45CE4878, IKE refcount 1
 for isakmp_initiator
*Nov 4 01:11:52.127: ISAKMP: local port 500, remote port 500
*Nov 4 01:11:52.127: ISAKMP: set new node 0 to QM_IDLE
*Nov 4 01:11:52.127: insert sa successfully sa = 44FACE7C
```

```
*Nov 4 01:11:52.127: ISAKMP:(0:0:N/A:0):Can not start Aggressive mode, trying
 Main mode.
*Nov 4 01:11:52.127: ISAKMP:(0:0:N/A:0):found peer pre-shared key matching
10.100.1.2
*Nov 4 01:11:52.127: ISAKMP:(0:0:N/A:0): constructed NAT-T vendor-07 ID
*Nov 4 01:11:52.127: ISAKMP:(0:0:N/A:0): constructed NAT-T vendor-03 ID
*Nov 4 01:11:52.127: ISAKMP:(0:0:N/A:0): constructed NAT-T vendor-02 ID
*Nov 4 01:11:52.127: ISAKMP:(0:0:N/A:0):Input = IKE_MESG_FROM_IPSEC,
IKE_SA_REQ_MM
*Nov 4 01:11:52.131: ISAKMP:(0:0:N/A:0):Old State = IKE_READY New State =
IKE_I_MM1
*Nov 4 01:11:52.131: ISAKMP:(0:0:N/A:0): beginning Main Mode exchange
*Nov 4 01:11:52.131: ISAKMP:(0:0:N/A:0): sending packet to 10.100.1.2 my_port
500 peer_port 500 (I) MM_NO_STATE
*Nov 4 01:11:52.179: ISAKMP (0:0): received packet from 10.100.1.2 dport 500
sport 500 Global (I) MM_NO_STATE
*Nov 4 01:11:52.183: ISAKMP:(0:0:N/A:0):Input = IKE_MESG_FROM_PEER, IKE_MM_EXCH
*Nov 4 01:11:52.183: ISAKMP:(0:0:N/A:0):Old State = IKE_I_MM1 New State =
IKE_I_MM2
*Nov 4 01:11:52.183: ISAKMP:(0:0:N/A:0): processing SA payload. message ID = 0
*Nov 4 01:11:52.183: ISAKMP:(0:0:N/A:0): processing vendor id payload
*Nov 4 01:11:52.183: ISAKMP:(0:0:N/A:0): vendor ID seems Unity/DPD but major 245
mismatch
*Nov 4 01:11:52.183: ISAKMP (0:0): vendor ID is NAT-T v7
*Nov 4 01:11:52.183: ISAKMP:(0:0:N/A:0):found peer pre-shared key matching
10.100.1.2
*Nov 4 01:11:52.183: ISAKMP:(0:0:N/A:0): local preshared key found
*Nov 4 01:11:52.183: ISAKMP : Scanning profiles for xauth …
*Nov 4 01:11:52.183: ISAKMP:(0:0:N/A:0):Checking ISAKMP transform 1 against
priority 1 policy
*Nov 4 01:11:52.183: ISAKMP: encryption 3DES-CBC
*Nov 4 01:11:52.183: ISAKMP: hash SHA
*Nov 4 01:11:52.183: ISAKMP: default group 2
*Nov 4 01:11:52.183: ISAKMP: auth pre-share
*Nov 4 01:11:52.183: ISAKMP: life type in seconds
*Nov 4 01:11:52.183: ISAKMP: life duration (VPI) of 0x0 0x1 0x51 0x80
*Nov 4 01:11:52.183: ISAKMP:(0:0:N/A:0):atts are acceptable. Next payload is 0
*Nov 4 01:11:52.223: ISAKMP:(0:1:SW:1): processing vendor id payload
*Nov 4 01:11:52.223: ISAKMP:(0:1:SW:1): vendor ID seems Unity/DPD but major 245
mismatch
*Nov 4 01:11:52.223: ISAKMP (0:134217729): vendor ID is NAT-T v7
```

```
*Nov 4 01:11:52.223: ISAKMP:(0:1:SW:1):Input = IKE_MESG_INTERNAL,
IKE_PROCESS_MAIN_MODE
*Nov 4 01:11:52.223: ISAKMP:(0:1:SW:1):Old State = IKE_I_MM2 New State =
IKE_I_MM2
*Nov 4 01:11:52.223: ISAKMP:(0:1:SW:1): sending packet to 10.100.1.2 my_port
50peer_port 500 (I) MM_SA_SETUP
*Nov 4 01:11:52.223: ISAKMP:(0:1:SW:1):Input = IKE_MESG_INTERNAL,
IKE_PROCESS_COMPLETE
*Nov 4 01:11:52.223: ISAKMP:(0:1:SW:1):Old State = IKE_I_MM2 New State =
IKE_I_MM3
*Nov 4 01:11:52.283: ISAKMP (0:134217729): received packet from 10.100.1.2 dport
500 sport 500 Global (I) MM_SA_SETUP
*Nov 4 01:11:52.283: ISAKMP:(0:1:SW:1):Input = IKE_MESG_FROM_PEER, IKE_MM_EXCH
*Nov 4 01:11:52.283: ISAKMP:(0:1:SW:1):Old State = IKE_I_MM3 New State =
IKE_I_MM4
*Nov 4 01:11:52.283: ISAKMP:(0:1:SW:1): processing KE payload. message ID = 0
*Nov 4 01:11:52.327: ISAKMP:(0:1:SW:1): processing NONCE payload. message ID =0
*Nov 4 01:11:52.327: ISAKMP:(0:1:SW:1):found peer pre-shared key matching
10.100.1.2
*Nov 4 01:11:52.331: ISAKMP:(0:1:SW:1):SKEYID state generated
*Nov 4 01:11:52.331: ISAKMP:(0:1:SW:1): processing vendor id payload
*Nov 4 01:11:52.331: ISAKMP:(0:1:SW:1): vendor ID is Unity
*Nov 4 01:11:52.331: ISAKMP:(0:1:SW:1): processing vendor id payload
*Nov 4 01:11:52.331: ISAKMP:(0:1:SW:1): vendor ID is DPD
*Nov 4 01:11:52.331: ISAKMP:(0:1:SW:1): processing vendor id payload
*Nov 4 01:11:52.331: ISAKMP:(0:1:SW:1): speaking to another IOS box!
*Nov 4 01:11:52.331: ISAKMP:(0:1:SW:1):Input = IKE_MESG_INTERNAL,
IKE_PROCESS_MAIN_MODE
*Nov 4 01:11:52.331: ISAKMP:(0:1:SW:1):Old State = IKE_I_MM4 New State =
IKE_I_MM4
*Nov 4 01:11:52.331: ISAKMP:(0:1:SW:1):Send initial contact
*Nov 4 01:11:52.331: ISAKMP:(0:1:SW:1):SA is doing pre-shared key authentication
using id type ID_IPV4_ADDR
*Nov 4 01:11:52.331: ISAKMP (0:134217729): ID payload
next-payload : 8
type : 1
address : 10.100.1.1
protocol : 17
port : 500
length : 12
*Nov 4 01:11:52.331: ISAKMP:(0:1:SW.:1):Total payload length: 12
```

```
*Nov 4 01:11:52.335: ISAKMP:(0:1:SW:1): sending packet to 10.100.1.2 my_port
500 peer_port 500 (I) MM_KEY_EXCH
*Nov 4 01:11:52.335: ISAKMP:(0:1:SW:1):Input = IKE_MESG_INTERNAL,
IKE_PROCESS_COMPLETE
*Nov 4 01:11:52.335: ISAKMP:(0:1:SW:1):Old State = IKE_I_MM4 New State =
IKE_I_MM5
*Nov 4 01:11:52.339: ISAKMP (0:134217729): received packet from 10.100.1.2 dport
500 sport 500 Global (I) MM_KEY_EXCH
*Nov 4 01:11:52.339: ISAKMP (0:134217729): received packet from 10.100.1.2 dport
500 sport 500 Global (I) MM_KEY_EXCH
*Nov 4 01:11:52.339: ISAKMP (0:134217729): received packet from 10.100.1.2 dport
500 sport 500 Global (I) MM_KEY_EXCH
*Nov 4 01:11:52.343: ISAKMP (0:134217729): received packet from 10.100.1.2 dport
500 sport 500 Global (I) MM_KEY_EXCH
*Nov 4 01:11:52.343: ISAKMP (0:134217729): received packet from 10.100.1.2 dport
500 sport 500 Global (I) MM_KEY_EXCH
*Nov 4 01:11:52.343: ISAKMP: Info Notify message requeue retry counter exceeded
sa request from 10.100.1.2 to 10.100.1.1 …
Success rate is 0 percent (0/5)
RND1#
```

It is kind of daunting to look at the whole thing, but like most debug outputs, there are a few things that you need to take notice of. We are not going to go through it line by line, but I'll point out a couple of key things. Take a look at something that shows that at least part of the debug is displaying correct behavior, and that is the line that says atts are acceptable. If you look right above that line, you will see the IKE (Cisco calls this ISAKMP) configuration.

Now let's move toward the end of the debug output and look at where you have problems. Note the MM_KEY_EXCH entry that repeats itself many times. Kind of looks familiar, doesn't it? This indicates that the key exchange failed.

Let's look at a different type of failure to see what changes in the debug output. In this case, a fault condition had been configured that prevented the VPN from coming up. Again, issue a ping from one end of the tunnel and watch the debug output:

```
*Nov 4 03:17:42.355: IPSEC(sa_request): ,
(key eng. msg.) OUTBOUND local= 10.100.1.1, remote= 10.100.1.2,
local_proxy= 192.168.23.0/255.255.255.0/0/0 (type=4),
remote_proxy= 192.168.24.0/255.255.255.0/0/0 (type=4),
protocol= ESP, transform= esp-3des esp-sha-hmac (Tunnel),
lifedur= 3600s and 4608000kb,
spi= 0x5449DE2B(1414127147), conn_id= 0, keysize= 0, flags= 0x400A
*Nov 4 03:17:42.359: ISAKMP: received ke message (1/1)
```

*Nov 4 03:17:42.359: ISAKMP:(0:0:N/A:0): SA request profile is (NULL)

*Nov 4 03:17:42.359: ISAKMP: Created a peer struct for 10.100.1.2, peer port 500

*Nov 4 03:17:42.359: ISAKMP: New peer created peer = 0x45CECB28 peer_handle = 0 x80000006

*Nov 4 03:17:42.359: ISAKMP: Locking peer struct 0x45CECB28, IKE refcount 1 for isakmp_initiator

*Nov 4 03:17:42.359: ISAKMP: local port 500, remote port 500

*Nov 4 03:17:42.359: ISAKMP: set new node 0 to QM_IDLE

*Nov 4 03:17:42.359: insert sa successfully sa = 44FACE7C

*Nov 4 03:17:42.359: ISAKMP:(0:0:N/A:0):Can not start Aggressive mode, trying Main mode.

*Nov 4 03:17:42.359: ISAKMP:(0:0:N/A:0):found peer pre-shared key matching 10.100.1.2

*Nov 4 03:17:42.359: ISAKMP:(0:0:N/A:0): constructed NAT-T vendor-07 ID

*Nov 4 03:17:42.359: ISAKMP:(0:0:N/A:0): constructed NAT-T vendor-03 ID

*Nov 4 03:17:42.359: ISAKMP:(0:0:N/A:0): constructed NAT-T vendor-02 ID

*Nov 4 03:17:42.359: ISAKMP:(0:0:N/A:0):Input = IKE_MESG_FROM_IPSEC, IKE_SA_REQ_MM

*Nov 4 03:17:42.359: ISAKMP:(0:0:N/A:0):Old State = IKE_READY New State = IKE_I_MM1

*Nov 4 03:17:42.359: ISAKMP:(0:0:N/A:0): beginning Main Mode exchange

*Nov 4 03:17:42.359: ISAKMP:(0:0:N/A:0): sending packet to 10.100.1.2 my_port 500 peer_port 500 (I) MM_NO_STATE

*Nov 4 03:17:42.411: ISAKMP (0:0): received packet from 10.100.1.2 dport 500 sport 500 Global (I) MM_NO_STATE

*Nov 4 03.:17:42.411: ISAKMP:(0:0:N/A:0):Input = IKE_MESG_FROM_PEER, IKE_MM_EXCH

*Nov 4 03:17:42.411: ISAKMP:(0:0:N/A:0):Old State = IKE_I_MM1 New State = IKE_I_MM2

*Nov 4 03:17:42.411: ISAKMP:(0:0:N/A:0): processing SA payload. message ID = 0

*Nov 4 03:17:42.411: ISAKMP:(0:0:N/A:0): processing vendor id payload

*Nov 4 03:17:42.411: ISAKMP:(0:0:N/A:0): vendor ID seems Unity/DPD but major 245 mismatch

*Nov 4 03:17:42.411: ISAKMP (0:0): vendor ID is NAT-T v7

*Nov 4 03:17:42.411: ISAKMP:(0:0:N/A:0):found peer pre-shared key matching 10.100.1.2

*Nov 4 03:17:42.411: ISAKMP:(0:0:N/A:0): local preshared key found

*Nov 4 03:17:42.411: ISAKMP : Scanning profiles for xauth …

*Nov 4 03:17:42.411: ISAKMP:(0:0:N/A:0):Checking ISAKMP transform 1 against priority 1 policy

```
*Nov 4 03:17:42.411: ISAKMP: encryption 3DES-CBC
*Nov 4 03:17:42.411: ISAKMP: hash SHA
*Nov 4 03:17:42.411: ISAKMP: default group 2
*Nov 4 03:17:42.411: ISAKMP: auth pre-share
*Nov 4 03:17:42.411: ISAKMP: life type in seconds
*Nov 4 03:17:42.411: ISAKMP: life duration (VPI) of 0x0 0x1 0x51 0x80
*Nov 4 03:17:42.415: ISAKMP:(0:0:N/A:0):atts are acceptable. Next payload is 0
*Nov 4 03:17:42.451: ISAKMP:(0:1:SW:1): processing vendor id payload
*Nov 4 03:17:42.451: ISAKMP:(0:1:SW:1): vendor ID seems Unity/DPD but major 245
mismatch
*Nov 4 03:17:42.451: ISAKMP (0:134217729): vendor ID is NAT-T v7
*Nov 4 03:17:42.451: ISAKMP:(0:1:SW:1):Input = IKE_MESG_INTERNAL,
IKE_PROCESS_MAIN_MODE
*Nov 4 03:17:42.451: ISAKMP:(0:1:SW:1):Old State = IKE_I_MM2 New State =
IKE_I_MM2
*Nov 4 03:17:42.451: ISAKMP:(0:1:SW:1): sending packet to 10.100.1.2 my_port
500 peer_port 500 (I) MM_SA_SETUP
*Nov 4 03:17:42.4.55: ISAKMP:(0:1:SW:1):Input = IKE_MESG_INTERNAL,
IKE_PROCESS_COMPLETE
*Nov 4 03:17:42.455: ISAKMP:(0:1:SW:1):Old State = IKE_I_MM2 New State =
IKE_I_MM3
*Nov 4 03:17:42.511: ISAKMP (0:134217729): received packet from 10.100.1.2
dport 500 sport 500 Global (I) MM_SA_SETUP
*Nov 4 03:17:42.511: ISAKMP:(0:1:SW:1):Input = IKE_MESG_FROM_PEER, IKE_MM_EXCH
*Nov 4 03:17:42.511: ISAKMP:(0:1:SW:1):Old State = IKE_I_MM3 New State =
IKE_I_MM4
*Nov 4 03:17:42.511: ISAKMP:(0:1:SW:1): processing KE payload. message ID = 0
*Nov 4 03:17:42.555: ISAKMP:(0:1:SW:1): processing NONCE payload. message ID =
0
*Nov 4 03:17:42.559: ISAKMP:(0:1:SW:1):found peer pre-shared key matching
10.100.1.2
*Nov 4 03:17:42.559: ISAKMP:(0:1:SW:1):SKEYID state generated
*Nov 4 03:17:42.559: ISAKMP:(0:1:SW:1): processing vendor id payload
*Nov 4 03:17:42.559: ISAKMP:(0:1:SW:1): vendor ID is Unity
*Nov 4 03:17:42.559: ISAKMP:(0:1:SW:1): processing vendor id payload
*Nov 4 03:17:42.559: ISAKMP:(0:1:SW:1): vendor ID is DPD
*Nov 4 03:17:42.559: ISAKMP:(0:1:SW:1): processing vendor id payload
*Nov 4 03:17:42.559: ISAKMP:(0:1:SW:1): speaking to another IOS box!
*Nov 4 03:17:42.559: ISAKMP:(0:1:SW:1):Input = IKE_MESG_INTERNAL,
IKE_PROCESS_MAIN_MODE
```

*Nov 4 03:17:42.559: ISAKMP:(0:1:SW:1):Old State = IKE_I_MM4 New State = IKE_I_MM4

*Nov 4 03:17:42.559: ISAKMP:(0:1:SW:1):Send initial contact

*Nov 4 03:17:42.559: ISAKMP:(0:1:SW:1):SA is doing pre-shared key authentication using id type ID_IPV4_ADDR

*Nov 4 03:17:42.559: ISAKMP (0:134217729): ID payload

next-payload : 8

type : 1

address : 10.100.1.1

protocol : 17

port : 500

length : 12

*Nov 4 03:17:42.559: ISAKMP:(0:1:SW.:1):Total payload length: 12

*Nov 4 03:17:42.563: ISAKMP:(0:1:SW:1): sending packet to 10.100.1.2 my_port 500 (I) MM_KEY_EXCH

*Nov 4 03:17:42.563: ISAKMP:(0:1:SW:1):Input = IKE_MESG_INTERNAL, IKE_PROCESS_COMPLETE

*Nov 4 03:17:42.563: ISAKMP:(0:1:SW:1):Old State = IKE_I_MM4 New State = IKE_I_MM5

*Nov 4 03:17:42.571: ISAKMP (0:134217729): received packet from 10.100.1.2 dport 500 sport 500 Global (I) MM_KEY_EXCH

*Nov 4 03:17:42.575: ISAKMP:(0:1:SW:1): processing ID payload. message ID = 0

*Nov 4 03:17:42.575: ISAKMP (0:134217729): ID payload

next-payload : 8

type : 1

address : 10.100.1.2

protocol : 17

port : 500

length : 12

*Nov 4 03:17:42.575: ISAKMP:(0:1:SW:1): peer matches *none* of the profiles

*Nov 4 03:17:42.575: ISAKMP:(0:1:SW:1): processing HASH payload. message ID = 0

*Nov 4 03:17:42.575: ISAKMP:(0:1:SW:1):SA authentication status: authenticated

*Nov 4 03:17:42.575: ISAKMP:(0:1:SW:1):SA has been authenticated with 10.100.1.2

*Nov 4 03:17:42.575: ISAKMP: Trying to insert a peer 10.100.1.1/10.100.1.2/500/, and inserted successfully 45CECB28.

*Nov 4 03:17:42.575: ISAKMP:(0:1:SW:1):Input = IKE_MESG_FROM_PEER, IKE_MM_EXCH

*Nov 4 03:17:42.575: ISAKMP:(0:1:SW:1):Old State = IKE_I_MM5 New State = IKE_I_MM6

*Nov 4 03:17:42.575: ISAKMP:(0:1:SW:1):Input = IKE_MESG_INTERNAL, IKE_PROCESS_MAIN_MODE

```
*Nov 4 03:17:42.575: ISAKMP:(0:1:SW:1):Old State = IKE_I_MM6 New State =
IKE_I_MM6
*Nov 4 03:17:42.579: ISAKMP:(0:1:SW:1):Input = IKE_MESG_INTERNAL,
IKE_PROCESS_COMPLETE
*Nov 4 03:17:42.579: ISAKMP:(0:1:SW:1):Old State = IKE_I_MM6 New State =
IKE_P1_COMPLETE
*Nov 4 03:17:42.579: ISAKMP:(0:1:SW:1):beginning Quic.k Mode exchange, M-ID of
-1948338380
*Nov 4 03:17:42.579: ISAKMP:(0:1:SW:1): sending packet to 10.100.1.2 my_port
500 peer_port 500 (I) QM_IDLE
*Nov 4 03:17:42.579: ISAKMP:(0:1:SW:1):Node -1948338380, Input =
IKE_MESG_INTERNAL, IKE_INIT_QM
*Nov 4 03:17:42.579: ISAKMP:(0:1:SW:1):Old State = IKE_QM_READY New State =
IKE_QM_I_QM1
*Nov 4 03:17:42.583: ISAKMP:(0:1:SW:1):Input = IKE_MESG_INTERNAL,
IKE_PHASE1_COMPLETE
*Nov 4 03:17:42.583: ISAKMP:(0:1:SW:1):Old State = IKE_P1_COMPLETE New
State = IKE_P1_COMPLETE
*Nov 4 03:17:42.591: ISAKMP (0:134217729): received packet from 10.100.1.2
dport 500 sport 500 Global (I) QM_IDLE
*Nov 4 03:17:42.591: ISAKMP: set new node -614552533 to QM_IDLE
*Nov 4 03:17:42.591: ISAKMP:(0:1:SW:1): processing HASH payload. message ID =
-614552533
*Nov 4 03:17:42.591: ISAKMP:(0:1:SW:1): processing NOTIFY PROPOSAL_NOT_CHOSEN
protocol 3
spi 1414127147, message ID = -614552533, sa = 44FACE7C
*Nov 4 03:17:42.591: ISAKMP:(0:1:SW:1): deleting spi 1414127147 message ID =
-1948338380
*Nov 4 03:17:42.591: ISAKMP:(0:1:SW:1):deleting node -1948338380 error TRUE
reason "Delete Larval"
*Nov 4 03:17:42.591: ISAKMP:(0:1:SW:1):deleting node -614552533 error FALSE
reason "Informational (in) state 1"
*Nov 4 03:17:42.591: ISAKMP:(0:1:SW:1):Input = IKE_MESG_FROM_PEER,
IKE_INFO_NOTIFY
*Nov 4 03:17:42.591: ISAKMP:(0:1:SW:1):Old State = IKE_P1_COMPLETE New
State = IKE_P1_COMPLETE
.
Success rate is 0 percent (0/5)
```

Once again, you see the atts are acceptable message, meaning that you matched an IKE policy. But a couple of things don't look right later on.

The first thing that looks wrong is the `peer matches *none* of the profiles` line. Okay, you have an issue there. The other thing is a little later in the debug that says `PROPOSAL_NOT_CHOSEN`. This would lead us to believe that something didn't match when an IPsec SA was set up. Often when you are setting up a VPN tunnel with a third party, you don't necessarily have access to the other side of the tunnel. Recognize the problem in the future when you run into it.

You have covered just a couple of the potential issues that could come up when troubleshooting a site-to-site VPN. There are many others to deal with. One of the best ways to help troubleshoot is to turn on debug, as I illustrated. If you see an error message that you aren't familiar with, check the Cisco website under Support and see if you can find out what that exact error message means. Examine many error messages, and over time, you will become very acquainted with specific issues.

Cisco Easy VPN

Because doing VPNs requires a great deal of coordination and expertise, Cisco saw the need for a method for reducing the administrative burden in configuring VPNs. Enter Cisco Easy VPN.

Cisco Easy VPN has a number of benefits over manual configuration:

- Centralized control over security policy
- Reduced dependence on remote access equipment
- VPN configurations held on central server
- Dynamic end user administration

 It might be helpful to review the difference between a site-to-site VPN and a remote-access VPN. A remote-access VPN is one where a PC is connecting individually to a VPN server of some kind. This is also known as transport mode. A site-to-site (or LAN-to-LAN) VPN connects hosts from one site to hosts at another site, without requiring VPN software on the host. A site-to-site connection is known as tunnel mode.

Let's talk a little about the architecture of Cisco Easy VPN. It resembles a typical client-server application; however, the server in this case can be any number of network devices, such as a Cisco IOS router, Cisco PIX or ASA firewall, or VPN concentrator. The client can also be any of these devices, but it also includes host workstations—such as those running Windows, MacOSX, and Linux—for remote access applications. The key is that the devices in question must support the Cisco Unified Client Framework, which allows the majority of VPN administration to be defined on the Cisco Easy VPN server.

Three types of operations are supported with Cisco Easy VPN:

Client mode   This is generally for remote access. NATs or PATs are in use here, and this is similar to the Cisco VPN client in terms of functionality.

Network extension mode   This configuration allows hosts at the remote end to have routable addresses within the network.

Network extension plus mode   This is the same as network extension mode, except that an additional IP is configured as a loopback address. This IP can then be used for troubleshooting or remote administration.

All three methods allow for split tunneling, which means that users and devices can reach all resources on the local subnet in addition to being able to access network resources on the other side of the VPN tunnel.

Configuring Cisco Easy VPN

Let's now use the SDM to configure a Cisco Easy VPN. Once again, in Figure 12.11, you see the familiar SDM Configure screen. In this case, you are going to configure the router as an Easy VPN server.

FIGURE 12.11   Cisco Router and Security Device Manager Create Easy VPN Server tab

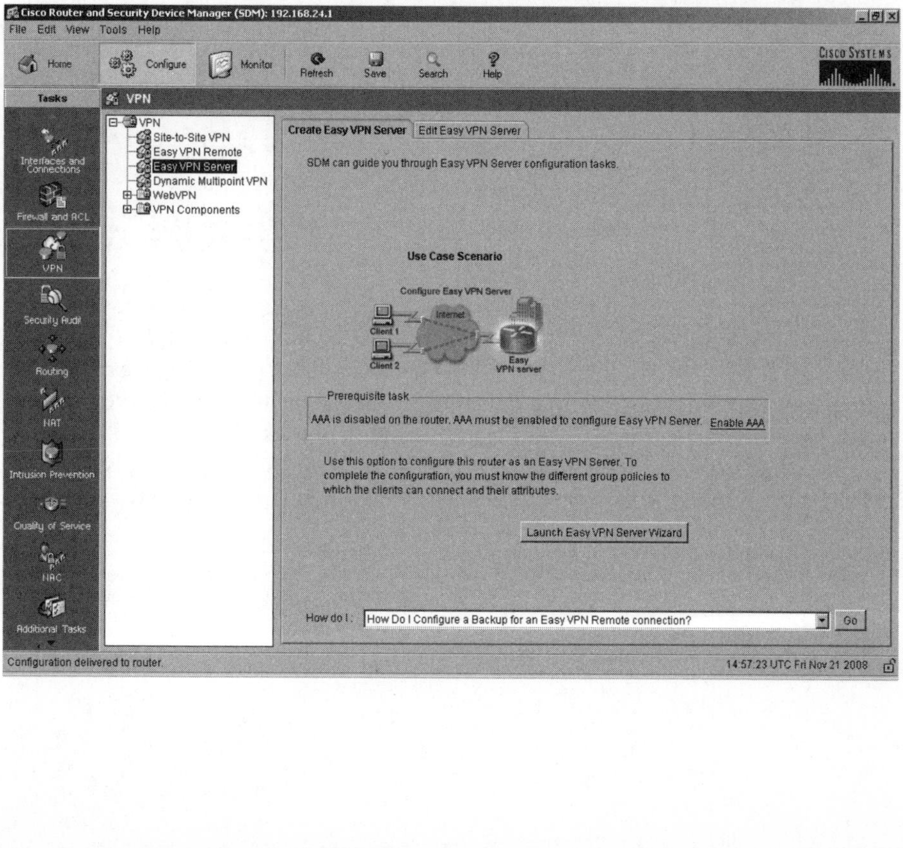

Notice that in order to configure an Easy VPN server you must have AAA enabled. For the purpose of this exercise, AAA has already been enabled. (AAA is discussed in Chapter 4.) So at this point, just be sure AAA is enabled and then click the Launch Easy VPN Server Wizard button to start the process.

The splash screen shown in Figure 12.12 gives you a summary of what you're going to be configuring in the upcoming screens. Take a moment to review it and then click the Next button.

FIGURE 12.12 Cisco Router and Security Device Manager Easy VPN Server Wizard

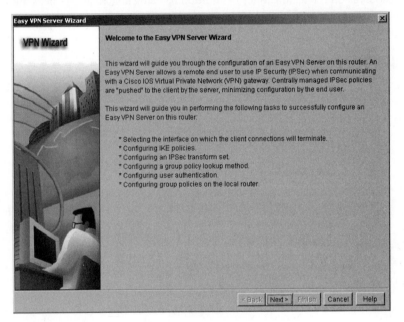

Similar to what you did to configure a VPN tunnel, you must select the proper interface to use for this VPN. In this case, as shown in Figure 12.13, use the FastEthernet0/0 interface. Again, for Authentication, select Pre-Shared Keys and then click Next.

The next screen defines what you'd like to configure as far as IKE proposals. In this case, take the defaults: 3DES for encryption, SHA-1 as the hash, and PRE_SHARE (preshared key) as the type of authentication, as shown in Figure 12.14.

FIGURE 12.13   Cisco Router and Security Device Manager Easy VPN Server Wizard Interface And Authentication screen

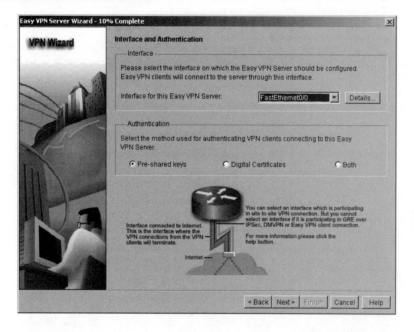

FIGURE 12.14   Cisco Router and Security Device Manager Easy VPN Server Wizard IKE Proposals screen

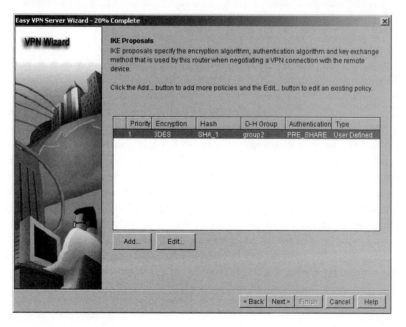

The next screen, shown in Figure 12.15, defines the transform set to be used. Just as when you configured a site-to-site VPN, select the default setting, which is ESP-3DES for encryption and ESP-SHA-HMAC for ESP Integrity.

FIGURE 12.15 Cisco Router and Security Device Manager Easy VPN Server Wizard Transform Set

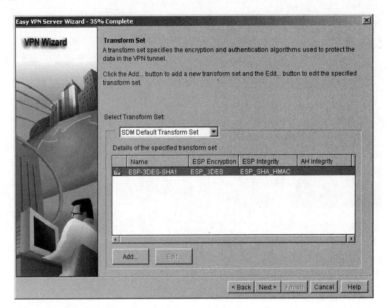

You might be noticing a pattern here—the SDM makes it very easy to configure and the defaults mean that you don't even have to specify anything. Just choose and go.

The next screen, shown in Figure 12.16, designates the group authorization and Group Policy choices. This might seem familiar to you, if you've ever configured a VPN concentrator. All of these choices must also be configured if you are setting up a VPN concentrator for remote access. Remember that you had to turn on AAA services to get to this option. Here you choose whether to make use of a local database on this server, use an existing or new RADIUS server, or use both services. RADIUS stands for Remote Authentication Dial In User Service. It evolved from the early days of the Internet, when thousands of remote dial-in users were connecting. There had to be a database of users that could be used to authenticate each connection. RADIUS served that need. Today's RADIUS is built into some operating systems and can be provided by stand-alone third-party services as well.

For the purpose of this exercise, select a local database to keep it simple. Also, assume that you don't have an existing RADIUS server.

FIGURE 12.16   Cisco Router and Security Device Manager Easy VPN Server Wizard Group Authorization And Group Policy Lookup screen

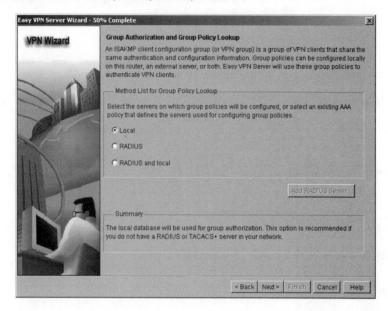

The Extended User Authentication, or XAuth, screen is shown in Figure 12.17. For this exercise, you will need to select Local Only authentication.

FIGURE 12.17   Cisco Router and Security Device Manager Easy VPN Server Wizard User Authentication (XAuth) screen

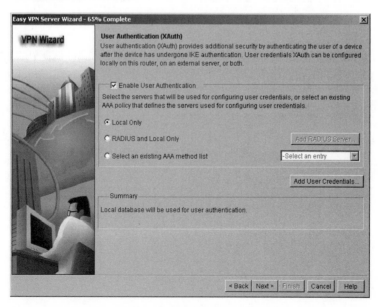

Group policies and group authorization settings are shown in Figure 12.18. Again, this is largely used for remote users. Add a placeholder default group policy by selecting the Add button.

FIGURE 12.18   Cisco Router and Security Device Manager Easy VPN Server Wizard Group Authorization And User Group Policies screen

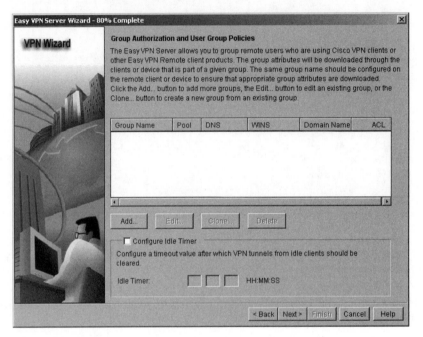

Once you click the Add button from the previous screen, you will see the Add Group Policy screen, shown in Figure 12.19. This screen has several tabs. The General tab gives you the opportunity to make preshared key assignments and IP DHCP pool assignments. These are the kind of assignments you need to make for VPN clients and other remote clients.

The DNS/WINS tab of the Add Group Policy dialog box shown in Figure 12.20 is pretty self-explanatory. Here you can enter the DNS and WINS servers that you would like to make available to remote users.

FIGURE 12.19 Cisco Router and Security Device Manager Easy VPN Server Wizard Add Group Policy General tab

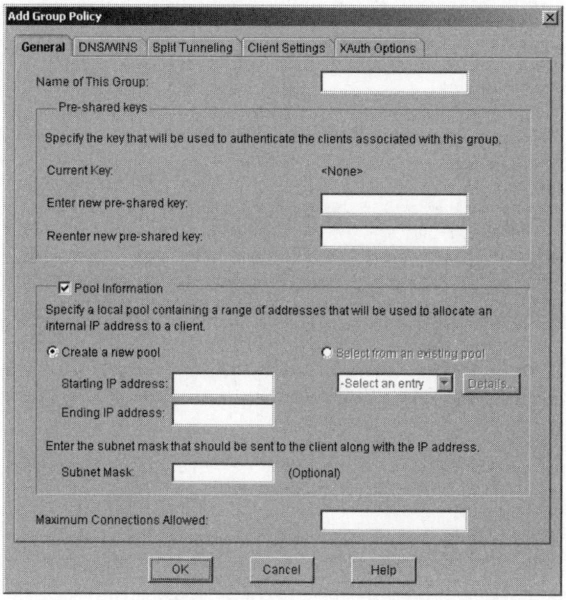

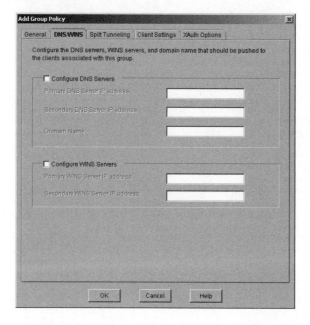

FIGURE 12.20 Cisco Router and Security Device Manager Easy VPN Server Wizard Add Group Policy DNS/WINS tab

The Split Tunneling tab of the Add Group Policy creation page is shown in Figure 12.21. Split tunneling is important if you want to be able to access local resources at the same time you are accessing the remote resources. To enable split tunneling, click the check box and define the networks that you would like to be able to access locally.

FIGURE 12.21   Cisco Router and Security Device Manager Easy VPN Server Wizard Add Group Policy Split Tunneling tab

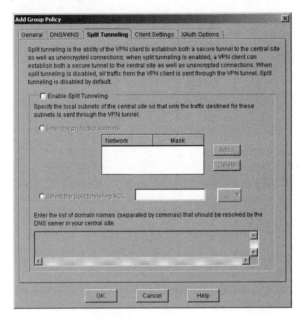

Moving right along to the Client Settings tab, pictured in Figure 12.22, you can make policy settings specifically for a client. You can configure the backup servers to be used in the event the primary Easy VPN server is unavailable. Next, if you enforce local firewalls on the client, select the Firewall Are-U-There option. The two local firewall options that are supported are Zone Alarm and Black Ice.

FIGURE 12.22 Cisco Router and Security Device Manager Easy VPN Server Wizard Add Group Policy Client Settings tab

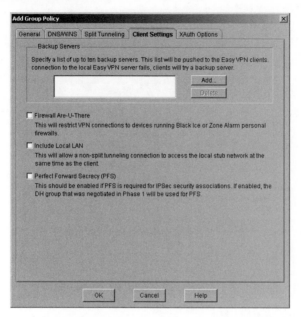

Remember that you just had the option to configure split tunneling. Well, suppose you wanted to configure just the local network that a remote user was on. There is a check box here on this screen, Include Local LAN, which allows you to include the local LAN, without configuring split tunneling explicitly. And the last option on this screen is Perfect Forward Secrecy (PFS). Only configure this if you have specified this at the server level.

Perfect Forward Secrecy (PFS) is another layer of security that ensures that a given IPsec SA key was not derived from any other secret. If a key is broken, PFS ensures that an attacker cannot use it to derive any other key. Each key would have to be broken individually.

The last tab on the Add Group Policy screen is XAuth Options, shown in Figure 12.23. The options here allow you to lock users into certain groups and allow VPN clients to save the XAuth passwords.

FIGURE 12.23 Cisco Router and Security Device Manager Easy VPN Server Wizard Add Group Policy XAuth Options tab

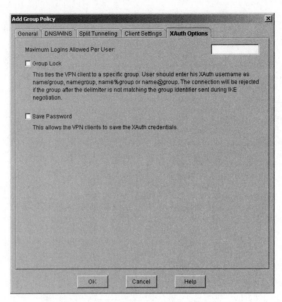

After you click OK in the Add Group Policy screen, take a look at Figure 12.24. Notice that you have added your group policy. It shows up in the policy window. Again, in this case, you have not specified any particular parameters for your policy.

FIGURE 12.24 Cisco Router and Security Device Manager Easy VPN Server Wizard Group Authorization And User Group Policies screen

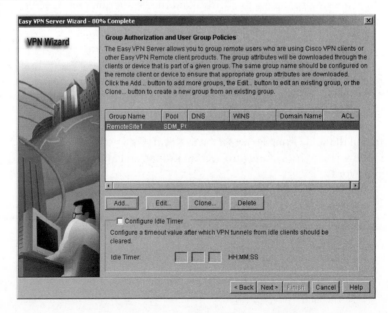

Click Next. And last, as before, a summary list of the configuration, as shown in Figure 12.25, is displayed. After completing the server portion, of course, you would have to do the remote devices as well, by going back to the beginning and choosing the tree selection Easy VPN Remote instead of Easy VPN Server.

FIGURE 12.25   Cisco Router and Security Device Manager Easy VPN Server Wizard Configuration Summary screen

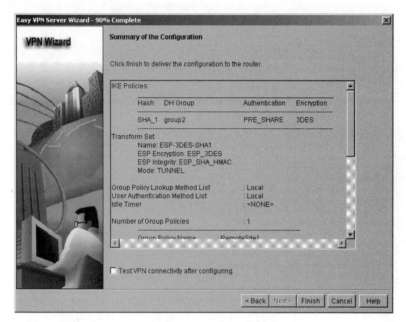

And once again, the wizard has delivered the commands to the router via SDM, as shown in Figure 12.26.

FIGURE 12.26   Cisco Router and Security Device Manager commands delivery status message

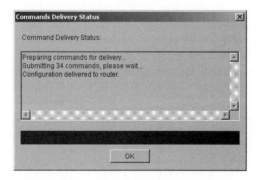

If you click the OK button from the delivery screen, you are taken back to the Easy VPN Server Edit tab, shown in Figure 12.27. You can now see the Easy VPN server that you have just configured. At this point, you have the option to add another one, edit the existing one, or delete it.

FIGURE 12.27   Cisco Router and Security Device Manager Edit Easy VPN Server tab

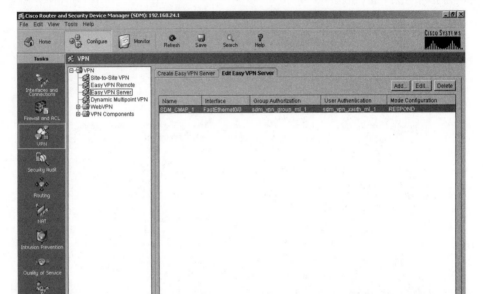

Redundant Connections and Equipment

VPNs are starting to become mission critical in today's business world. For that reason, it is important to cover a few of the techniques and technology used to keep those connections available at all times.

The concept of having redundant Internet service provider (ISP) connections is a design consideration that is important for a number of reasons. Generally, when you have more than one ISP connection to your network, you would use BGP for more information. Next, if you want to have VPN redundancy, this generally means having more than one network device available for this connectivity. You saw in the Easy VPN server configuration that you could configure multiple servers to give to the client. Depending on how large your network is and how diverse you want to be, you may want to have equipment in multiple geographical locations as well as redundant equipment at your primary location.

Summary

In this chapter, you learned about IPsec and used it to configure a site-to-site VPN using Cisco Security Device Manager. Then, you examined the VPN configuration from the command line and learned some troubleshooting techniques. And last, you used SDM to configure an Easy VPN server. Although there are many things to learn about VPNs, I covered the basic techniques and knowledge you need to get started with configuring your networks with VPN.

Exam Essentials

Remember the key IPsec protocols.   In particular, remember what AH and ESP are and what they are used for. Then remember that there are two types of protocols used when configuring a VPN, an encryption algorithm such as 3DES or AES and an integrity protocol such as SHA or MD5. These are deployed as a transform set in the router configuration.

Know the components of a VPN configuration from a command-line configuration.   The command-line configuration is important to know, even if you use SDM to configure your VPN. You have to have an ISAKMP policy that stipulates what protocols to use, including a preshared key. Then you must have an access list that calls out your interesting traffic to flow through the tunnel. Then you must have a crypto map that states your remote peer address, applies the correct transform set, and states what access list to use. Finally, you must apply the crypto map to the correct interface.

Understand the Cisco SDM for deploying a site-to-site VPN.   By this time you should be very familiar with the Cisco SDM. Know that you use the Configure menu to get started and then use the site-to-site VPN wizards to build your VPN. Know what options you will have to configure for proper operation.

Be able to perform some basic troubleshooting using the command-line interface (CLI).   Be able to use debug commands to help you troubleshoot VPN connectivity. Be familiar with the command-line configuration to identify any potential missing or incorrect configuration statements. Be familiar with the debug output so that you can quickly identify issues.

Be familiar with the Cisco Easy VPN configuration using the Cisco SDM.   You should be able to determine what menus are used to configure an Easy VPN using the SDM. The Configure menu is used to get started and then a wizard is available to help you configure the Easy VPN.

Written Lab

Write the answers to the following questions:

1. Using the CLI, which command would you issue if you wanted to verify a crypto map?
2. Using the SDM, what would you initiate to configure a site-to-site VPN?
3. What do you use to define interesting traffic to traverse your VPN tunnel?
4. If you needed to allow Encapsulating Security Payload (ESP) through your firewall, which protocol/port would you configure in your access list?
5. What is the command to create a transform-set in CLI with a name of HomeSET and using ESP-3DES for encryption and ESP-SHA-HMAC for integrity?
6. Which ESP mode is in use if the ESP header appears *after* the IP header?
7. In the Site-To-Site VPN Wizard, what are the two types of setups that can be performed?
8. When you see an MM_NO_STATE in your debug output, what does that typically mean?
9. What is negotiated during IKE Phase 2?
10. What are the default IKE proposals used in the Cisco Easy VPN configuration?

   (The answers to the written lab can be found following the answers to the review questions.)

Hands-on Lab

In this lab we will configure a site-to-site VPN using the command line interface.

Hands-on Lab 12.1: Configuring a Site-to-Site VPN

1. Log into your router and go into privileged mode by typing **en** or **enable**.
2. Enter global configuration mode by typing **config t** or **configure terminal**.
3. First configure a crypto policy for ISAKMP. Here you will designate the number of the policy, in this case 1. Then configure 3DES as your encryption type. You'll then configure preshared keys as the method of authentication used. And finally, configure Diffie-Hellman Group 2, which denotes 1024 bits will be used.

```
Router# config t
Enter configuration commands, one per line.  End with
  CNTL/Z.
Router(config)# crypto isakmp policy 1
Router(config-isakmp)# encr 3des
```

```
Router(config-isakmp)# authentication pre-share
Router(config-isakmp)# group 2
```

4. Now configure a transform set named VPN1. This shows that you will be using ESP-3DES for encryption and SHA-HMAC for integrity:

```
Router(config)# crypto ipsec transform-set VPN1 esp-3des esp-sha-hmac
```

5. Next configure a preshared key of t0ps3cr3t and the peer address of the remote end by typing the following while still in global configuration mode:

```
Router(config)# crypto isakmp key t0ps3cr3t address 10.100.1.1
```

6. Next you will need to define an access list that allows the interesting traffic that you want to flow over your VPN tunnel. You are going to allow a complete subnet on your end, with the IP address of 192.168.100.0, to talk to a complete subnet on the remote side, which will be 10.100.100.0. Once again, still in global configuration mode, type the following:

```
Router(config)# access-list 100 permit ip 192.168.100.0 0.0.0.255 10.100.100.0 0.0.0.255
```

7. Now you will configure a crypto map that defines some of the parameters you will use. Type the crypto map command with the name CM and the number 1, which is the number of the crypto map, and then the type, which is IPSEC-ISAKMP. Next you will set the peer address of 10.100.1.1. The next statement says that you are going to use the transform set named VPN1 that was defined earlier in the configuration. And finally, you are going to match traffic based on that access list 100 that was just defined. This time you will type the first command while in global configuration mode to define the name of the crypto map, and then you will notice that your mode changed to crypto-map mode to set the rest of the commands. Type the following:

```
Router(config)# crypto map CM 1 ipsec-isakmp
Router(config-crypto-map)# set peer 10.100.1.1
Router(config-crypto-map)# set transform-set VPN1
Router(config-crypto-map)# match address 100
Router(config-crypto-map)# exit
Router(config)#
```

8. Finally, apply the crypto map to an interface. You will need to enter interface configuration mode to apply the crypto map that was just configured. Type the following:

```
Router(config)# interface Serial0/0/1
Router(config-if)# crypto map CM
```

9. At this point, you are ready to press Cntl+Z and write your running configuration to startup configuration. You have now configured a site-to-site VPN using the command-line interface.

Review Questions

1. When an IPsec VPN tunnel is configured, how does the router determine what traffic is to traverse the VPN tunnel?

   A. Policy map

   B. Access list

   C. Transform set

   D. Tunnel list

2. Which IPsec protocol does both encryption and authentication?

   A. AH

   B. ESP

   C. PPTP

   D. GRE

3. What is the default encryption type when using SDM to configure an IPsec VPN tunnel?

   A. DES

   B. AES

   C. 3DES

   D. RSA

4. In Cisco Easy VPN, what is the advantage of network extension plus mode over network extension mode?

   A. A loopback address is configured.

   B. An access list is required.

   C. NATs are in use.

   D. Routable addresses are used.

5. If you were working in the IOS command-line interface and needed to check on the status of a VPN tunnel, what command would you enter?

   A. `show interface`

   B. `show access-list`

   C. `show crypto isakamp`

   D. `show crypto ipsec sa`

6. If you were working in IOS command-line interface, in a single command, what could you do to determine the interesting traffic for a particular VPN tunnel?

   A. `show interesting traffic`

   B. `show access-list`

   C. `show crypto map`

   D. `show ip interface`

7. What is the "peer address" when discussing a VPN tunnel?

A. The remote device VPN endpoint

B. The interesting traffic

C. The local outside interface

D. The remote end loopback address

8. What is split tunneling?

A. A dual tunnel to two locations

B. The ability to access both local resources and those over the VPN

C. The ability to access only remote locations

D. None of the above

9. True or False? You can have only one transform set to define the type of authentication and encryption.

A. True

B. False

10. Name a debug command that's commonly used when troubleshooting VPN connectivity. (Choose all that apply.)

A. debug ip

B. debug crypto isakmp

C. debug crypto ipsec

D. debug vpn

11. What command is used to designate that you will use Diffie-Hellman Group 2 for your key exchange?

A. DH group2

B. group 2

C. dh-group2

D. ipsec group-2

12. What is the name of the set of both the encryption algorithm and the integrity protocol used in the crypto map?

A. Transform

B. Crypto set

C. Transform set

D. Crypto-set

13. Which of the following modes encrypts the entire packet and adds a new header for IPsec?

    A. Transport mode

    B. Encrypt mode

    C. Header mode

    D. Tunnel mode

14. When configuring a crypto map for a VPN tunnel, what is the command to configure the remote end IP that you need to communicate with?

    A. `peer address ip address`

    B. `set peer address ip address`

    C. `peer ip ip address`

    D. `set peer ip address`

15. What purpose does the preshared key serve?

    A. Authentication

    B. Integrity

    C. Confidentiality

    D. Authorization

16. Put the following steps in the order in which they occur.

    A. Traffic matches interesting traffic ACL.

    B. Phase 2 or IPsec tunnel is set up.

    C. Traffic flows over the VPN tunnel.

    D. Phase 1 ISAKMP SA is formed.

17. When configuring a site-to-site VPN, what is the type that is designated when using a crypto map?

    A. IPSEC

    B. ISAKMP

    C. IPSEC-ISAKMP

    D. ISAKMP-IPSEC

18. You've just configured a VPN tunnel with a remote site. When looking at the output from the `show crypto isakmp sa`, you notice the message MM_NO_STATE. What might be the problem? (Choose all that apply.)

    A. Access lists don't match

    B. Preshared keys don't match

    C. ISAKMP policies don't match

    D. Encryption protocols don't match

19. What is another name for a Phase 2 IKE tunnel? (Choose two.)

    A. Phase 2 SA

    B. IKE 2

    C. IPsec

    D. IPsec tunnel

20. What protocol would you use if you needed both encryption and authentication and what port number would you open? (Choose two.)

    A. ESP

    B. AH

    C. 51

    D. 50

Answers to Review Questions

1. **B.** An access list is used to define interesting traffic, which is the traffic that is allowed to traverse the VPN tunnel.

2. **B.** ESP (Encapsulating Security Payload) does both encryption and authentication. Remember that AH does only the authenticating and no encryption.

3. **C.** The default encryption type is 3DES—this is what SDM uses when you choose the default configuration.

4. **A.** The network extension plus mode allows you to configure a loopback address, which is helpful in troubleshooting connections.

5. **D.** The command you would enter is `show crypto ipsec sa`. This displays any IPsec security associations. You can also use this to determine some error conditions to do further troubleshooting.

6. **C.** The `show crypto map` command displays all components of the crypto map, including the access list that controls interesting traffic. Note: Option B could be used if you knew which access list was related to the crypto map.

7. **A.** The peer address is the remote endpoint of the VPN device to which you are connecting.

8. **B.** Split tunneling is the ability for a remote VPN client to be able to access resources across the VPN tunnel and also those on the local network.

9. **B.** False. When defining VPN tunnels to different business partners and sites, it's often advantageous to have different transform sets to describe what parameters you are using with each partner.

10. **B, C.** The two used in the chapter that were described are `debug crypto isakmp` and `debug crypto isakmp`.

11. **B.** The Diffie-Hellman group 2 key exchange is part of the ISAKMP configuration and is a submenu under the ISAKMP policy command.

12. **C.** The transform set denotes the encryption protocol to use and then the integrity protocol.

13. **D.** IPsec tunnel mode encrypts the entire packet but adds another header on top of the packet.

14. **D.** You configure several variables under the crypto map configuration, including the peer IP address.

15. **A.** The preshared key is used for authentication between the two parties of the VPN tunnel. If they do not match on both sides, the tunnel will not be formed.

16. A, D, B, C. Traffic must match the interesting traffic ACL, then the Phase 1 ISAKMP SA is negotiated and formed, the Phase 2 or IPsec tunnel is then formed, and finally, traffic flows over the tunnel.

17. C. The correct answer is IPSEC-ISAKMP.

18. A, B. MM_NO_STATE typically means that either the preshared keys don't match at both ends or the access list that defines interesting traffic doesn't match. Or it could mean both of those don't match.

19. A, D. A Phase 2 IKE tunnel is also known as a Phase 2 SA (security association) or an IPsec Tunnel.

20. A, D. You would use ESP because it supports both encryption and authentication. ESP uses IP Protocol 50.

Answers to Written Lab

1. `show crypto map`

2. The Site-To-Site VPN Wizard

3. An access list

4. IP protocol 50

5. `crypto ipsec transform-set HomeSET esp-3des esp-sha-hmac`

6. Transport mode

7. The quick setup and the step-by-step option

8. Either the preshared keys don't match or the interesting traffic doesn't match on both sides.

9. An IPsec SA

10. 3DES and SHA1

ppendix

A

Securing Voice Solutions

A scant 10 years ago or so, the overriding technology used in voice solutions at most organizations was Private Branch Exchange (PBX), which required a wiring infrastructure separate from that of the data network. Over the last 10 years, a major shift in direction has occurred, which allows the commercial sector as well as the residential consumer to take advantage of transmitting voice signals and calls over IP packets, commonly called Voice over IP, or VoIP. This shift is in part due to newer technology, but it's also driven by use of the Internet and the broadband movement. Most households now have a home network and an Internet connection, which allows them to use VoIP. Most companies have an internal network, which can carry IP packets, also advancing the use of VoIP.

The mixing of voice and data over the same network is called *convergence*. Not only can we send voice and data over the same network, we can also send video. Also of interest is a feature that is called *Unified Presence*, which is essentially similar to the chat functionality used by content providers like Yahoo! and MSN. You can see when people are online and available and then call them, text them, chat with them, and in some cases do an ad-hoc video conference.

Organizations like all these features, especially the voice features, because they can potentially save money on wiring, on charges from the phone company, and by allowing remote offices to send intracompany calls over their own network for no charge. Sure, some of these features have been around for awhile, but doing it over an existing IP network is relatively new.

I bring this up because with every new technology, there are new challenges to securing them, and VoIP is no exception. We will look at the technology itself and then discuss some of the ways that are used to exploit vulnerabilities and then some of the ways that can be used to secure and defend a voice network.

Voice over IP Essentials

To learn about how to secure something, it is usually wise to invest some time learning about the technology itself. Here we look at what Voice over IP is and how it works. There will be a discussion of the common voice protocols and their operation. Also covered will be the components that make up a Cisco Voice over IP solution and some of the features that can be used.

What Is VoIP?

Voice over IP, or *VoIP*, is one of those terms that a lot of people have heard and know, but they might not really understand what it is and how it works. Defined simply, it is a voice conversation that has been broken down and put into a series of IP packets. Because IP packets are usually carried over an existing data network, there are concerns that need to be addressed to make the VoIP solution a solid one.

Data networks usually carry lots of different types of traffic, and voice is one of them. It is, however, different than other types of traffic. Most data can tolerate some level of delay or interruption, and there are mechanisms within the IP protocol itself to address some of these issues. Voice conversations, however, don't sound very good if a packet needs to be retransmitted for one reason or another. We've all been on cell phone calls where every other word is dropped. VoIP has the same problems if precautions are not taken. On the plus side, if done right, VoIP can sound just like a traditional wired phone. Cisco offers varying levels of quality of service (QoS) to ensure that there is guaranteed bandwidth for your voice conversations.

Also of concern is security, which is part and parcel to any data network and why we are discussing VoIP in this appendix. Voice is not immune to security vulnerabilities and requires the same level of protection that would be offered to any other data on the network. Cisco offers measures to protect voice data, and we will discuss some of them later.

For the purpose of this book, the terms *Call Manager*, *Unified Call Manager*, and *Unified Communications Manager* are one and the same. The Cisco Call Manager line of products was an acquisition from Selsius and was first named Cisco Call Manager (CCM) with version 3.0. Then the product was renamed Cisco Unified Call Manager with version 4.2, and in 2007 it became Cisco Unified Communications Manager (CUCM), and that's where it is today. You will find all three terms in use among Cisco users and engineers.

Let's look at a typical VoIP setup from a Cisco perspective. In Figure A.1, we have a Unified Communications Manager, or Call Manager, that connects to the network infrastructure. In this case it is a Cisco switch with Power over Ethernet (PoE) capabilities. This is necessary if you want to avoid having an external power supply for your IP phone. An IP phone is also connected to the network infrastructure. There is a gateway router that connects to the public switched telephone network (PSTN). And finally, we add in a Unity voicemail server.

FIGURE A.1   Typical VoIP configuration

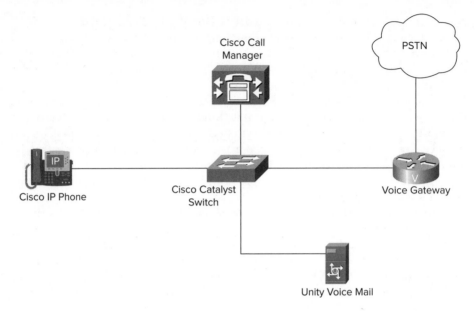

Components of VoIP

What makes up a Voice over IP system? We've examined a typical setup, but there are more components that can be used. Table A.1 describes the most common components. The component names are industry-standard terms, but there are Cisco-specific counterparts that match up to each one.

TABLE A.1   Components of VoIP

Component	Description
IP phone	IP phones are connected to the local LAN and provide voice services to the desktop.
Call agent	A call agent is responsible for the call setup and control, call admission control, bandwidth utilization, and management. A call agent can be any of the Cisco Unified Messaging platforms, formerly called Call Manager.
Gateway	A gateway provides connectivity between the IP-based network and the PSTN. A typical gateway is a router with connections to both the IP network and the PSTN (usually through a primary rate interface, or PRI, connection).

Component	Description
Application server	An application server provides ancillary services to the VoIP network, such as voicemail and intelligent routing services.
Gatekeeper	A gatekeeper provides address translation and controls access for H.323 devices.
Multipoint control unit	This is a device to connect users in various locations to the same resources, such as in a videoconference.
Videoconference station	A videoconference station is a device that connects users via video and audio stream. It uses a video camera and microphone to capture each end of the conference.

These components are shown in Figure A.2.

FIGURE A.2   Components of a VoIP system

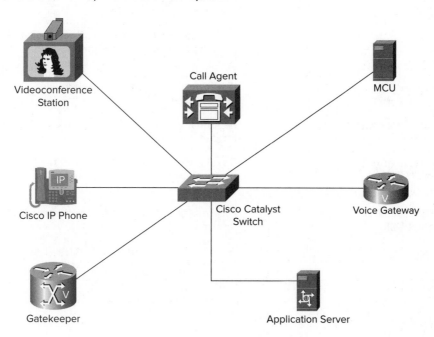

Other components that are typically part of an enterprise Voice over IP solution include Cisco switches that have Power over Ethernet (PoE) capability, which is used to power the phones directly through the Ethernet cable. This is not a hard requirement because the phones can be connected to a power supply; it's a matter of convenience as well as safety. In the event of a power outage, enterprise switches are usually connected to a UPS battery backup, whereas the desktop power supply is typically not.

Common Protocols Used in Voice over IP

There are a number of protocols in use with a Voice over IP solution. Many of them are described in Table A.2. Some are responsible for signaling and others for the actual voice conversation.

TABLE A.2   Protocols Used in Voice over IP

Protocol	Description
Session Initiation Protocol (SIP)	Can use TCP or UDP to provide audio, video, streaming media, instant messaging, and presence capabilities
Media Gateway Control Protocol (MGCP)	Used to control gateway operations both on the network and with the PSTN
H.323	An ITU standard for a suite of protocols that govern voice and video communications
Skinny Call Control Protocol (SCCP)	Also called just Skinny, a Cisco-proprietary protocol for connectivity between a Cisco IP phone and Call Manager
Real-Time Transport Protocol (RTP)	Responsible for carrying the audio and video streams
Secure Real-Time Transport Protocol (SRTP)	Developed as a method to secure the RTP protocol, providing encryption, authentication, integrity, and anti-replay capabilities
Real-Time Transport Control Protocol (RTCP)	Provides out-of-band statistics and control information for RTP flows
H.248 (aka Megaco)	An IETF/ITU collaboration that is a form of the Media Gateway Control Protocol

Threats to Voice over IP

Emerging technologies are especially vulnerable to threats before they are completely understood or have matured to a point where security isn't the hottest issue. (Let me know when we get to that point with anything.) In this section, I will discuss some of the threats facing those who have deployed or are about to deploy VoIP. Table A.3 lists the most common VoIP threats.

TABLE A.3 Common VoIP Threats

Threat	Description
Toll fraud	An unauthorized person makes toll calls that end up costing the organization.
Phishing and vishing	Phishing and vishing are both methods of eliciting information from a person. Phishing is email based and vishing is phone or voice based.
Denial of service	A denial of service attack overutilizes resources that are required to make the VoIP environment operate correctly.
Unauthorized access	Unauthorized persons might gain access to any VoIP resource, such as a phone or server, without the correct authorization.
Eavesdropping	Voice packets can be captured, which can allow re-assembly and playback of an audio conversation.
Spam over IP telephony (SPIT)	SPIT is mostly an annoyance. An example is ringing a phone constantly or at certain intervals.

Toll Fraud

Toll fraud happens when a user or attacker is able to place long-distance calls (frequently international calls from the United States) without the authorization to do so. In its simplest form, someone inside a company might be violating policy by placing long-distance calls. Toll fraud is a big deal in corporate America today, especially in large corporations that might not have tight control on their long-distance calling structure. Indeed, there are companies whose sole existence is based on saving money for other companies. Their payoff? A cut of the savings. Talk about an incentive program. These companies typically start their investigation of savings by looking at toll fraud.

Other methods of toll fraud typically involve hackers breaking into a phone system. If you can gain access to the system, you may be able to program it to allow toll calls on certain numbers, or you might be able to call a number and then call out from the same number. You might recall the Kevin Mitnick case. He manipulated phone company switches so that his phone number was the only one that could respond to a contest held by a radio station. This was before the days of VoIP, but the concept is the same. Only the technology has changed.

Phishing and Vishing

Most everyone has heard of phishing by now. In a phishing attack, an email is sent to many users, for example, appearing to be from someone of trust, such as a bank or e-commerce site. The email contains a link that appears to go to the trusted site but actually goes to a malicious site. The idea is to get the user to click the link and enter personal or confidential information, which the owner of the site will use maliciously or sell to a broker of such information. In other cases, clicking the link might initiate a download of a virus, Trojan horse, or other malware. A special kind of phishing, spear phishing, is targeted to certain individuals or groups.

Now that *phishing* has entered the mainstream, there's a new term. *Vishing* is an attempt to collect personal and/or confidential information over the phone. This isn't a new form of fraud, and it's a problem because people seem to have a greater confidence in communicating over the phone versus the Internet. The game changer is the ability to use VoIP technology to spoof caller IDs and numbers, which is relatively new.

Denial of Service

Denial of service attacks are popular today and can also apply to the VoIP environment. A denial of service attack is basically an attack in which someone sends packets that usually cause issues by taking up an excessive amount of resources, therefore causing an interruption or delay of services. In a VoIP environment, this could mean chewing up the bandwidth of a communications link carrying VoIP traffic, or it might mean an attack against a single IP phone or perhaps even a Cisco Unified Communications Manager server by overloading the resources there or attempting to exploit vulnerabilities on the operating system or application.

Unauthorized Access to VoIP Components

Attackers may try to gain access to various VoIP components such as an IP phone or the Cisco Unified Communications Manager by attempting to guess passwords and usernames or break into the login screens. Or there may be resources that are not secured adequately, allowing access that shouldn't be allowed.

Eavesdropping

Eavesdropping on a traditional phone conversation used to involve planting bugs or perhaps tapping the line by physically connecting to the actual wire pairs that the phone line used. In today's VoIP environment, it is much easier to eavesdrop. All you need is to be able to capture packets of an RTP or other voice stream and you will be able to re-create the stream and save it in a format that you can listen to. This can be done very easily using several inexpensive or free tools that are out there.

SPIT

It sounds unpleasant, but it's just an acronym for Spam over IP Telephony. Most everyone knows what spam is, so what is Spam over IPT? Basically it's the same as email spam, only it applies to your phone. You could receive messages on your phone's display, or it might ring many times in a short period. Although it's an extreme example, you might receive spoofed caller ID information that would mislead you to believe that you were connected to a trusted phone number.

Methods of Securing the Voice over IP Environment

You can secure your Voice over IP environment with a combination of good security practices, taking advantage of security features built into Cisco devices, and hardening endpoints such as application servers.

Separating Your Voice Traffic

In a Voice over IP network, it is always advisable to separate your voice traffic from your data traffic for security purposes. In a Cisco switched environment, this is a trivial task. Voice traffic on a Cisco Catalyst switch is usually carried on either a voice virtual local area network (VLAN) or an auxiliary VLAN. This allows voice traffic from the IP phone and data to use different VLANs. Separating the voice VLAN from the data VLAN in and of itself is a strong deterrent to layer 2 type attacks. In particular, this prevents a *man-in-the-middle* attack, where attackers can spoof their media access control (MAC) address, masquerading as a forwarding address to the victim. Because attackers cannot usually attach the MAC-spoofing data device to the voice VLAN, this attack is thwarted.

However, there are other attacks that can overcome the separation of voice and data traffic. One such attack is VLAN hopping, which can be achieved in three different ways:

MAC address overflow attack   MAC address overflow attack is the most primitive form of VLAN hopping. The attacker uses a tool that generates numerous MAC addresses, filling the MAC table of the switch to overflowing and causing the switch to turn into a hub. Newer switches have built-in protection against these attacks, or you can manually mitigate them by allowing only a small number of MAC addresses to attach via any one port.

One tool used for VLAN hopping is called VoIP Hopper. VoIP Hopper can emulate IP phones from various manufacturers, including a Cisco IP phone. In the Cisco environment, the tool captures a CDP packet and then determines the voice VLAN. More information on this tool is at http://voiphopper.sourceforge.net/.

Double-tagging attack   In a double-tagging attack, the attacker sends crafted packets with two VLAN tags, one encapsulated within the other. The concept is that the first VLAN tag is seen by the switch when it reaches the port and is stripped off. Then the packet is forwarded. When it reaches the intended VLAN, it is seen as being intended for that VLAN and is allowed onto that VLAN, accomplishing the end goal. Mitigation for this type of attack is described in Chapter 7.

Switch spoofing   The third method is called switch spoofing and requires a host to be capable of communicating via the trunking protocol in use. The host can then attach to the victim switch and be able to see all the VLANs. The mitigation technique to avoid this is to make sure that any unused switch ports are turned off. That way, if anyone were to gain access to a switch port, they could not carry out this attack. Mitigation techniques for switch spoofing are discussed in Chapter 7.

Let's examine the phone and PC connection. Most Cisco IP phones have a separate data port on the back. Cisco IP phones allow a single connection to a switch port, pulling their power from that connection, if that switch has PoE capabilities. The Cisco IP phone acts as a specialized switch, sensing that there is an auxiliary or voice VLAN configured and using this VLAN to communicate. But it also has the intelligence to recognize a PC plugged into the port and carries this traffic over the data VLAN, as shown in Figure A.3.

FIGURE A.3   Typical IP phone/PC connection

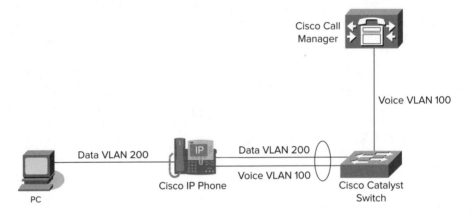

Utilizing Security Devices

Part of your overall security architecture should include protection for your voice network. It's no different from any other element of the network that you would protect. Probably one of the first things you would think about would be using firewalls to segregate your voice infrastructure. Sounds easy, right? But one thing about using VoIP is that it utilizes a wide range of ports. How do you know which ports are being used? Because ports are dynamically assigned during call setup, it can be difficult to set static rules for them.

Not to fear, however, because the Cisco ASA (and PIX) firewalls can dynamically inspect call setup traffic and allocate User Datagram Protocol (UDP) ports as needed for the conversation. In fact, the ASA performs a number of duties to secure voice communications. The following list shows some of the features that are used:

- Enforce voice standards on MGCP, SIP, H.323, and SCCP protocols—this keeps any nonstandard traffic from reaching the voice equipment.

- Allow only registered phones to be enabled for calling. This keeps rogue phones from using the network.

- Enforce SIP message rate limits. This prevents SIP messages from being used to perform a denial of service attack.

- Policies such as white lists, black lists, and using caller ID can mitigate threats.

- Protection to dynamically open ports is necessary and part of a voice call.

- Enable inspection of encrypted calls. SRTP calls can be inspected.

Encrypt Traffic with VPNs

Virtual private network (VPN) technology is used for a great many purposes, providing both encryption and authentication services. While Cisco IP phone communication can be encrypted and authenticated, other devices that make up the Voice over IP communications suite do not have this capability. A VPN can be utilized to perform this function. Illustrated in Figure A.4 is a VPN connection between the Unified Communications Manager and a voice gateway.

FIGURE A.4   VPN connection for voice servers

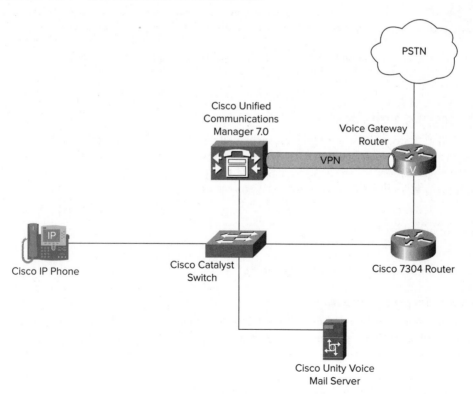

In this case, the communications that would be IP based and that travel between the gateway (connected to the PSTN) and the Unified Communications Manager are being protected. That would be any outbound or inbound calls, either local or long distance, utilizing the PSTN. This affords you the same protection that you would have with any wired telephone.

Remember that one of the reasons you might use VoIP is for flexibility and telecommuting. What if you extended your voice network to telecommuters or those whose office is at home? You would generally use a VPN to connect those users to the office network, thereby protecting the connection from eavesdropping.

You might protect your communications with a VPN for the following reasons:

- Using VPN for encryption.

- Using VPN for authentication.

- Protecting organization and physical boundaries. For example, you can use a VPN to separate connectivity from one organization to another.

- Allowing for secure remote users.

 A vendor-agnostic document that covers in-depth security considerations for deploying VoIP systems is the National Institute of Standards and Technology's "Security Considerations for Voice Over IP Systems," which can be obtained at `http://csrc.nist.gov/publications/nistpubs/800-58/SP800-58-final.pdf`.

Protecting VoIP Devices

And what of protecting the endpoints, such as IP phones, Unified Communications Manager devices, Unity voicemail servers, and gateways? They are as important to protect as the conversations themselves. Besides using the methods that I've already discussed, let's look at the ways that these devices can be protected:

- Secured server architecture

- IP phone hardening

- Server hardening

- IPS/IDS systems (discussed in Chapter 8)

Secure Server Architecture

Let's look at a secure server architecture for voice. Placing the servers in a secure location so that only traffic that is destined to communicate with them (such as IP phones) can access them is a first step.

There are a couple of schools of thought on what that architecture should look like:

Servers in the same VLAN as the IP phones   One secure architecture, illustrated in Figure A.5, is to place the servers into the same VLAN as the IP phones themselves. The thought is to not allow any traffic into this VLAN from the outside because the devices that need to converse are all located within the same VLAN. This method doesn't scale well and doesn't work for larger organizations, but it's a good fit for smaller businesses.

FIGURE A.5   Servers in the same VLAN as IP phones

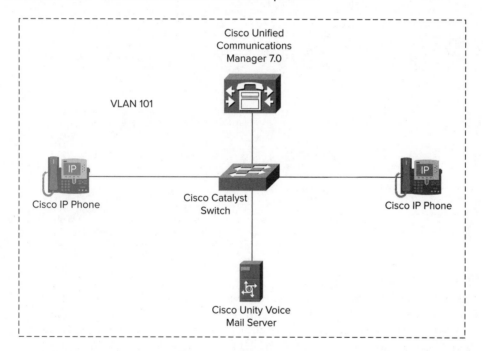

Servers in separate VLAN with access to IP phone VLANs   Another method would be to segregate the servers into their own VLAN with access allowed to and from IP phone VLANs. This might be a good solution for larger organizations where IP phone VLANs are numerous and scattered physically and logically throughout. This is shown in Figure A.6.

FIGURE A.6 Servers in a separate VLAN

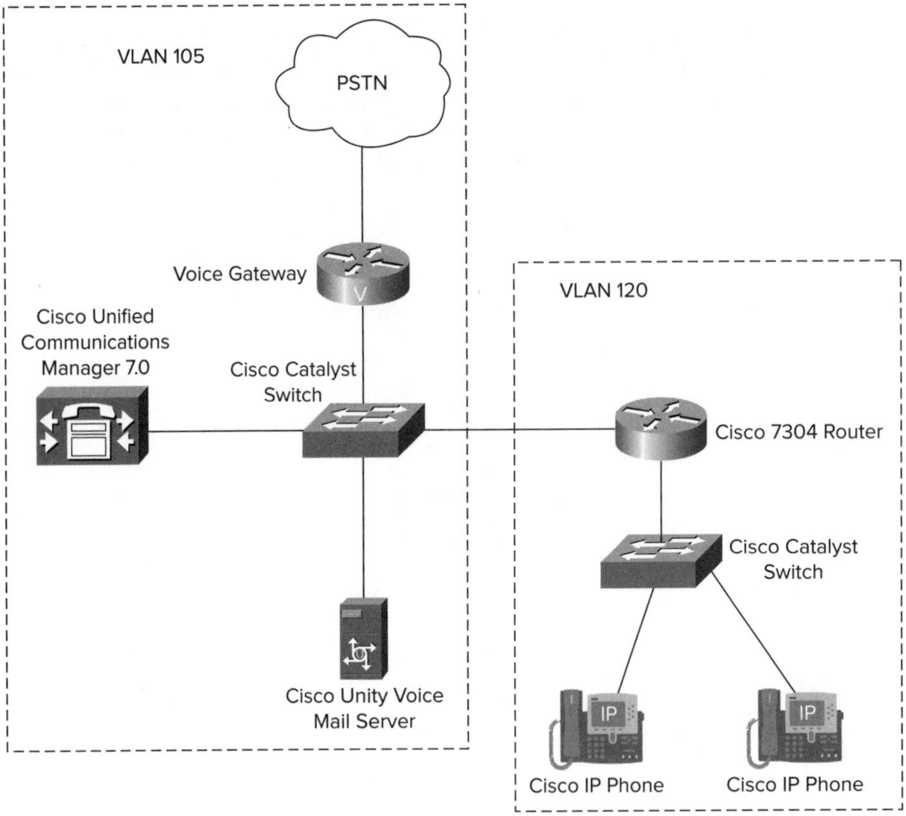

IP Phone Hardening

Beyond looking at the architecture of where the servers are located, we can look at the IP phones themselves. Did you know that IP phones have a web browser built into them? What information could an attacker glean from the information provided on a browser? This is a feature that can be disabled, but it is turned on by default. It gives information such as IP address, DHCP server, DNS server, IP address of the Call Manager device that it's attached to, and the default gateway. All of this is assuming you have access to the voice VLAN in the first place, but it's good to be aware of the default settings so that you can take the appropriate action.

Another way in which Cisco has taken measures to secure the IP phone is to use signed binary images. What does this mean? Basically, this allows the phone to reject any image that has been tampered with or to prevent a "homebrew" image from being loaded onto the phone. This is a configuration change within the Cisco Unified Communications Server and has been available since Call Manager 3.0. Another option that became available in Call Manager 4.*x* is that of configuration file authentication. This is where the IP phone configuration has to be validated prior to loading.

There are some configuration options within the IP phone itself that allow an administrator to prevent an attack against an IP phone. Inside the Call Manager Administration screen, you can enable or disable the following features:

Web Access—On by default. Gives information such as IP address, DHCP server, DNS server, IP address of the Call Manager device that it's attached to, and the default gateway. Disabling Web access prevents unauthorized users from obtaining information about the phone and network that they could use to attack.

PC Port—On by default. You may want to disable the PC port on a public phone that you want to provide only voice access.

Settings Access—Disable this if you do not want users to be able to change their individual settings on the phone.

Gratuitous Address Resolution Protocol (ARP)—Disabling this will prevent a man-in-the-middle attack as described earlier in this appendix.

PC Voice VLAN Access—If this option is set to disable, the Cisco IP phone will insert VLAN tags (802.1q header) on ingress packets from the PC port. The behavior can be different for different IP phones.

Server Hardening

As far as the Unified Communications server goes, it has already been prehardened by Cisco. Most unneeded services have been turned off by default. You may elect to turn off other services, if not needed, depending on the role and functionality of the server in question.

To summarize what has been discussed in this section, please refer to Table A.4.

TABLE A.4   Summary of Security Features/Techniques

Feature/Technique	Description
Separating your voice traffic	Using a separate voice or auxiliary VLAN is a best practice for voice security.
Utilizing security devices	Utilizing Cisco PIX or ASA firewalls can automatically protect and inspect voice traffic and dynamically permit traffic based on the stream.
Encrypting traffic with VPN	Where you don't have protections that are natively built in, it is a good practice to connect those devices/streams with an IPsec VPN.
Protecting VoIP devices	Hardening IP phones using the Cisco Unified Communications Manager Administration screen is a good practice as well as reviewing any application servers for services that might not be used.

This appendix included a brief discussion of Voice over IP technology, the components and protocols used in a Voice over IP solution, some of the attack vectors used against VoIP technology, and finally, ways to mitigate the threat to the VoIP infrastructure.

Appendix

B

Introduction to SAN Security

THE FOLLOWING CCNA SECURITY TOPICS ARE COVERED IN THIS APPENDIX:

✓ Introduction to storage area networks (SANs) and the benefits from using a SAN

✓ Components of a SAN

✓ SAN security techniques

Every day that goes by, it seems we increase our need for storage. One only needs to look at the social networking sites like YouTube and Facebook to see that we as a society have an ever increasing need to interact online. This equates to more and more storage. Our enterprises aren't any different. We need to fuel the drive for more data with more storage. Today's enterprise uses storage area networks (SANs) for their storage needs.

Introduction to Storage Area Networks

You can use storage area networks to extend the amount of storage beyond the capacity of the file server and share the services across a dedicated network. Some people have basic SANs at home, which could be as simple as a couple of servers with a second NIC card attached to an external storage array. The more sophisticated, enterprise version often has dedicated network resources that extend the size of your storage to many terabytes, even up to a petabyte of storage.

Figure B.1 shows how a typical SAN is connected.

FIGURE B.1 Typical SAN configuration

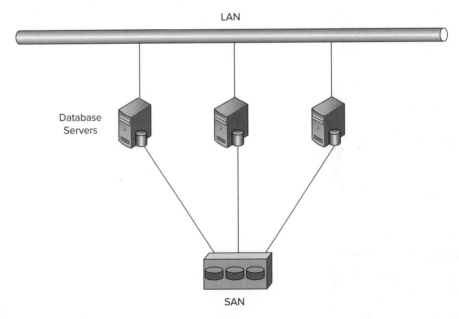

If you think of a traditional network with VLANs or subnets, a SAN can actually be storage that is accessed over a specific VLAN or subnet. It doesn't necessarily have to be a completely separate, distinct network for storage. However, many proprietary systems do implement their own network to use exclusively for the SAN.

An advantage of using a separate network is that you don't have to share the network with production traffic such as email, file sharing, and web traffic. A SAN could be used for such things as dedicated backups, file storage for email or other systems, and general-purpose storage.

The beauty of using a SAN is that you don't suffer the performance issues that you can experience when you share your storage-related traffic with other types of traffic.

Benefits of a SAN

Data storage is a critical element to an organization, and a highly available abundance of storage is a boon to IT managers looking for increased uptime among their servers and applications. SANs with lots of storage space allow servers and applications to continue operating without a hard limitation on disk storage space.

SANs are continuing to evolve as disk space continues to increase in size and decrease in cost. However, the business requirements that a SAN needs to meet have remained somewhat static. Those requirements are as follows:

- Reduce operational and capital expenses of information technology.

- Increase the performance of replication, backup, and recovery.

- Improve the IT Governance goals as they relate to regulatory bodies and industry best practices.

- Meet ever-changing business priorities, revenue growth, and application requirements.

SAN Transport Methods

SANs rely on the Small Computer System Interface (SCSI) protocol as the basis of most, if not all, types of SAN transport methods.

SAN transport methods are listed in Table B.1 and discussed in the following sections.

TABLE B.1   SAN Transport Methods

Type	Description
Fibre Channel	Today's most-used SAN transport method for host-to-SAN connectivity
Internet Small Computer System Interface (iSCSI)	A standard for transporting SCSI commands over TCP/IP
Fibre Channel over IP (FCIP)	Used for SAN-to-SAN connectivity, primarily over a WAN or other remote network
Fibre Channel Over Ethernet (FCOE)	The up and coming way to transport Fibre Channel over Ethernet for a layer 2 implementation

Fibre Channel

Fibre Channel is a first-generation gigabit SCSI-based technology used for storage area networks. It has evolved with the technology to support greater speeds over the years. Fibre Channel is a layered protocol, similar to TCP/IP or the OSI model. It has five layers, of which the first three are the same as the first three layers of the OSI model—Physical, Data-Link, and Network. The other two layers are the *Common Services layer*, which is similar to the Presentation layer of the OSI model and the *Protocol Mapping layer*, which is where the SCSI commands get encapsulated.

One thing to note is that even though the technology has the word *fibre* in the name, it can be carried over either fiber-optic cables or twisted-pair copper cables.

iSCSI

Internet Small Computer System Interface (iSCSI) is based on the SCSI interface, used in computer systems for years. iSCSI adds the functionality of being able to encapsulate SCSI commands into IP packets, thereby allowing almost endless capabilities in terms of where the devices can be and how they can communicate.

FCIP

Fiber Channel over IP (FCIP) allows much the same capabilities as iSCSI, encapsulating Fibre Channel commands into IP packets. However, FCIP is used for SAN-to-SAN connectivity only. FCIP was developed by the IETF and is defined in RFC 3821. FCIP forwards FC frames between FC fabric elements without being aware of the underlying IP infrastructure.

That means you could have SANs in many disparate locations and they could communicate over the IP network just as if they were located next to each other.

Unified fabric is a concept where, instead of servers having many cables coming out of them, the server switch connects every server with a single high-bandwidth, low-latency network cable (two cables for redundancy). Unified fabric is part of Cisco's Data Center strategy.

FCOE

Fibre Channel Over Ethernet (FCOE) was just recently approved for an ANSI standard in mid 2009. One of the driving reasons for the standard is that it will work with 10 Gbps Ethernet and allow a much higher transfer rate than before. FCOE brings the following benefits:

- Unified Fabric over Ethernet is available today from industry leaders.
- FCOE is the next evolution of SCSI/Fibre Channel.
- Unified Fabric will transform the economics of server deployment and network connectivity.
- Unified Fabric will contribute to extending the life of data centers.

FCOE operates over the Ethernet layer, which means that it has no routing capabilities. However, it is designed for use within a data center environment and can utilize both existing and new hardware.

The data center environment constitutes a layer 2 and layer 3 network with typically a large number of servers. Other connectivity usually involves Internet and/or private communication links.

All of these features are now being targeted for use within a single switching environment such as the new Cisco Nexus platform. If you can upgrade your platforms from 1 Gbps to 10 Gbps within largely the same infrastructure, you can preserve the hardware you have for years to come. Also, by integrating switch fabric and server fabric in the same platform, you can achieve economies of scale.

Elements of a SAN

The following sections discuss some of the technology that helps make up a SAN.

Logical Unit Numbers (LUNs) and LUN Masking

In the context of data storage, a logical unit number (LUN) is a numerical address for an individual disk drive and for the disk device itself. A LUN comes from the SCSI world and is used as a way to differentiate individual disk drives within a common SCSI target device, such as a drive array.

With LUN masking, you can enable a LUN for specific hosts while denying access to other hosts. LUN masking is implemented primarily at the host bus adapter (HBA) level. An HBA is an I/O adapter that sits between the bus of the host computer and the Fibre Channel network and manages the communications between the two channels.

LUN masking that is implemented on the HBA is only as secure as the HBA. With HBAs it is possible to force source addresses. If the HBA is compromised, then the LUN masking process could be compromised as well. This means that LUN masking cannot be considered a serious security feature by itself.

The primary benefit of using LUN masking is that it is a way to keep improper server behavior at bay by restricting server activity that might otherwise corrupt disks that are part of other systems. For example, Windows servers that are attached to a SAN will occasionally corrupt non-Windows volumes such as Linux volumes by attempting to write Windows volume labels to them. Masking the LUNs of the Linux volumes hides those volumes from the Windows servers and prevents this problem.

Fibre Channel Zoning

Fibre channel zoning is the partitioning of a Fibre Channel fabric into smaller pieces. A SAN can contain multiple storage devices, but not all devices should be able to communicate with the other devices in the SAN. Zoning is one way to accomplish this security task.

Zoning is sometimes confused with LUN masking because they seek the same objectives. However, zoning is implemented on fabric switches while LUN masking is performed on endpoint devices. Zoning is also potentially more secure. Zone members are able to view only other members of the zones they belong to. The zone segregates users by zone. (That means anyone in a single zone can see every other member in that zone, but not outside the zone.) However, devices can be members of more than one zone.

In the example in Figure B.2, there are three zones that have anywhere from three to four members per zone. All the members of Zone Z are also members of the other two zones. Zone X has three members: Disk 1, Disk 2, and Disk 3. Zone Y has four members: Disk 4, Host 1, Host 2, and Host 3. Zone Z has three members: Host 2, Disk 1, and Disk2.

FIGURE B.2   Fibre Channel zoning example

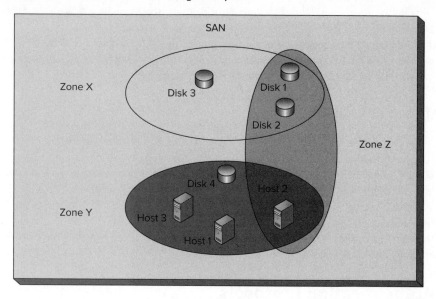

World Wide Names

A World Wide Name (WWN) is a 64-bit address that Fibre Channel networks use to uniquely identify each element in a Fibre Channel network. Figure B.3 shows a WWN that might belong to a Cisco MDS 9000 SAN switch.

FIGURE B.3   World Wide Name example

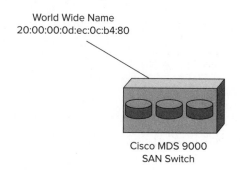

WWNs are used within zoning to configure security permissions. Zoning also make use of name servers within the switch fabric to permit or deny access to World Wide Names within the fabric.

World Wide Names do not represent a solid security practice, largely because the WWN can be spoofed. This means that if someone can compromise an HBA, they may be able to spoof a known HBA address and overcome the security measure.

VSANs

A virtual storage area network (VSAN) is an aggregation of ports from a group of connected Fibre Channel switches that form a virtual fabric. You can partition ports within a single switch into multiple VSANs. Additionally, multiple ports on many switches can be combined to form a single VSAN. In this manner, VSANs are very similar to VLANs. Also, as with VLANs, tagging is used and a VSAN is tagged with the VSAN ID as it crosses Inter-Switch Links.

VSANs were a proprietary protocol originally, invented by Cisco, but they have now been adopted as an ANSI standard.

Port Authentication Protocols

There are two primary port authentication protocols for working with VSANs:

- DHCHAP (Diffie-Hellman Challenge Handshake Authentication Protocol)
- Challenge Handshake Authentication Protocol (CHAP)

DHCAP is one option to authenticate devices that connect to a Fibre Channel switch. It allows only trusted devices to be added to a switch fabric. DHCHAP has support for both switch-to-switch and host-to-switch authentication. It uses a password-based, key-exchange authentication protocol, as you would expect with a name such as Diffie-Hellman. Prior to authentication, DHCHAP negotiates hash algorithms and Diffie-Hellman groups. It also supports authentication based on Message Digest 5 (MD5) and Secure Hash Algorithm 1 (SHA-1).

CHAP is used as the mandatory protocol in iSCSI, which was mandated by the Internet Engineering Task Force (IETF). The Challenge Handshake Authentication Protocol uses a three-way handshake to authenticate.

SAN Security Essentials

In SAN security, there are three technologies that are worthy of your security efforts. The SAN fabric, the hosts, and the disk drives are the three components that need to be secured.

Within these boundaries there are six areas of security on which to focus:

- SAN management access
- Fabric access (secure access from devices)

- Target access (secure access to LUNs and targets)
- SAN protocols (secure protocols used in intra-SAN communication)
- IP storage access (secure FCIP and iSCSI)
- Data integrity and secrecy (encrypting data in motion and data at rest)

Let's examine each of these in more detail.

SAN Management Security Risks

Threats to SAN management security include the following three main areas of vulnerability:

Switch fabric compromise   Switch fabric can be compromised by altered or modified configurations, lost configurations, or changes to ports, services, or the like. This can result in loss of service, system downtime, and so on.

Data confidentiality and integrity compromise   Data can be compromised by a breach in the system, potentially damaging the confidentiality and/or the integrity of the data.

Switch processing disruption   Switch processing disruption can be performed by using a denial of service against the switch, causing the CPU to exhaust its resources.

Fabric and Target Access Security Risks

When you look at securing access to the fabric and targets, there are three main areas of concern:

- The data itself should be secured at all costs. The issue at hand is loss of confidentiality and/or integrity. A breach could lead to the compromise of the data.
- LUN integrity must be ensured. If the LUN configuration itself is tampered with, there could be a loss of data and potentially availability. If data were lost, restoring from a backup (if one exists) would take time. Any changes to the configuration could compromise fabric stability.
- Disruption of the switch itself—for example, a denial of service condition—could cause a disruption to the availability.

Secure SAN Protocols

You need to secure the SAN protocols that are used in switch-to-switch communication. Encapsulated Security Protocol (ESP) is a protocol that is used for optional encryption within Fibre Channel networking. Fibre-Channel Security Protocol (FC-SP) is a security framework that provides multiple protocols to enhance security of the Fibre Channel network. Fibre-Channel Authentication Protocol (FCAP) is an optional authentication method between two devices using either certificates or keys.

Secure IP Storage Access

The features within iSCSI are used to secure IP storage access, which uses some of the same techniques that are available to IP networking. For example, ACLs are akin to Fibre channel zones, VLANs are similar in nature to VSANs, and 802.1x port security is similar to Fibre Channel port security.

Secure Data

You need to encrypt the data as it rests on a SAN device and also as it is transferred from one place to another. There are a number of ways to secure your data with a Cisco SAN solution. As previously mentioned, you can use CHAP, DHCHAP, FCAP, and FC-SP, to name a few.

Cisco MDS 9000 Features

In a Cisco environment, the Cisco MDS 9000 series SAN switches make up the core of the SAN environment and run the Cisco SAN-OS operating system. The following are some of the salient features of the Cisco MDS 9000 SAN switch:

InterVSAN routing   InterVSAN routing facilitates communications between initiators and targets on different virtual SANs (VSANs) without merging them into a single logical fabric. This is similar to VLANs on an Ethernet switch. SAN Fibre Channel control traffic doesn't go between VSANs and initiators cannot access resources outside of InterVSAN routing.

VSAN access control   Role-based access control can be assigned to specific SANs so that administrator privileges to the entire SAN do not need to be assigned to operators of specific VSANs. In other words, operators of specific VSANs have access only to those VSANs that they own.

LUN zoning   LUN zoning can be enforced by Cisco SAN-OS whereby LUNs can be accessed only by specific hosts.

Read-only zones   Cisco SAN-OS can provide read-only zones using SCSI commands within a zoning attribute. A read-only zone is useful for sharing volumes across servers for backups, for example.

Quality of service   Not unlike other traffic on a router, data on the SAN switch can be classified into specific levels of service. For example, you might want to give high priority to control traffic as well as latency-sensitive applications, whereas you might want to give a lower priority to backup traffic.

Switch-to-switch and host-to-switch authentication   Fibre Channel Security Protocol (FC-SP) is used within the Cisco SAN-OS to provide authentication for switch-to-switch and host-to-switch communications.

Port security   Port security on a SAN switch is similar to port security on a regular Ethernet switch. You can lock down a specific entity to a specific switch port. Specific entity types include a target, a host, or a switch and can be identified by the World Wide Name (WWN).

Appendix

C

Exploring Endpoint Security

THE FOLLOWING TOPICS ARE COVERED IN APPENDIX C:

- ✓ Introduction to endpoint security
- ✓ Buffer overflow threats
- ✓ Cisco endpoint security products
- ✓ Endpoint security best practices

Earlier in the book, I discussed intrusion prevention, primarily from a network perspective. In this appendix, we'll look at security from the perspective of the host, what has been called endpoint security. An endpoint is defined as anything that can be construed to be a host, such as a desktop computer, a laptop computer, a smartphone, and so on. For the purpose of this discussion, a server can also be an endpoint. For example, a host intrusion prevention system is a form of endpoint security. It guards against an attack to host computers and servers and is usually deployed in an enterprise setting. In addition to an introduction to endpoint security, we will look at the threat posed by buffer overflows. Then we will look at the various products used by Cisco to address endpoint security. Finally, I will discuss endpoint security best practices.

Introduction to Endpoint Security

Endpoint security is another part of a layered approach to an enterprise's security posture. I've talked about network security a great deal in this book, but there's also the need to secure hosts. With the multitude of threats that exist today, there's always the chance that a host can be infected by a virus or a user might inadvertently download malware from a website. Many other types of host threats exist.

The enterprise network used to be an entity with a hardened security perimeter around it and that was it. But today's network is used by telecommuters, business partners, and wireless users. This network needs demilitarized zones (DMZs). In other words, the perimeter is everywhere and nowhere, all at the same time. So there needs to be a way to secure the host as well as the network. This is where endpoint security comes into play.

Cisco has a number of security elements, as shown in Table C.1, which are geared to protect the host device.

TABLE C.1 Cisco Host Security Elements

Protection Feature	Description
Endpoint protection	Cisco Security Agent (CSA) protects against unknown threats to hosts by using behavior-based technology. CSA provides endpoint protection against threats such as worms, viruses, and Trojan horses.
Cisco Network Admission Control (NAC)	Network Admission Control ensures that endpoints conform to existing policies for entry into the network. If an endpoint does not meet policy, it can be denied access, quarantined, or granted restricted access.
Network infection containment	Network infection containment is achieved using a combination of Cisco Security Agent, Cisco NAC, and Cisco Self-Defending Network.

Buffer Overflow Threats

Buffer overflows are a common security attack vector. They are difficult to guard against without an endpoint security product such as Cisco Security Agent. It's important to know what a buffer overflow is and why an endpoint protection product can thwart the attack.

A buffer overflow attack can take place when an application does not properly control all the input that is provided. That is, there can be too much input, embedded commands, or improper formats or encoding. All of these conditions have the capability to cause a buffer overflow within the application. That means the memory space allocated to the application has been overrun. Why is this a problem? If the memory space that is allocated is overrun, you may intrude upon space used by the operating system. And that is precisely what the attacker is hoping to do.

If the attacker can cause the overflow, then they may be able to drop into a command shell and, more often than not, have administrator (on a Windows box) or root (on a Unix box) privileges. Once that happens, the attacker can do almost anything they want. Some people like to refer to this situation as "game over."

While this section is about buffer overflows, the following types of attacks can also give an attacker administrator or root privileges. Therefore, they also need to be considered:

- Worm attacks
- Virus attacks
- Trojan horses

These attacks differ from buffer overflows in how they act and how they are delivered. Some are delivered via email in the form of attachments. If the user opens the attachment, the attacking program can gain access. Some are also delivered in an URL embedded in email. If the user visits the URL with a browser, the host can be exploited. Still others are sent via open holes or ports that are available on the host, have some kind of vulnerability, and are thus capable of being exploited.

One way to prevent the overflow condition is to implement proper input handling when developing an application. But often a previously unknown issue in a system program or application surfaces and there isn't time to patch or correct the problem before an attacker exploits this vulnerability. That's where having an endpoint solution in place can protect you against so-called "zero-day" attacks.

Cisco Endpoint Security Products

Cisco offers many technologies to help protect endpoints from the threats that have been discussed here. In the following sections, we will explore some of these technologies and how they work together with other security devices and software to form a more secure enterprise. In particular, we will look at IronPort, Cisco Network Admission Control (NAC), and Cisco Security Agent (CSA).

IronPort for Email and Web Protection

IronPort is a technology that was acquired by Cisco in early 2007. It targets web and email security and is used by some of the largest organizations in the world. However, IronPort appliances are available to meet the needs of smaller organizations as well.

The email protection appliances protect against spam and perform antivirus filtering. A high-performance web security appliance is also available. The web security appliance performs spyware filtering, URL filtering, and anti-malware protection. There is also a security management appliance, but we will focus on email and web security appliances here.

IronPort email protection appliances, also known as the C-Series of the IronPort line of products, use a technology called the IronPort SenderBase Network to collect data on over 100,000 Internet service providers (ISPs), universities, and other organizations. Over 120 different email server parameters are collected, giving this database the most accurate view of email sending patterns of any on the Internet.

Two of the pieces of technology behind the Cisco IronPort email security appliance are the IronPort Reputation Filters and the SenderBase Reputation Score. These allow users of the appliance to score email entering the system. Only email with a high enough score is allowed through the system.

The email appliance also contains the IronPort Virus Outbreak Filters, which protect an enterprise in real time from viruses as they appear on the Internet. These filters can often protect against viruses before antivirus software vendors are able to create updated signatures to cover the threat.

In the IronPort web security appliance, also known as the S-Series, the SenderBase Network is also used, with Reputation Filters and a Web Reputation Score. The appliance offers URL filtering and exploit protection. This technology allows protection for enterprise customers without waiting for updates.

The SenderBase collects data on more than 25 percent of the world's email and web traffic. Over 100,000 organizations, including the largest networks in the world, contribute information on over 5 billion queries per day. The SenderBase network of organizations gives mail and web administrators real-time visibility into security threats from around the globe.

The simple breadth of data makes for a great sample size. There are more parameters to look at than just a high volume of mail being sent. You might assume that any organization sending a high volume of email would be a spam house. However, there are legitimate senders of high volumes of email, such as senders delivering news alerts. What about a large retailer such as Amazon.com, who might send out hundreds of thousands of emails, for both orders and advertisements? Volume cannot be the only indicator. If you look at other parameters in conjunction with the volume, a more accurate picture of the emailer emerges. These parameters might include end user complaint data, zombie characteristics, and country of origin.

Cisco IronPort has more than three years operational experience managing data quality and integrity. It developed the Data Quality Engine to assess the quality of a given data feed by cross-correlating multiple different data streams with known references or benchmarks. This system allows the SenderBase to access questionable data streams and weigh them based on quality.

Cisco Network Admission Control

Cisco Network Admission Control (NAC) is a complementary product for other security devices and software. Cisco NAC is available in two types of products:

- The NAC appliance sits on your network and makes admission decisions based on certain criteria.

- The NAC framework is a software component that lives on Cisco's and other vendor's equipment.

Cisco Network Admission Control allows you to enforce a security policy on your network. This means you can strictly control who is on your network and under what conditions. You can implement admission control whether you have managed systems, unmanaged systems, or guest systems from contractors, vendors, and so on.

The Cisco Network Admission Control system can provide the following features to further the security of your network:

- Authentication, authorization, and accounting

- Scanning

- Quarantine

- Remediation

Table C.2 describes the differences between the NAC framework and the NAC appliance.

TABLE C.2   NAC Product Differences

Category	Description
NAC Framework	The Cisco NAC Framework is a software-based solution that uses Cisco network components merged with other third-part products to form a framework of security. The NAC Framework can enforce strict compliance across a multitude of platforms, including remote access, wireless, WAN, and extranet.
NAC Appliance	The NAC Appliance is used for medium-sized business that requires a turnkey solution. It does not require a Cisco network to run and can implement the solution without software.

Cisco Security Agent

Cisco Security Agent (CSA) offers effective threat protection not just for desktops, but also for servers, point-of-sale (POS) systems, and any stand-alone system that lives on the network. The Cisco Security Agent can scale up to 100,000 agents on a single management console.

The Cisco Security Agent product consists of two components, which are described in Table C.3.

TABLE C.3   Components of the Cisco Security Agent Product

Component	Description
Cisco Security Agent	Cisco Security Agent is software that is installed on a host system, such as a desktop computer. It monitors the local system continuously and analyzes system operation.
Management Center for CSA	Management Center is administrative software that allows you to manage groups of CSA users. Users can be grouped according to specific job functions. Different security policies can be deployed on different groups. The CSA clients periodically communicate with the Management Center to see if there are updates.

Administration of the Management Center is done from a desktop using a secure web session over SSL. Communication between CSA client and the Management Center is also encrypted with SSL.

Cisco Security Agent uses the concept of interceptors. When an application attempts to access a system resource, it makes a call to that resource. An interceptor listens to that call to the resource and compares it to security policy. If the call does not violate an existing policy, it is passed to the kernel for execution. If a violation is found, two different actions can be taken:

- The application request is refused and an error message is sent back to the application.
- An alert is generated and sent to the Management Center.

Because Cisco Security Agent uses behavior-based pattern recognition, it can discern between normal behavior and something that could be perceived as malicious. Behavior-based technology is more accurate than signature-based technology and doesn't require updated signature files.

Table C.4 describes the four distinct interceptors used within Cisco Security Agent.

TABLE C.4   Cisco Security Agent Interceptors

Type	Description
File system interceptor	Intercepts file read and write requests and either denies or allows them, depending on security policy.
Network interceptor	Used in conjunction with the Network Driver Interface Specification (NDIS) to control changes to the interface. Security policy can control changes as well as rate limit the number of connections to prevent a denial of service attack.
Configuration interceptor	Read and write requests to Unix rc files and Windows Registry files must pass through this interceptor. This is to limit changes to the operating system.
Execution space interceptor	Controls access to memory space used by the application. This interceptor detects and blocks attempts to write to memory space not owned by the application. Other attacks that this interceptor prevents are buffer overflow attacks and code injection attacks.

By having all of the different interceptors, Cisco Security Agent is capable of performing the functions of many security technologies in one product:

- Worm protection is afforded through the use of execution space interceptors and the network interceptor.
- File system integrity is protected with the file system interceptor and the configuration interceptor.
- The file system interceptor, the configuration interceptor, and the execution space interceptor provide an application sandbox where you can test suspect programs to determine if they meet security standards.
- The network interceptor and the execution space interceptor work together to form a type of Host Intrusion Prevention System (HIPS).
- Cisco Security Agent acts as a host firewall using the network interceptor.

With these interceptors and their default policies in place, Cisco Security Agent can thwart attacks without waiting for updated signatures and policies. This allows the users of CSA to be able to defend against so-called "zero-day" attacks before anyone knows about them.

Attacks are constantly changing, and security administrators cannot possibly keep up with all the latest attack vectors. Using Cisco Security Agent is an effective method of controlling attacks by intercepting them before they happen.

Endpoint Security Best Practices

The following sections describe some of the practices you should follow to improve the security of your hosts.

Operating System and Network Security

There is such a thing as a trusted operating system, but it is usually expensive or difficult to administer. The typical organization must choose an off-the-shelf operating system such as Microsoft Windows or various flavors of Unix/Linux. Each of these typically has security vulnerabilities right out of the box and require constant patching to keep up with exploits. We are making strides in the right direction, but we're still not there yet in terms of a "secure" operating system.

After you load an operating system today, often the first thing you have to do is install patches that were released after the software shipped, often many in number. Once that is finished, system hardening needs to occur, which often involves the following:

- Turning off unnecessary services
- Eliminating default settings
- Making sure applications do not use an elevated privilege account
- Removing unnecessary software
- Disabling or removing unnecessary usernames and passwords

It is important to keep up with new and evolving security vulnerabilities, so being informed is paramount. There are many security vulnerability mailing lists, such as those on SecurityFocus or from vendors such as Cisco or Microsoft. You should join one or more of these lists to keep up-to-date.

There are other organizations that track security vulnerabilities, such as the SANS Institute, OWASP, and WASC. You can often find the latest vulnerabilities by checking their sites regularly.

Once you have hardened your operating system, you should use firewalls to filter traffic from insecure external sources such as the Internet. Only necessary traffic should be allowed to reach internal devices and sensitive machines. There are security tools that should be used in addition to the steps previously mentioned. Using file integrity check programs, deploying an IPS, and using host firewalls would be a wise move when dealing with mission-critical systems. Inspection of protocols can be done using the Cisco ASA and IPS appliances.

Application Security

Applications should be designed, built, and deployed with security in mind. In the development phase, focus should be placed on the following tenets:

- Least privilege
- Modularization

The principle of least privilege means an application should be limited to the least amount of access possible. In other words, to prevent an attacker from accessing it, the application should not run as root or administrator unless it is absolutely necessary. You should develop a modular, multiple-tier application that runs on more than one server. This ensures better security for the application. A three-tier application is a great example of this. Setting up the application as a set of layers makes it much harder for a hacker to gain access—there are three layers to get through. The three tier application works like this:

- The web layer is offered to the public, for example. This might live on an Internet DMZ.
- The middleware layer could be on the Internet DMZ also, but it could live inside the core network too.
- The database layer usually has a firewall protecting it separately.

As you have seen, one layer of security isn't enough. You need to use multiple levels so that if any one layer of security is compromised, there is another way to thwart the attack. This multilayered approach is sometimes referred to as defense in depth.

To round out our discussion of application security, here are some of the key methods for securing your application:

- Use application access controls.
- It is important to encrypt sensitive data such as personal data and credit card numbers, both while in transit and also while at rest, such as in a database.
- When you are programming, it is important to perform input filtering, both on the server side and on the client side. You cannot assume that users of the application are going to enter only those parameters that you are expecting. If there are characters that exceed the input length, you will want to filter those as well as any type of character (such as a control code) you would not be expecting. This prevents unexpected results and also prevents commands from being sent to a database to do injection attacks.

Appendix

D

Capstone Exercise

Now that we've covered all the topics of the CCNA Security exam, it's time to do one final practice exercise. This exercise will cover many of the topics of the previous chapters, but they will be part of what could be considered a real-world scenario. In this scenario, a corporation with headquarters in Chicago is connected to a remote office located in San Francisco. The remote office also has an Internet connection, rather than going back to headquarters for this service. The San Francisco remote office also has a business partner in Oakland that will come into play later in the exercise.

Many of the topics that we have studied will be applicable to this exercise:

- Layer 2 security
- IOS firewall
- IOS intrusion prevention system (IPS)
- Authentication, authorization, and accounting (AAA)
- Securing the router
- Virtual private networks (VPNs)

Let's take a look at the network diagram that we will be working with in this exercise, shown in Figure D.1.

FIGURE D.1   Remote network exercise diagram

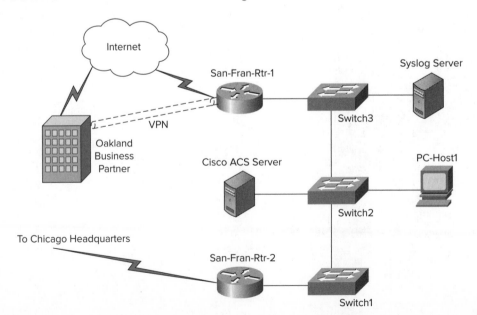

As you can see, we have a total of two routers to work with, three switches, and there is a PC as well as a few servers. As this is a high-level diagram, we will get into more detail as we go over the individual steps.

Let's get into the exercise now. Since we have several switches to work with, we will start with layer 2 security.

Layer 2 Exercise

Refer to Figure D.2 for the layer 2 detailed information relating to this section. It's just a drill down to show more detail at the switch level.

FIGURE D.2   Layer 2 detail

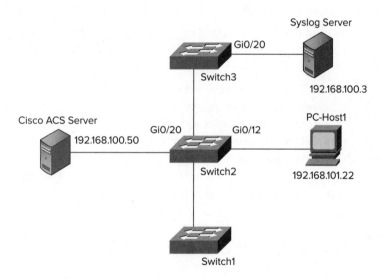

Follow these steps:

1.   Starting with Switch2, configure the port where the PC is attached to be an access port in VLAN 100. Also configure Portfast on the port with bpduguard to ensure that the port is not used as an attack vector for switch spoofing.

```
Switch2(config)# interface gigabitethernet 0/12
Switch2(config-if)# switchport mode access
```

```
Switch2(config-if)# switchport access vlan 100
Switch2(config-if)# spanning-tree portfast bpduguard
```

2. On this switch, configure DHCP snooping on the entire VLAN.

```
Switch2(config)# ip dhcp snooping vlan 100
```

3. Next, configure port security on the port labeled PC-Host1. Use a sticky MAC address configuration with a maximum MAC of 1. Also configure the port security to protect the port on violation.

```
Switch2(config)# interface gigabitethernet 0/12
Switch2(config-if)# switchport mode access
Switch2(config-if)# switchport port-security
Switch2(config-if)# switchport port-security maximum 1
Switch2(config-if)# switchport port-security mac-address sticky
Switch2(config-if)# switchport port-security violation protect
```

4. Look at Switch3 and the port into which the Syslog server is plugged, which is Gigabit0/20. Configure port security and lock it down to only the MAC address of the server itself.

```
Switch3(config)# interface gigabitethernet 0/20
Switch3(config-if)# switchport mode access
Switch3(config-if)# switchport access vlan 100
Switch3(config-if)# switchport port-security
Switch3(config-if)# switchport port-security maximum 1
Switch3(config-if)# switchport port-security mac-address 0000.1f02.003e
Switch3(config-if)# switchport port-security violation protect
```

IOS Firewall Exercise

In this exercise, you will configure an IOS firewall on the router facing the Internet to guard against attacks. You will configure this using the Cisco SDM graphical environment. We will walk through this one screen at a time, as we have in the past:

1. Click Configure; then in the taskbar at the left, click the Firewall And ACL task (see Figure D.3).

FIGURE D.3   Choosing the Firewall And ACL task

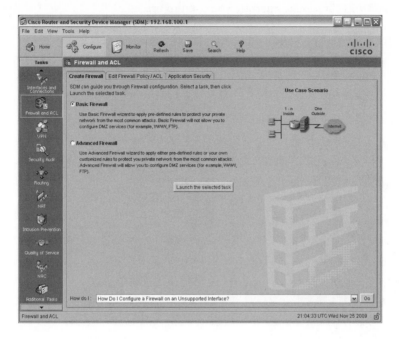

2. Launch the Basic Firewall Configuration Wizard. The introduction screen is shown in Figure D.4.

FIGURE D.4   Basic Firewall Configuration Wizard introduction screen

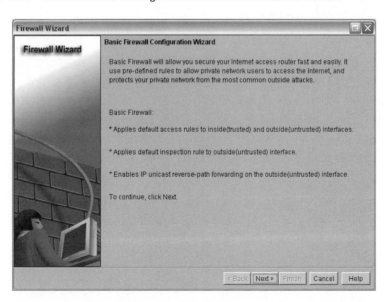

3. Click Next to see the interface configuration screen, shown in Figure D.5. On this screen you will choose the interface you want to use.

FIGURE D.5   Choosing the interface for the basic firewall

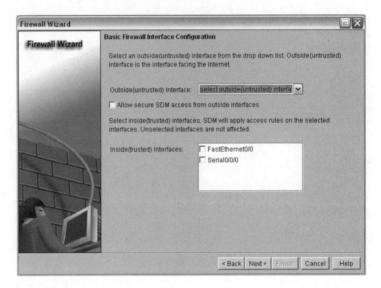

4. Staying on the same screen, choose Serial0/0/0 as the outside interface and FastEthernet0/0 as the inside interface, as shown in Figure D.6.

FIGURE D.6   Selecting the outside and inside interfaces

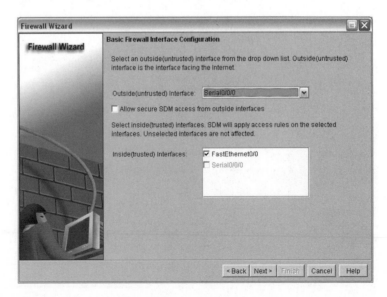

5. Click the Next button and you will see the Firewall Configuration Summary screen, shown in Figure D.7.

FIGURE D.7 The Firewall Configuration Summary screen

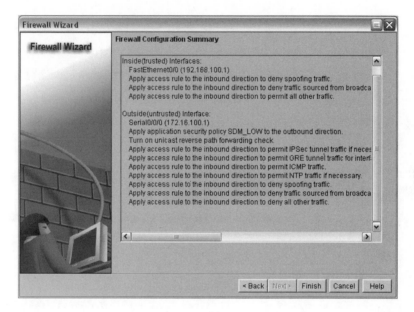

6. Click Finish. The Commands Delivery Status screen appears (Figure D.8).

FIGURE D.8 The Commands Delivery Status screen

When you are finished, the Edit Firewall Policy/ACL screen appears (Figure D.9). You can see the rules that were deployed as part of the basic firewall here.

FIGURE D.9   The Edit Firewall Policy/ACL screen

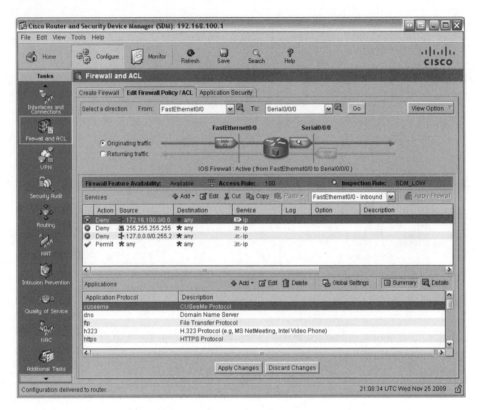

Secure Management Access Exercise

Since we have a connection to the Internet on router San-Fran-Rtr-1, we have decided to use auto-secure to enhance the security of the router.

Use the parameters in the following example as a guide to fill in the user interaction portion of auto-secure.

```
San-Fran-Rtr-1# auto secure
            --- AutoSecure Configuration ---


*** AutoSecure configuration enhances the security of
the router, but it will not make it absolutely resistant
to all security attacks ***
```

AutoSecure will modify the configuration of your device.
All configuration changes will be shown. For a detailed
explanation of how the configuration changes enhance security
and any possible side effects, please refer to Cisco.com for
Autosecure documentation.
At any prompt you may enter '?' for help.
Use ctrl-c to abort this session at any prompt.

Gathering information about the router for AutoSecure

Is this router connected to internet? [no]: yes
Enter the number of interfaces facing the internet [1]:

Interface	IP-Address	OK?	Method	Status	Protocol
FastEthernet0/0	172.16.100.1	YES	NVRAM	up	down
FastEthernet0/1	192.168.100.1	YES	NVRAM	up	down
Serial0/0/0	unassigned	YES	NVRAM	administratively down	down

Enter the interface name that is facing the internet: FastEthernet0/1

Securing Management plane services...

Disabling service finger
Disabling service pad
Disabling udp & tcp small servers
Enabling service password encryption
Enabling service tcp-keepalives-in
Enabling service tcp-keepalives-out
Disabling the cdp protocol

Disabling the bootp server
Disabling the http server
Disabling the finger service
Disabling source routing
Disabling gratuitous arp

Here is a sample Security Banner to be shown
at every access to device. Modify it to suit your
enterprise requirements.

Authorized Access only
   This system is the property of So-&-So-Enterprise.
   UNAUTHORIZED ACCESS TO THIS DEVICE IS PROHIBITED.
   You must have explicit permission to access this
   device. All activities performed on this device
   are logged. Any violations of access policy will result
   in disciplinary action.

Enter the security banner {Put the banner between
k and k, where k is any character}:
%
WARNING: Authorized users only!
All access is logged and monitored.
Violators will be prosecuted to the full extent of the law!
%
Enable secret is either not configured or
 is the same as enable password
Enter the new enable secret:
Confirm the enable secret :

Configuration of local user database
Enter the username: **admin**
Enter the password:**g0ldeng4t3**
Confirm the password: **g0ldeng4t3**
Configuring AAA local authentication
Configuring Console, Aux and VTY lines for
local authentication, exec-timeout, and transport
Securing device against Login Attacks
Configure the following parameters

Blocking Period when Login Attack detected: **30**

Maximum Login failures with the device: **3**

Maximum time period for crossing the failed login attempts: **10**

Configure SSH server? [yes]:
Enter the hostname: **San-Fran-Rtr-1**

Enter the domain-name: **myrouter.com**

Configuring interface specific AutoSecure services
Disabling the following ip services on all interfaces:

 no ip redirects
 no ip proxy-arp
 no ip unreachables
 no ip directed-broadcast
 no ip mask-reply
Disabling mop on Ethernet interfaces

Securing Forwarding plane services...

Enabling CEF (This might impact the memory requirements for your platform)
Enabling unicast rpf on all interfaces connected
to internet
Tcp intercept feature is used prevent tcp syn attack
on the servers in the network. Create autosec_tcp_intercept_list
to form the list of servers to which the tcp traffic is to
be observed

Enable tcp intercept feature? [yes/no]: **yes**

This is the configuration generated:

no service finger
no service pad
no service udp-small-servers
no service tcp-small-servers
service password-encryption
service tcp-keepalives-in
service tcp-keepalives-out
no cdp run
no ip bootp server
no ip http server
no ip finger
no ip source-route
no ip gratuitous-arps
no ip identd

```
banner motd ^C
WARNING: Authorized access only.  Violators will be prosecuted!
^C
security passwords min-length 6
security authentication failure rate 10 log
enable secret 5 $1$u7lI$OLIOAS7.rnTRAiZICkHz91
username admin password 7 15001E1F01387A
aaa new-model
aaa authentication login local_auth local
line con 0
 login authentication local_auth
 exec-timeout 5 0
 transport output telnet
line aux 0
 login authentication local_auth
 exec-timeout 10 0
 transport output telnet
line vty 0 4
 login authentication local_auth
 transport input telnet
line tty 1
 login authentication local_auth
 exec-timeout 15 0
login block-for 30 attempts 3 within 10
hostname San-Fran-Rtr-1
ip domain-name myrouter.com
crypto key generate rsa general-keys modulus 1024
ip ssh time-out 60
ip ssh authentication-retries 2
line vty 0 4
 transport input ssh telnet
service timestamps debug datetime msec localtime show-timezone
service timestamps log datetime msec localtime show-timezone
logging facility local2
logging trap debugging
service sequence-numbers
logging console critical
logging buffered
interface FastEthernet0/0
 no ip redirects
 no ip proxy-arp
```

```
 no ip unreachables
 no ip directed-broadcast
 no ip mask-reply
 no mop enabled
interface FastEthernet0/1
 no ip redirects
 no ip proxy-arp
 no ip unreachables
 no ip directed-broadcast
 no ip mask-reply
 no mop enabled
interface Serial0/0/0
 no ip redirects
 no ip proxy-arp
 no ip unreachables
 no ip directed-broadcast
 no ip mask-reply
ip cef
access-list 100 permit udp any any eq bootpc
interface FastEthernet0/1
 ip verify unicast source reachable-via rx allow-default 100
ip tcp intercept list autosec_tcp_intercept_list
ip tcp intercept drop-mode random
ip tcp intercept watch-timeout 15
ip tcp intercept connection-timeout 3600
ip tcp intercept max-incomplete low 450
ip tcp intercept max-incomplete high 550
!
end


Apply this configuration to running-config? [yes]:

Applying the config generated to running-config
The name for the keys will be: router1.myrouter.com

% The key modulus size is 1024 bits

San-Fran-Rtr-1#
000018: *May 15 20:40:13.071 UTC: %AUTOSEC-1-MODIFIED: AutoSecure configuration
has been Modified on this device
```

Cisco IOS IPS Exercise

On the Internet router, San-Fran-Rtr-1, you want to configure IOS IPS to mitigate the risk from Internet traffic. In this case, you will use Cisco SDM to configure the IPS:

1. Starting up Cisco SDM, you will need to navigate to the Configure button to bring up the taskbar.

2. Choose Intrusion Prevention to configure IPS. You will see the screen shown in Figure D.10.

FIGURE D.10 Choosing the Intrusion Prevention System (IPS) task

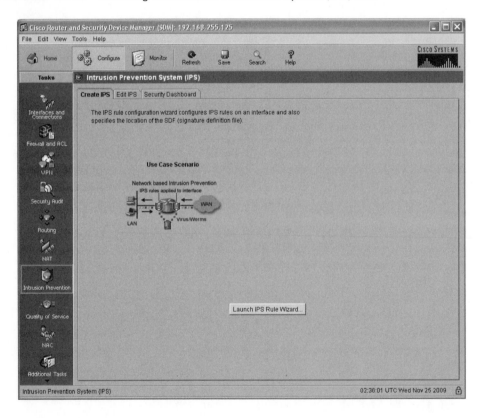

3. On this screen, choose Launch IPS Rule Wizard. Clicking the button brings up the informational message shown in Figure D.11.

FIGURE D.11   Informational message

4.   Click OK in the message box. The next screen, shown in Figure D.12, is the IPS Policies Wizard opening screen, which outlines what will be configured in the next few screens, including the interface to be used, the direction of flow, and the location of the SDF file to be used.

FIGURE D.12   The IPS Policies Wizard welcome screen

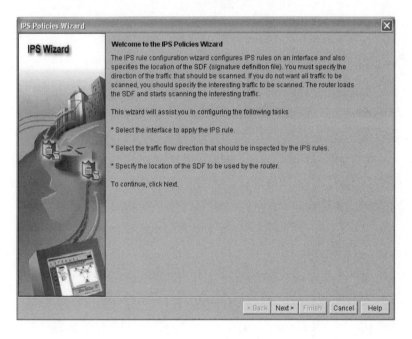

5.   In the next screen, shown in Figure D.13, you will select the interface(s) that you want to use and the direction that you want to use. Choose the inbound direction on the Serial0/0/0 interface by checking the box, as shown in Figure D.14.

FIGURE D.13   Select Interfaces, part 1

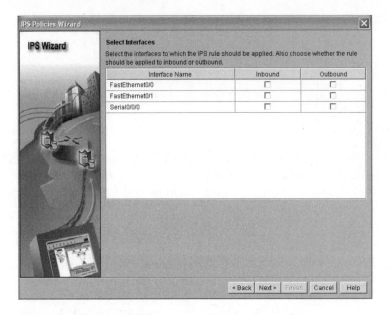

FIGURE D.14   Select Interfaces, part 2

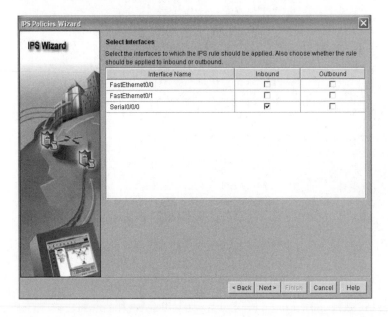

6.   Click Next. Then choose the default signature definition file (SDF), as shown in Figure D.15. Also check the box to use the built-in signatures if the first one fails.

FIGURE D.15 The SDF Locations screen

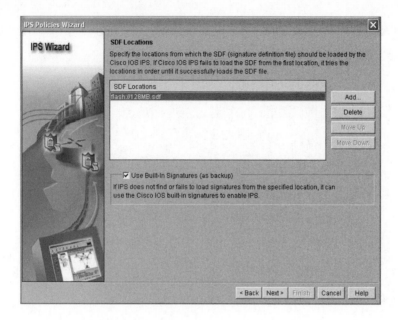

7. Click Next and you will see the summary screen (Figure D.16).

FIGURE D.16 The Summary screen

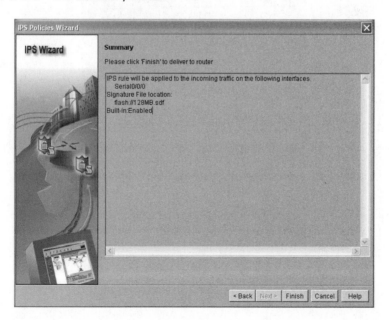

8. Click Finish and you see the Commands Delivery Status screen, shown in Figure D.17.

FIGURE D.17   The Commands Delivery Status screen

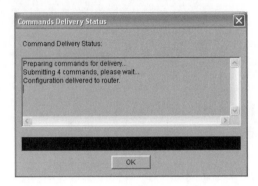

9. Click OK, and finally you see that the IPS signatures are ready to go (Figure D.18).

FIGURE D.18   The Signature Compilation Status screen

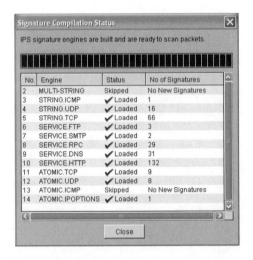

The Edit IPS status screen appears again (Figure D.19), and you can see that the rules are enabled on the inbound direction of the Serial0/0/0 interface.

FIGURE D.19   Edit IPS tab of Intrusion Prevention task

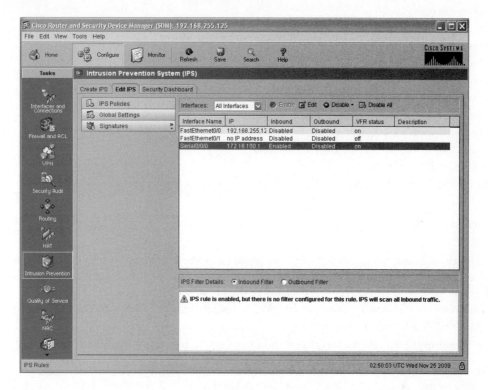

AAA Exercise

In the secure management access exercise earlier in this appendix, you configured AutoSecure from the command line. One of the things that is configured when you use AutoSecure is AAA. Let's examine what was configured for AAA services back in that section by looking at a snippet of the configuration:

.
.
.

```
username admin password 7 15001E1F01387A
aaa new-model
aaa authentication login local_auth local
line con 0
 login authentication local_auth
 exec-timeout 5 0
 transport output telnet
line aux 0
```

```
 login authentication local_auth
 exec-timeout 10 0
 transport output telnet
line vty 0 4
 login authentication local_auth
 transport input telnet
line tty 1
 login authentication local_auth
 exec-timeout 15 0
login block-for 30 attempts 3 within 10
hostname San-Fran-Rtr-1
ip domain-name myrouter.com
.
.
.
```

If you will notice, a local username and password were configured as part of AutoSecure. Then AAA was enabled and authentication for all access methods was configured for local. For the purpose of this exercise, refer back to the primary diagram (Figure D.1), where there is a Cisco ACS server running TACACS+. Let's assume the ACS server is at IP address 192.168.100.50. Follow these steps:

1. Enter in the TACACS+ server and the key using the following command:

```
San-Fran-Rtr-1(config)# tacacs-server host 192.168.100.50
San-Fran-Rtr-1(config)# tacacs-server key cisco
```

2. Change the AAA configuration to use the TACACS+ server that you just configured. So now you will be using TACACS+ for authentication in place of the local account. Use the following command:

```
San-Fran-Rtr-1(config)# aaa authentication login default group tacacs+
```

Site-to-Site VPN Exercise

The San Francisco office uses a local business partner in Oakland for some of its needs and needs a way to securely transmit orders and confidential information to them. You have proposed a site-to-site VPN over the Internet connection that you have at the office.

For this exercise, you will use the command-line interface to configure the VPN. You must coordinate the technical details with the partner's technical staff so that you know the parameters to be used when configuring the VPN tunnel. Follow these steps:

1. Based on the information that you have gained, configure the following ISAKMP policy in global configuration mode.

```
San-Fran-Rtr-1(config)# crypto isakmp policy 1
San-Fran-Rtr-1(config-isakmp)# encr aes 256
San-Fran-Rtr-1(config-isakmp)# authentication pre-share
San-Fran-Rtr-1(config-isakmp)# group 2
```

These commands configure the following:
- A crypto policy with AES 256-bit encryption
- A preshared key, which you chose mutually with your counterpart at the business partner
- Diffie-Hellman Group 2

2. You have decided to configure an access list with the number of 110 to define the interesting traffic for use on the tunnel. Only the traffic defined in the access list can traverse the tunnel. You will be permitting all local traffic that is part of the network of 192.168.100.0/24 to the remote network of 192.168.200.0/24. Enter the following access-list command:

```
San-Fran-Rtr-1(config)# access-list 110 permit ip 192.168.100.0
0.0.0.255192.168.200.0 0.0.0.255
```

3. The next part of the configuration is where you specify the preshared key and the remote side peer IP address that you need to connect to. (The preshared key is not starred out when you enter it, but it will be when you save the configuration and display it later.) You may want to compare notes again after you've done the configuration to see that preshared keys and other parameters match up. Enter the following command:

```
San-Fran-Rtr-1(config)# crypto isakmp key ********* address 10.100.1.1
```

4. The next step is configuring the transform set. As you will recall, the transform set is where you designate the type of authentication and encryption you will be using. The transform set in this case is named AES_1. You have defined the transform set to use AES 256 for encryption and SHA-HMAC for the authentication type. Enter the following command:

```
San-Fran-Rtr-1(config)# crypto ipsec transform-set AES_1 esp-aes 256esp-sha-hmac
```

5. The next phase of the configuration is to define the crypto map. In the first line of the configuration, you define the type of crypto map as ISAKMP and name it SFO-OAK to show that the tunnel originates at San Francisco and terminates in Oakland. The next line has a description that says it's a VPN tunnel and terminates at the remote IP address. Enter the following commands:

```
San-Fran-Rtr-1(config)# crypto map SFO-OAK 1 ipsec-isakmp
San-Fran-Rtr-1(config-crypto-map)# description VPN Tunnel to 10.100.1.2
San-Fran-Rtr-1(config-crypto-map)# set peer 10.100.1.2
```

6. In the next line you will designate which transform set is actually being used. Last, you will define the access list that you are going to use to determine the interesting traffic. You configured this earlier in this section and now you apply it to the crypto map. Enter the following commands:

```
San-Fran-Rtr-1(config-crypto-map)# set transform-set AES_1
San-Fran-Rtr-1(config-crypto-map)# match address 110
```

7. The last step is to apply the crypto map to the proper interface. In this case, the proper interface is the one connected to the Internet, which is interface Serial0/0/1. Enter the following commands:

```
San-Fran-Rtr-1(config)# interface Serial0/0/0
San-Fran-Rtr-1(config-if)# crypto map SFO-OAK
```

8. Now you have completed the configuration of the VPN tunnel. Once the other end of the tunnel is configured, run a show command to see whether it's working correctly. If so, the command and results will look something like this:

```
San-Fran-Rtr-1# show crypto isakmp sa
dst              src            state          conn-id slot
10.100.61.1      10.100.1.2     QM_IDLE              1    0
```

Appendix

E

About the Companion CD

IN THIS APPENDIX:

✓ What you'll find on the CD

✓ System requirements

✓ Using the CD

✓ Troubleshooting

What You'll Find on the CD

The following sections are arranged by category and summarize the software and other goodies you'll find on the CD. If you need help with installing the items provided on the CD, refer to the installation instructions in the "Using the CD" section of this appendix.

Some programs on the CD might fall into one of these categories:

Shareware programs are fully functional, free, trial versions of copyrighted programs. If you like particular programs, register with their authors for a nominal fee and receive licenses, enhanced versions, and technical support.

Freeware programs are free, copyrighted games, applications, and utilities. You can copy them to as many computers as you like—for free—but they offer no technical support.

GNU software is governed by its own license, which is included inside the folder of the GNU software. There are no restrictions on distribution of GNU software. See the GNU license at the root of the CD for more details.

Trial, *demo*, or *evaluation* versions of software are usually limited either by time or by functionality (such as not letting you save a project after you create it).

Sybex Test Engine

For Windows

The CD contains the Sybex test engine, which includes all of the assessment test and chapter review questions in electronic format, as well as two bonus exams located only on the CD.

PDF of the Book

For Windows

We have included an electronic version of the text in .pdf format. You can view the electronic version of the book with Adobe Reader.

Adobe Reader

For Windows

We've also included a copy of Adobe Reader so you can view PDF files that accompany the book's content. For more information on Adobe Reader or to check for a newer version, visit Adobe's website at www.adobe.com/products/reader/.

Electronic Flashcards

For Windows

These handy electronic flashcards are just what they sound like. One side contains a question or fill-in-the-blank question, and the other side shows the answer.

System Requirements

Make sure your computer meets the minimum system requirements shown in the following list. If your computer doesn't match up to most of these requirements, you may have problems using the software and files on the companion CD. For the latest and greatest information, please refer to the ReadMe file located at the root of the CD-ROM.

- A PC running Microsoft Windows 98, Windows 2000, Windows NT4 (with SP4 or later), Windows Me, Windows XP, or Windows Vista
- An Internet connection
- A CD-ROM drive

Using the CD

To install the items from the CD to your hard drive, follow these steps:

1. Insert the CD into your computer's CD-ROM drive. The license agreement appears.

> *Windows users:* The interface won't launch if you have autorun disabled. In that case, click Start ➢ Run (for Windows Vista, Start ➢ All Programs ➢ Accessories ➢ Run). In the dialog box that appears, type **D:\Start.exe**. (Replace *D* with the proper letter if your CD drive uses a different letter. If you don't know the letter, see how your CD drive is listed under My Computer.) Click OK.

2. Read the license agreement, and then click the Accept button if you want to use the CD.

The CD interface appears. The interface allows you to access the content with just one or two clicks.

Troubleshooting

Wiley has attempted to provide programs that work on most computers with the minimum system requirements. Alas, your computer may differ, and some programs may not work properly for some reason.

The two likeliest problems are that you don't have enough memory (RAM) for the programs you want to use or you have other programs running that are affecting installation or running of a program. If you get an error message such as "Not enough memory" or "Setup cannot continue," try one or more of the following suggestions and then try using the software again:

Turn off any antivirus software running on your computer. Installation programs sometimes mimic virus activity and may make your computer incorrectly believe that it's being infected by a virus.

Close all running programs. The more programs you have running, the less memory is available to other programs. Installation programs typically update files and programs; so if you keep other programs running, installation may not work properly.

Have your local computer store add more RAM to your computer. This is, admittedly, a drastic and somewhat expensive step. However, adding more memory can really help the speed of your computer and allow more programs to run at the same time.

Customer Care

If you have trouble with the book's companion CD-ROM, please call the Wiley Product Technical Support phone number at (800) 762-2974. Outside the United States, call +1(317) 572-3994. You can also contact Wiley Product Technical Support at http://sybex .custhelp.com. John Wiley & Sons will provide technical support only for installation and other general quality-control items. For technical support on the applications themselves, consult the program's vendor or author.

To place additional orders or to request information about other Wiley products, please call (877) 762-2974.

Glossary

A

AAA   Authentication, authorization, and accounting, the service associated with determining who is accessing a resource, what rights they have, and how long they have accessed it.

ACL   Access control list, a list to filter traffic based on protocol, layer 3 address, and so on. An ACL can also be used to identify traffic that matches some other feature.

AES   The Advanced Encryption Standard (AES) is the current U.S. government encryption standard.

authentication   A way of validating the identity of someone attempting to access a resource.

authorization   The granting of rights to a user based on their identity.

accounting   The process of tracking usage of network resources.

asymmetric encryption   Another name for public key encryption; it uses a public and a private key to encrypt and decrypt data.

AutoSecure   One-statement command used in the Cisco command-line interface to secure the router. It replaces individual configuration for each item you want to secure.

B

bootset   The combination of the router image and configuration files, stored securely and used as part of the Cisco IOS Resilient Configuration.

blocking mode   On a switch port, the state in which frames are blocked as part of the Spanning-Tree Protocol.

brute-force attack   An attack in which the attacker simply tries each and every combination of a particular character set in order to crack a password or ciphertext.

C

CA   Certificate authority, a third party that's trusted to provide signed keys for a Public Key Infrastructure (PKI).

Caesar cipher   An encryption technique that is also known as a substitution cipher or shift cipher. It is so named because it was used by Julius Caesar to send messages to commanders in the field.

Content Addressable Memory (CAM) table   Internal table in a switch that captures the MAC address and which port it was seen on as a source.

CBAC   Context-Based Access Control, a feature of Cisco IOS that provides a stateful packet inspection on routers.

CHAP   Challenge Handshake Authentication Protocol, a means of authentication that was originally used in PPP, which uses a three-way handshake that is verified periodically. Instead of sending the password across the wire, it sends a hash of the challenge, hostname, and password.

ciphertext   Text that has been encrypted using some algorithm.

community string   Text-based "password" used in conjunction with SNMP version 1 and 2 to allow access. There are both read-only and read-write community strings; each is used for different purposes.

D

DHCP snooping   A security feature in Cisco IOS to prevent a DHCP snooping attack.

Diffie-Hellman algorithm   Asymmetric key exchange algorithm invented by Whit Diffie and Martin Hellman, often used to provide a secure key exchange over the Internet.

digital signature   A form of asymmetric encryption using a public and private key to verify signatures.

DAI   Dynamic ARP Inspection, a security feature used to prevent man-in-the-middle attacks.

double-tagging   Attack that involves an additional 802.1Q tag to an already tagged packet for the purpose of attempting to hop from one VLAN to another.

E

EAP   Extensible Authentication Protocol, an authentication method used by 802.1x and RADIUS.

ESP   Encapsulating Security Payload, used for authentication and encryption of IPsec packets.

exploit   A program written specifically to take advantage of a vulnerability.

F

Fibre Channel   A transport method used in storage area networks (SANs).

FCIP   Fibre Channel over Internet Protocol, an implementation of Fibre Channel using IP as a transport method, to allow physically disparate devices to communicate over the network.

firewall   A device that can segment off traffic, allowing only the communications that you want to allow between the segments.

forwarding mode   On a switch port, the state in which frames are forwarded.

G

gatekeeper   An IP telephony device that monitors VoIP traffic and the available bandwidth.

H

hash   A one-way mathematical function that is used in data integrity.

HMAC   Hash Message Authentication Code, uses a hash with a secret key to create an authentication code. This can be used for integrity and authenticity. A hash function such as MD5 or SHA-1 can be used to calculate the HMAC; this is used in IPsec.

HIPS   Host Intrusion Prevention System, an IPS written specifically for an operating system.

HBA   Host bus adapter, used in a SAN environment to connect to storage.

I

IKE   Internet Key Exchange, a protocol used to help create an ISAKMP key exchange for IPsec.

ISR   Integrated Service Router, a Cisco router that contains numerous service capabilities such as voice and security.

IDS   Intrusion detection system, a system that detects intrusion events that match certain criteria. This is a passive system that generally reports on events. Some systems do have the ability to perform TCP resets.

IPS   Intrusion prevention system, an inline system designed to prevent intrusions by, based on either signatures or anomaly detection strategy, blocking packets from entering the network.

IP telephony   Another name for Voice over IP or having voice packets travel over an IP network.

L

LEAP   Lightweight Extensible Authentication Protocol, an authentication protocol that is used in Cisco wireless environments and uses username/passwords.

M

MGCP   Media Gateway Control Protocol, a VoIP protocol developed by Cisco to use in its Unified Communications system.

MD5   Message Digest 5, a 128-bit hash function commonly used to provide data integrity.

method list   Used in AAA in Cisco IOS, a list of the methods that can be used to authenticate. They are listed in order of precedence; if a method fails, the next method on the list is tried.

MS-CHAP   Microsoft's version of CHAP.

N

NAS   Network access server, which can be any network device that can send authentication requests to a TACACS+ or RADIUS server.

NAT   Network Address Translation, a method of translating an IP address from (usually) an RFC 1918 or private address to a public address. This is typically used to preserve public IP space.

NAC   Network Admission Control, a security system designed to regulate who accesses a network. Cisco has many NAC products.

P

private   Default read-write community string in an SNMP setting on a device. It's called private because the private string should not be public knowledge because someone with access and the read-write string can makes changes to a device.

private key   Half of the public/private key system that is part of asymmetric encryption or a digital signature. This key is known by only the owner of a public/private key pair.

privileged mode   Also known as enable mode. The mode in which an administrator is allowed to configure the router.

PKI   Public Key Infrastructure, an entire system that uses public-key cryptography to provide services to an organization.

public   Default read-only community string in an SNMP setting on a device. It's called public because someone utilizing a read-only SNMP community string can only monitor and observe, not make changes to a device.

public key   Half of the public/private key system that is part of asymmetric encryption or a digital signature. This key is made public and is used to encrypt by someone other than the owner and then the owner decrypts using the private key.

R

RTP   Real-Time Transport Protocol, an IP telephony protocol commonly used for delivering audio and video streams.

RADIUS   Remote Authentication Dial In User Service, a standard first used for dial-in users. It can now be generally used for any kind of remote access system for authentication.

RC   Rivest ciphers, a series of ciphers created by Ron Rivest. The most common one is RC4, which uses a variable key stream cipher.

root bridge   The bridge in the network with the lowest-priority value. It is elected by exchanging Bridge Protocol Data Units (BPDUs) with all the other switches in the network.

root port   The port closest to the root bridge, determined by the lowest cost to the root bridge.

S

SDF   Signature definition file, a file that is used by the Cisco IOS IPS and contains a collection of signatures used by the router to identify threats.

SDM   Cisco Security Device Manager, a graphical user environment for configuring and monitoring routers, in particular security features of routers.

self-defending network   Cisco's idea of a network using features within to protect itself against attacks.

SSH   Secure Shell, a protocol that is used as a remote terminal and provides encryption and authentication.

SHA-1   Secure Hash Algorithm 1, a common hashing algorithm to provide a fixed-length message digest.

SNMP   Simple Network Management Protocol, a protocol used to monitor and manage network devices.

SPAN   Switched Port Analyzer, a feature of Cisco Catalyst switches that allows traffic to be monitored, either on a port basis or an entire VLAN.

switch spoofing   Attack in which the attacker forces a connection to another switch using a trunk port.

T

TACACS+   Terminal Access Controller Access-Control System Plus, a system used to perform AAA services for access to network devices.

transport mode   One of the two modes used in Cisco's IPsec implementation. Transport mode maintains the original IP header and just encapsulates the data payload.

tunnel mode   One of the two modes used in Cisco's IPsec implementation. Tunnel mode encapsulates the entire packet and has a new IPsec header.

U

UDP   User Datagram Protocol, a layer 4 connectionless protocol.

user mode   The initial entry point into the router. In user mode, an administrator is able to do show commands but not configure the router.

V

vishing   Using a phone to gather user information for further attacks.

VoIP   Voice over IP, packetized voice over an IP network.

W

WWN   World Wide Name, a 64-bit address used in Fibre Channel environments to uniquely identify every element.

Z

zeroize   A command used in conjunction with RSA crypto keys on the router. Zeroize removes any previous keys that might have been present.

Index

T

The Best CCNA Security Book/CD Package On The Market!

Get ready for your CCNA Security certification with the most comprehensive and challenging sample tests anywhere!

The Sybex Test Engine features:

- All the review questions, as covered in each chapter of the book.

- Challenging questions representative of those you'll find on the real exam.

- Two full-length bonus exams available only on the CD.

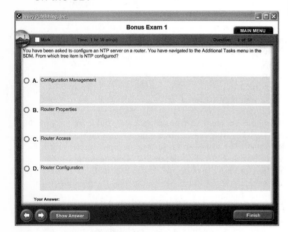

- An Assessment Test to narrow your focus to certain objective groups.

Search through the complete book in PDF!

- Access the entire *CCNA Security Study Guide* complete with figures and tables, in electronic format.

- Search the *CCNA Security Study Guide* chapters to find information on any topic in seconds.

Use the Electronic Flashcards for Windows to jog your memory and prep last-minute for the exam!

- Reinforce your understanding of key concepts with these hardcore flashcard-style questions.

- Download the Flashcards to your Palm device and go on the road. Now you can study for the CCNA Security exam (IINS 640-553) anytime, anywhere.

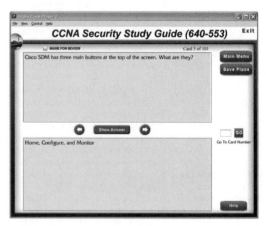